THE GOSPEL SOUND

25th ANNIVERSARY EDITION

THE GOSPEL SOUND

GOOD NEWS AND BAD TIMES

UPDATED AND REVISED

ANTHONY HEILBUT

LIMELIGHT EDITIONS   NEW YORK   1997

Fifth Limelight Edition, May 1997

Library of Congress Cataloging in Publication Data

Heilbut, Tony.
  The gospel sound.

  Reprint. Originally published: Garden City, N.Y.: Anchor Press/Doubleday, 1975.
  Discography: p.
  1. Gospel music—United States—History and criticism. 2. Afro-American musicians. I. Title.
ML3187.H44   1985   783.7   84-26122

Manufactured in the United States of America

THE GOSPEL SOUND was first published in hardcover by Simon and Schuster in 1971. A 1975 paperback edition of that book, published by Anchor, contained a new Preface and Postscript by Anthony Heilbut. This edition contains new material and a new discography by Anthony Heilbut.

CONTENTS

PREFACE

This book first appeared in 1971. At that time, the assertion that gospel singing supplied the roots for much of contemporary music was not widely accepted; today it seems a received truth. But, paradoxically, though the gospel sound is now universal, the culture that produced it appears increasingly a thing of the past. At its best, the black gospel church provided the richest form of American folklore. Its language combined the stately periods of eighteenth-century prose with the richness of southern country talk and ghetto slang. More than this, the gospel culture with its rituals, images, and psychological assumptions allowed generations of untutored artists to express themselves in a manner as free and improvisatory as they cared to make it. Virtually alone among popular forms of folklore, it recognized the importance and creative capacity of women. A cynic may scoff at the gospel church as matriarchal—though some of gospel's greatest exponents are male—but the indisputable fact is that in church singing women could be peerless artists, not by denying their social situation, but by drawing upon all its elements as resources.

It is to these great folk artists that this book is dedicated, especially the older singers, "the ones who didn't sell out" but stuck with their music despite the encroachments and temptations of the world. Their "gospel bird" may be an endangered species but it still keeps flying.

Anthony Heilbut
1975

INTRODUCTION:

The Gospel Moment

In January 1969, 50,000 black Chicagoans trooped through Mount Pisgah Baptist Church on the newly named Dr. Martin Luther King Drive. They were viewing the body of Roberta Martin, a gospel singer whose obituary did not appear in *The New York Times* and whose funeral not even *Jet* reported. Roberta Martin had grown rich from her gospel group and publishing studio. But she began her career in store-front churches, singing for nickels and dimes, and the poor who supported her then gathered now to pay their final respects. Roberta Martin belonged to them, to all the impoverished singers who tell you, "We're not here for form and fashion. We're here to be ourselves." She'd helped give them a way to be themselves through a musical style that could lure the most depressed. While she reigned they rejoiced; now they honored her as someone who'd "stuck with her own." Miss Martin's origins and struggles meant a lot more that week than all her worldly success. And all over America, gospel fans who had shared vicariously in her route, who could all testify, "My soul looks back and wonders how I got over," celebrated her for, as they said, opening doors and moving mountains. They mourned as they'd supported, without benefit of any mass media but their own: radio broadcasts and word of mouth.

Church people like to say, "There's none so blind as he who will not see." For forty years America has nurtured unacknowledged a cultural form as imposing as jazz, and a life style as peculiarly native as the hippie's. Yet while the mass media devour anything new, subverting the avant-garde simply by making it available, an area of American life crucial to millions of people is never gobbled up as news.

The gospel sound Roberta Martin helped inaugurate is everywhere. All rock's most resilient features, the beat, the drama, the group vibrations derive from gospel. From rock symphonies to detergent commercials, from Aretha Franklin's pyrotechnique to the Jacksons' harmonics, gospel has simply reformed all our listening expectations. The very tension between beats, the climax we anticipate almost subliminally, is straight out of the church. The dance steps that ushered in a new physical freedom were copied from the shout, the holy dance of "victory." The sit-ins soothed by hymns, the freedom marches powered by shouts, the "brother and sister" fraternity of revolution: the gospel church gave us all these. But if gospel music is obliquely important to Middle America, it's central to any study of the black ghetto. The huge turnout for Roberta Martin's funeral—reportedly the largest ever held in Chicago—is a small sign of gospel's hold on its followers. Consider the ghetto store windows cluttered with gospel placards, the city stadiums packed with gospel fans. One would think these signs alone would clue America that a formidable underground identifies itself with a unique musical style, especially now that rock has done something similar for an entire generation. But gospel singers and their audiences remain the best-kept secret of ghetto culture.

"The world never did love us," they say, "but we're going on *anyhow*." Along the way they have constructed a world complete unto itself. Obviously gospel lovers have their own music, but the music is just a part of the gospel style. There's also a distinctive language, special rhythms, a complex sense of ritual and decorum. Gospel has its own very superior aesthetic standards. The audience's musical sophistication is remarkable; it's nothing rare to see thousands of people roaring their approval for the subtlest change in tune, time, or harmony. But the most universal approval comes for honesty of emotion. Church people understand spirit, "soul" if you will, better than anyone: "After all, we invented it. All this mess you hear calling itself soul ain't nothing but warmed-over gospel."

Behind all the dignity, the great emphasis on posture and wardrobe traditional to the black church, is an implicit sense of bad news in bad times. The special tribulations of the singers, the most underpaid in America, and the fans, surely the poorest of any mass audience, get entangled. Gospel lyrics may sound banal, but they talk about the things that matter most to poor people. When you're well off, you can write songs about individual neuroses. But a poor man's concerns are simply staying alive ("I could have been dead sleeping in my grave"; "It's another day's journey and I'm glad about it"); healthy ("I've been sick and I couldn't get well"; "I woke up this morning in sound mind and with the blood running *warm* in my veins"); and financially solvent ("I've been down and out, you know I didn't have a dime"; "When your meal gets down low and you have no place to go"). Combine these pressing demands with a diction made up of the most vivid idioms and some of the most old-fashioned imagery, and the gospel language begins to make sense. The character is never in doubt; gospel singers look the part. "It's how we carry ourselves," says Mahalia Jackson. Once you get to know them, you learn that gospel singers are experts in all the ugliest sides of American life. But they always stand tall and walk upright: "We're Marching to Zion" on a "Highway to Heaven," which takes all the best of them, those who don't sell out, through hell.

The old cliché about suffering for your art is confirmed

every day by gospel singers. And what an art they produce! Good gospel can be warm, funny, sad, sexy, deadly serious and playfully ironic. There's scarcely an emotion that can't be touched upon. Though the churches are ruthless in their rejection of singers who switch to blues, it's easy to see a gospel singer sneaking in love references. During the time Mahalia Jackson had public marital problems, she'd sing in church, "He Never Left Me Alone"; when another great singer, Marion Williams, sang to college students "This Too Shall Pass," she intuited their burdens and ad-libbed, "Students, it can't be that hard, no matter what's your trouble. Your love life, you'll find someone else . . . it'll pass." And gospel singers are easily the most physical performers alive. When they romp through audiences, "getting down with the people," their sheer physical presence broadcasts all kinds of messages for saint and sinner both. "I sing with my body, it's the only way I know." All the dance steps from twist to popcorn to robot and Brooklyn strut are duplicated every Sunday by church saints who shut James Brown off when they see him.

It's a hard assessment to accept, but gospel has as much variety as any popular musical form extant. We're all familiar with the great-voiced soloists symbolized by Mahalia Jackson. Likewise "O Happy Day" by the Edwin Hawkins Singers introduced to the world the fiery, adventurous harmonies of the young peoples' choirs. But there's so much else. Gospel influences, reflects and mimics blues, jazz, and even country and western. There are male quartets who sound like the Golden Gate Quartet, the jubilee group with the impressive close harmonies that first turned America on to swinging pop-gospel versions of the spirituals we learn in public school. Then there are male groups who can and do teach James Brown and Wilson Pickett lessons in frenzy. There are the Edwin Hawkins Singers and dozens of new choirs into jazz chord progressions and Mormon Tabernacle decibels. But equally big sellers are the duo F. C. Barnes and Janice Brown of Rocky Mount, N. C., pure and rural as any street singer. Sullivan Pugh's guitar sounds like simple blues; Howard Carroll used to jam with Wes Montgomery and B. B. King. In Chicago they call the pianist Geraldine Gay "the Errol Garner of gospel," and in Philadelphia, Pearl Williams Jones is cited as "our Nina Simone." Periodically an old Atlanta preacher, Dr. C. Johnson, issues records in which he leads his congregation in *a cappella* hymns that sound like field recordings from the twenties. But there's also J. Robert Bradley, "Mr. Baptist," soloist for the huge National Baptist Convention. He's gospel's Paul Robeson, with a glorious, trained baritone. You'd think him too rarefied for gospel, but when he sings the most beloved gospel hymn of all, "Amazing Grace," he causes pandemonium. "Big Bradley sang for us," a Chicagoan says, "and the folks couldn't stand it. We had to call an intermission, the folks shouted so bad." The gospel voices are easily the most phenomenal outside of opera. And even classical singers daren't take such risks; gospel is filled with male sopranos and female basses. Lately gospel groups have begun singing protest material, though as early as 1942 the Golden Gates sang "No Segregation In Heaven," and in 1950 the Soul Stirrers, still tired from World War II and then scared about Korea, sang:

> *How long will this world stand?*
> *Will it be destroyed by man?*

About that time a Miami disc jockey, Otis Jackson, who previously had composed the topical song "Pearl Harbor," recorded a survey of black historical figures from Solomon* to George Washington Carver, "greatest genius ever known." Church once provided the only outlet for black expression. All that is changed, but it allows gospel singers an extensive tradition and almost unlimited artistic freedoms.

Gospel singers need an audience that shares their feelings and acknowledges their efforts at self-expression. The

* Some gospel songs describe Christ as black. These lyrics present him as having hair like lamb's wool and feet like polished brass.

black church provides the best training in the world, and
these singers have become the supreme showmen of our
time. On a visceral, emotional level, gospel's directness can
reach anybody. Virtually every time gospel singers appear
anywhere, they tear up. This near-perfect track record
hasn't noticeably enriched them, and they are veterans of
winning the war and losing the peace. When two of the
best groups, the Gospel Harmonettes and the Dixie Hummingbirds, appeared at the 1966 Newport Folk Festival,
the folkies applauded like mad, but if they wanted to see
more of the Nettes or the Birds, the groups have yet to
hear about it. Marion Williams makes a decent living singing in colleges. But in 1969 she broke up festivals in Europe and Africa, where good gospel was immediately
recognized as one of the world's great black arts. A year
later the Staple Singers, a folk-rock group once famous for
down-home gospel, went churchy in Iran and opened
Asia's ears to the gospel beat. "Yet our very own soul stations won't play us," complains a Hummingbird. Lately
white America has bought a slew of neo-gospel rock discs
but they can't be bothered with the real thing. "Besoever,"
as they say in church, the musical industry knows where
it's at. Rock stars turn up at gospel concerts complete with
tape recorders and stenographers. In big studios, record
producers sit listening to gospel, counting beats, figuring
how to convert all that raw energy into profits.

"They used to talk about us like dogs, call us crazy and
Holy Rollers," says Marion Williams, "and now those
white children are carrying on worse than we ever did."
She's right to the extent that the ambience of rock festivals
—free, spontaneous, anarchistic—is a mirror image of gospel churches. The embodiment of the Woodstock Experience, getting the freaks together, was Sly Stone, a graduate
of store-front churches who sang "I Want to Take You
Higher." Change his slang and his clothes, and Sly's a
stoned gospel singer, teasing, worrying, provoking a congregation to shout themselves happy. Real gospel singers
are never invited to rock festivals and are plain bewildered

by hippies. (When you remind them Jesus had long hair, they'll say, "My Jesus was clean.") But the resemblances are clear. Gospel singers don't say "Do your thing" but "We're coming to you in our *own* way. We're not singing for form or fashion or for outside show of this world . . . but we came to work out our own souls' salvation." Nor of course do church audiences "freak out," but they do let a song "get all over them" with responses as wild, varied and idiosyncratic, often consciously so, as any rock listener's special trip. Gospel audiences also respond as one to their music. Applause can follow a skillful change in melody or rhythm, a distinctive reading of a specific line, even a musical note, hit exactly right exactly when. Each listener brings some private testimony, but a good singer can take the stalest lines and make them fit anybody's life. In a phrase, gospel gets a church "on one accord"—just what rock does for its celebrants.

Plus ça change, plus c'est la même chose: everything changes, everything stays the same. The musical community that heralds the alternate culture has origins as old as America. For hundreds of years Americans have been getting religion and "getting happy" in the process. During the Great Awakening that spread from New England to Kentucky, millions of pioneers shouted, danced, barked and jerked, getting release, entertainment and, incidentally, salvation. Nor were the preachers slaves and illiterates, but those early lights of American literature and theology Jonathan Edwards and Cotton ("Yours in the bowels of Christ") Mather. Slaves attended these services and were profoundly influenced. They combined the revival hymns of eighteenth-century England with an African song style and created our greatest national music. They also turned the Puritan orgies of hysteria into the most moving communal gatherings. A young Atlanta singer says what's common knowledge: "Church has always been the one place we could be ourselves, be really black. Outside we go through all those changes, trying to be like some movie star or somebody on television. In church we ain't ashamed to be *real*."

The spirit is an elusive thing. Sometimes a church service strains to invoke it for several hours. Other times it comes almost as soon as the congregation gathers. Suddenly the entire church is on one wavelength, caught up in the same moment that expands to contain the smallest, most personal detail. In a kind of emotional shorthand, the hums, moans, and screams make profound sense: "That's all right, honey," "Help yourself, son," the church calls to itself. In Southern Baptist churches, a group of oldtimers sits in the amen corner and "moans" the spirit into presence by wailing lines that predict the blues. "It's getting late in the evening and the sun is going down," moans an old deacon. He repeats the line, his voice slurring every word, each syllable a blue note. Other members extend the syllables in the intricate note bending that scholars call melisma and the church calls "curlicues and flowers and frills." Then his voice descends to a summing up at once bitter and resolved: "If it wasn't for Jesus I'd have no friend around."

Each moaner sings his own story; as Moaning Bessie Griffin says, "It ain't the voice. Sometimes somebody with the squeakiest voice can say what we want to hear." The spirit, invisible but palpable, roams about the church. One moaner chants, "Everytime you see me crying, that's my trainfare home." Someone else picks up and announces, "Keep on telling you, it's a God somewhere." And, acknowledging his presence, the people begin to get happy, each person in his own way, responding sometimes simultaneously, sometimes a second apart, to a force that overwhelms the room, compressing all cries into one moan. Then everyone is indeed in one accord, and the spirit descends, as the Bible says, "Like the rushing of a mighty wind." Often a moment of absolute silence will be charged with such intensity that the church may shudder and roar as one, "Whoo," "Hah," "Yessir," "My Lord my Lord."

The *a cappella* moaning still persists in some smaller

congregations. But today the larger churches contain pianos, organs, drums, guitars, and tambourines. In earlier times, rhythmic songs known as ring shouts were performed in circles, each participant dancing in unison with his neighbors. Today shouting is more individual. Although a shout usually comes out in a dance, the spirit can announce itself in laughing, walking, running, arm-waving, and fainting.

The great singer Dorothy Love describes the process in song:

Some get happy, they run.
Others speak in an unknown tongue,
Some cry out in a spiritual trance,
Have you ever seen the saints do the holy dance?

The saints she refers to belong to the comparatively recent sects known as Holiness, Pentecostal or Sanctified. The real saints are "saved, sanctified and filled with the Holy Ghost," a spirit possession defined by "speaking in tongues as the spirit gives utterance." Negro religion was always emotional, but when the saints came marching in, they put Baptists and Methodists to shame. It is said with awe and perhaps derision, "Sanctified folk can shout *for days.*" In the spirit, out of self, but not out of control.

Each saint has his own distinctive step. "You can tell your readers," one lady said, "I didn't get my shout by copying anybody. I got this on my knees." Some rock gently, lightly swinging their hips and shoulders in counterpoint to the music. Others contort violently, cutting steps in time to the music until their contortions knock them to the floor. Some wave their hands in the air, others hold one hand or arm erect. Most people shout with their eyes shut to the world, but a few point ecstatically to their private vision.

In a Sanctified church, the spirit can be called up by song and dance alone. One Sunday in Philadelphia's Greater Zion (formerly Little Zion) Church of God in Christ, the choir sang so fervently that the guest preacher couldn't speak. Each time she rose to give her message, the fire descended again. "Well, we're certainly having a marvelous time in the Lord," she said once, and a moment later, people began to holler and dance. Ten minutes later, she tried again, but briefly, "I'm feeling good this evening. Somebody's here now . . . must be the Lord," and she found herself shouting too. The song itself was long forgotten—each round of shouts seemed a spin-off from the one preceding, until the spirit and the hand-clapping and the community became the message. A little boy with a bandaged foot got up shouting. A sympathetic lady came to his rescue, holding his hand as he danced, until she caught the vibrations and shouted herself. After an hour of periodic shouts, the congregation became subdued, softly praising God with blue-noted hums and unknown tongues. Then several began applauding, as if the Holy Ghost had announced itself to them alone. The spirit traveled from their hands to their arms to their feet, and the shouts started again. By now the guest preacher's bus had arrived. She gathered her flock; some marched out still shouting, and she apologized for them with grace. "I couldn't speak to you this evening, beloveds, but that's all right. We've had some *good* church."

It's this feeling of a community caught up in the spiritual moment that turns gospel into a "foretaste of glory," makes saints say "We were really going to heaven . . . we were sure nuff going home." It's what Prince or Michael Jackson, or any group, black or white, tinged by 1960s soul, are after when they try to "get a thing going, babies, let's get together." Of course, they almost never succeed as well as most gospel preachers or congregations. But the supreme architects of the gospel moment are the great gospel singers. With them, spirit and community are welded by art. Their phrasing distills the best in folk expression, while adding unparalleled style and talent. All by themselves, the best singers can invoke as much spirit as a cathedral of saints. R. H. Harris, the father of gospel quartet and the originator of Sam Cooke's style, recently returned to the small Texas town where he first sang. "It was a deeply spiritual service. Folks came from all over. They came down from Houston, that's 101, and Beaumont, that's 85 miles away. During the intermission when they ask the strangers to speak, one lady got up and said she'd come 165 miles all the way from Dallas. She say, 'It's been so long since I've heard Brother Harris. I just wanted to get that something, that spiritual lift I knew he'd give me. I've been longing for it,' and do you not know, the people started shouting right off what she said?"

The modern gospel style is barely sixty years old, but it continues a tradition of singing, preaching, and shouting familiar to generations of black people. Any gospel singer, even the hippest, can summon up feelings of nostalgia for a simpler time when everybody believed and participated in the old-time religion. This identification is an imposing asset since the religion he embodies once provided a universal *rite de passage* for black youth. Most Southerners know about the ritualized sequence of adolescent conversion. After "tarrying" on the "mourner's bench," being prayed over by the old-timers in the "amen corner," the young sinner would accept "Jesus Christ as my Lord and Saviour." The baptism that ensued, "going down in the muddy creek and coming up shouting," was probably a supreme moment in his life, the kind of experience around which cluster our deepest emotional and physical memories. Adolescence hurts the body and confuses the mind. No wonder conversion, uniting ecstatic physical response with firm moral commitment, becomes a thrilling moment, permanently registered and communally sanctioned. "You may not remember the hour," Edna Gallmon Cooke used to say, "but you can't forget about that day." Gospel singers remind the forgetful by citing the weekday and spot of their own conversion: "I got my religion one Tuesday evening in the clay hills of Alabama." And invariably people shout, as the whole overwhelming experience is recalled. The old song says, " 'Tis so sweet to be saved," and magically all that sweetness returns.

Is this spiritual renewal or merely a repossession of lost time? No matter. The singers are evoking a real experience, acting, as it were, as the custodians of tradition. In so doing, they can induce a camaraderie that quickly draws together a churchful of strangers. "You know I didn't always come from Chicago," the lead for the Pilgrim Jubilees tells a crowd. "Didn't always have it easy. My brothers and I grew up in a little three-room shack in Houston, Mississippi. We didn't have much back then, church, but we had a family altar. Aw, you all don't know what I'm talking about . . ." everybody laughing because everybody does.

Militants keep crying for a black awareness of life on this continent. In its own way, gospel has always been defiantly conscious of its history. An old popular song in southern churches is precisely about tradition:

Oh the people don't sing like they used to sing,
The mourners don't moan like they used to moan,
The preachers don't pray like they used to pray,
That's what's the matter with the church today.

As early as 1926 Sister Sallie Sanders begins her recording "Shall These Cheeks Be Dried" with the admonition "Let's go back to the old-time singing of our grandfathers and grandmothers." The old-fashioned style Sister Sanders' congregation demonstrates is permanently identified with a group of songs millions of black Americans were raised on. Today the choirs sing Motown tunes and Thelonius Monk chords but when the new arrangements fall flat: "The old Dr. Watts hymns will always *bother* a church." The first songs slaves sang on this continent were probably those sturdy eighteenth-century English hymns depicting amazing grace, Jordan's stormy banks, and fountains filled with blood. Traditionally a leader would recite the line, after which the congregation sang in a slow, languorous man-

ner called long or common meter, which allowed for intricate embellishments by each singer.

Isaac Watts was only one of several hymn writers, but
his name personifies the *a cappella,* moaning style from
which all Afro-American music derives. By an obscure
twist of cultural history, that dour Methodist hymn

> *Father I stretch my hand to thee*
> *No other help I know.*
> *If thou withdraw Thyself from me*
> *Whither shall I go?*

became an ancestor of modern blues. Its mood of isolation
and loss, of having tried the world and found it wanting, is
in itself a kind of cosmic lament, while its simple metrical
structure anticipates the sixteen-bar blues, a form so common in gospel I call it the Baptist blues. The despair implicit
in this hymn can deeply move any church audience. Five
years ago a Mississippi couple were captured by Klansmen who threatened to kill the husband. Convinced that
no help was forthcoming, the wife fell on her knees and
recited the words of "Father I Stretch My Hand to Thee,"
and eventually the Klansmen let them go. Such a story
seems almost apocryphal, but it *was* reported in *The New
York Times* and it suggests why these hymns remain the
truest songs for rural blacks.

The most popular of the "Dr. Watts hymns," "Amazing
Grace," was actually composed by another Englishman,
John Newton. No matter. "Amazing Grace" has become
a Negro spiritual. Southern whites singing the tune prefer
the stanza

> *When we've been there ten thousand years,*
> *Bright shining as the sun,*
> *We've no less days to sing God's praise*
> *Than when we've just begun.*

Black congregations are attuned to more pressing concerns.
The verse they prefer may sound like doggerel, but in gospel churches it is *the* universal testimony:

> *Through many dangers, toils and snares,*
> *I have already come.*
> *'Twas grace that brought me safe thus far*
> *And grace will lead me home.*

A good singer can make the phrase "dangers, toils and snares" resonate with specific experience. "Amazing Grace" is the song for all those who came up "the rough side of the mountain"; young singers can't really execute it: "I don't want to pay those kind of dues." Dorothy Love understands the song's meaning. "Look, we didn't have any money, and how much luck is the white man gonna let you have? The government just started waking up to the fact we're here, and nobody's fooled they care. So now tell me, if it wasn't *grace* that brought us safe thus far, show me what did it." No song so moves black congregations. Even young people like "Amazing Grace," though they can't sing it with their parents' conviction: "I'll cry too because it reminds me what we've all had to go through," a striking example of the group consciousness that gospel cultivates. And "dangers, toils and snares" clearly don't disappear in the big city where they assume the guises of pushers, loan sharks, number runners and thieves.

The best-loved Dr. Watts hymns—"The Day Is Past and Gone," "A Charge to Keep I Have," "I Heard the Voice of Jesus Say," "I Love the Lord, He Heard My Cry," "That Awful Day Will Surely Come," "Must Jesus Bear the Cross Alone"—are similarly blunt metaphors of physical trouble and spiritual transcendence. "The Day Is Past and Gone" may be the most terrifying evocation of death in American folklore.

> *The day is past and gone,*
> *The evening shades appear.*
> *O may we all remember well*
> *The night of death draws near.*

We lay our garments by,
upon our beds to rest.
Though death may soon disrobe us all
Of what we now possess.

The very existence of hymns like "Amazing Grace" and "The Day Is Past and Gone" symbolizes the awful consciousness black Americans have always lived with. It also should forever banish the notion of the "contented darkie" still propagated by some historians. People who moan about dangers, toils and snares, and death disrobing us all, are scarcely unaware of the lives they lead. The Dr. Watts hymns seldom contain the lavish imagery of the spirituals, but the stark language speaks to the most desperate side of black life. In bad times, gospel lovers always go back to "Amazing Grace" or "Must Jesus Bear the Cross Alone." The public keeps hearing about new civil-rights laws. But the fact that Dr. Watts hymns continue to matter tells something about the political and social conditions in this country. For the gospel poor, things have scarcely changed.

The basis of the gospel repertoire remains these hymns, just as the essence of the gospel style is a wordless moan. But through the years, congregations have adopted other songs, spirituals, plaintive nineteenth-century hymns ("What a Friend We Have in Jesus," "Pass Me Not O Gentle Saviour," "Jesus Keep Me Near the Cross") and a large body of "tabernacle songs," anonymously composed tunes common to rural Southerners of both races. Any churchgoer in the Deep South states should be familiar with a good two hundred of those, some sung only in the community where he lives. In big cities, when singers revive a tune like "Ain't No Grave Can Hold My Body Down" or "There's a Man Over the River," church members will chuckle appreciatively, "Lord I haven't heard that kind of singing since I don't know when."

Another of gospel's most striking traditional resources is the male quartet. Self-styled "gospel groups" are a recent phenomenon, but quartets were traveling and singing

church music long before Thomas A. Dorsey and Sallie
Martin helped dream the traveling groups into existence.
Quartet, whether barbershop or gospel, has always been
the most popular and common form of singing among
black men. The great modern blues singers owe their controlled frenzy to quartet leads. Similarly, the rhythm-and-
blues groups of the fifties with their doodling bass and
tin-whistle falsetto secularized a traditional quartet sound.
For men in Baptist churches, quartet is the conventional
option, the aim of talented boys long before their voices
change. Black neighborhoods are filled with men who discuss quartet with the same expertise and partisanship they
extend to boxing or baseball, down to the smallest details
of local origin. "Them's my boys," fans say, and quartets
exploit this loyalty by listing their home base in the manner of hillbilly troupes or calypso bands. "I'm gonna sing
this song the way we used to do in the clay hills of Alabama," says Claude Jeter of the Swan Silvertones; Reverend Willingham of the Swanee Quintet used to say, as he
demonstrated a funky dance step, "We shouts like that in
Georgia."

The verbal and physical manner, the overall posture, of
quartet singers says much about what black communities expect and admire in their husbands and fathers.
What with quartet harmony defined by four male voices
(women quartets call their top singers, tenors, their bottom singers, bassos) and Baptist and Methodist preachers
invariably men, religious song and sermon were very early
identified with the male sex. The Dr. Watts hymns often
grew out of the moan of some preacher or deacon, acting
as both individual supplicant and congregational leader.
These deacons may have been the forerunners of the "gospel men," the name jubilee quartet singers gave, in the
1930s, to singers who "hooped and hollered" in a style suitable to the fervor of hard gospel. To this day, many Southerners consider gospel music a male province. Like Samuel
Johnson, ridiculing the notion of a woman preacher, these

conservative Southerners will not accept religion as women's work. "Women don't belong in the pulpit," they say, and they do not enjoy them growling like preachers, moaning like deacons, or "clowning" like "gospel men." Even the conspicuous consumption and self-advertisement of the evangelist are acceptable male behavior—one Alabaman observed, "Sure, the minister's supposed to dress good and drive good. Men of God are supposed to be fine."—though a woman who carried on accordingly might be branded "whore" or "gypsy." Now, the greatest individual artists produced by gospel are, with a few exceptions, women. But this, paradoxically, proves the rule of male domination. The men didn't have to assert themselves so distinctively because they already had an accustomed status and identity.

Since gospel usually implies matriarchy, the mere existence of quartet debunks most easy generalizations. It also underlines the fact that gospel contains two distinct styles. Quartet is the oldest, but not the best known. The newer style is called simply "gospel" and as a category includes soloists, groups, and choirs. The two styles obviously feed off each other but they're still easy to distinguish. Quartet uniforms are street clothes, their instruments guitars, their harmonies precise and geared to the extremes of the male voice—heavy bass and wailing falsetto. Gospel singers are, more often than not, female. They sport willowy robes, a kind of sanctified lingerie both elegant and functional: "We sweat easier in robes." Unlike the traditionally unaccompanied quartets, gospel singers have always featured a lot of music, and every city has its virtuoso pianists and organists. The harmonic sound is usually female; gospel is probably the only musical form boasting a battalion of male sopranos. Nobody who follows gospel could confuse the groups and the quartets any more than he'd call pumpkins pears. Quartets outdraw all but the very top attractions, yet so far as national exposure goes they lag behind. Their resentment at this lopsided situation is understandable. "When they say somebody's the world's greatest gospel singer, that don't faze me because I'm singing quartet.

INTRODUCTION

I'm not doing what Mahalia or Clara Ward did, so don't put them up with me."

Though Sanctified church groups recorded during the twenties, the professional gospel groups first began traveling in the thirties. They received their initial impetus inspired by the compositions of writers like Lucie Campbell, A. L. Haskell, and Thomas A. Dorsey, who distributed their songs at the annual Baptist and Holiness conventions.

Dorsey ("Georgia Tom" in his earlier incarnation as a blues singer) consciously decided to combine the Baptist lyrics and Sanctified beat with the stylized delivery of blues and jazz. Together with his partner, Sallie Martin, he set out to revive a church gone "cold and dry." During the thirties, the all-black National Baptist Convention sold its paperback collection of hymns, *Gospel Pearls,* by the tens of thousands. Taking a cue from the Convention's ministers of music, Dorsey began publishing his songs. The public was ready for something new. By 1942, gospel supported a good half-dozen publishing houses with Sallie Martin, Dorsey, and their discovery, Roberta Martin, running the largest. These three, touring America with groups and soloists trained to sing the new songs, made converts everywhere. Their early sheet music is thick with dedications to groups and choruses from Brooklyn to Denver. Where once every black Baptist home kept its copy of *Gospel Pearls* with the family Bible, Dorsey's sheet music took over, with Bible and *Pearls* both gathering dust.

In gospel, to paraphrase Yeats, it's the singer, not the song. When the spirit's right, the simplest lyric can stir a crowd. Still, the songs of Dorsey and his fellows acted as catalytic agents. Something about the new material with its dominant blues riffs and swinging beat turned on a whole generation thrilled by blues, yet not ready to disown its religious training. Singers who might have been content to solo each Sunday were moved to turn professional. The richly eclectic style they cultivated proved irresistible even for intellectuals who blanched at the religious homilies. A slew of critics moaned in the subjunctive when they first heard Mahalia, "If only she'd sing some decent songs." They never bothered to think that perhaps those awful songs brought out the best in her. If America's greatest singers require certain songs to release their talents, something must be right with the songs. Between 1940 and 1950 gospel presaged the golden age of rock, as over a dozen prolific songwriters—W. H. Brewster, Lucie Campbell, Kenneth Morris, R. H. Harris, Abe Windom, Beatrice Brown, Antonio Haskell, Virginia Davis, Roberta Martin, Robert Anderson, Clevant Derricks, Clifford Davis, H. J. Ford—joined Dorsey in turning out superb songs. Remember, this was the period when much of pop veered between the lifeless witticisms of Broadway and the mindless spewings of Tin Pan Alley. Country and western had still to graduate from its rococo period, and even rhythm and blues was in a rut. Yet all this time, the young peoples' choirs were singing new songs that galvanized the ghetto.

Singers selected their songs as much for message as for beat: "I like a song that tells a story." The songs hit home because they told a persuasive story; as Sallie Martin says, "They were songs written out of somebody's burden, not just to make money." Constructed with uncanny attention to emotional cadence, they built line by line to an emphatic, victorious release. The best tunes were filled with vivid imagery, the writers evidencing great subtlety in finding Bible passages relevant to black life. Yet, as all great songwriters do, they "kept it plain," by writing lines that either exploited or extended the folk vocabulary.

> *The mean things you say don't make me feel bad,*
> *I can't miss a friend that I've never had,*
> *I've got Jesus and that's enough.*

Sometimes the singers discovered implications hidden in the lyrics. Lucie Campbell's "In the Upper Room" is a lyrical depiction of communion inspired by Christ's final appearance to his disciples. Marion Williams ad-libs verses closer to home:

In the upper room with Jesus,
I had to tell him "Make my enemies leave me alone, make
  them behave."
But he took me on up and my load got lighter,
Well my burden got lighter in the upper room,
Came walking on out and everything was all right,
When I came out of the room,
The upper room, just talking with the Lord.

In Robert Anderson's brilliant "Prayer Changes Things,"
the first verse operates by suggestion:

> *I've heard the story of David,*
> *I've heard of Daniel in the lion's den.*
> *I've heard of Job and his affliction,*
> *How they all kept the faith to the end.*
> *But when all hope had seemed to fail,*
> *My God's power did prevail,*
> *I know, yes I know, prayer changes things.*

The next verse makes it all plain:

I've traveled through sorrow valley,
So many times my heart's been made to bleed.
By some friends whom I thought were with me,
Through disappointment, I was knocked down to my knees.
But I rose with faith and grace,
I found nobody to take God's place,
I know, yes I know, prayer changes things.

The melancholy of "Father I Stretch My Hand to Thee"
gives way to the triumphant "I rose with faith and grace,"
really something to shout about. And with the popularity
of sheet music and records people began calling such
tunes "my song." Of course, rock listeners gauge their development by their response to Dylan songs, as an earlier
generation made fumbling puppy love to Glenn Miller
records. In gospel, however, a song doesn't mark a stage
in life, it's an assertion of identity. I've been betrayed by
enemies, I've found nobody better than God, so . . . as

some singers like to say, "I've got a song that can't nobody sing but *me*."

As gospel attracted the best singers with the most compelling tunes, it became the most important black musical form since early jazz. By 1940, a smoother version was even receiving national attention. Three jubilee quartets, the Golden Gate, the Charioteers, and the Deep River Boys, and a spiritual chorale group, the Wings Over Jordan, broadcast each Sunday over the three radio networks. Though the quartets were basically entertainers and the Wings never soared too high in the spirit, their programs inspired dozens of local broadcasts by more authentic groups. Gospel also entered the world of theaters and nightclubs. Sister Rosetta Tharpe and her bluesy guitar were featured with several big bands; in 1939, her record of Dorsey's tune "Rock Me" with Lucky Millinder's band was a pop hit. The same year, the Georgia Peach, a stately contralto, the Mahalia of her day, surrounded herself with jubilee quartets and a miniature choir for appearances at Radio City Music Hall and the World's Fair.

Meanwhile Dorsey and Sallie and Roberta Martin were constructing the "gospel highway," a circuit punctuated by churches and auditoriums where gospel groups were welcome. Their efforts paid off. By 1945 the Roberta Martin Singers were earning three thousand dollars for a week's revival in California. The public and the singers were obviously ready for records. America is filled with petty capitalists who cater to ghetto needs, whether these be magic ointments in New Orleans, love potions in East Harlem, or polka records in Milwaukee. After World War II, this enterprising breed discovered gospel. By 1950 there were dozens of gospel hits heard everywhere in black neighborhoods, on street corners, through open windows, down alleys, in bars and restaurants. A whole generation grew up listening to the Trumpeteers' "Milky White Way," the Georgia Peach's "Shady Green Pastures," the Angelic Gospel Singers' "Touch Me Lord Jesus," Mahalia's "Move On Up a Little Higher," the Martin Singers' "Old Ship of

Zion," the Pilgrim Travelers' "Mother Bowed," the Ward Singers' "Surely God Is Able," the Five Blind Boys' "Our Father" and the Bells of Joy's "Let's Talk About Jesus." Not everyone remembered the singers' names, but because a good gospel record can be played for years, they all absorbed the styles and standards of these early hits.

The records became identified with personal histories: "my song" became "my record." Gospel d.j.s would warn their listeners, "All right, children, here's 'Surely God Is Able.' Better put on your shouting shoes." Sometimes the records encroached too much on the listeners' lives. Edna Gallmon Cooke made her mark with song-sermonettes that were invariably about death. Her evocations of heaven, almost sensual to some listeners, gave others the creeps. One Alabama lady remembers, "I'd just left my grandmother lying in her sickroom. I turned on the radio, and they were playing 'When the Evening Sun Goes Down' by Madame Cooke. Just as it ended, here comes my brother, shaking his head and telling me, 'We lost Mama.' I'm sorry but I never could stand Edna Cooke after that."

From 1945 to 1960, while gospel's golden period lasted, all things worked for good. Audience and singers intuitively understood each other, accepting and applauding the most daring improvisations as self-expression determined by the moment's demands. Showmanship abounded, but the hard stylization of later years was absent. Everything was fresh, sweet, and vital. People came prepared for "a time . . . a good time . . . a marvelous time in the Lord." For the record collector it was bliss to be alive. He could buy any new record by a major group, quartet, or soloist, and expect a work of art—"We wouldn't record if we didn't have something to say—" and the best records advanced the number of ideas and techniques available to gospel. Singers today still live off the mannerisms developed by the gospel pioneers, just as rock bands echo the jazz and blues of thirty years ago. The imitators can almost duplicate the fervor and the surface mannerisms. But they completely lack the sweetness and spontaneity that made for real power. "We had some rare stuff back then."

For those who saw them, the greatest gospel performances became moments that could haunt or even change their lives forever. "I heard somebody say the minister's the man because nobody ever got saved off singing," says a disgruntled Roberta Martin Singer. "That's not so, singing has saved *many* souls." One didn't have to be saved to be haunted by the sheer generosity, vocal, emotional and physical, of those gospel moments. All the great soul singers grew up trying to equal them. But where are the young artists with heart and soul great enough to shout hundreds of people at one time? Even in the forties, many singers were scared to "move out that deep. When the spirit got too high, some of us used to run away from it." Those who moved on while people screamed and hollered and fainted—and in a few instances died—were simply the most powerful performers of the century.

The real gospel legends are these singers, the ones who gave all of themselves to move the people. Between 1940 and 1955, the "baddest men on the road" were the quartet leads—R. H. Harris, Silas Steele, Walter Latimore, Ira Tucker, Archie Brownlee, Kylo Turner, Sam McCrary, Julius Cheeks. But male gospel singers like Norsalus McKissick, J. Robert Bradley, Robert Anderson, and Joe May also left churches in shambles. Most thrilling of all were the female singers. Queen C. Anderson, Willie Mae Ford Smith, Sallie Martin, Mahalia Jackson, Ernestine Washington, Rosetta Tharpe, Roberta Martin, Sadie Durham, Edna Gallmon Cooke, and Mary Johnson Davis were the champions of gospel's first generation. But the second, those singers born during the twenties, produced such formidable church wreckers as Marion Williams, Bessie Griffin, Dorothy Love, Myrtle Scott, Deloris Barrett Campbell, Clara Ward, Ruth Davis, Bessie Folk, Albertina Walker, and Inez Andrews. That's a lot of names, but gospel is a huge field with more gifted adherents than any other popular music form in America. And even though all these singers had their own ways of doing everything, from bending notes to taking breaths to moving across a stage, to a man they insist the woods and hamlets are filled with "folks who can beat us all with their own original style."

Gospel singers complain, "We keep telling folks gospel's as good and big as any music." The claim shouldn't be necessary: the immense attention to details required in gospel should bespeak their art. But the world considers them naïve, wrongheaded, vocally athletic sorts who'd be wiser singing blues. So, turning in on themselves, the gospel singers move in their own world with its special experiences, standards, and language. There's so much good humor, spirit, and energy in the gospel life that ex-church singers keep coming back. "The church will take you in when nobody else will" is an old saying. But soul singers don't return for a spiritual retreat. A ghetto church is no monastery, and some gospel singers lead lives of resolute abandon. Even the straightest know all about bad times. "When you're out here on this highway," they say, "you don't miss a thing." Gospel singers aren't supposed to be worldly, but the world holds no surprises for them.

When they talk among themselves, their language is a compound of tradition and innovation. Like the singing itself, it employs all manner of nonverbal aids—moans, hums, chuckles—to enhance communication. If the basis of gospel is a moan, the basis of soul speech must be a hummed *hmmm*. A hum can speak volumes, as when Dorothy Love sings, "Lord you've been a mother for me, you've been a father, *hmmm*," implying her family's history in an emotional shorthand. The next step after *hmmm* is the three-part sequence *hmmm, hmmm, hmmm;* imagine it said in a downward scale like "mi re do" in half steps. These three moans can convey pleasure, surprise, sympathy, bewilderment. Obviously they don't mean anything by themselves—moment and tone make them eloquent. Much like the abrupt staccato chuckle "hah," which concentrates a complex of private associations, as if to say "I know what I know" or "If you think that, you're foolish." Always these sounds render the indescribable, implying, "Words can't begin to tell you but maybe moaning will."

Gospel talk begins there, in an emotional sound system, stable in form and infinitely flexible in content. But its own idioms are bristling with verbal wit. The most common refer to singing itself. A good singer can "tear up," "clean," "plumb demolish the place," "leave nothing standing, not even dust." When the spirit's high, it's "judgment," "doxology" (the last song in the hymnal), or "time for church to be dismissed." A hit number is called a "house wrecker," a "song for Sister Fluke" or a "stick." There's an easy self-parody. Completely secure in their roles, gospel singers may act sanctified—cry "Thank You Jesus" or cut some holy dance steps—under the most secular circumstances.

So gospel language can be as outrageous as the lives the singers lead. One Sunday, a pair of robbers stuck up Robert Anderson shortly after he left church. He was unharmed but still shaken when he told his friends, "Baby, I sang 'Just a Closer Walk with Thee' last night, but I didn't know how *close* he was." Albertina Walker thanks the church workers who cooked dinner for her group: "Chickens died that we might live." Alex Bradford tells of the time a big-name group appeared at his Newark church. "The local groups had sung and left the fire burning. The people were really ready for the girls, and they dared to get up singing she-bop-a-she-bop. Let me tell you, Jesus took the Q-17 bus." For two decades, Evangelist Shirley Caesar's big number has been "Sweeping Through the City." She says of her repertoire, "The new numbers are selling but the stick is still sweeping." A mistress of this eccentric idiom is that gospel trouper, eighty-nine-year-old Sallie Martin. In Cleveland, some time ago, Miss Martin rose to sing, following a band of popular young groups. "Well," she said in her characteristic portentous way, "The Caravans came to you. They got up to bat and hit a single. They made it to first base—yessir. The Pilgrim Jubilees stopped by this evening. They hit a triple, that carried them to *thoid* base, *hmmm*. Now it's time for a home run. Son—give me a C."

Sometimes even the language of apocalypse, of "doxology" and "judgment" squares exactly with the facts. Bessie Griffin, a female Job, barely survived an illness during which her temperature soared to 108.2. Shortly after her return from the hospital, she was awakened "right in the bed" by the Los Angeles earthquake. "I woke up screaming 'Jesus!' My cousin ran in yelling 'Cousin, cousin!' I told her, 'Don't call on me, call on the Lord.'" Through it all, Bessie remained a gospel pro. "When my husband Spencer got all upset, I told him

This old world can't last much longer,
Reeling and rocking so early in the morning."

Bessie makes the old gospel blues sound like a news bulletin. Later she prophesied, "I'm looking for all the churches to be filled this Sunday. You talk about many dangers, toils and snares! Baby, Jesus himself will be circling the block trying to get in."

Through the years the sheer act of gospel singing has become a metaphor for itself, confirming the old hymn lines about "taking my way with the Lord's despised few" and being "sometimes up, sometimes down, sometimes almost level with the ground." All the veterans have their testimonies. They've all traveled hundreds of miles on Maypop tires ("may pop any moment") to confront empty churches and penniless promoters. They all know about broken homes and dispossessed furniture and unpaid bills and segregated facilities (something that really matters if you travel by car). "I hate to sing those trouble songs," said one. "They'll get next to me in a minute."

So it would seem that nobody needs the music like those who make it. Commercial favor is the last thing one can count on in gospel. A popular group last year may sit home for months, waiting for promoters to call. The only thing that stays constant in their lives is the music. So their song becomes a testimony, evoking public role—"I've come to lift your burdens"; and private needs—"I can't sing your story but I can moan mine." Marion Williams says of "Prayer Changes Things," "If anybody can sing that, God knows I can." Dorothy Love won't sell her classic "I've Got Jesus and That's Enough" to the rock hustlers: "That's my whole story, I'd be selling out everything I am." And even Roberta Martin, the wealthiest gospel lady in Chicago, stuck with her store-front faith. Till the end, she refused to take pain-killing drugs. "Mrs. Martin expected the Lord to work a miracle in her life," explains Robert Anderson. "And she wept so hard when she got worse. She felt that she'd let us down. We tried to tell her the doctors were the miracle but she wanted to show us God's still the greatest healer, just like she used to say in her songs."

How do gospel singers view themselves? "We're the ones who came up on nothing but mother wit and Jesus," says one old-timer; another replies, "You better hush." "Mother wit and Jesus," "Came up," "Nothing but," even "We're the ones": every phrase distills the isolation, pride, and insecurity that comprise the gospel singer's self-image. The song line that defines their situation is from that dreary Methodist hymn, "Blessed Assurance, Jesus Is Mine":

"This is my story, this is my song."

PART ONE

BUILDING THE GOSPEL HIGHWAY

1

"Sallie Martin's Outta Sight"

"I've never been the greatest, nobody ever called me the greatest, never claimed to be the greatest, yet and still I've been everywhere the greatest have *been* . . . and that's just the way it go." Indeed, nobody could call Sallie Martin the greatest gospel singer. Her voice is all wrong, rough, gnarled, wide-ranging and shaky in all its registers from bass to second tenor. But "yet and still," Sallie Martin is the embodiment of true gospel music. She is one of its oldest practitioners, the founder, together with Thomas A. Dorsey, of the Gospel Singers Convention, the head of the largest Negro-owned gospel publishing company in America. More than this, she is an overwhelming performer, impossible to "outshout." Sallie's authority derives from the bad voice, the palpable sense that she's got nothing going for her but energy and will. "If Mahalia's a Cadillac and Roberta's a Buick," she tells Chicago churches, "I'se just a Model T Ford. But I makes it over the hill without shifting gears, and that's what counts, church, I makes it over the hill."

Most of the gospel pioneers who started out with Sallie came equipped with much more talent—Theodore Frye,

Mahalia Jackson, Sadie Durrah, Willie Mae Ford Smith had immense, blues voices—and much less gumption. At eighty-nine, Sallie has outlived most of them and sponsored all the significant musical changes gospel has since undergone. In 1940 she hired and trained a flighty teen-age pianist, Ruth Jones, who later became the mother of rhythm and blues, Dinah Washington. The first tune Sallie published, "Just a Closer Walk with Thee," is the one gospel song everyone knows. In gospel she has championed the most sophisticated young musicians, though her own singing resembles early field recordings. Sallie's done her share, "been everywhere the greatest have been." And lasted, outlasted the musical fads, stuck to the Baptist hymnal when the children started gospelizing Beatles tunes. So the people always know what to expect. "Ain't got nothin' new for you this evening. None of this *maw*dern music. Same old Sallie Martin, same old Jesus."

Above all, Sallie has presence. She is short, not quite stout, and charged with nervous energy. At home, she manifests a peculiar kind of country regality, all still and sober. But as soon as she hits church, she begins turning and twitching. When she sings, practically every note has its physical brother. Is it showmanship or Holy Ghost possession? "Somebody said, I wahnder . . . if you're gonna do that little *mooove* [the word beautifully syncopated] you do. I told her I don't do a move. Whenever I know anything, that thing that's *moved* me already *moved* me." The move is Sallie Martin, and to know and admire her is to mimic her ways. The physical and vocal shocks, the pet phrases scattered like verbal rest stations—"*Well*, I don't *know, Yes*sir, *mmm, hmmm,* see, that the way it go," and most of all, that voice. In private, Sallie's characteristic tone is low, pensive, almost disengaged from her words. The voice, like Sallie, seems to have comprehended all it ever will and now retains, almost reflexively, its distance and irony. It is shrewd, laconic, willful, on rare occasions, charming. Her severity turns off some people, but the authority is unmistakable. "They say I'm strict, I say they won't do right."

If Sallie retains an endearingly amateur quality, it may be because professional singing came rather late in her life. Before it did, she went the full round of ghetto experience: "I've had it, I really have," she now says without emotion. She was born in Pittfield, Georgia, a tiny black hamlet made up of a few houses, a store, and a combination church-schoolhouse. Her father died when she was young, but her mother and grandparents did not neglect her. "I really think my folks did pretty good on a little common sense. They just lived an ordinary life with a house with two rooms and a chimney in the middle and that's just how it was, farming, but my grandfather just didn't take no foolishness from nobody, white or colored." For Sallie, church and school became inseparable, one picking up where the other left off. The old hymns equate reading with praying, and she apparently saw anything religious as an extension of her education. "My mother used to go from place to place singing. They never had pianos but if they sang a ballad, she could remember the tune. This gave me a great desire to travel and sing. I had a cousin with whom I played and I told her I would never live in the country when I grew up, for I had seen a dress in a Sears Roebuck catalogue and I told her if she wanted to, I would show it to her just how it wore."

Black people were clearly deprived and terrorized—Sallie tells one horror story of a man who escaped a mass lynching by letting corpses fall on his prostrate body. But judging by her comments, there was also considerable race pride. When Sallie says, "I think the people lived a little better then," she sounds a recurrent gospel note: our forefathers were wiser, stricter, more devout. (One gospel standard admonishes "Let Us All Go Back to the Old Landmark.")

There's nothing passive about this old-time power; it comes from survival under pressure, and the tightest self-control. Southern elders are notoriously strict, brooking no dissent, quick to whip an unruly child. So severely disciplined is Sallie that she prefers these old ways; no modern mollycoddling for her. "I *think* we had better . . . *lessons* then because we knew the paddle would reach our hands if we failed."

Her most frightening experience involved a Wintersville, Georgia, clan of Snopeses. "The Smith brothers had been noted for if Negroes would pass, they would stop them and make them dance or make them do this. So then one of the brothers was going with a white girl and he tried to overpower her, and her father shot him, and one of the brothers shot the father. Now that calmed them down *just a little.*" Not enough, because they began making passes at Sallie. She was staying with a typically stern cousin. "He told Mr. Smith, 'I don't like no joking, I don't joke because one morning I might not be feeling well and you might not be feeling well, so we're just going to do our business. Now you all don't give me any trouble about this girl. You all leave here.' So for the rest of the summer, if I'd see Mr. Smith, cause he would always ride a horse, I'd make it my business to hide in the bushes or go someplace else."

Sallie quit school in the eighth grade, moved to Atlanta and began the long, wearying succession of black jobs: babysitting ("We called it nursing"), day work, night work, laundries and doctors' offices. She was raised a Baptist, but in 1916 she joined the Fire Baptized Holiness Church. "I'm very happy I was saved in a Holiness church, cause I got some principles from them that I'd *never* lose, *never* lose, never." The Holiness churches first flourished in the 1890s as a more evangelical, sanctified antidote to a dried-up Baptist church. Thus their first period is called the "Latter Rain Movement." In Holiness theology, fire and flood are commingled; Fire Baptized denotes an outpouring of Pentecostal fire. Sanctified folks have always been dubbed religious fanatics, "borned again" Holy Rollers. That's a painful onus for some, but Sallie probably relished the extra fillip of joining the "Lord's despised few." The singing she remembers was spirited and unprofessional. "We didn't have no soloists. We would all sing together or if you felt like you were going to testify, you might start out with a song, yourself." Such spontaneous expression is what gospel's all about. It can't be dictated or directed, as Sallie knows. "I always tell these young folk, be original, be *yourself*." The wonder of the Sanctified churches is that they let people be themselves, and they become original along the way.

In the twenties Sallie moved, with her husband and son, first to Cleveland ("where the Polish people made it so hard for us to work") and then to Chicago. Hers was not a saved home. The couple rented rooms and sold barbecue to the church next door: "We were making fifty dollars a week and that was good money then"; but her husband decided to "add on moonshine and gambling." Of course Sallie objected, but he ignored her, importing a new girl friend to mix the drinks while he cut the cards. In a huff, Sallie walked out with her son. It was 1929, and the only work she could get was at the "Contagious Hospital." "Mr. Cermac was the mayor and he simply wasn't paying anybody, but at least I had my room and board."

Meanwhile she began hearing about Thomas A. Dorsey, a former blues pianist whose gospel songs were laying Chicago church members in the aisles. "I had continued thinking about singing, and it just happened to be my good fortune that I heard about a lady named Mrs. Dennis. She knew Professor Dorsey and had him to hear me sing. He said, 'I think you have a wonderful opportunity if you can get with somebody who can trans*pose* for you.'" On February 7, 1932, Sallie made her debut with Dorsey's group at the Ebenezer Baptist church. Not surprisingly, Dorsey ignored Sallie's less than lustrous contralto. It was a year before her first solo. "I was so determined that I would get where I was going, I didn't bother him. But one night we went to Danville, Illinois. I told him I'd like to sing a solo." Her voice becomes harsh and gruff: "'You reckon you can do a solo?'" then cedes to sweet reasonableness. "'I can try' and I sang 'I Claim Jesus Foist and

That's Enough for Me.' I never had to ask him another single time. We traveled for eight years with me doing all the solos without any grief."

Dorsey's genius and Sallie's fervor proved an irresistible combination. Within a year's time, gospel choruses especially trained to sing Dorsey's tunes began sprouting all over Chicago's South Side. In 1933, Sallie traveled to Cleveland and organized their first gospel chorus. "Mr. Dorsey asked me 'You think I ought to write a paper to recommend you?' I told him, *No,* anyplace I've ever lived I can go back to, I don't need no one to recommend me." On that trip she sold ten dollars' worth of sheet music, enough to clue her to the business Dorsey was missing. "People would come into Mr. Dorsey's home to buy music, and so one day after they had finished, you see, he was living with his uncle, you see, he had a sack on his drawer in which he'd keep his money, and if his niece wanted to go to the store, she'd just go and get the money out, and never say how much out and how much in and I noticed that. 'Really you have something here but you don't know what to do with it.' 'You think you could do better?' 'I know I can.' 'I'll pay you four dollars a week,' and I said, 'All right, that's a deal.' "

Sallie's mother wit translated easily into organizational skill, an impetus Dorsey scarcely lacked. The two set up choruses in all the major ghettos of the South and Midwest, sponsored scores of talented young singers like Mahalia Jackson and Roberta Martin, and set up the Gospel Singers Convention, an annual convocation of America's gospel choristers. (Typically, the once-revolutionary Convention now seems a bit hidebound; a more progressive version was founded in 1969 by the "Crown Prince of Gospel," James Cleveland.) In 1937, Dorsey's University Gospel Singers began broadcasting over Chicago's WLFL. About that time the two traveled to Philadelphia, where Madame Gertrude Ward and her daughters Clara and Willa helped introduce the newer gospel tunes to the East Coast. California alone remained virgin territory.

On her own, Sallie traveled to Los Angeles. Here, logically, she performed at the Angelus Temple of Aimee Semple McPherson. Evangelist McPherson's services were a happy blend of old-time religion, sex, and showmanship. For all her Elmer Gantry tactics, she had a sense of humor ("All right, ushers, clear the one-way street for Jesus") and a real compassion for the working-class migrants who comprised her followers. "She was *wahn*derful. She used to say like 'Now who's here tonight for the first time? Now come up cross the pulpit, I'm gonna give you a rose.' She's gone now but they're carryin' it on for her in a beautiful way." The reactionary elements in Evangelism from Gerald L. K. Smith to Billy Graham are well known. But Evangelism also contains an element of populism. The revival churches sing, "You've got to love everybody if you want to see Jesus," and Aimee McPherson's services were completely integrated. So, in 1936, blacks and whites shouted together—"They always did get happy there"—off the songs of Sallie Martin. Gospel has toured Europe and America's colleges, but that much integration will never occur at Harvard or the Montreux Jazz Festival.

Having colonized California for Mr. Dorsey, Sallie returned home. But relations between the two began to cool. Sallie's imperious ways turned off Dorsey's friends, who found her arrogant and overbearing. She in turn resented their sly insinuations and interference: "Well I don't know, everybody's got to be a leader." After one lady confronted her, Sallie took a tack from her Georgia cousins. "It just provoked me so bad that I didn't say anything because I knew if I'd said anything I wouldn't be where I am today because I knew by the time I said it, I'd have hit her. And she's dead today and don't even know." Finally, in 1940, Dorsey himself confronted her with the various complaints. "I told him, 'I'll tell you the truth, brother, I wouldn't care to hear *nothin'* that *anyone* said.' 'Well that's what you always say, why don't you prove it?' and I said, 'O.K., here's your dawn, I'm gone.' And I walked out, and that was at the corner of Oakwood and Cottage Grove, and I was at the Ritz Hotel on Martin Luther King's Drive. And when I was back on the street waitin' for the bus I said, 'Lord, liveordie, sinkorswim, I'll never go back *there.*' "

By now Sallie knew every gospel route in the country, having opened up most of them herself. She experimented for a while, traveling first as a soloist, accompanied by the volatile Ruth Jones. "She could really sing but, shoot, she'd catch the eye of some man and she'd be out the church before the minister finished off the doxology."

Sallie next joined forces with Roberta Martin. Roberta was a talented pianist and musician. She had trained at Northwestern and could write, read, and, above all, arrange gospel music. (Sallie eventually learned to read music. "I know it was nothin' but the Lord, because I only took six weeks of piano lessons," she says, playing like someone who's taken six weeks of piano lessons.) Where Sallie's roars could carry for city blocks, Roberta's contralto was refined, subdued, achieving its greatest effects through timing and phrasing. Artistically and temperamentally she was Sallie's polar opposite, but her group contained the finest young male singers in Chicago: Robert Anderson, Norsalus McKissick, Eugene Smith, Willie Webb. Once again, Sallie's willpower and connections eased the way for more talented singers. "We were called the Martin and Martin Gospel Singers. No, we weren't together very long because they were too narrow-minded, they were too afraid that somebody would say Sallie and don't say Roberta." Not that the Martin Singers don't respect Sallie. Robert Anderson feels that with Roberta and Mahalia gone, Sallie is the last living symbol of the old-time gospel tradition. But Sallie had to be her own woman, and, doubtless inspired by her namesake, formed the Sallie Martin Singers, the first female group in gospel.

Right after leaving Dorsey, Sallie was advised by Reverend Clarence Cobbs to form her own publishing house. Reverend Cobbs was the flamboyant pastor of the First Church of Deliverance, a Spiritualist congregation whose

members range from all walks of life, crooked and straight.
His fiery broadcasts, punctuated by ecstatic outbursts and
lusty choir singing, are probably the most famous in gospel.* Cobbs was more Sallie's speed. "He told me, 'Sallie,
why don't you go into business? I've got a man named
Kenneth Morris over at church and he's not doing anything but throw his talent away, selling his songs for three
dollars.'" Aided by Reverend Cobbs, Sallie and Kenneth
Morris formed the Martin and Morris Publishing Company, Sallie providing the contacts and the busy work,
Morris, a tubercular pianist, writing the songs. Morris began where Dorsey left off. An early Morris hit, sung to the
kind of blues riff that links Count Basie and Chuck Berry:

I want to dig a little deeper in God's love,
Dig a little deeper in God's love,
Dig a little deeper in the storehouse of God's love.
Gonna walk on like a Christian should,
Talk on like my Jesus would,
Dig a little deeper in the storehouse of his love.

"Dig a Little Deeper" seduced the Sanctified churches but
America wasn't ready for that much sensual fervor. More
universally palatable was Morris' arrangement of "Just a
Closer Walk with Thee," the company's first hit. By 1945,
even without recordings, gospel sheet-music sales num-
bered in the hundreds of thousands. While Mahalia Jackson was traveling with Thomas A. Dorsey, featuring all
Dorsey programs, and the Roberta Martin Singers performed tunes published by Roberta's Martin Studio of Mu-

---

* Cobbs's church, bedecked with flowers, reeking of incense, and
studded with grand pianos and Radio City-style organs, is a perfect
setting for the gospel drama. Spiritualism emphasizes the "spirit,"
rather than God or Jesus, and the spirit is unpredictable. Cobbs's
members never know what to expect. One Sunday he refused to
preach. The spirit had told him to take off his robes, which he did,
exposing undershirt and slacks, put on an old country preacher's
robe and sat and prayed. "I want you all to walk out of church and
touch the sleeve of my robe. God's going to work a miracle." The
ensuing pandemonium brought smiles of pleasure from Sallie, acknowledging an old friend's work well done.

sic, the Sallie Martin Singers featured Martin and Morris songs exclusively.

The group had a neat background harmony, a sweetly soaring soprano, Dorothy Simmons, and a first-rate gospel soloist, Sallie's adopted daughter Cora Martin. Where Sallie's approach was straightforward and lowdown, Cora's style was sophisticated and a bit tricky. Her broken notes, half-sobs, and intricate note bending influenced Sallie not a bit. No matter—all the public wanted from Sallie was spirit and new material, and with Kenneth Morris back home composing, she had plenty of both. Even without records, the group did well cross-country, achieving a success never duplicated in gospel—with both black and white church audiences. "We always seemly . . . did have marvelous services, especially in Los Angeles. Nobody had been going out there. And especially with the white people." Item from *The King's Ambassador,* a white Los Angeles Baptist newspaper, January 1944:

SALLIE MARTIN COLORED LADIES AT CENTER
A special feature of the musical program of the Oswald P. Smith campaign will be the singing of the Sallie Martin Colored Singers of Chicago who are making a tour of the west. This splendid group of colored ladies recently made an appearance at the L. A. Evangelistic Center and delighted the packed auditorium with their inspiring, soul-stirring music. The Sallie Martin Colored Ladies Quartet possess not only the traditional and characteristic enthusiasm of their race but they also possess exceptionally fine voices nicely blended together to present enjoyable singing.

Did Sallie mind such patronizing commentary? "No, didn't think anything about it, because I'd never heard anything else."

While out in L.A., Sallie made contact with the more down-home black churches. The largest, St. Paul Baptist Church, had taken over the California airwaves much as Cobbs' church had in Chicago. Sallie attached herself to the choir and in 1946 acted as their narrator in the first gospel television broadcast. The choir's director, a flamboyant baritone named J. Earle Hines, once said, "All those white folk wanted me to go and sing Schubert and Schumann and all that shit," and he could have, too. Instead he stuck to Kenneth Morris'

> *I'll be somewhere around God's altar,*
> *I'll be somewhere around God's throne,*
> *Look just look for me in Heaven somewhere,*
> *I'll be there.*

The choir made several great records including "Just a Closer Walk with Thee" performed by the Sallie Martin Singers. On the record, Sallie's voice drops gracefully to the bass register, to the immeasurable glee and satisfaction of her vocal audience. She did have one other hit, "He'll Wash You Whiter Than Snow," performed with the group of Alex Bradford, a baritone even more flamboyant and gifted than Earle Hines. The disc maintains a crunching rock beat with Sallie listing, to a blues riff, the items God will wash: "He'll wash my heart, he'll wash my mind, etc." But somehow the recording medium was not friendly to Sallie. "God's love is better felt than told," she likes to say, and she's better seen than heard. The recording voice is strident and off key; in person, Sallie's personality swamps aesthetic criticisms.

For gospel groups traveling has never been easy. Sallie probably experienced first and most all the characteristic disappointments: small crowds, swindling promoters, broken contracts. Yet, "I held on. Didn't make me no difference if we didn't have but ten people there, we went on and *sang.*" As usual, she bore her burdens alone. If her girls had to sit with her during the humiliating procedure of free-will offering—"I'm looking for one hundred but I'll settle for twenty-five. Won't you give? The Lord will bless you"—they were always assured of getting their money. "From the beginning I paid *all* the bills for my girls, and the ending too. They didn't know what a bill looked like."

Sallie showed more concern for her group than most leaders, for while other groups saved their money by traveling long and uncomfortable journeys by car, Sallie sent her group by train. "I remember one time we had closed out a meeting in Washington. We made it to the train station just in time but I couldn't find the tickets. We only had three minutes, so I told the conductor, 'Let the girls go on, I'll find the tickets.' He tried to act cute: 'What if I let them on and you ain't got the tickets?' 'Man, I'll *buy* de *train*, don't worry about it,'" and for once, Sallie's voice bursts into falsetto giggles.

Sallie retired the group in the mid-fifties. She remains a vivid presence in Chicago churches. She is the best kind of gospel m.c., one who prepares the spiritual reception for the artists. "I tell the people, 'Now just don't sit there and wait on your special singer. You get with *every*body, because this is just like serving a dinner. We're starting out perhaps with soup. After awhile we'll give you a little something else, and we'll finally move on up until we get to . . . the dessert but if you sit chere and do nothin' about it, you won't get anything. You'll be just as hungry as when you started.' "

Occasionally she will favor the public with a solo. Her songs are usually old hymns, pre-Dorsey, performed the old-time way. "I heard the voice of Jesus say," Sallie sings, and suddenly twists to the side, struck either by the Holy Ghost or a severe colic. "Come unto me and rest," another turn, a wave of her handkerchief. "Lie down thy [sic] weary one, lie down, thank God," she hollers. "Thy head—" a big note—"upon my breast." By the end of the first verse, ushers are carrying the saints out. Singers joke over Sallie's voice but they hate to follow her. "Why does she make it so hard for us?" wonders Jessy Dixon. "Sallie Martin's outta sight," say the young choir singers, slapping palms. Sallie can't keep up with their strange time signatures and key changes, since she makes so many herself. But she knows what they'll never know, and they know it.

Sallie's done and seen it all in gospel and she's distilled something out of her life very close to art. On a recent album she uses the text of "Amazing Grace" as the starting point for a set of verbal improvisations. In the background drone an organ and an electric saw (!). When Sallie reaches the lines

> *I once was lost but now I'm found*
> *I was blind but now I see.*

she interpolates, "I was blind, that's the trouble with so many folks today, they're blind, they can't see." It's all spoken but it's a daring, exquisitely musical convolution of the tune, ending exactly where it should. Sallie can shock one with these reminders that, yes, she does hear the tune, even if she can't always carry it. Later she says, "I hope you really felt something. I hope you didn't join the church because you heard a minister say, Well . . . give me your hand and God your heart," parodying the old communion invitation. The old phrases are just slogans to Sallie, and her voice discriminates between lip service and spirit possession.

Sallie is a rich woman; she owns several houses as well as Martin and Morris. (A false rumor had her owning the ground on which the Los Angeles Dodgers played.) She makes good use of her money, giving private scholarships and aiding the less fortunate singers. In the late fifties she took up the plight of a Baptist missionary school. "Every Sunday over at Pilgrim, the minister used to say, 'We're gonna lift the Foreign Mission offering because we'll never be free till Africa puts on her clothes.' And of course, everyone put in a dollar or a dime, and this went on for a number of years and I began thinking, I said, *Well* now, I don't *know,* as much *money* as we've raised for the Foreign Mission, seem like to me if they been getting it, they ought to have their clothes on. I'll send my money direct to Dr. Martin's mission in Nigeria, West Africa." In 1960 Dr. Martin invited her to celebrate Nigerian independence.

When she arrived, Lagos was packed with tourists. The only route to the mission was by taxi. So Sallie went out and hired herself a taxicab. After a two-day trip, she discovered the mission school without lights. "I told Dr. Martin to find out how much the lightnin' cost. I'll pay for it if I have to pay a dollar down, a dollar a week." Of course, she did better than that, and one of the mission buildings now carries her name.

She now lives in a modern apartment building she is in the process of buying. Her own apartment is cluttered with furniture, the rococo stage of various periods, with a few old rotogravure photos of Cora and her son in Army uniform (he was killed in 1942). The windows were tightly shut one August afternoon as Sallie sat, regal and isolate amidst her vases and couches, musing on where she'd been. "You've got to have it within you that you can make it. See, and with the help of the Lord, ain't nothing can keep you from it." Her naturally conservative disposition does not take kindly to the militants. "Just like I get kind of provoked with these folks now worrying about my identity and my this and my that. You better stop worrying about your identity, and do something for yourself. As for me, I've just been myself, never tried to be like anybody else. They say we've been brainwashed. I haven't been brainwashed because I've never tried to be like anybody else, because I always really thought myself *somebody*. I've been somebody all my life. Like I told that girl I'm going to Chicago, I just *believed* that, I'm gonna be somebody." She's the incarnation of old-time religion, but she treats accusations of Thomism with lowdown disgust. "Like this lady on TV. I know what she was saying with her big words was everybody that believed in God was dumb and ignorant, see. But, you see, you have to know for yourself. As *smart* a man and as *intelligent* a man as Paul was, they criticized him. We haven't kept ourselves back, if you know anything you know you haven't kept yourself back. Just didn't have the opportunity. It's being opened up, Martin Luther

King died that we might have it; of course they're messin'
it up." Once again, it's Sallie Martin against the world. She
apparently has little faith in modern ways, politics or gospel. For her, it's the old songs every time. "I like the old
songs, I do, I really do. I think the old songs were written
out of some kind of burden. The old songs wasn't some
song some person sat down and said, I'm gonna get me
some kind of song together to make me some money.
Nowadays nobody has no worry or struggles."

Sallie is equally critical of the gospel folk who don't live
like her. "There isn't but one thing that I say will keep us
back and that is singing one thing and then doing so different when you get out of your service, that will really
hinder anybody. I heard a man say, 'Some of you do your
devilment and want to bring it into the church. Regardless
to what I do, I'm certainly not gonna bring it into the
church.' Well what does he mean? That wooden building
means nothing. *He's* the church. The only way you don't
bring it into the church is you leave it *off*. Now if folks see
somebody trying to do the right thing—" and the identity
of "somebody" is very clear—"they say, 'Well, some people
try to be *sooo nice,'* " the word hard like a slap—" 'and
they try to be *soo ho—lay* and *ev*—everybody's got a skele-
ton in the closet.' " Her voice becomes pinched and mean:
"Well, how do you *know?*" Then having routed the en-
emy, it becomes calm again. "Somebody is wrong. If we
can't live right, then why did Jesus leave it here with us?"

Sallie will keep on being herself, singing the old songs,
criticizing the new ways, and pushing people to live right.
There's no danger of the voice getting worse, but that's
never been the problem. Sallie Martin is real, and everyone trusts her to be herself. "I can't sing just any song. A
song that carry a message got to have some kind of absolutely *common* sense, and a whole lot of songs sing about
my mother's gone and my father's gone, well we don't
need all of that. They're playin' on emotions, that don't
mean nothin'. They're not tellin' them you got to live right,

and if you're not right, you need to get right, see." On her
album, Sallie sings the lines

> *Some folks may doubt, some folks may scorn,*
> *All can desert and leave me alone.*
> *But as for me, I'll take the part,*
> *For God is real, and I can feel him in my heart.*

After singing "But as for me," she lets go with a heartfelt
"Yeah Lord" because that's how Sallie sees herself.

Sallie's is not a faith that soars on bromides; the nub of
"absolutely common sense" is always present. "I claim
Jesus, I believe Jesus. I don't need to play uh horse races
or whatever they come around with. In the first place, I
don't need to stoop to live. If God's got everything, I'm his
child, then why do I have to do different?" There's nothing
passive, or quietist about the voice now; if this is Thomist
theology, its speaker is a contentious old lady. Sallie has
achieved a faith which belies all the facile pieties. "At funerals I like to sing 'What a friend we have in Jesus, all
our griefs and sins to bear.' Because he'll bear *all* your
burdens, *sooo* . . . lift up your heads. You go on singing
about he's everything to me, the Lord will make a way,
but once a burden comes around, you look somewhere
else." Sallie, however, will stick because "Joy, comfort, I
found all of that," and the voice now is emotionless and
matter-of-fact. In church the joy may turn Sallie into a gospel windmill, but at home she describes it casually, famil-
iarly.

Even the outrageous Sallie is assimilated at home. When
she remembers the remark about the Model T Ford, she
says, without a grin, "That's the truth, the Lord has always
proved true. I'll tell you one thing, I've never craved to be
rich, but I can really tell you this, whatever I desired from
a child the Lord has given it to me. Because I didn't ask
for a whole lot, and yet in a way I think it's a great big
blessing I said when I was sixteen, I'd like to go to Paris,
I want to go to London, I really would like to have a
home. All of it come to pass. *Now,*" she says decisively,

"I've been to Paris three or four times." Sallie's earned what she owns and accepts loneliness as her lot. When she travels cross-country to see Cora, she names her crew "me, the Lord, and the car." Old age hasn't tempered the grim disposition that sees bad coming out of all earthly good. "Like when this old head finally hits the papers," she begins smiling, "some of my folk come by and say, 'my God, if some drops are falling, they ought to fall on all of us.' I tells 'em, 'Babies . . . whatever drops fallin' on you, still waitin' in your treasure.'" The grin disappears, "And that the way it go."

2

"I Get These Special Vibrations":
Thomas A. Dorsey

The 1969 Gospel Singers Convention was held in Philadelphia at Tindley Methodist Church, the same church where Bessie Smith was buried. To Thomas A. Dorsey, whose eclectic faith embraces reincarnation and spiritual vibrations, it must have seemed a journey through time. C. A. Tindley, the church's founder, was Dorsey's inspiration as a songwriter. "I feel I became part of Dr. Tindley just like he became part of me." Dorsey also shared a special understanding with Bessie Smith. He wasn't always saved, and during the twenties, as "Georgia Tom," accompanist for Ma Rainey and the Empress, he was notorious for his double-entendre blues. Though he later gave up the world, he knows "Blues is a part of me, the way I play piano, the way I write." Since Dorsey's Convention rose out of the success of his tunes, inspired by Tindley and nourished by Bessie Smith, the old man was indeed "retracing the bridge that brought me over," surrounded by only the friendliest ghosts.

Dorsey is a perfect foil for Sallie Martin. Where she is all nervous energy and commotion, mother wit and down-

home humor, he has the wizened, laconic manner of a
New England merchant. He likes to go hunting, owns a set
of vacation cabins, drops big words with preacher's facility,
and is given to poems and epigrams of a fairly audacious
nature: the motto for *Thomas A. Dorsey's Poem Book* is
"A solemn promise with faith, appraise the state of security
and bind one's self to his or her promise." He is a slim,
dark man, slightly stooped, with a small kernel of a head.
In the dozens of pictures taken for the Convention he is
usually dwarfed by the massive women surrounding him.
In most of these pictures he appears glum and suspicious.
Actually he has a charming smile and his enthusiasm often
lifts his voice into an irrepressible falsetto. Thomas A.
Dorsey is a wise old man, perhaps the only Chicago pioneer
to remain above the internecine gospel feuds. Though he
renounced the blues years ago, he keeps many friends in
the field, is proud of his achievements, and seems much
less entwined in the gospel mystique than Sallie. Where
she distrusts everyone, his disposition is open and friendly.
"I can walk into a room and pick up these special vibrations. That's why I've never had no trouble from white or
black."

In 1935, Dorsey's life was celebrated in poetry by Mrs.
Ruth A. Smith of Brooklyn. The first stanza would have
delighted Mark Twain:

*I now write of Thomas Andrew Dorsey, who in eighteen
     ninety-nine*
In Villa Rica, Georgia, below the Mason-Dixon Line,
*Was born to Reverend T. M. Dorsey, a Baptist minister of
     renown,*
And Mrs. Etta Dorsey, a jewel of that town.

Dorsey was raised in Atlanta, where he heard the old Dr.
Watts hymns, early blues, and jazz. Like most Southern
Baptists, his parents disapproved of the theater, but as a
child he worked as a water boy for the circus, welcoming
any byway to show business. One of the great moments of
his childhood was a revival conducted by Billy Sunday on

the circus grounds. Dorsey attended on "Colored Night" when the circus tent was packed. "When Sunday got hot, he'd take off his coat and loosen his collar and everybody would holler Amen and Hallelujah. It must have been just a gesture but the people went wild." Dorsey was equally impressed by Sunday's musician, Homer Rodeheaver. "Homer played a sweet trombone. You know, at that time, they didn't allow too much music in church. We became fast friends in later years when he ran the Rodeheaver Music Company, here in Chicago." Clearly, something secular about the revival, about Sunday's showmanship and Rodeheaver's music, attracted the youth.

Dorsey was a child prodigy, mastering several instruments, and while still in his teens he began playing blues and ragtime. He heard Bessie Smith as early as 1912 and joined Ma Rainey a few years later. Throughout the twenties Georgia Tom was a most prolific blues composer. His erotic numbers exhibit a cunning wit and verbal playfulness that is so absent in his sub-Edgar Guestian poetry. His melodies are among the loveliest of that era; one of them, "It's Tight Like That," is still heard on underground radio stations. Yet the minister's son was not contented. In 1921 he was saved at a Baptist convention off the tune "I Do, Don't You?" Though composed by a white man, the song manifested the same qualities as Tindley's compositions—and, more than anyone, Tindley was Dorsey's idol.

Neither spirituals nor hymns, Tindley's songs comprised a whole new genre. Amidst the most banal sentiments, Tindley incorporated folk images, proverbs, and Biblical allusions familiar to black churchgoers for over a hundred years. For example,

Courage my soul and let us journey on,
Though the night is dark, it won't be very long,
Thanks be to God, the morning light shines through,
And the storm is passing over, hallelu.

Hallelu, oh hallelu, the storm is passing over, hallelu.

In that refrain Tindley created a modern spiritual wedded to the kind of church verse respectable publishers like Homer Rodeheaver would use.

Another Tindley tune is not remarkable for its verse, but the chorus:

> *I'll overcome, I'll overcome, I'll overcome some day,*
> *If in my life I do not yield, I'll overcome some day.*

was easily transformed into the greatest of all freedom songs. Thousands of Southern blacks were raised on "I'll Overcome," a sentiment one step away from militant protest. Indeed, Tindley's songs are specifically addressed to the poor and downtrodden:

> *If this world from you withhold,*
> *All its silver and its gold*
> *And you have to get along on meager fare,*
> *Just remember in his word*
> *How he feeds the little bird,*
> *Take your burdens to the Lord and leave 'em there.*

> *Leave it there, leave it there,*
> *Take your burdens to the Lord and leave it there,*
> *If you trust and never doubt,*
> *He will surely bring you out,*
> *Take your burdens to the Lord and leave them there.*

The victory implicit in "surely bring you out," one of the standard black idioms, is a master stroke.

Another Tindley composition blends rather pretentious metaphors with a moving climax and an archetypal gospel chorus.

> *We're tossed and driven on this restless sea of time,*
> *Somber skies and howling tempests often hide the bright*
> *   sunshine,*
> *But there is a land of fadeless day*
> *And when the mists are rolled away*
> *We'll understand it better by and by.*

By and by when the morning comes.
When all the saints of God are gathered home,
We'll tell the story how we've overcome,
We'll understand it better by and by.

Tindley's greatest composition contains no excess metaphors. "Stand By Me" combines the fervor of a Dr. Watts hymn with the terse economy of a spiritual:

When the storms of life are raging, stand by me,
When the storms of life are raging, stand by me,
When the world is tossing me,
Like a ship upon the sea,
Thou who rulest wind and water, stand by me.

In the midst of persecution, stand by me,
In the midst of persecution, stand by me,
When my foes in battle array
Undertake to stop my way,
Thou who rescued Paul and Silas, stand by me.

When I'm growing old and feeble, stand by me,
When I'm growing old and feeble, stand by me,
When my life becomes a burden,
And I'm nearing chilly Jordan,
O thou Lily of the Valley, stand by me.

As the format may suggest, the melody is a blues variant, the sixteen-bar blues, the form so ubiquitous in mournful gospel that I have dubbed it the Baptist blues. With the era of soul and rock, the sixteen-bar blues infiltrates even detergent commercials. But Tindley was composing in 1905, and his merger of black folk tunes and sentiments with the music of shabby white Evangelism is one of the great chapters in American popular music. Dorsey considers Tindley the first gospel songwriter. His songs contain blues modes, easily adjusted to jazz syncopations, and offer implicit opportunities for improvisation. "Stand By Me," especially, allows for elaborations on the vocative: "Thou . . . Mary's baby, Thou . . . meek and humble lamb,

Thou . . . my mountain mover, Thou . . . my hell-hound chaser, Thou . . . my walking cane to glory," etc.

Tindley's songs are gospel, though years before gospel's first flourishing. Likewise, all during the twenties and early thirties, religious recordings were produced for the "race" market. Most of these records featured jubilee quartets or shouting preachers, and some of them—Reverend J. M. Gates's "Death's Black Train," Reverend F. W. McGee's "Jonah in the Belly of the Whale," Reverend J. C. Burnett's "Handwriting on the Wall," Elder Lightfoot Michaux' "Happy Am I"—were smash hits, selling hundreds of thousands of copies. The most celebrated shouting preachers would usually preach a brief sermonette to hieratic encouragement from the sisters. Then everything climaxed in a rhythmic shout accompanied by snycopated hand-clapping and quasi-Dixieland instrumentation, much resembling the Sunday services still broadcast from many Sanctified churches. The religious field also included itinerant guitar-playing minstrels like Blind Willie Johnson and Reverend E. W. Clayborn and a slew of amateur soloists discovered by record scouts in the major churches. One pianist-soloist, the blind Arizona Dranes, later became a power in the Holiness church, but most of the artists were endearingly unprofessional. Their records still contain a certain charm (a few collectors specialize in early gospel and refuse to touch anything past 1929). Their appeal was limited almost exclusively to church folk. Unlike later blues singers who start in church and seldom lose their affiliations, Ma Rainey and Bessie Smith are described by Dorsey as completely uninterested in gospel. "Now they were masters in their day. And if they came on the scene today singing gospel, nobody could touch them. They had that special cry. Still, like I said, nobody talked about church music then. Not even me, and I was brought up under it."

In private, Dorsey had never left the church. As a boy in Atlanta, he had known both Reverend Gates and Clara Hudmon, a magnificent contralto who recorded first with

Gates and in later years under the name "The Georgia Peach." "I always said Georgia Peach could have been the next Bessie Smith, if they'd pushed her right." He continually wavered between the two fields, secular and sacred, delighted to have either Bessie Smith or Clara Hudmon perform his compositions. (Dorsey feels another gospel pioneer, Willie Mae Ford Smith, could have surpassed even Bessie, had she switched fields.)

"In the early 1920s I coined the words 'gospel songs' after listening to a group of five people one Sunday morning on the far south side of Chicago. This was the first I heard of a gospel choir. There were no gospel songs then, we called them evangelistic songs." In 1926, he composed his first gospel hit, "If You See My Savior, Tell Him That You Saw Me." "That song was written out of a sad condition. I had been ill for two years. My wife would work in a laundry and come home and nurse me. I lived in an apartment building under a fine young man, a taxi driver. He went to work one morning and came home *so* sick. They put hot packs on his stomach and we stayed up all night with him. But by then appendicitis had set in. They took him to the hospital and he died that very night. I was in a quandary. I'd been sick six to eight months and this boy'd been ill not twenty-four hours and died. So the message came to me, the spirit told me, 'If you see my Savior . . .'" Dorsey borrowed five dollars and mailed five hundred copies to churches throughout the country. "It was three years before I got one single order. I felt like going back to the jazz field of music. The flower of dawn blossomed in 1930 when the National [all black] Baptist Convention met at their Jubilee Session at Chicago's Coliseum. There was a girl from St. Louis, had a good heavy voice, she was laying them in the aisles singing 'If you see my Savior tell him that you saw me.'" The musical directors of the Convention, Lucie Campbell (a great early gospel songwriter) and E. W. Isaac, then invited him to sell his music. From 1929 on, Dorsey committed himself exclusively to gospel.

The next ten years were his most prolific period. During the worst of the Depression, he kept turning out dozens of optimistic songs aimed to lift the spirits of the unemployed laborers and domestics who comprised his audience. The gospel of Tindley and Dorsey talks directly to the poor. In so many words, it's about rising above poverty while living humble, deserting the ways of the world while retaining its best tunes. Many Dorsey songs borrowed the blues-tinged melody of Tindley's "Stand By Me"; others had a bounce straight out of early vaudeville. One of his early partners was the ex-blues shouter Sara Martin, famous for her "Death Sting Me Blues," who gave up the world to sing gospel. For Miss Martin Dorsey composed a variation of the old "There'll Be Some Changes Made," calling it "I Surely Know There's Been a Change in Me."

Dorsey combined the good news of gospel with the bad news of blues in a form worldly singers called the gospel blues. Some saints objected, but the imagery of the blues obviously resonates through such fine lyrics as

> *When lights go out, crowds get thin,*
> *Friends move out, He steps on in,*
> *What could I do if it wasn't for the Lord?*

or

Often there's misunderstanding out of all the good I do.
I go to friends for consolation and I find them complaining
    too.
So many nights I keep tossing in pain,
Wondering what the day's gonna bring,
Then I say to my soul take courage,
The Lord will make a way somehow.

Not even Tindley had better employed folk idioms for musical effect. Dorsey says he didn't deliberately use blues melodies and rhythms *but* "You see, when a thing becomes a part of you, you don't know when it's gonna manifest itself. And it's not your business to know or my business to know."

Sallie Martin, Chicago, 1969.

Thomas A. Dorsey.

Mother Willie Mae Ford Smith, St. Louis, 1975.

Mahalia Jackson, New York, early fifties.
Photograph by Otto Rothschild

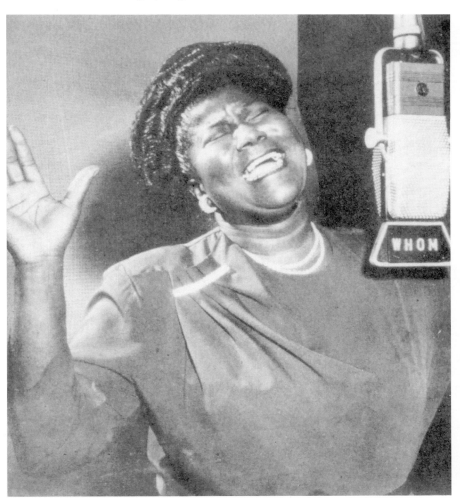

Bessie Griffin, Los Angeles, 1969.

Sam Cooke, New York, 1955.
Photograph by Lloyd Yearwood

Sister Rosetta Tharpe, Europe, 1970.
Photograph by Gunther Rakete

Golden Gate Quartet, early forties.

The Sensational Nightingales, New York, 1958. Julius Cheeks at mike; *background left to right:* unidentified member, Dewey Young, Jo Jo Wallace, David Edrington. *Photograph by Lloyd Yearwood*

Clara Ward and Marion Williams, New York, 1958; Kitty
Parham on tambourine.
Photograph by Lloyd Yearwood

The Dixie Hummingbirds, New York, 1958. *Left to right:*
James Davis, Ira Tucker, William Bobo.
Photograph by Lloyd Yearwood

Dorsey's tunes also owed plenty to the old Dr. Watts hymns, and he published the most beautiful and chilling "The Day Is Past and Gone." The archetypal moan, this hymn eloquently illustrates the proximity of blues and sacred music. It also placed Dorsey's controversial gospel blues in a respectable black Baptist tradition. Conversely, he composed a few songs white publishers like Homer Rodeheaver could accept on sight. Two of them, "It's My Desire" and "When I've Done the Best I Can," are indistinguishable from pop ballads of the "I Believe" ilk; in the late forties, Guy Lombardo popularized "My Desire." Dorsey's tunes frequently exhibit a double bind to low-down gospel and a more sentimental middle-class music. This tendency is even more apparent in his *Poem Book*, e.g.,

> *I have a great respect for father;*
> *I love my sister and brother.*
> *I have a world of love for my wife,*
> *But I'm fonder of my mother.*

Many of his lyrics are exceptionally sentimental ("To the blind man give him glasses, to the cripple give a crutch"), though an occasional abrasive image rises above the treacle: "I see the window, I see the door, This world don't seem like home anymore." Dorsey's tunes revealed the full spectrum of show-business influences, from Ma Rainey to Guy Lombardo; Mahalia called him "our Irving Berlin."

Gospel appeared at the right time. The Depression was at its cruelest mark, and the churches apparently couldn't reach the people. "I wrote to give them something to lift them out of that Depression. They could sing at church but the singing had no life, no spirit. The preacher would preach till his collar would melt down around his neck but there wouldn't be no money in the oblations." Dorsey and Sallie Martin "livened up the churches," and enriched them too, as they observe with pride. By 1932, when they held the first Gospel Singers Convention, the three-thousand-seat Pilgrim Baptist Church was packed. "We had so many voices in the chorus we had to put the director's stand halfway up the aisles, back of the church." During gospel's golden period, from 1945 to 1960, the Convention attracted the finest singers in America. For years it was the only institution dedicated to advancing gospel as both an art form and a way of life. In 1974, despite the inroads of James Cleveland's gospel workshop, the Convention drew three thousand people to its St. Louis meeting. By then it had absorbed the energies and talents of three generations. Most of the original members were gone. "I went over my first Convention photo. Out of one hundred one voices, only four are left. Seventy of those folk are dead. But we keep carrying on."

In 1932, Dorsey's first wife and child died while he was on the road. At first, like Job, he cursed his lot, but within a week's time he'd rallied enough to join his friend, Theodore R. Frye, for an evening of music. That night he composed his masterpiece.

Precious Lord take my hand,
Lead me on, let me stand,
I am tired, I am weak, I am worn.
Through the storm, through the night,
Lead me on to the light,
Take my hand precious Lord, lead me on.

When my way grows drear,
Precious Lord linger near,
When my life is almost gone,
At the river, Lord I'll stand,
Guide my feet, hold my hand,
Take my hand precious Lord and lead me home.

Dorsey wanted to change the title to "Blessed Lord Take My Hand" but Frye insisted, "No, call him 'Precious Lord.' " The melody of this song has the simplicity of a mountain hymn or "Amazing Grace," except for a haunting blue note on the word "lead." Dorsey later composed more imaginative songs, but the simple eloquence of "Precious Lord" eclipsed them all. It has been translated into thirty-two languages and recorded by virtually every gospel singer, black and white. Perhaps no other song has so matched the group of Dr. Watts and Tindley hymns in popularity. Since it's the best-known gospel song, it was perfectly natural for Dr. Martin Luther King to request its performance the night of his death. The assassination of King may well have hastened the demise of the faith that sustained gospel music. But for the few days following his death, "Precious Lord" seemed the truest song in America, the last poignant cry of nonviolence before a night of storm that shows no sign of ending.

From the start, Dorsey's music was popular with white Southerners. A couple of Kentucky evangelists began purchasing his yearly output in the early thirties. By 1939, Stamps-Baxter and R. E. Winsett, two leading white publishers of gospel music, were anthologizing Dorsey tunes. That year, Dorsey adapted the old spiritual "We Shall Walk Through the Valley in Peace" into a plaintive semi-hillbilly hymn.

There the bears will be gentle and the wolves will be tame,
The lions will lay down by the lamb.
And the host from the wild
Will be led by a child,
I'll be changed from the creature I am.

There'll be peace in the valley for me someday,
There'll be peace in the valley for me I pray,
No more sadness, no sorrow, no trouble I'll see,
There'll be peace in the valley for me.

Next to "Precious Lord," this song is Dorsey's biggest hit, though its greatest success has been in the white market. Both Red Foley and Elvis Presley sold a million records of the song. Dorsey may be the only black member of the white National Gospel Singers Convention. Morton

Downey and the right-wing commentator Fulton Oursler, Jr., gave him a brief flurry of publicity in the early fifties. In fact, Dorsey, who views the more torrid gospel tempos with alarm, told *Ebony* that some white singers perform his tunes better than blacks. The Dorsey of the pop ballads may have a case.

But his best tunes are the lowdown, hard gospel songs. He obviously calculated their effect on church audiences. When asked if people shouted off Sallie Martin's performances, he says in rousing falsetto, *"Sure.* We were upset if they didn't shout." He may not have anticipated the possible variations, but he left his songs sufficiently open-ended to allow all manner of interpretations. Dorsey created a body of songs that turned on scores of gifted singers, as rock was to do thirty years later. And like rock, Dorsey's tunes helped create a community of musical adherents whose styles, tastes, and vocabulary were influenced by the repertoire. In 1931 the Blue Jay Quartet became the first gospel group to record a Dorsey tune, "If You See My Savior." In 1937, Elder Beck on Decca and The Heavenly Gospel Singers on Bluebird became the first to record "Precious Lord." In 1938, Rosetta Tharpe swept America with

> *Hide me in thy bosom till the storm of life is over,*
> *Rock me in the cradle of thy love.*
> *Feed me until I want no more,*
> *Then take me to my blessed home above.*

the sanctified offspring of Tindley and Ma Rainey. Another early Dorsey composition begins in a minor, bluesy mode:

> *How many times have I wounded his heart,*
> *How many times have I disobeyed,*
> *How many times have I fallen,*
> *How many times have I faltered, have I strayed.*

Then the tempo and key change to a rousing major melody:

How many times did my Jesus lift me up?
How many times did He my burdens bear?
So many times has He forgiven my sins,
That when I reach those pearly gates, He'll let me in.

This is great, compelling music, and "How many times" has become a catch phrase among gospel singers to suggest what's better left unsaid.

One of Dorsey's best tunes, "I'm Gonna Live the Life I Sing About in My Song," was prompted by a commercial take-over of gospel. "So many people, when gospel began to pay off, got in who weren't interested in soul saving. I had quite a few friends who quit the other field, figurin' they could make some money in gospel. I thought someone needed to advance some kind of idea to those folk who seemed to be forsaking their principles for the good money out there. They tried to get me to write some more blues. That's where I got the idea, 'Fair day or rainy day, dark night or moonshine night, I've got to live the life I sing about in my song.'"

If by day, if by night,
I must always walk in the light.
Folks mistake me, under-rate me,
Because I'm trying to do what's right.
I can't go to church, shout all day Sunday,
Go out and get drunk and raise hell on a Monday,
I've got to live the life I sing about in my song.

While other Dorsey tunes—"Singing in My Soul," "If You Sing a Gospel Song," "I Thank God for My Song"—celebrate the joys of singing gospel, this bluesy anti-blues became both his testimony and his notice to the bloodsuckers that gospel wasn't for sale.

After Sallie and Dorsey established the Singers Convention, they opened up the gospel highway, previously restricted to *a cappella* quartets. Between 1932 and 1944, Dorsey toured America in self-advertised "Evenings with Dorsey." These were the first concerts exclusively devoted

to the new music, performed by singers trained by the
master himself. Admissions ran from a penny to a dime;
ballads sold for a nickel. Theodore Frye and Sallie Martin
sang for him during the thirties. In 1936 he sponsored a
gospel-song battle between Sallie and Roberta Martin, the
two "sisters." At fifteen cents a ticket, they packed Chicago's DeSable High School. Who won? "Oh, nobody won,
the one who sold the most tickets won." From 1939 to
1944, Dorsey traveled with Mahalia Jackson.

At seventy-five, Dorsey no longer writes or travels, but
he continues to direct the Convention. He retains his
theatrical instinct and has become a popular after-dinner
speaker. Like Sallie, he prefers the impromptu, but with
him improvisation is instinctual. "When I enter a meeting,
I don't know what I'm gonna say. As I walk in, I get the
vibrations of the people in the place and then it comes over
me. . . . *And yet,* we were taught in the theater you always want to be ready to put something in a new place.
You have to cover a mistake. In a serious role, you throw
in something witty, funny, create a little risibility and then
duck back into your *role.* What it does, it changes the vibrations of the *whole.*" He is completely secure in his several roles and feels no qualms about his life in show business. He remains a member in good standing of the Chicago
Musicians Union, and his attic studio is filled with pictures
and records of Georgia Tom. "No, no," his voice cracks
calmly, "I'm not ashamed of my blues. It's all the same
talent, a beat is a beat whatever it is."

Yet for Dorsey, like Sallie, the best music is about hope
for the present and power in the gospel. "I just hope they
don't desecrate gospel by putting in too much double jazz
beat. Fast is all right, slow is all right. But double time
won't work in this type of music. Gospel is good news, St.
Mark, St. Luke, St. Paul, and so forth. All this new beat,
I don't know how much *power* that has on the *soul* of the
individual." In an era when trouble surfaced in a less complex way, Dorsey's songs had a magical effect. "We intended gospel to strike a happy medium for the downtrod-

den. This music lifted people out of the muck and mire of poverty and loneliness, of being broke, and gave them some kind of hope anyway. Make it anything than good news, it ceases to be gospel." Today's young need other forms of rescue than a gospel tune. Dorsey's optimistic "When I've Done My Best" and "Life Can Be Beautiful" seem hopelessly dated. But his bluesier, more personal lyrics continue to inspire musicians. Everything contemporary music aims for, Dorsey accomplished, welding gospel, blues, jazz, and country music into a distinctive musical style. In the mid-fifties, rhythm-and-blues groups began using simple, funky melodies swiped from Dorsey tunes. Dorsey, in turn, had adapted the plaintive refrains of the twenties. So longest way round is shortest way home. By way of Thomas A. "Georgia Tom" Dorsey, the blues of Bessie Smith and Blind Lemon Jefferson live again in the songs of Aretha Franklin and the Rolling Stones.

Needless to say, Dorsey earned only a fraction of the money due him. He long ago gave up tracing the singers who plagiarize his material. Old age and his family provide satisfaction enough. He stands by his work and trusts in his vibrations. "When I wrote, I wrote about hope and love. Living the life we sing about should be the idea of every individual who wishes to demonstrate this *love*. I do love everybody because I was *taught* to love. It's something that grows up on and in you."

From *The New York Times,* April 19, 1971. JACKSON, MISS., April 18—James Charles Evers became the first Negro candidate for governor in the 154-year history of this state today. . . . The rich, resonant voice of Mrs. Fannie Lou Hamer, the founder of the Freedom Democratic party in Mississippi and a familiar figure in civil rights circles across the country, filled the crowded [convention] hall with "Precious Lord, Take My Hand," a song she dedicated to Mr. Evers.

He strode to her side on the broad stage, they embraced and both began to weep as the audience joined in singing.

3

The Head of the House:
Ira Tucker

What group anywhere has the track record of the Dixie Hummingbirds? Since 1939, the Birds have been the favorites of gospel quartet fans. For versatility, imagination, and harmony few groups play in their league. Their bass, William Bobo, is the lowest, their guitarist, Howard Carroll, gospel's answer to B. B. King. But the Birds' most powerful member is their lead singer, Ira Tucker. Tucker is the virtuoso of quartet. He looks to seduce his audience vocally. So, within a few bars of his opening note, he will scoop down between beats in a dizzying combine of wit and breath. It takes a split second before the audience responds, and then orgiastic "Oohs" and "Help yourself, son" inform Tucker he's home safe.

Scores of brilliant black male singers have performed with quartets through the years. Indeed, now that country blues has waned into a senile echo, quartet alone retains the rough, down-home intensity of a Blind Lemon Jefferson or a Robert Johnson. So many great quartets—yet among black Southerners, the Dixie Hummingbirds have always been the leaders. The Birds are conscious artists,

especially Tucker. "I'm a firm believer in giving people
something for their money. Talent. A variety—fast, slow,
something sad, something with a lot of laughs." He can beat
any blues singer alive, then turn around and subtly parody
the hillbilly gospel he's heard since childhood. Tucker's
talent is no secret among black singers. He helped train
Bobby "Blue" Bland, a blues shouter whose work became
eminently satisfying under Tucker's tutelage. The Temptations' harmonies are shot through with Hummingbirds
echoes, and the soul singers Jackie Wilson and Brook
Benton owe plenty to the quartet master.

Yet quartet is Tucker's metier and he pays most attention to his fellow singers. The Birds feature an amusing
"Let's Go Out to the Program," in which they mimic the
major traveling quartets. The number allows Tucker to
wail a blues about Mother like the late Archie Brownlee
of the Five Blind Boys, preach funkily like Reverend
Reuben Willingham of the Swanee Quintet, and then hi-
lariously take on the Mighty, Mighty Clouds of Joy, the
youngest, most flamboyant and most popular quartet.
Moaning with more power than the Clouds' lead can summon up, Tucker lets the world see oldest is still best. The
audience, which had been shouting frantically a few moments before off Tucker and his co-lead James Walker,
now collapses in visceral giggles. "Whew," one lady says
in a fit of laughter, "those Birds *tickle* me." Since many
of his fans sing with local quartets, Tucker is making musical jokes for professionals. In so doing, he's discovered a
purely local source of gospel wit. And by parodying their
friends, the group also reminds us of their own distinctive
postures. James Walker's right shoulder is always tilted
higher than his left, Beechie Thompson stoops over the
mike, James Davis standing in profile moves his arm in
circular motion, and Tucker—Tucker comes on with a silly
grin and his arms hanging loosely away from his sides. In
one stirring routine, Tucker and Walker move their heads
counterclockwise to emphasize their already ferocious
musical dialogue. The dizzying gymnastics will upset any

audience, but as yet no group has seen fit to parody them. The Birds mimic in good fun, but nobody else could get away with it.

Tucker has sung with the Birds for over thirty-five years. He was born in Spartanburg, South Carolina, and raised by a widowed mother. Like so many gospel singers, he had a strong man at home in the person of his grandfather, Ed Moore, an ex-farmer who worked during the Depression for the Spartanburg WPA. Moore wasn't much of a public man but he was, says Tucker, one great singer. He owned an intricate red accordion, imported from Germany sometime in the nineteenth century. Tucker's earliest memories are of Ed Moore sitting barefoot on their porch, singing "Let's Go Round the Walls of Zion" and "Dig My Grave with a Silver Spade," making up verses as he went along. "Man, he was *everything* to me. He was out of *sight*. He had fore*sight*. He told me in 1937 when I'd just started singing, he used to call me Ketta, that was my nickname, he say, 'Ketta, don't you get disgusted. You keep on singing and one day you'll be down in Florida,' and that was the *first* big place I sang at with the Hummingbirds." Tucker raised his three children on Ed Moore's songs, employing the accordion as a symbol of their musical roots. In memory, Moore's powers seem almost uncanny. Mrs. Tucker never met him, but shortly after her marriage, "I had this dream. I was walking down a road and I came to a tree. I looked up and sitting there in the tree, smiling for *days,* was this big friendly fellow saying, 'You know me, I'm Ed Moore.' Next day I described the man to Ira and he said, 'That was him.'" Other singers like to resurrect Mother as their source of inspiration, but when Tucker begins to run dry, he still communes with his grandfather. "Say I'm writing a song and the words don't come like they should. I just sit in a room in the dark and focus on him."

Ed Moore started Tuckers' fascination with song styles. The boy sang the standard anthems in school. "I opened up the chapel. I was you might say the less dressed person in school but I had a strong voice and, hah hah, they went for the voice." "Less dressed" is an understatement. His mother worked for a shoe salesman, and "I'm not ashamed to say I was one coming up who used to wear shoes, two for the same foot. I did this for five winters." As a little boy, to earn money and possibly to show off, he'd go from door to door singing "Amazing Grace" and "I'll Preach the Gospel Everywhere I Go." On these treks he befriended an old blues singer, Blind Simmie. "He passed in 1945, must have been eighty. Never did get any breaks. The whites had it covered, all you'd hear on the radio was hillbilly, and no scouts came in our neighborhood. But for blues, he was the greatest." Tucker spent those early years "scuffling to find my own style." His greatest influence outside his grandfather was South Carolina quartet. "Where you're from makes a difference in your singing, don't let nobody tell you otherwise." Any quartet lover can spot a group's origin by their style. Tucker sees South Carolina quartet as "this country and western deal mixed up with gospel, blues and geechee." (Geechee is the dialect of the lowland people, resembling West Indian speech.) "They'll say, That's my favor-right. Like that. You know, even the whites in Charleston will talk geechee." Tucker has always perceived connections between black and white music. "When you sing, you focus your mind on the things you didn't have coming up. Believe it or not, the hillbillies do the same thing." He likes to write tunes in a country bag, and the two biggest hillbilly quartets, the Statesmen Quartet and Blackwood Brothers, often record his compositions.

The approved style for young black males was quartet, and Tucker formed his own group, the Gospel Carriers, before his voice changed. They began performing at "silver teas," a sanctified version of the rent party. To support his family, Tucker worked after school in a grocery where "I got the reputation for plucking ninety chickens in half an hour." The most famous local quartet, the Heavenly Gospel Singers, whose bass, William Bobo, lived on Tucker's street, made a few dozen discs for Bluebird and achieved a

fair amount of prestige. They were Tucker's idols until one
night when he went to a silver tea song battle between the
Heavenlys and an unknown quartet operating out of
Greensville, the Dixie Hummingbirds. The Birds won hands
down and Tucker joined them that night, Bobo shortly
after.

At the time, the Birds were a smooth, quasi-jubilee
group. Their leader and founder, James Davis, was raised
with Josh White in Greensville, and White had promised
to open doors for the group in the big city. In 1939 they
recorded a series of discs for Decca, including one regional
hit, "Joshua Journeyed to Jericho." The Birds could easily
have switched to "folk," the term quartets use for all the
artists from Josh White to the Staple Singers who deliberately gear their performances to the desires and expectations of folk audiences. Yet James Davis was a bit
too sanctified to sell out. Under his aegis, the Hummingbirds have remained the straightest, most respected quartet
on the road, the "gentlemen of Song." Tucker's son remembers from childhood knowing Davis as *Mr.* James
Davis. "That's what we were raised to call him. Not because he was mean but by the way he carried himself. You
know, those men are scared of him. He doesn't curse, he
doesn't yell, but he keeps them in line." To this day, the
group has codified rules and regulations. Infractions are
fined: five dollars for each five minutes late for rehearsal,
etc.

When Tucker joined the group, conditions were bad.
Transportation took up most of their earnings; when a shirt
got dirty, they'd wear it inside out; good food was a loaf of
bread, dough piled out and sardines stuffed in. They gradually developed a reputation as the best Southern quartet,
with Tucker their boy wonder. While singing in Green-
wood, South Carolina, Tucker met and wooed Louise
Archie, a beautiful girl who had planned to be a teacher.
While still teen-agers, they were married; recently Mrs.
Tucker returned to paraprofessional work in the Philadelphia school system.

In his first five years of professional singing, Tucker saw quartet undergo several major stages. The earliest is represented on records by the Heavenly Gospel Singers of Spartanburg, South Carolina, and Mitchell's Christian Singers of Kinston, North Carolina. Tucker calls their style "folk." Their harmony is precise and self-conscious but shot through with blue notes, the flattened quarter tones which derive from moans and inform every black song style. To some white collectors, Mitchell's Singers are the most primitive of all quartets. Tucker finds their style more familiar, just "less dressed up than the later groups. Lots of quartets can still do that kind of harmony, it's not hard." The Heavenlys, a much more successful group, employ some of the vocal instrumental sounds later identified with the Golden Gates. They included Dorsey compositions and their lead singers are more striking than the Mitchells, who never lost what some consider an endearing amateurism.

The next stage was jubilee, notable not for any major change in repertoire but for a marked leap forward in professionalism. Tucker's idols were the Norfolk Jubilee Singers. Their hit recordings of the early twenties, "Gambling Man," "Cool Down Yonder," and "My Lord's Gonna Move This Wicked Race," cunningly combined jubilee and blues. Like several other Virginia groups—the Silver Leafs in the twenties, Golden Gates in the thirties, and Harmonizing Four in the forties—the Norfolks concentrated on close harmony and sophisticated arrangements, with little diminution of their origins in southern folklore. Their lead, Norman "Crip" or "Highpocket" Harris, was Tucker's idol, not for hard singing but for technical skill. "Crip's" high-pitched, staccato phrasing, and intimations of jazz riffs distinguished the Norfolks' hits of the thirties, Dorsey's "Standing by the Bedside" and "Shine for Jesus," and can still be detected in Tucker's own approach to song. "Crip was the only one I ever met who could take eight different groups and give them completely different arrangements of the same songs. The Norfolks were twenty-five years ahead of their time. You know the Four Freshmen and the Hi-Los? I wish I had Crip's records to play you. You'd hear that very same sound. It might be a little different, but you could hear it like you could hear my doorbell ring."

The most famous jubilee practitioners were the Golden Gate Quartet. "They used to snatch their words. At the end of a song, they blended harmony and would hold a note sometimes for fifteen seconds." The Golden Gates' first records and radio broadcasts were such successes that by the early forties they were touring with swing bands. Their harmonies were far more sophisticated and consciously jazz influenced than their predecessors'; next to the Mills Brothers, they were the best vocal exponents of instrumental sounds. Their lyrics were, like most jubilees, optimistic, Bible-derived, occasionally arresting, as in "Jezebel":

> *Then death came leaping, she jumped in hell,*
> *Great God almighty, I heard them tell*
> *Nine days she lay in Jerusalem street,*
> *Her flesh was too filthy for the dogs to eat.*

By the mid-forties, their repertoire had expanded to include comic, love, and topical songs ("Comin' in on a Wing and a Prayer"). Despite all these worldly signs, the Gates played a major role in gospel history. Their lively syncopations were borrowed from the Holiness churches in Virginia. While their most notable lead singer, Willie Johnson, an ex-law student, sang their witty jubilees or Popular Front anthems

> *Stalin wasn't stallin' when he told the Beast of Berlin*
> *That he'd never rest contented till he'd driven him*
> *from the land*

the Gates also featured two proto-gospel leads Henry Owens and Bill Landford. Owens' melancholy tenor was best suited for mournful spirituals like "Anyhow" and "See

How They Done My Lord." He slurred and moaned with an understated tact that still moves a listener. Landford was more showmanly; a baritone, he was switching registers to falsetto as early as his 1938 recordings of "Precious Lord" and "When the Saints Go Marching In" (slowed down, almost contemplative, incorporating the verses of the hillbilly hymn "Life Is Like a Mountain Railroad"). Landford's tone is sly, satisfied, oily with vibrato, yet unmistakably southern. He may be the first example of a stylized lead singer in gospel quartet. With their superb arrangements and lead singers like Owens, Johnson and Landford, the Gates set a high standard for later groups. Today, still under the aegis of the original tenor and bass, Clyde Reddick and Orlandus Wilson, they coolly harmonize for European and Israeli audiences.

The Selah Jubilee Singers, led by Thurman Ruth, were the third major jubilee quartet of Tucker's youth. Less obviously comic "entertainers" than the Norfolks or Gates, they recorded some early gospel compositions, their biggest hit being the lovely "I Want Jesus to Walk Around." More special were the Wright Brothers, a Texas quartet, who recorded in 1940 a beautiful series of early gospel songs, heavily characterized by falsetto and melisma; their style is unmistakably gospel, both in its repertoire and the group's general seriousness. Perhaps on a level with the Golden Gates themselves were The Golden Eagles of Chicago, a quartet distinguished by both male and female lead singers (including Thelma Byrd, a gospel pioneer in the Midwest), Dr. Watts moaning, polyrhythms, unusual harmonies triggered by the mixed membership, compositions by Dorsey and the Soul Stirrers, and—oddest of all—occasional harmonica accompaniment.

Tucker considers the next category "strictly gospel," though with its note bending, blue notes, and moans it is actually a more harmonious retexturing of the Baptist hymn style. Some white people blanch at the thought of hymns, imagining Billy Graham chorales pleading in semaphore, but any sensitive listener who hears an old-time gospel quartet will understand why hymns are the favorite songs in black churches. Beginning with a cry that seems preverbal, the group builds to an emotional pitch that can be as intricately, if spontaneously, orchestrated as an avant-garde jazz ensemble (as in jazz, this is spontaneity resulting from years of practice). The baritone might start off, "It's getting late in the . . ." upon which the group comes in wailing "e–e–e–evening," each syllable attached to a desperately wavering note, "and the sun is going down," each man bending the last note home his own way. The word "down" is followed by a husky, breathy *whoo-hoo*, the hardest, most virile sound imaginable. The vocal dynamics can scare, cajole, evoke things best forgotten.

The gospel quartets sang the compositions of Dorsey and Lucie Campbell, but their repertoire always included the Watts and Tindley hymns "The Day Is Past and Gone," "Amazing Grace," "Stand By Me," and

> *I love the Lord, he heard my cry*
> *And pitied every groan,*
> *Long as I live and my trouble rise,*
> *I'll hasten to his throne.*

Trouble is always rising in the old quartet songs. When they don't sing directly of hard times—"Ain't Got Nobody to Depend On but the Lord," "My Trouble's So Hard"— they mourn Mother—"She Left Me Standing Out on the Highway," "Mother's Prayer Followed Me All the Way" in a musical mode one step removed from blues. During the Depression and war years, while the low comedy high jinks of the Gates and Norfolks entertained the masses, hard-gospel quartets were wrecking the churches. For Tucker, the masters of the style were the Kings of Harmony of Alabama. "Look, I saw two people jump out of the balcony at Lawson's Auditorium off those boys' singing."

The Kings of Harmony were originally a jubilee act until their lead singer, Carey "Squeaky" Bradley, moved to

Chicago, heard the Soul Stirrers and opted to convert the Kings' sound to hard gospel. In their masterpieces, "Poor Pilgrim of Sorrow," "Give Me Wings," "Precious Lord," and "God Shall Wipe All Tears Away," it seems as if each member—lead, tenor, baritone, and bass—contributes a sensational phrase or harmonic twist. The Kings' only peers were the Blue Jay Singers of Alabama. They first recorded in 1931, debuting with the first recorded version of Dorsey's "If You See My Savior." Unlike the fluting falsetto quartets of today, the Blue Jays emphasized intense, low harmonies. Because they kept things in the basement, they come across roaring like lions, not whistling like birds or yowling like cats, the standard animal analogues for later quartet singers. Their hits "Canaan Land" and "Standing Out on the Highway" contained dialogues between the two leads, Charlie Bridges and Silas Steele, that would erupt in frenzied syncopations always swallowed up, as it were, by the bass harmonies. Bridges had the calibrated delivery of an ex-vaudevillian (he was), but Steele's preacher shouts may be the most impassioned of any quartet lead on records. His habit of rephrasing words ("over there, *o*ver there, over *there*, way over there") duplicates a standard preacher tactic, but I haven't heard anybody do it on records before him. In his masterpiece, "Sign of the Judgment," an old Dr. Watts hymn, Steele sings

Can't you hear God calling, calling by the thunder,
He formed the world on a wonder,

and the voice is thunder and wonder itself, the Burning Bush in song.

It also demanded Steele-like lead singers from the competition, men whose sole task was to growl, moan and shout while other leads assumed more "versatile" assignments. The best lead singers—Tucker, R. H. Harris, Claude Jeter—were eventually forced into harder singing, but they all began as sweet, jubilee crooners. The "gospel man"

was a whole new category, required by the change in religious music, and pioneered by men like Steele, Walter
Latimore and Carey Bradley of the Kings of Harmony,
Joe E. Union of the Flying Clouds, and Leroy Barnes of
the Evangelist Singers. Tucker calls these men "legends,
like Wyatt Earp." Like outlaw heroes, quartet singers could
take over a town and leave the slain stretched out. Who was
the toughest, the deepest, the most spiritual? Who shouted
the most people? Whoever, nobody since has equaled the
emotional impact of these early gospel men. The old hymn
style virtually disappeared with the demise of *a cappella*
singing, as if a cry so pure couldn't accommodate any
sound more mechanical than the human voice.

The style flourished on records up to 1955. Among its
best later practitioners were the Five Blind Boys, Fairfield
Four, Spirit of Memphis, Pilgrim Travelers, Chosen Gospel Singers, Soul Stirrers, and Swan Silvertones. The famous Five Blind Boys of Mississippi were an early influence on Ray Charles. Their lead, Archie Brownlee, would
demolish huge auditoriums with the bluesiest version of
the Lord's Prayer ever recorded. Brownlee would interrupt
his songs with an unresolved falsetto shriek that conjured
up images of witchcraft or bedlam. "Archie started that
scream you hear all the soul singers do. Now plenty of us
used to scream but Archie really brought it out." Brownlee,
completely blind, died of a perforated ulcer in 1960, but his
group still coasts on his reputation as "the baddest man on the
road."

Among the most beautiful quartet records in this style
were those issued in the early fifties by the Spirit of
Memphis Quartet. The group's powerhouse was the ever-
dependable Alabaman, Silas Steele, late of the Blue Jays
and Bright Stars. Steele's thunderous baritone could shake
a church, the subdued lead of Jet Bledsoe and the ringing
tenor of Willie "Little Ax" Broadnax blended gloriously
with his roars. Often James Darling, the group's baritone,
would improvise a melodic counterpoint to Steele's lead,
while the bass "boom-de-boomed" in accustomed style.

With all this music, one didn't need instruments. Latter-day aces in this style were the Chosen Gospel Singers of California. Their showy leads were often in the Sam Cooke tradition and included Lou Rawls and Joe Hinton, but the down-home, Dr. Watts moaning of the tenor Fred Sims and magnificent bass J. B. Randall rivals the group team-work of the Kings of Harmony. For a while Tucker sang these "touching" numbers too, and the effect must have been thrilling. Too much so, for one Sunday in Steuben-ville, Ohio, a lady died during his performance of "I'm Still Living on Mother's Prayer." (When gospel singers speak of "killing," they speak with authority. Bessie Griffin once sang "I'm Going Over the Hill" in Louisiana, and a lady did just that.) "After the lady died, I didn't bother too much with the hymns." He was content with the last style—his own.

In 1942 the Hummingbirds moved to Philadelphia. When Tucker arrived, he brought something new to gospel. Unlike the earlier "flat-footed" singers who stayed posi-tioned in one spot, Tucker would run up aisles and rock prayerfully on his knees. "I started this hip-slapping all the quartets do." In 1944 he went gospel showmanship one step further. "I jumped off my first stage in Suffolk, Vir-ginia. I was singing 'I Don't Know Why' by Thomas A. Dorsey, and the folks had fits." The teen-age Tucker an-ticipated all the frenetic workings out of soul music. "Shoot, what James Brown does, I've *been* doing." Besides ex-hibiting his showmanship, the Birds enthralled audiences with their advanced harmonies; Rebert Harris remembers that "The Hummingbirds were always ten years ahead of every other quartet." For Tucker, the vocal complexity obviated instrumentation. "Man, there was nothing like singing then. Today it's gospel *music,* then it was gospel singing. It all went down so *easy,* everybody came together on a key. It was like you were floating."

Tucker's showmanship basically derived from country preachers. Up North he received new inspiration when Paul Owens joined the Birds. Owens, another South Carolina native, had made the trip to Philly before him. When Tucker arrived, the two boys found their musical mirror. "Paul was making a lot of changes, what we called 'trickeration.' That got me started on my own." Their kind of "trickeration" meant note bending of a dazzling complexity executed with a lyrical skill bordering on the erotic. "We knew the range of each other so good until I could always depend on him to pick a note up where I left it off. A split second before I finished, he got it. We understood each other just that close. In other words, it was just like cropwork." Seldom in quartet history have two such similar musical temperaments collaborated.

The mid-forties were the golden age of *a cappella* quartet. Even without records, major groups could pack stadiums in the South. One weekend in Richmond, Virginia, the Hummingbirds earned nine hundred dollars apiece. Yet they still yearned for the success of Josh White or the Golden Gate Quartet. They began singing on WCAU in Philadelphia, appearing as both the Jericho Boys and the Swanee Quintet. As the Jericho Boys, they auditioned for John Hammond, the brilliant producer who has sponsored artists from Count Basie and Billie Holliday to Aretha Franklin and Bob Dylan. "We were shocked. Hammond didn't dig our jubilee stuff but he flipped when Bobo did this thing about 'Lord Don't Drive Your Children Away.' That's original, he told us." In 1942 Hammond booked them at Café Society Downtown, the Greenwich Village showcase for black talent. (The Hummingbirds triumphed at Café Society, as they did twenty-four years later at Newport; then they retired, as in 1966, to the obscurity of the churches.)

In 1945, the group began recording again. Judging by Tucker's early records on Apollo and Gotham, he was already an extraordinary stylist. He seems compelled not to repeat himself, and it is astonishing to hear, on a recent album of reissues, "Move On Up a Little Higher," the variety of vocal colorations he was already achieving. Since 1952 the Hummingbirds have recorded for Don Robey's

Peacock label. Their first disc revived a World War II
"hymn":

> *Our boys are wading through blood and water*
> *Trying to get home.*

The next disc was an old spiritual, "I Know I've Been
Changed." Tucker's vocal convolutions here involve zoom-
ing down from falsetto to near-bass while unraveling blue
notes. The other side is a Hummingbirds masterpiece,
"Trouble in My Way."

> *Trouble in my way, I have to cry sometime,*
> *Jesus will fix it by and by.*

The initial format is close to a twelve-bar blues, but it
segues into a steamy "working" chorus. Coming on like a
Southern preacher, Tucker growls, "Hey Father, Father of
Abraham," repeats the phrase, then throws it to the Birds,
who chant it fervently while he interpolates a new set of
couplets before reverting to the original tune. The resemblance to jazz improvisation is obvious. With each disc
Tucker expanded the freedoms available to quartet singers.
The Birds' harmonies were equally adventurous. Paul
Owens left the group in the early fifties and was replaced
by James Walker, a splendid baritone. He and Tucker do
most of the composing for the group, but "each man has
his own vision of the final sound." In the early fifties, when
a cappella quartets picked up guitar accompaniment, the
Birds added Howard Carroll, a former co-worker of Paul
Owens'. Carroll supports and expands the Birds' harmony,
making his own comments, often at a deliberately ironic
tangent to their song.

The Hummingbirds' best album, "In the Morning,"
demonstrates all these musical talents. The title tune, "In
the Morning," begins where most records end, in mid-
climax, with Tucker squalling at peak power. Twice he
doubles up and syncopates the words, "morningmorning,
morningmorning, morningin the morning," achieving

rhythmic effects from the consonant interplay. After a shouting ending, "In the morning when the dark clouds roll a—" Tucker relaxes into a gentle, low "—way," at peace with the spirit and himself. The next tune, "My Prayer," approximates the tense, dense manner of the Kings of Harmony. The tempo is very slow, as Tucker chants in fervent vibrato, "Heavenly Father, Lord have mercy Jesus," and one of the Birds claps his hands to an invisible beat, "I want you to hear my plea." Tucker chants the lines and the Birds respond virtually *a cappella,* with Carroll's guitar coming in a split second after their responsive "whoos." Despite Tucker's volume, the mood is quietly introspective, and Carroll's guitar responds to one line, "I can't make this journey, Father, if you don't see me through," by dropping to the bass register, as if moaning to itself. Another rouser, "Jesus Walked the Water," begins with a relaxed recitation of Jesus' more miraculous exploits. At the break, Tucker starts yelling, "He walked the mighty water." The passion is undeniable but there's also a bit of fun in the lilted "water"; the pleasure comes in the very saying. Toward the end, as Tucker hollers, "Walk with me, walk with me, walk with me," he breaks momentarily on the final "walk" to chilling effect. Now he starts crowding words to a syncopated vocal line while the background is subtly retarded, and Bobo's bass becomes a subliminal foil to his fury. The last tune, "This Evening," is a rearrangement of the Birds' first record for Apollo, "Every Knee Surely Must Bow."

> *This evening our heavenly Father,*
> *Once more and again,*
> *A few of thy handmade servants*
> *Come bowing down before thee.*
> *Throw your loving arms around me,*
> *Prop me up on every leaning side,*
> *Every knee surely must bow.*

Tucker takes the old hymn sound, subtly revamping it to capture the old intensity in a new guise. The harmonic sophistication impelled by Beechie Thompson's tenor, all nasal and plangent, and Bobo's wide-open bass, is really a period gesture; as with the old moaning quartets, every change in vocal texture elaborates and refines the emotion. For example, when Tucker sings the line "You know a *few* of your handmade servants," Bobo's bass underlines the word "few" with an evocative power that lies beyond words. Tucker sings with the melismatic expansiveness of a Dr. Watts song, while Carroll's guitar interpositions are in waltz time, adding the missing, implicit beat. The first verse ends with Tucker floating from falsetto to bass on a cloud of quarter tones. Then he yells out in his preacher voice, "Sometimes you just have to fold your arms and moan it out," and ends the song and the album with some intricate and quiet hums. So the album returns to its proper source, the moan, at the core of all good quartet. Tucker has touched all bases, but his shoes are still in the clay hills of South Carolina.

One night after a knockdown concert at the Philadelphia Met, Tucker expressed his delight in moving an audience. "I get happy just knowing I'm making somebody happy. My spirit comes on me when I focus on whence I came. I always say shouting people is secondary for me. I just like being up there. When I sing, I feel like I'm the head of the house, getting that *good* feeling from the people." If he comes out looking a bit awkward and sheepish, there's a point being made. "You have to get right down with the people. It's like I'm saying, 'O.K., now, here I am, ol' country me.' So when I leave 'em, they'll say, 'Old Tuck's great, he's all right.'"

That night's program had been a bit unusual. "I feel like I can look at an audience and base my mind on that audience, like. Like tonight, I introduced some brand-new songs. Now I could have done the old familiar things and gotten in much quicker. But I felt like a change. And if you noticed, I came in later than the Birds. So when I came out, I was fresh. I did this new number and it went over big and I sat down again. Then when it came time to do the working numbers I could feel a coolness in the audience. I wanted to do this thing where I line twenty people up to hold the people who're shouting. I did this one time in Mississippi and people shouted who wasn't even going to shout. But the first two rows were young people, they wouldn't know nothing about that kind of stuff. So I went into my thing, didn't try to shout the house, and did three encores anyhow. This is what keeps the Hummingbirds at our age at the bracket we're in. *Strategy*."

Many fans feel Tucker and the group don't need to "clown" like the less talented quartets. Tucker claims the routine's no act. "I look at it this way, if I get to stretch a thing hard, I've got the spirit with me. Cause sometimes during the first song, I'm out of breath. Sometimes even cool singing will do you that way." He'll build an audience to any emotional peak, but he'll carry himself along with them. Like all great showmen, Tucker wants to be remembered. "If the hard shouts don't get you, then the bluesy stuff or the imitations will." The strategy is self-serving but it's also a public service. Tucker is out to lift an audience, give them their money's worth, and, not incidentally, expand their appreciation of gospel. In the middle spaces between professional routine and spirit-feel, the Hummingbirds fly alone.

In church, Tucker feels himself the head of the house. "And I've *always* been the head of my house." This past Thanksgiving, Tucker's three children, Ira, Sandra and Linda, returned home. For twenty years Tucker's family has lived in the same house. The home itself is neat and unpretentious with some imaginative wall remodeling executed by Tucker. It's a good home off a bad street, Columbia Avenue, a place where "you don't miss a thing about nothing." All three of Tucker's children are musicians. When Linda was eight, she appeared at Harlem's Apollo Theatre with the Hummingbirds, singing "The

Lord's Prayer." Now she sings show-biz soul, sentimental ballads and Motown beat tunes, when not touring with Stevie Wonder's vocal group. Sandra got her first recording contract when she was fourteen. "The man wouldn't believe I wrote the songs. He said they were too mature for my age." Very precocious—but remember, their father was headlining Café Society at seventeen. Over the dinner table, Sandra and Linda discuss the raw breaks soul singers have in a rock-dominated market. Linda winks, "Yet I guess we shouldn't gripe, Daddy outsings us all and look where he is."

Ira Tucker, Jr., also known as "Gramp," is there with his best friend, Birdis Coleman. Both are graduates of the Philadelphia Conservatory of Music, and now working in the music division of the Philadelphia school system. Coleman's admiration for the Birds helped bring Ira around "because man, there was a time I was ashamed my father sang gospel. I used to tell the kids in school my father was on the road, like he was some kind of salesman." Gramp's was the first generation to rebel en masse against everything the Hummingbirds represent. The strict Southern upbringing was only one obstacle. "I used to think all their fancy stuff was a lot of jive." Like all quartets, the Hummingbirds once wore konked hair and walked on stage in the skins of swamp beasts. "My father tried to get me a process and he wanted to give me some of those corny, country shoes." What bothered him more were the Elmer Gantry tactics of gospel preachers, "phonies *all* of them," and the music itself. "I didn't want to hear nothin' but Beethoven." Thanks to Birdis, he's changed. "Bird made me listen. And what really blew my *mind* were all those changes the group makes. They did some stuff years ago all the rock groups still haven't caught up with." Ira, Jr., is no Ira Tucker. He's a good musician with a pleasant voice but he seems more at home with Stevie Wonder than with Dr. Watts. "I can't do that stuff. I haven't lived it, plus you don't find too many young people into that kind of hard singing." Tucker looks up: "They can't do it." His son nods his head without emotion. "We don't have that kind of *control*." Ira likes pop, his father likes gospel. Tucker is politically cautious, Ira, Jr., a militant. Yet some rapprochement has been effected. When Ira, Jr.'s, mother-in-law died, he took her five small children into his home. He speaks of the gesture in radical terms, "We need to keep together *now*," but his father has a simpler expression: "Church folk have always looked after their own."

The Tuckers are a beautiful family, and somebody asks if they ever sing together. "Oh, we sing around the house all the time," says Sandra. "Daddy likes Mama and me to back him up. Usually we sing blues." "You mean soul," I say. "I mean *blues*," says Sandra. "Old-time *blues*. And *funkaaay*." Tucker's tight with several blues singers and jazz musicians; he and Howard Carroll still remember when B. B. King introduced them to the records of Django Reinhardt in Lake Charles, Louisiana. But Tucker won't sing blues outside of the house. His daughters keep him informed of all the musical trends, and he'll tease one with plans to get some well-known group in hand, make them really sing. The mind boggles at the possibility of Tucker's arranging for the Temptations or the better rock groups. Yet in the world of sixteen tracks where sessions last for months, how could he remain the head of the house? Some brilliant gospel singers have floundered before the alien requirements of rock or jazz, when they could beat the world sticking to their own musical turf. "You can do anything in gospel, but not out of it," Tucker says. "You see, there's a lot of routine in pop. That doesn't apply to gospel. You do what you feel. I might come on and make fifty mistakes as far as my steps are concerned, and another group comes out like they're beating time. But they got a routine *against* feeling, it stands out like the V for victory."

In 1966, the Hummingbirds tore up the Newport Folk Festival and received a standing ovation. No college festivals or Fillmore bookings ensued. But the Hummingbirds have already made their own legends. Quartet is the manly art of song, and Tucker seems the quintessence of proud black manhood when he says, "We do what we like." He looks outside the window at kids scrambling through the slush. "I'm a mediocre liver today. I could have been rich. But I didn't choose it." Other singers will talk about the Lord's blessings, salvation, victory in Jesus. But the reason Tucker sticks is simpler. "Gospel's the greatest music there is. Someday I'd just like to get that across to the people."

4

Mahalia the Queen

If America knows no other gospel singer, she has conferred a blessed status on Mahalia Jackson. All by herself, Mahalia was the vocal, physical, spiritual symbol of gospel music. Her large, noble proportions, her face contorted in song into something resembling the Mad Duchess, her soft speaking voice and huge, rich contralto, all made her gospel's one superstar of the late fifties and early sixties. Equally impressed on the public's consciousness was her religious devotion. Pious before the TV cameras, always looking somewhat north of the cathode rays, then breathily defending her old-time religion to Arthur Godfrey and Dinah Shore, Mahalia came across as both humble servant and religious scold. In a Herbert Gold story, a cynic says to a disheartened writer, "Trust in the Lord," and gets as reply, "You sound like Mahalia Jackson."

Mahalia is not merely one of the supreme gospel singers —even she balks at the press-agent's gimmick, "world's greatest"—she has easily broadcast gospel's appeal more widely than anyone else in history. Not necessarily in the church, where she's only one of many pioneers. But in Europe and white America, Mahalia is the single most important gospel singer—not, alas, without some diminution of her distinctive manner. Mahalia, the musical daughter of Bessie Smith, was effectively modified into a black Kate Smith. The lady once known as the most volatile mover in Chicago churches—"Mahalia was our original belly dancer," says an old accompanist affectionately—became the stately, classic, "flat-footed" presence who enthralled white critics with her instinctive maternity—though indeed Mahalia has no children—while those who really knew her could sense the repressed itch to rock and shimmy with the beat.

Or take her latest incarnation as operator of the Mahalia Jackson Chicken Diners, a franchise committed to warfare with Colonel Sanders. "The Colonal calls his food finger-lickin' good," Mahalia tells Johnny Carson, "I say mine is *tongue*-lickin' good," and then obligingly adds, "I learned to cook and keep house down South." Another pet project is the Mahalia Jackson Scholarship Foundation —"For years I gave out of my own personal money to send the young folk to college." With Bobby Darin and Mike Douglas breathing assent, she observes, "I believe we should have *compassion*," the gentlemen nodding at the received truth. One regrets the transmutation of Mahalia from shouter to huckster, but hardest to deal with are her public defenses of Mayor Daley. Again to Mike Douglas, Mahalia says, "Don't you go around criticizing Mayor Daley, that's a wonderful man." The TV commentator truthfully admits he'd be the last to tackle Chicago's porcine ruler, while Mahalia continues the litany of Daley's virtues. Now when she moved into an all-white neighborhood, Daley sent police guards to protect her home from snipers. And when she brought Dr. Martin Luther King to Chicago, Daley assisted her. Not to mention her fervent attachment to the Democrats. "Roosevelt fed me when I was *hongry*," she tells Joey Bishop. "*A*-men."

But whatever the explanations, it's definitely a confusing image projected by the lady. Says a Chicago friend, "Why don't they just leave Mother alone and let her sing?"

Everything about Mahalia, her diction, build, manner, bespeak New Orleans. She was born there in 1911, the daughter of devout Baptists but the niece of professional entertainers. She grew up poor by the levee, playing with Italian and Irish kids, absorbing all the musical noises of the city. Her idol was Bessie Smith, whose open-voiced belting and chilling blue notes she incorporated in her style. She could have been the greatest blues singer since Bessie but opted to remain in the church. Years later, Robert Anderson recalled, "Mahalia was the first to bring the blues into gospel," and there's no doubt her bluesiness contributed to her spectacular success.

Her initial repertoire consisted of the Baptist hymns, especially the Dr. Watts songs "Amazing Grace" and "The Day Is Past and Gone." "Dr. Watts? Now you're talking about the *power*. Those songs, *hmmmm*, they come out of conviction and suffering. The worst voices can get through singing them, cause they're telling their experiences." Every Sunday she'd sit with the other children around the altar, listening to the old-timers moan, "Before This Time Another Year I May Be Dead and Gone" or "How Can I Sink with Such a Prop?" She especially remembers a local workman, Willie Jackson, who used to hit "Nearer My God to Thee" as soon as he struck the church floor. "Years later when I recorded my album with Percy Faith I thought to Willie and made 'Near-oh to Thee.'" In church, they held all-night wakes before a member's funeral, during which they sang dire pronouncements of "revelations." Mahalia's first record, "God's Gonna Separate the Wheat from the Tares," came out of those wakes. Besides the Baptist church on Sunday, and the blues and jazz of the streets, Mahalia had the incalculable advantage of living next door to a Sanctified church. Like Sallie Martin, she witnessed Holiness in its first stages, though unlike Sallie, she never converted. Still, her terrific bounce owes as much to Sanctified shouting as to New Orleans jazz.

Mahalia had to quit school in the eighth grade, and like many black Southerners she headed North. When she left

New Orleans in 1927, she was a big, beautiful girl, "stout like they like them at home," stubborn and combative, a mistress of all the down-home sounds, and vocally accomplished. Within a few months of her arrival in Chicago, she was singing leads with the choir of Greater Salem Baptist Church. She supported herself as maid and laundress but was clearly too talented to remain a domestic. Her pastor's son, Robert Johnson, was equally ambitious. Together with his brothers Prince and Wilbur, a young soprano, Louise Barry Lemon, and Mahalia, he formed the Johnson Gospel Singers. Though other small groups formed from church choirs had recorded during the twenties, the Johnsons may have been the first professional gospel group. Their theatricality demonstrated itself in a series of plays, *Hellbound, From Earth to Glory,* and *The Fatal Wedding,* written by Robert, and starring him and Mahalia in the lead roles. Their song style was advanced and free; Prince Johnson played a distinctive boogie-woogie piano geared to the Dorsey bounce. During the early thirties, the group toured local churches, earning as much as eight dollars some nights. By the mid-thirties the Johnsons had split up, and each member was singing solo.

In 1936 Mahalia married Isaac Hackenhull, a graduate of Fisk and Tuskegee reduced by the Depression to working as a bookie. Hackenhull wanted her to sing jazz and classics, and she even tried out for *The Jazz Mikado,* singing "Sometimes I Feel Like a Motherless Child"; she quit mid-audition, swept by guilt. The marriage eventually broke up, and Mahalia Hackenhull, surely one of the most consonant-vowel-laden names in history, became plain Halie Jackson again. Hackenhull's mother was a beautician with a huge store of recipes and formulas for cosmetics, ointments, emollients, and hair oil. Mahalia, always gifted at figures—"I'm a mathematics," she tells a crowd, "I can look out and tell just how many of you here"—adapted the Hackenhull formulas and after training at the Scott Institute of Beauty Culture opened Mahalia's Beauty Salon; a few years later she started a small florist shop. Again like

Sallie Martin, her talent was matched by business sense. "You must give Mahalia one thing," says a Chicagoan, "she's earned everything herself."

She began to acquire a following in the Midwest, and in 1937 "while Sally Rand was right here at the World's Fair," cut her first records for Decca. The characteristic Mahalia style is already evident in these. Her voice is high and nasal, not quite the awesome instrument of later years. But the heavy breathing and irresistible swing, the Bessie Smith slurs and Willie Jackson groans are unmistakable. "God's Gonna Separate the Wheat from the Tares," a tune adapted from the New Orleans wakes of her childhood, was a hit in the South. The song is old; what's new is Mahalia's freedom and theatricality. She growls and moans; one immediately visualizes her face contorting as she hollers,

> *If you never hear me sing no more,*
> *Aw, meet me on the other shore,*
> *God's gonna separate the wheat from the tares,*
> *Didn't he say.*

The other side, "Keep Me Every Day," is a Baptist hymn, and anticipating her later style, Mahalia phrases with a wonderfully artless purity and conviction, breathing between words and adapting the old Dr. Watts manner to a more recent composition. At the same session she recorded a new gospel tune, "God Shall Wipe All Tears Away," composed by a St. Louis musician, Professor Antonio Haskell.

> *When we reach that blessed homeland,*
> *Where 'tis ever lasting day.*
> *On that bright, eternal morning,*
> *God shall wipe all tears away.*

The song is a gospel masterpiece, one of several Mahalia was to introduce on records, and she sings it with a full-throated assurance that could wreck any church. Yet despite the evident vocal power, she didn't record again until 1946.

In the years between, she may have done her best singing. Chicago was filled with the great pioneer gospel shouters, some on tour, many resident: no other city boasted
so many great soloists. The greatest of the period was
probably Willie Mae Ford Smith, a Sanctified lady from St.
Louis who worked with Dorsey and Sallie Martin in their
Convention. There was also Madame Lula Mae Hurst, a
concert artist—"Whew, she could sing" recalls Mahalia—
who tore up Baptist Conventions with "Amazing Grace"
and was eventually stabbed to death. The Georgia Peach,
by now a New York contralto, had tremendous power, as
did Mary Johnson Davis, a Pittsburgh soprano who used to
wail "Holy Spirit Surely Is My Comfort." In Chicago, Sallie and Roberta Martin were hustling every bit as much
as Mahalia, and her old colleague, Louise Lemon, ruled
her share of the church turf.

But Mahalia had a power and self-assurance of her
own. Ironically, the lady often cited by critics as an example of gospel dignity, was initially criticized for her physical gusto. From the start she was a "stretch-out" singer,
breaking all the rules, changing the melody and meter as
the spirit dictated. Robert Anderson remembers, "Mahalia
took the people back to slavery times." She was unasham-
edly Southern, moaning and growling like the down-home
congregations, skipping and strutting like the Sanctified
preachers. The other singers may have influenced her—"We
learned from each other. I think everybody on this earth
has a mate somewhere"—but her style remained special.
Some churches exiled her for her rocking beat, others for
her "snake-hips." So, in the small churches where anything
goes, Mahalia was herself. "The girl always had a beautiful
voice but she was known for her hollering and getting
happy and lifting her dress," remembers a man who followed her during the thirties. When the spirit presumes,
Mahalia lifts her robe an inch or two: "Mahalia always was
the sexiest thing out there."

Even then, her most powerful performances were reserved for "going to heaven" tunes, especially "When

I Wake Up in Glory," in which she'd wail, "I shall *see*
God's blessed face, he's kept *me* . . . all by his grace,"
patting her ribs with gusto decried by the more "seditty"
churches but sweetly familiar to the store-fronts. Of
course, she sang the Dr. Watts hymns, and those on her
recordings, but she also sang "Have You Any Time for
Jesus?" and Willie Mae Ford Smith's "If You Just Keep
Still," both pure blues with religious lyrics. Equally bluesy
and close to her spirit were "Just One Moment" (. . . "In
God's kingdom will pay for it all, Glory Hallelujah!" she
says, remembering the song, "That's all I'm living for"),
and "I'm Gonna Tell God All About It One of These
Days," an opportunity to sing of heaven while deriding
earthly enemies:

> *I'm gonna tell him how my friends and enemies*
> *Brought me to my bended knees,*
> *And the doors that were open for me,*
> *Sometimes closed, Lord, in my face.*

In the early forties she joined forces with Thomas A.
Dorsey. Poor Dorsey—from the commanding Sallie to
the equally stubborn Mahalia, his singers doomed his efforts to train them. "I tried to show Mahalia how to breathe
and phrase, but she wouldn't listen. She said I was trying
to make a stereotyped singer out of her." She may have
been right. Instead, she chose to sing "Precious Lord"
and "If You See My Savior" her own way to an invisible
beat and a metrical sense that has defeated scores of musicians. (On a recent Columbia album, Mahalia sings a
favorite hymn, "I'd Rather Have Jesus than Silver or
Gold." The note bending and spirit are magnificent, the
metrics typically loose and formless. An orchestra is clearly
dubbed in; no violins could ever play so lethargically without direction.) In Dorsey's rocking "What Could I Do?"
she interpolated "Lord have mercy on me," her standard,
down-home refrain, by then her vocal trademark. Dorsey
carried Mahalia with him all over America. Dorothy Love
remembers seeing her in Birmingham. "It was amazing.

Mr. Dorsey would just keep handing Mahalia these ballads, and she'd stand there reading the words while she sang. She'd do fifteen, twenty songs a night like that." By 1945, the gospel churches all knew Mahalia for her glorious contralto, her fiery spirit, her flirtatious manner ("Surely out of all these handsome men," she used to say, "I can find me a good husband"). Above all, she was always one of the people. While other singers criticized her for breaking rules, the Southern migrants recognized their own free-form song style. While Chicago giggled over her "Lord have mercys" and "Well, well, wells," Mississippi and Louisiana heard their native twang.

Then, as ever, Mahalia was most expressive when reminded of her past origins. Like every great gospel singer, her best work is a musical testimony. One evening, after a program, she returned to her hotel room with some friends. While counting her change, it came upon her that she could now buy a doll. "You know, when I was coming up, we was too poor to afford a doll. I always did want to have one, but you know how times were down South. But I stuck with the Lord, and now he's given me money to buy a doll. Lord," she started hollering, "I want to thank you for giving me enough money to buy a doll." The friends there say Mahalia never sang better, and that in the streets people shouted "like it was church." The words hardly mattered. Mahalia's diction has always been erratic; but her special cry carried, as it always carries.

In 1946, Mahalia signed with Apollo Records, a small New York outfit run by the imperious Mrs. Bess Berman. For over eight years the two feuded, particularly over Mahalia's questions about royalty statements. But the series of records by Mahalia that Bess Berman produced were uniformly brilliant. "Move On Up a Little Higher," her third Apollo disc, sold over a million copies, and made her, after years of struggle, the Gospel Queen. The song was composed by W. Herbert Brewster, a Memphis minister and songwriter who also composed "Just Over the Hill" and

"How I Got Over." These three succeeded "When I Wake Up in Glory" as Mahalia's "going to heaven" workouts. Her power on records and in person was downright terrifying. At her best, Mahalia builds these songs to a frenzy of intensity almost demanding a release in holler and shout. When singing them she may descend to her knees, her combs scattering like so many cast-out demons. (One time in the Atlanta Stadium, she sang "I Bowed on My Knees and Cried Holy," and commenced to do so. She descended from the platform to floor level; by her third bow on her knees, "folks were falling out in the fifth balcony.") Or she may lift up her skirt as she calls the ones she'll meet when she moves up higher.

Move on up a little higher, meet with Paul and Silas,
Move on up a little higher, meet the lily of the valley!

Or, climaxing "How I Got Over" with ebullient "Thank Gods," she may run and skip halfway down the church aisles. There were other house wreckers: Brewster's "These Are They" (with Mahalia's most thrilling lines on record, "They're coming on up, *coming on up* through great tribulation"), Robert Anderson's "Prayer Changes Things," or Kenneth Morris' "Dig a Little Deeper" wherein Mahalia, her hand firmly planted on her belly, strutted with the beat, "I want to dig a little deeper in the storehouse of God's love." But the going-to-heaven trilogy established her as a gospel powerhouse; on some nights she'd sing "Move On Up" for twenty-five minutes.

She was equally beloved for her slow hymns, the descendants of "Keep Me Every Day," on Decca. Her voice then was at its loveliest, rich and resonant, with little of the vibrato and neo-operatic obbligatos of later years. On Apollo records like "Even Me," "Just as I Am," "City Called Heaven," and "I Do, Don't You" the phrasing is perfect, the contralto sturdy and grainy, angelic but never saccharine. On these records she doesn't growl; "City Called Heaven" alone makes any special vocal demands.

But the power, control, and feeling remain awesome. The spiritual depth of Mahalia's best hymns has seldom been surpassed. Together with her jubilant shouts, they made her a towering force in gospel's greatest era.

Now her style and manner became the stuff of mimicry and legends. She has a characteristic vocal habit of combining slurs and blue notes in a disembodied soprano. It's a weird, ethereal sound, part moan, part failed operatics: "Lately I've been learning all these terms. You know, I half-moan and bring forth those head tones with a groan . . . the tone is still sustaining. Child—" she gives up—"I don't know how I do it myself." The young singers imitated the slurs and the ubiquitous "lordys," and "my luhds," and "yeah yeah yeahs." A few, like Cleophus Robinson, even duplicated her physical manner. When ending a song Mahalia frequently twists to the side, as if hit in the belly; some of her gestures are dramatically jerky, suggesting instant spirit possession. The gestures often combine with her multiple endings, as when in New York's Mount Morris park she closed the song "I Have a Friend" with "His love is deeper and deeper, yes deeper and deeper, it's deeper! and deeper, Lord! deeper and deeper, Lord! it's deeper than the se–e–e–e–a, yeah, oh my lordy, yeah, deeper than the sea," breaking up the last word into a dozen syllables, "Lord," another scale run from falsetto to near-bass.

Just as Sallie Martin collects legends about her, Mahalia is the subject of many gospel tales. One describes her performance of "Prayer Changes Things" in Washington's Uline Stadium. Some of her Chicago friends, including James Cleveland, Alex Bradford and Robert Anderson, were there, as was her old pianist, James Lee, who used to sing soprano in duets with the contralto Mahalia. She placed her pocketbook in Lee's hands and proceeded to sing. Midway through the song, Lee caught the spirit, yowled and fell out, slain by the Holy Ghost with a dead man's grip on her money. The story goes that Mahalia ad-libbed:

Do you know prayer (Get the pocketbook, Robert)
changes things,
Child I know (Get the pocketbook, James) *prayer changes
things,*
I've been out (Alex, get my pocketbook) *out on the
stormy . . . yes Lord* (Pocketbook, babies) *raging
sea . . .*

All to no avail. Lee was trundled off stage, Mahalia marching in the funeral train. Ten minutes later he was revived,
and Mahalia returned to the stage, complete with pocketbook, and assured the saints, "Excuse me, beloveds, but I
was so spirit-filled I had to leave you."

In 1950 Studs Terkel, the Chicago journalist, began
featuring Mahalia on his local TV program. She acquired a cultist following among jazz critics who detected
her dramatic resemblance to Bessie Smith. In 1952, her
Apollo recording of "I Can Put My Trust in Jesus," an old
Kenneth Morris blues-gospel song she used to duet with
James Lee, won a prize from the French Academy, and
she made her first European tour. It was a smashing success; her record of "Silent Night" became an all-time best
seller in Norway, and she was immediately recognized as
one of the greatest American voices. But she suffered a
physical collapse and returned home after six weeks. Now
she seemed more guarded in her manner. She warned
younger singers not to work so hard: "The people don't
appreciate your sweat," and dropped "Just Over the Hill"
from her repertoire ("I saw that pale rider, I almost went
over the hill.")

She continued to tour the churches, accompanied by
ambitious young singers and booked by her nephew, Allan
Clark (he more recently booked James Cleveland, the current king of gospel). But she was now a national property,
celebrated in white America, with press agents on her pay-
roll. In 1954 she appeared on her own radio and TV
programs. By all accounts they were magnificent. One time

she sang "City Called Heaven" and cried out ecstatically, "Glory!" Afterwards she apologized: "Excuse me, CBS, I didn't know where I was," though she obviously knew *who* she was. The major national advertisers were scared to sponsor her—"My God, I'm only singing hymns!"—and the programs were canceled. But she "moved to higher heights and deeper depths." In 1954 Columbia Records signed her with a terrific publicity campaign. On her first album note, George Avakian remarked that calling Mahalia "the world's greatest gospel singer" was like calling Babe Ruth a fair base runner—a statement not calculated to win him the affection of Chicago gospel singers. Mahalia appeared on the major TV programs and was featured in *Life* magazine cooking soul food for Duke Ellington. Columbia recorded some pure gospel, including her old hit "When I Wake Up in Glory," but they also burdened her with the inspirational dung heap, "Rusty Old Halo" and "The Lord Is a Busy Man," among other winners. In interviews Mahalia tried to set things right. "I can't get with this commercial stuff. I'm used to singing in church till the spirit comes. Here they want everything done in two or three minutes."

By now she had priced herself out of the black church. Almost all her appearances were before white audiences. Though she still featured a few hard gospel numbers, especially "How I Got Over," the bulk of her repertoire was pop-gospel, lively, up-tempo versions of the most familiar spirituals: "Down By the Riverside," "Didn't It Rain," "Hold On," "Joshua," and "When the Saints Go Marching In." Her efforts were greatly abetted by her pianist, Mildred Falls. Miss Falls is perhaps the only pianist who completely understands and anticipates Mahalia's shifting moods and rhythms. By Chicago choir standards her chordings and tempos were old-fashioned, but they always induced a subtle rock exactly suited to Mahalia's swing. Though the material couldn't compare with her former hymns, Mahalia sang brilliantly. In "He's Got the Whole World in His Hands," she might interpolate

If religion was a thing money could buy,
The rich would live and the poor would die

with the same bluesy abandon that formerly graced "I
Gave Up Everything to Follow Him." Mahalia became a
most regal gospel queen. She'd sing twenty, twenty-five
songs a program, treating her audience like subjects. Sometimes, as Mildred Falls started her gospel rock, she'd put up
her hand. "That's enough, darlins, I know you're enjoying
yourself, but you just ain't clapping right. If you don't stop
clapping," she'd tease, "I'm gonna sing something slow."
One time a white minister requested "The Crucifixion,"
and she asked ingenuously, "Which one? I know three."

She could do no wrong. In 1958, she sang at the Newport Jazz Festival in the rain. "You make me feel like I'm
a star," she flirted with the rain-soaked, ecstatic fans.
Whitney Balliett, the *New Yorker* critic, was especially
enraptured with her performance of "The Lord's Prayer."
But gospel friends seeing the film of that concert thought
otherwise. "Just look at her. You can tell Mother knows
she's jiving. Mahalia should be singing 'Prayer Changes
Things,' not no 'Lord's Prayer.'" Mahalia was the latest
victim of the show-business juggernaut. When her album
with Percy Faith became a best seller, Columbia deluged
her with orchestras and choirs, light years removed from
the Greater Salem Baptist Church. And what songs: "The
Velvet Rose," "I Thought of You and Said a Little Prayer,"
"A Perfect [Puf-fickt] Day," even "Guardian Angels" accompanied by Harpo Marx on harp.

So her gospel fans became accustomed to the occasional
wheat amidst the tares, the one "How I Got Over" on a
program of "Riversides." At home she continued to sing as
the spirit moved her. "One Sunday I was singing 'Soon I
Will Be Done with the Troubles of the World,' and me
and the spirit and the people got all tangled up. Some fellow from the movies happened to be there and that's how
I got into *Imitation of Life*." Mahalia's performance of
"Troubles of the World" was the emotional climax of that

film; her flamboyant "I want to see my mother" provoked floods of weeping in suburban theaters.

Meanwhile the "jealous-hearted gospel singers" smirked with resentment at her success—"I keep telling them I just got out here myself—" but they continued to press her for contacts and engagements. She seldom appeared with them, though when she did, she always mustered the old fire. Her press agent, Joe Bostic, became New York's major gospel disc jockey, and for several years she appeared at his annual concerts at Madison Square Garden. One year, at the peak of her fame, she sang "How I Got Over" and descended to her knees, while all over the Garden women shrieked and fainted. In 1961 she closed her hour with "When the Saints," her customary climax. Realizing church folks might misapprehend, she ad-libbed, "They call that jazz, but that's all right. After awhile it'll all be over." She began moaning and suddenly started roaring the chorus of "Just Over the Hill," after all those years of not having sung it, until she forgot the words and walked out, waving queenfully to the fans. In 1962 Bostic's anniversary was held at Randall's Island. Nobody came; the night Mahalia sang, perhaps three hundred people heard her. She began slowly, hoarse and bitter. But in the middle of "Said I Wasn't Gonna Tell Nobody" she renewed herself and began hollering "I Cried Holy." One fan says, "I have hay fever and I got a seizure while Halie was singing. I must have sneezed twenty-five times, and when I was done, do you know she was still crying Holy?"

During the sixties, Mahalia was a loyal friend and supporter of Dr. Martin Luther King. Though King was not the shouting Baptist preacher of her childhood, he loved her music, and she in turn was devoted to him. She began featuring "We Shall Overcome" at her concerts; though, typically, forgetting the words, she would wind up singing the old hymn "I'll Be All Right," from which it derived. At King's funeral, Mahalia sang his last request, "Precious Lord," a song she'd sung countless times on her tours with Thomas A. Dorsey. With the death of King and her friends the Kennedys—she sang at the 1961 Inauguration—Mahalia retired from politics.

Till then, she had been a black spokesman, a living institution, news copy for the mass media. In her public pronouncements, she tried to retain her folksy disposition; in *Jet,* especially, she studded her talk with down-home sayings. In Chicago she continued to involve herself with Greater Salem's fund-raising campaigns. "Come on over," she said on the radio, "and let Halie cook you her fine New Orleans gumbo." But her regal status had obviously isolated her. Her generous, lonely spirit acknowledged the children of impoverished gospel singers as her godchildren by the score. The late Princess Stewart, a partially blind ex-concert singer who later appeared in *Black Nativity,* once brought her child along to see Mahalia, hoping for a handout. "Mahalia kept calling my child, 'Come here, Mahalia, right here, Mahalia.' Baby didn't know what to do. I should have told her Mahalia was her middle name."

In 1965, Mahalia married Sigmund Galloway, a handsome musician, most definitely not a gospel person. She seemed very happy. Her autobiography appeared with dedications to her husband and stepdaughter. *Ebony* showed her and Galloway sprawling on the floor, mooning over their scrapbook.

But the gospel life is seldom kind. Mahalia divorced her husband in a sensational, much publicized trial, full of ugly details that marred the saintly image of thirty years. After a series of heart attacks, she lost a hundred pounds. In spring 1967, when she sang at Philharmonic Hall, her voice was barely a whisper. Whitney Balliett accepted even this loss as gain, but for everyone else the program was heartbreaking. Yet the gospel life can strengthen as well as kill. By summer, Mahalia had regained some of her weight and voice. She sang in Oakland, confiding in the audience as "My family. I've been serving you for thirty years. I'm married to you, not to that man." She sang "How I Got Over" with more spirit than ever, stopping midway to "thank God" and yell "He brought me out . . .

God brought me out." The audience gasped "Yes" after
each line, and clearly on the verge of shouting, Mahalia
left the stage, whooping a falsetto "Whoa," while the audience of deserted women, with none of Mahalia's money,
but some of her troubles, roared with delight. Mahalia was
herself again, relaxed and charming. She introduced a local
minister, apologizing for her way with words, "You know
I can't speak, baby darlins. But this man, he has grace
. . . and the letter. Folks like me, we just have grace." Of
course the minister bumbled his way, while the naturally
eloquent Mahalia smiled out at Oakland.

Lately Mahalia seems more relaxed and outspoken than
ever. "Mahalia, how do you feel about growing old?" asks
Mike Douglas. "I don't feel nothing—I am old," she says,
"but I look pretty good for an old girl, don't I?" She is
back to her old size, telling the church workers, "You sweet
people put all this lovely fat on me," and singing with consequent energy. Twice, on television, she has skipped and
shouted as if back in the store fronts; and Newport 1970
was graced by her holy dancing off "Just a Closer Walk
with Thee" to the amazement of jazz critics who had
canonized her as the still, stolid gospel Buddha. On a Harlem program with Reverend Jesse Jackson of Operation
Breadbasket, she was especially outspoken: "Sometimes we
act a bit cute, but we're being ourselves today." As if in
reply to the current attacks on the black matriarch, an
image she universally embodies, Mahalia roared, "Don't
you knock the black woman. She gave the greatest thing
she had, her *body,* for her man." The crowd gasped,
stunned, then cried "Right on!" as she added, "and you
know who brought Martin Luther King to Chicago when
all the *Negro* ministers were too scared? It was a *black*
woman, *me.*" In Chicago they say, "Better not mess with
Mahalia, she'll read you for days"; and Mahalia's fiery,
New Orleans tongue read that afternoon.
    She continues to record inspirational drivel, but her heart
remains with the Dr. Watts hymns. "They say those songs

are old. They're brand new to me. Man, I was down South. You should hear those choirs in South Carolina and Georgia. They sing those hymns, and tears run from my eyes. I just want to jump up and shout. Looks like I find myself when I hear them. We lose something up North, ain't no need fooling ourselves. But when I hear those folk, I sort of get refilled, get what I had when I was a child." She has little patience with the young people's choirs, their modern jazz progressions and Top Forty repertoire; to them she's a gospel legend, two or three generations removed. "You go to church now and you don't know where you're at. I guess I'm of the old school but I just can't feel this new stuff." Alas, she continues to feature all kinds of "new stuff," almost always with unhappy results. But let her moan Dr. Watts, wail Sanctified, and rock New Orleans, and the old Mahalia fire rekindles itself.

Amidst her business and philanthropic projects, Mahalia remarried Sigmund Galloway. He now introduces her recitals and sometimes performs an initial solo on flute. Her current audiences are largely composed of middle-aged Baptists who came up with her shouting "Move On Up a Little Higher," grew prosperous with her crooning "The Lord's Prayer," and now regret the spirit they all left down home. For them Mahalia sings the old hymns—"I can't get above what made me—" and preaches her native gospel. One night she sang "He Never Left Me Alone" with such power that she nearly collapsed. Afterward, when an admirer commented on her wild, expressive freedom, she nodded. "I'm a mood singer, I sing by feeling. Looks like I get more so by the year. I think when we're old, we become like David and look back over our life like it was a story. God knows I've something to sing about." (Mahalia Jackson died in January 1972. See postscript.)

5

"The Women Had Fits":
The Soul Stirrers

The first things that will strike any newcomer to gospel are its stylistic similarities to soul music and the obvious, if not overwhelming, sexual presence of its performers. In these respects the Soul Stirrers are the most representative quartet around. Their arrangements smack of the rock and roll the group both spawned and spurns. Their lead singers have always given women fits: in 1947, R. H. Harris sang "I Thank You Lord" so hard a woman suffered a laughing seizure; ten years later, Harris' successor, Sam Cooke, had teen-age girls lined up around 125th Street waiting to see "that pretty child" at the Apollo; after he too had left the group, Johnnie Taylor, Cooke's successor, shook up America with "Who's Making Love to Your Old Lady While You're Out Making Love?"

The Soul Stirrers are the real creators of the modern quartet sound. Their history vividly demonstrates the leap gospel made in a generation's time from backwoods churches to million-dollar show business. In 1936, when they were still Texas farm boys, Alan Lomax recorded them for the Library of Congress. Lomax remembers their

music "as the most incredible polyrhythmic stuff you've
ever heard." Less than ten years later, this same group
sang on the White House lawn for President Roosevelt
and Winston Churchill. They got there via their appearances at USO shows, and their repertoire included "Precious Lord" and "I'm a Soldier." (It's gratifying to know
that before he died Winston Churchill heard a little Dr.
Watts.) And then, in the fifties, Sam Cooke so modified
the barriers between spiritual and secular music that when
he stepped out to become the father of soul music, he carried with him a generation of stylists, from David Ruffin
to Jerry Butler, who swore by him in either field. So, sneaking behind the most rococo excesses of modern soul
music, the Moog Synthesizers and casts of thousands, is
something rural and clean. That essence preserved beneath
layers of psychedelic schmaltz is the quartet sound. It
makes folklorists of all lovers of black quartet singing.
Even the monomaniac collectors of fifties rhythm and
blues, those intense late adolescents who wouldn't be
caught dead with anything older than 1948 or younger
than 1955, celebrate a "close-harmony thing" that derives
directly from rural quartet. And, "different strokes for
different folks," Motown soul is equally shot through with
quartet influences. So a musical history of the Soul Stirrers
is also a condensed survey of the entire quartet tradition.
Sam Cooke was the greatest sex symbol in gospel history.
Now gospel is, in some ways, a sexual music. Its performers
sing with their bodies and move with a thrilling grace and
physical abandonment. This sexuality is taken for granted,
and is, I think, largely innocent. (Only a dirty mind could
delight over the buxom Gospel All Stars trumpeting "He's
all over me and he's keeping me.") Like the itinerant blues
singers, quartet members are notorious lovers, blessed if
they so desire with women in every town. But Cooke's sex
appeal had nothing to do with friendly local sponsors. It
was the allure of the professional showman. Even in gospel,
he was a bobby-sox idol, the first singer to bring in the
younger crowd as well as the older shouting saints.

In 1964 Cooke died violently under highly suspicious circumstances. A few years later another Stirrer, Jimmy Outler, was accidentally killed. Now the Soul Stirrers are not violent men—R. H. Harris, for one, quit the road because he found it too crooked—yet the deaths of Cooke and Outler bring home the constant dangers that plague all black entertainers, most especially gospel singers. For all their leaps at Mammon, the group's history confirms the old gospel line, "When you sing for Jesus, you have nothing but trouble."

Jesse Farley, the only original member of the Soul Stirrers still left in the group, is an amiable, low-keyed man. He delights in playing old records and takes the Soul Stirrers' career pretty much for granted. Yet his determination has kept the Soul Stirrers' name "out there" despite every conceivable disaster. The original group banded together in Trinity, Texas, where Farley joined them in 1935. "Back then, we took things as they came. I can remember one time in 1936, the Soul Stirrers held a revival in this all-colored town, Boley, Oklahoma. Do you not know the whole group made $2.65 for the entire week? But nobody was married, everybody was young, the fellows wanted to travel." Two of them, Farley and the tenor, S. R. Crain, could read shaped-note music, and from the start "we were a venturesome group." While other Southwestern quartets would be singing spirituals and jubilees, the Soul Stirrers' repertoire was based almost exclusively on the newer gospel compositions. "They'd be singing 'It's Cool Down Yonder by Chilly Jordan,' and we'd turn around and do 'Precious Lord,' you see. In fact, when we first came to Chicago, we were criticized in the *Chicago Defender.* They didn't think a quartet should sing church songs."

Determined to sing gospel anyhow, the group began composing their own tunes. Farley remembers Crain reading his Bible and compiling the words for a modern spiritual, "He's My Rock, My Sword, My Shield."

Well Isaiah said he saw him with his dyed garments on,
Coming from the land of Bozrah, treading the wine press
alone.
Daniel said he saw him as a chief cornerstone,
I'm gonna wait right here for my Jesus till he comes.

Rebecca said she saw him while kneeling down in prayer,
He came down through the elements and his glory filled
the air,
With a rainbow on his shoulder and the government in
his hand,
I'm gonna wait right here on my Jesus till he comes.

One imagines that the great spirituals were composed in
similar fashion. The Stirrers were also the first quartet to
take traditional tunes and revise them in the new style.
R. H. Harris turned the old "I'm Gonna Tell God How
You Treat Me" into a sixteen-bar blues, and added the
wonderful couplet

I'm gonna tell him if it wasn't for your grace,
Many times I'd quit this old race.

Among them, Crain, Harris, and James H. Medlock wrote
many gospel standards and never collected a penny. "One
firm told us nobody could get a copyright on a song unless they had a publishing house. So we gave them our
songs, and they give us five hundred copies of sheet music,
free. No royalties, no nothin'."

At first, Chicago attacked them for their repertoire and
their most extraordinary innovation—a second lead singer
who effectively turned them into a quintet. Previously a
quartet lead was stationed with his three partners around
the mike, not emphasized in any special way. As a result,
he had few long solo passages. The *Five* Soul Stirrers
changed all that: "We brought the lead singer out front."
The second lead could take his place, so the four-part
harmony was never neglected. This may have been the
most revolutionary step in quartet history.

The Soul Stirrers have featured many great lead singers —Cooke, James Medlock, Leroy Taylor, Paul Foster, Willie Rogers—but their first and best was Rebert H. Harris. "Mr. Harris, a great gentleman," says Farley with elaborate emphasis, "he never left the stage like they started doing lately. But that man could just stand and *move* a church. He had the ability to make up verses as he went along. If the people were really shouting, he'd keep on. We would just chant the standard refrain, he would go where he wanted to go. . . . He started all that."

At sixty-nine, Rebert Harris retains the high, clear voice of an adolescent. Like Marion Williams, Ira Tucker, and very few others, Harris can alternate between a lyric sweetness and a grainy, passionate intensity. He sings and talks with all the laconic authority of a Sallie Martin. He's entitled, for Harris simply created the entire gospel quartet tradition. "I always say every singer out there, pro or con, is singing the R. H. Harris style. Somewhere along the line, they got a touch of me even if they don't know me." In every way, Harris reformed quartet. Lyrically, he introduced the technique of ad-libbing: "I didn't know what I was doing. One day Kenneth Morris said, 'I like that ad lib.' I didn't even know the term. I thought he was criticizing me." Melodically, he originated the chanting background repetition of key words. As for rhythm, "I was the first to sing *delayed time*. I'd be singing half the time the group sang, not quite out of meter," but enough askew to create irresistible syncopations. "The group would start one meter, and I'd be in and out, front and behind, all across there." Such an explosion of vocal possibilities deserves comparison with the great jazz musicians' liberation of their horns.

Harris was raised on a small Texas farm. He grew up, isolated and independent, musically precocious. "I used to listen to the birds sing. Whatever tune they'd make, I trained myself to make. So my tunes and my vocal control, I just impersonated the birds." When he was eight, he composed his first song, "Everybody Ought to Love His

Soul." A year later, he composed the lovely "I Want Jesus
to Walk Around My Bedside." "Some quartet out of New
York stole it, but that was the pioneer song to feature a
group singing background words, 'Walk around, walk
around,' while the lead, me, would be singing the verses."
With some brothers and cousins, he formed the Friendly
Five, and between the ages of ten and twelve, "I became
the first male ever to sing falsetto." Outside of church,
falsetto was as old as field hollers but Harris claims, "Even
women didn't sing falsetto in church back then." If Harris
is right, the falsetto sound that traveled from gospel
to soul to the Beatles began as a Texas birdsong mimicked
by a latter-day Mozart.

Harris' family was the tough, hard-working, mother-
wit-endowed sort Sallie Martin remembers. "They were just
common farmers . . . nothing was accumulated. But I
want you to mention our church, Harris Chapel C. M. E.
Methodist was named for my father. They raised me to be
very disciplined. That's why I believe there's this *virtue*
that goes along with gospel. There's more to it than good
singing. It's a beaconing thing that other folk can see without you talking it." He worked himself through high school
and a couple of years at Mary Allen Seminary in Crockett,
Texas, supported by athletic scholarships. But a boy so precocious and talented was wasted in a backwater college. "I
always did have a traveling mind, and when the Soul Stirrers asked me to join them, I just went. Though I want
you to know they had to get sole permission from my parents for me to leave the house." He was a solid, husky
youth, already balding at eighteen, and so settled that a
year later, they were calling him "the most spiritual man
on the road."

Harris claims he had no musical influences—"I came up
on my own. Out in the country, wasn't no quartet to influence me. All of my singing career is original with me"
—and certainly nobody sounded like him before. But once
he moved to Houston with the Soul Stirrers, he was surrounded by great blues singers. He listened to the country

blues of Blind Lemon Jefferson ("I just couldn't see a blind man singing blues and not spirituals. Onliest thing, Lemon kept insulting black women in his songs") and the citified double entendres of Leroy Carr ("He was my man. I just wished he'd been in the spiritual field"). His special friend was Lil Green, the same girl who later sang with Ira Tucker at Café Society Downtown. At that time, Lil was in jail for killing a man in a roadhouse brawl. She used to sing every Sunday during the prison church service, and Harris would go out each week to hear her do "Sleep On, Mother" and "Is Your All on the Altar?" Eventually Lil sang herself out of prison, and her first record hit, "Romance in the Dark," combined blues and gospel phrasing in a completely modern way three years before Aretha Franklin was born. Leroy Carr and Lil Green impressed Harris as "colorful" singers, in other words, as stylists. In 1939, the Soul Stirrers shared radio time with the white Stamps-Baxter Quartet (Stamps-Baxter is the largest white publisher of gospel music). With prime exposure to Texas blues and hillbilly music, and his own solid grounding in gospel, Harris had influences enough to whet any singing career.

Brilliantly, uniquely, Harris not only created but defined the terms of good quartet singing. "Most lead singers do not study the e–ssential word or phrase in the song. They don't read, don't define, don't insert themselves into the composer's condition and bring the thing to a picture. You must say it so clearly, so expressional . . . so forceful that it demands a fellow to accept it." The great records Harris made in the late forties still sound modern despite the *a cappella* harmonizing of the Soul Stirrers. The background harmonies are pleasing and undistinguished, but Harris' voice comes through with the timeless urgency of a Robert Johnson or a Billie Holliday.

Though "I was the first quartet singer to bring out the old hymns; that's my meat, a sad slow minor song," Harris is also a great rhythm singer. He can take the old hymn "His Eye Is on the Sparrow" and, like he says, sing all

around the barbershop "clang-a-lang-a-langs" of his group.
It's all, as Harris knows, in accenting the right words and
syllables. He'll sing a line, "Whenever I am tempted, whenever clouds rise," and simply by pausing after the first
"when," and then, by preceding the second "when" with a
"said uh," syncopate the whole line. Then he'll bisect the
word "clouds," lifting to a slur resolved by the next word,
"rise," and instruct all gospel singers how to swing lightly
and moan at the same time. Later he'll let loose his falsetto
"I sing because I'm free, ohhh," and convey the elements
of Sam Cooke's style.

On "By and By" (Specialty LP), Harris sings the old
Tindley verse with unparalleled intensity. The parentheti-
cal words are his additions:

> (*Whoa*) *trials dark on every hand,*
> *We just can't understand,*
> *The way* (*Lord*) *my God will lead us,*
> *To his blessed* [*pause*] *promised land,*
> *He'll guide us* (*Lord*) *with his eye,*
> *Every child of God will follow* (*on*) *till we die,*
> *We'll understand it better,* (*by, by*) *by and by.*

This is art almost immune to criticism. Every single syllable is charged with feeling, every added note is perfectly
weighted, exactly right. Elsewhere Harris' voice can be
winsome light; here it has the heavy impact of a farmer
broadcasting bad news about crop failure or drought. It
is sweet, manly, and terrifying, all at once. On its own,
Harris' solo part could shake a church, but it exists primarily to set up matters for Paul Foster's screaming
chorus. Like the great jazz musicians remembered for scattered solo choruses, Harris' performances were usually surrounded by the good work of less gifted men.

After leaving the Soul Stirrers, Harris continued making
great records. He recut a Stirrers hit, "I'm Willing to
Run," with his next group, the Christland Singers. On the
later disc, he manages a splendid melodic transformation.
The verse, as written, goes:

Mother and father gone on before me,
Leave me lonesome as I can be.
Our parting at the river of Jordan I sure recall.
But I told them, broken-hearted,
I'd be faithful to the end,
Lord I'm willing to run on all the way.

Before getting there, Harris ad-libs in the same key,

After a while crying days sure be over,
You won't buke me no more.

By keeping in time and anticipating the melody, he effectively expands a six-line into an eight-line verse. It's all done with consummate ease—no shock, no sweat, merely musical genius. Harris' most recent records with his current group, the Gospel Paraders, contain more rhythmic innovations. "Have you heard the opening to 'Sometime'? It's very extreme for quartet. . . . I always pride myself on saying I was in the forefront, and I stays in the forefront." He's right, too.

The Soul Stirrers were probably the first traveling quartet exclusively committed to gospel. Their early travels convinced many other groups to switch from jubilee to gospel, and Harris wound up competing with men who learned their styles from him. In the late forties the Soul Stirrers battled for the gospel championship with the Pilgrim Travelers. The Travelers also headed from Texas. Like most quartets, they sprang from family groups, and their two lead singers, Kylo Turner and Keith Barber, were cousins. Both men had R. H. Harris marked all over them. Turner's falsetto crooning contrasted with Barber's harsh growls; Harris could beat them at both styles, having named their games. The Pilgrim Travelers were known for their "walking rhythms," their foot-pats obviating the need for other percussive effects. Their strongest harmonic asset was their baritone, Jess Whitaker, who had the most beautiful quartet baritone I've heard. A fine, insidiously seductive vocalist up front (his "How Jesus Died" was copied note for note by Ray Charles in "Lonely Avenue," though Whitaker's decibels are the more erotic!), Whitaker produced unique harmonic effects with his voice. Kylo Turner's big hit was a sixteen-bar blues, "Mother Bowed," filled with dramatic R. H. Harris shifts in tone and register. The Travelers were masters at "resurrecting Mother." And here, despite their musical debts to Harris, the two groups parted company. "I believed in giving you a message. Didn't believe in preying up on an audience with a sympathetical move. I tried to stay away from 'My mother's dead' and all that. If I'd sing a song about Mother, I'd be praising her. I can't stand to hear folks sing a lie, I'd soon to hear a hummingbird *hum*. No sir, I don't believe in singing a lie. I could never sing 'O Mary Don't You Weep,' cause Mary and Martha wasn't even born when Pharaoh's army got drownded."

As early as 1942, his sound had progressed from individual idiom to folklore. In that year, in Clarksdale, Mississippi, a farm worker named Bozie Sturdevant was recorded in church, singing "Ain't No Grave Can Hold My Body Down" with a combination of slurs, falsetto, and portamento that remain the wonder of folklorists and blues collectors. Despite his place in the Library of Congress archives, Sturdevant was no untouched primitive. In the late thirties, he had migrated to Chicago, and so assimilated Harris' style that church audiences detecting the resemblance would cry out, "Sing Harris, dig that grave, R. H.," as if the other man were performing. In 1937, the Library of Congress had recorded some blind Mississippi schoolboys singing comical game songs. The students eventually became the Five Blind Boys and their lead, Archie Brownlee, the "baddest man on the road." What turned Brownlee from folk patter to gospel shout was the R. H. Harris sound. His first records were songs identified with Harris, "Lord I've Tried" and "One of These Days," and Brownlee remained "the only singer out there who'd credit me. On any old program, Archie would stand up and say, 'You know, you all carry on how mother taught

you how to sing. But I got mine from Pop Harris, and I
ain't ashamed to tell who inspired me.' No matter how
terrible he got, no matter how drunk, Archie Brownlee is
the onliest one who didn't forget me."

Harris refused to "clown," to leap off stages and run
down aisles. Not that he needed to—no one has gotten
more shouts. But he believed his points were best made
easily: "I'd sing the folks happy." People trusted him. One
witness to Harris' power is Dorothy Love Coates. In 1948,
she suffered a severe bout of pneumonia while pregnant.
Her child was born palsied, and Dorothy was prostrate
with grief and exhaustion. "Dot hadn't gotten off the bed
for months. We came to her home, there in Birmingham,
and sang Old Man Brewster's song, 'I Never Reached Per-
fection . . . Lord I've Tried.' That girl got up and been
up ever since." Dorothy remembers that bad time: "Yes,
what Harris said is the truth. There was something about
that man, he seemed so real, he seemed to be singing to
you." Like the pioneer female singers—Queen C. Anderson, Sallie Martin, Willie Mae Ford Smith—Harris embod-
ied integrity. No wonder his tasteful, rugged but
understated song seems to express so large a measure of
personal goodness.

But by the late forties, the gospel highway was dense
with moral snares, most of them female. Harris hadn't
found it so in the early days. "Here's what you gotta realize. Women became more far-ward, they came to the
front faster, they were more open in their push. In my
young days coming on, women were more fearful." Jesse
Farley says something similar: "It was the middle forties
when I began to notice the congregation would be filled
with these eager women to take the men out to dinner
and, say, entertain them. It happened when records began
to make it. The average woman when she sees a man, and
he's sharp and he's clean . . . and a whole lot of people
be shouting off him because he's so emotional, well it just
motivates the whole thing. The ladies would start a differ-

ent shout, and the way they shouted, they'd be trying to say something."

Harris wasn't listening. He was a happily married man and his wife, Jeanette Harris, sang lead with the greatest female quartet, the Golden Harps.* "Women? Lord I had to run from them instead of running to them." It was a good time for Harris. He was the most moving singer on the road, the Harrises were gospel's most talented couple. The Soul Stirrers packed houses everywhere. Then, in 1950, he quit the group "because the moral aspects of the thing just fell out into the water. The singers didn't care anything about it. They felt they could do anything they wanted." He stayed off the road for a while, but "I couldn't help it by running away from it. I had to keep myself involved, help lift the image."

So together with two ex-Soul Stirrers, Leroy Taylor and James Medlock, he formed the Christland Singers. The group left us some exquisite discs, but they never caught fire like the Soul Stirrers. In later years, Harris has sung with the Gospel Paraders. "My boys in the Paraders are real young, stretching down to twenty-two. You know how young men do, but these fellas stays straight with me. I guess that means, somewhere in my life span I must have stood for something." Sam Cooke recorded the Paraders on his label, Sar, and they had a mild hit, "Pass Me Not," in the early sixties. Since then, Harris has not recorded. He now works for a florist, gives occasional music lessons, and keeps morally and vocally in trim. His absence from recording is a great pity; his voice and style remain as fresh as ever. But at least he's still out there, keeping up with the changes in quartet style, and singing with the Paraders of an occasional weekend. Other quartet giants don't do half as much. At last report, Keith Barber was driving a

---

* The Golden Harps recorded only two singles for Peacock, but one of them, "I'll Make It Somehow," featuring the straightforward contralto wailing of Ann Grant and the stylized, husky replies of Jeanette Harris, is as deep a quartet record as the post-Kings of Harmony/Blue Jays era has produced.

school bus in Houston, Jess Whitaker was a janitor in Los Angeles, Paul Foster a vegetable trucker in Las Vegas, and James Medlock a doorman in Chicago.

The Soul Stirrers adjusted to life without Harris by developing a new sound, style, and image. While nobody ever considered them a top-flight harmony group, their sound was always distinctive. In a field of darkly grained solid-rock voices, their blend is light and casual. The typical quartet tenor in the thirties, inspired by the legendary "Highpocket" of the Norfolk Jubilees, used to sing "very outside and loose," Harris remembers, "way off by himself, in no way blending." Harris and the Stirrers hated "when those voices split and you could drive a wagon between each channel." S. R. Crain, their tenor, either couldn't or wouldn't travel those marvelous scale lines. Instead he blended as precisely as a hillbilly tenor. Says Ira Tucker: "The Soul Stirrers were always a western group, they never did care too much about harmony nohow." Similarly, Jesse Farley is no overwhelming bass. ("Listen at me trying to sing bass," he'll laugh when playing the old records.) But again, less meant more. Great quartet bassos like Bobo of the Hummingbirds, Caruthers of the Fairfield Four or Bossard of the Swan Silvertones might employ their voices as instruments, from whence derives the "boom-de-de-boom" of rock and roll. Farley and Crain, dividing the extreme harmonic assignments between them, decided to pursue a more "versatile" sound, easier, more secular.

Their biggest asset was Sam Cooke. R. B. Robinson, the group baritone, had been training a group of Chicago teen-agers, the Highway QCs, as a sort of Little League Soul Stirrers. The training paid off; three of the Stirrers' leads have come out of the QCs. The first was Cooke. When he initially came on, imitating his idol, Harris, it didn't work. To begin with, the physical images were not the same. Harris was tall, balding, and settled. "I never did appeal to the real young folk, because I was always a very conservative type. I wasn't flashy, very steady." Not that Sam Cooke was hot-headed. But he was barely twenty, moderate-sized, and gifted with exceptionally regular, almost pretty, features.

At first, Cooke was just a boy out there doing a man's job, and not too well either. Then, in the early fifties, he discovered himself. Farley recalls: "Sam started as a bad imitation of Harris and wound up with his own yodel: *Whah–ah–oh–ah–uh–ah–uh–oh.* After that, he could sell what he had better than any other member of the Soul Stirrers." Sam was singing pop style, over a quasi-hillbilly background, while Paul Foster was singing the most rugged hard lead outside of Tucker, June Cheeks, and Silas Steele. The Stirrers were among the first groups to switch from *a cappella* to instrumental accompaniment.

Theirs was a new kind of gospel. "Sam did it in a different way. He didn't want to be that deep, *pitiful* singer, like 'My mother died when I was young,' you know, Blind Boys, Pilgrim Travelers stuff. He made up different kinds of verses." Harris says, "Sam was a great thinker. He was a singer who could stand and within the process of just singing create without throwing the background off. I taught him that." Sam could holler too, though with Paul Foster and the phenomenal Julius Cheeks (who sang briefly with the Stirrers), there was no need to do so. Instead, his biggest hits, "Nearer to Thee" and "Touch the Hem of His Garment," are story songs, familiar sermons set to a moderate rock beat. His two gospel masterpieces, "Wonderful" and "Jesus Wash Away My Troubles," are both pure gospel tunes, but the phrasing, breath control, and polish are a library of hymns removed from the Kings of Harmony. "Wonderful," Cooke breathily croons, "God is so wonderful . . ." tactful pause—"Wonderful . . . God is so wonderful," the phrase yodeled with sensual sweetness. As good pop singers are supposed to do, Sam grabbed you with his first notes. One could say he didn't build much from there, but nobody cared. Merely sustaining the falsetto grace of the initial "Jesus" in "Jesus Wash Away My Troubles" was enough.

Everybody loved Sam, especially the young. The teenagers who followed the popular rhythm-and-blues heroes Clyde McPhatter and Johnny Ace also formed Sam Cooke fan clubs. Up to then, gospel's appeal had rested mainly with adults. "In the old days, young people took seats six rows from the back, the old folks stayed up front. When Sam came on the scene, it reversed itself. The young people took over," Farley remembers. "They started this pattern of standing up when the lead singers start bearing down." Congregations had always risen to their feet, but not like this. Sam became the idol of scores of young men, because he proved one could be both soulful and contemporary. After all, he was old Pop Harris' successor, yet there was nothing country or old-fashioned about him.

The legend goes that Specialty Records owed their head producer, Bumps Blackwell, and in lieu of money, Bumps asked for some pop tapes Sam had recorded. Blackwell released Sam's first singles on his own label, Keen, and they were instant smashes. From 1957 to his death in the mid-sixties, Sam was a superstar. Harris' musical offspring became the father of soul, as Harris had fathered gospel quartet. Yet Sam never seemed completely satisfied in pop. He recorded the Soul Stirrers and Harris' Paraders on his own label, Sar, and whenever the Stirrers were in his neighborhood, he'd go out to hear them. Perhaps only one time as a single did he reach the artistic heights of his gospel days. That was on his last recording, the prophetically named "A Change Is Gonna Come," a great song whose last chorus is still waiting the definitive interpretation some gospel singer will give it:

> There have been times that I thought
> I couldn't last for long,
> But now I think I'm able to carry on,
> It's been a long time coming but
> A change is gonna come, yes it will.

The semi-yodel "yes it will" is pure Sam, but the words could be the universal gospel testimony. "Of course, Sam did his best work in gospel," says Dorothy Love. "How you gonna take somebody who loves what he's doing and turn him around and put him in something unfamiliar and he's gonna be as free and natural as he was at *home?*"

There came a time in the mid-sixties when Cooke thought of returning to gospel. For about six weeks he managed to attend Soul Stirrers concerts, and, coincidentally, they always asked him to sing. But gospel followers are a hard, unforgiving lot, and the scheme didn't work. The saddest occasion was the Soul Stirrers' anniversary in Chicago. All the old members attended, and Harris himself emceed. "While the Soul Stirrers were on stage, they called Sam up. I was the emcee but I didn't know nothing about it. Somehow when Sam hit the stage, the crowd went dead and stayed dead till Jimmy Outler and Paul Foster came back. Folks were hollering, 'Get that blues singer down. Get that no good so-and-so down. This is a *Christian* program.' And it pierced me to my heart, it *shamed* me how he was rejected by the home people. He walked off stage, tearin'. He was hurt badly."

In gospel, it seems nothing good lasts for long. Sam's attempted comeback actually hurt the group, and a couple of years later everything collapsed. Sam died under gruesome circumstances, shot by a landlady while supposedly pursuing an exotic dancer. "That don't make no kind of sense," says Harris. "Here's a man who has to run from women, and they say he's raping some woman in a fleabag hotel, shoot. . . ." It's rumored that Sam, like the late Otis Redding, was really the victim of a mob killing. Sam Cooke's enterprises were big business, and the Mafia's involvement in the record industry is common knowledge.

After that, it was all downhill for the Soul Stirrers. Cooke's replacement, Johnnie Taylor, another ex-Highway QC, had long since gone into pop. From a carbon copy of Sam he developed into a lusty, full-voiced shouter, achieving some fair success in the early seventies. With Taylor's replacement, Jimmy Outler, it was the typical story of the country boy too green for the road. An ex-fruit picker, Outler couldn't adjust to the two-bit glamour and back-room temptations. He kept getting in trouble over women, and in 1967 was accidentally killed in a fight. Meantime, a couple more Stirrers died of natural causes, and Paul Foster was forced to quit for health reasons. In the mid-sixties the group's guitarists, Leroy Crume and Sonny Mitchell, who had developed the Stirrers' pop-hillbilly sound, decided a meager road had lost its charms. Some-how Farley kept the group together. He feels that their current lead, Willie Rogers, yet another QC, has "a better voice than Sam Cooke ever dared to have." Rogers' key influence was Ira Tucker, and his phrasing is gutsier and more intricate than Sam's, in keeping with the Tucker tra-dition. One would think the Soul Stirrers were all ready for the pop sound. For thirty years, their easygoing har-monies and sexy, crooning leads set the pace for pop groups. But they still celebrate paydays no grander than in 1957 and, alas, far fewer.

Through it all, R. H. Harris kept the real quartet tradi-tion alive. In the late forties, he founded the National Quar-tet Convention. Today the group numbers 32,000 members in twenty-five states, and the 1970 Convention drew 2,600 delegates. "Our sole purpose is to help the less fortunate. We give four scholarships a year to senior graduates, and five maturity bonds to five babies each year. We don't have no stored-up money, it all goes to benefit the destitute and poor." Over half the delegates are under thirty, and lately the Convention has featured art exhibits, poetry readings, and seminars with social and political topics.

Harris runs the convention to glorify quartet. Even the Convention choir sings four-part harmony. His personal integrity and standards dominate the proceedings. "We have many blues singers to come each year. B. B. King, Bobby Blue Bland, Brook Benton. Dinah Washington was a member for years. But we won't let them sing. We ad-

vocate you can't sing the two things." One year he directed
a seminar on the subject "Which is most valuable, to bring
singing or let singing bring you? It's the general public
who puts you up. We tell the singers, be aware of the fact,
don't let yourself get beyond the singing. Let the singing
bring you. Be mindful of being a *servant* of the public."

With his unconscious imitators scattered everywhere, it's
safe to say Harris helped create the modern vocal sound.
His efforts haven't paid off. He and Jeanette were divorced
a few years ago and he now lives in a rooming house in
the plush Chicago area that Mahalia Jackson and Roberta
Martin opened up to gospel singers. His room is clean and
spare, a student's digs, and, in fact, his neighbors study at a
local college. He owns some property in Texas and visits
there annually. "Every year I give a recital in Trinity,
at the Methodist Church, and folks turn out better each
time. This year I reached back and did the old songs like
'Willing to Run' and 'Precious Lord' and 'Amazing Grace,'
and they just couldn't understand it. They wouldn't stop
shouting, even if it was a Methodist church. It was very
deeply spiritual." Harris remains the most moving quartet
singer around, at once the sweetest and most spiritually
powerful, and he'll probably go back to the Texas farms,
his genius unrewarded except for the affectionate nickname "Old Pop Harris."

"You know Sam didn't know nothing when I brought
him into my home and set him down and gave him point-
ers how he should control his voice, how his personality
should be on stage. I was scorned and buked for taking
time with him when he was just a little baby child." But
babies learn, and Sam conquered the world with R. H. Harris' style.

In the end, loss outweighed gain. Sam died, and the Soul
Stirrers went back to calling six hundred dollars a day good
pay. At times, it seems quartet's over. This once most popular form of religious music can no longer support young
singers, and there aren't many Rebert Harrises left to hold
the fort. Yet, look at all the soul quartets harmonizing

like second-flight Hummingbirds or second-string QCs.
Who has the answer? Perhaps the disillusionment with
quartet traces to Sam Cooke's death. Folks knew quartet
singers had women and drank and carried on like blues
singers. But what hurt gospel followers most was the seedi-
ness of it all. Gospel trains one to bear himself with pride:
"It's how we carry ourselves," Marion Williams says. "God
means his children to be *beautiful.*" Even in pop, Sam
maintained his wholesome, fresh-scrubbed image, as if to
tell the church mothers he had switched but hadn't back-
slid. Now he was gruesomely, publicly dead, and for all
R. H. Harris' efforts, "They must think the gospel singers
are the worst people in the world."

PART TWO

THE
GOSPEL
PIONEERS

6

Reverend Brewster and the Ward Singers

By the mid-fifties, the gospel sound had invaded every area of popular music, including even country and western. In 1955, Elvis Presley, a young Mississippian, sprang on the pop scene by way of Memphis with a musical composite of Southern song styles, most of them black. Because Presley looked the part of the hillbilly racist, he received some criticism for his musical borrowings. He vehemently denied any prejudice against black people and offered as proof his attendance every Sunday at the East Trigg Baptist Church in Memphis. Presley later went on to notoriety as a Wallace supporter, so his disclaimers of prejudice are a mite questionable. But at least he knew good gospel music. East Trigg was not just another black gospel church. Its leading soloist, Queen C. Anderson, is by legend the greatest gospel singer the South has produced. And its preacher, Reverend W. Herbert Brewster, is a magnificent songwriter, at the very least a Milton to Thomas A. Dorsey's Shakespeare.

Reverend Brewster is a beautiful example of the progressive impulses nurtured by gospel and developed in the freedom movement. His lyrics have always been the most ambitious in gospel, blending a conscious literary sensibility with the most vivid, immediate folk imagery. "A gospel song is a sermon set to music. It must have sentiment and doctrine, rhetorical beauty and splendor," he says. To elaborate his doctrines, Brewster gave wide currency to the folk sentiments of his rural childhood. This most articulate of gospel preachers is also the deepest, most lowdown songwriter. It's a marriage of "doctrine and sentiment" celebrated by all the great black leaders from Marcus Garvey to Dr. Martin Luther King and Malcolm X. Reverend Brewster himself has always been a political radical. For years, he wrote pamphlets and books urging "a greater freedom for the black man." He composed pageant plays commemorating the black struggle, *From Auction Block to Glory*. Irritated by the Uncle Tom gestures of his colleagues, his motto became "Out of the Amen Corner onto the Street Corner." And he freely acknowledges what's apparent in all his best songs—that the metaphors of progress involve moving up higher in this life as well as the next. "I always loved challenges, to meet them and extend them."

Brewster was born in the small farm town of Somerville, Tennessee, in 1897. His father farmed a few acres, and the boy began working when "I was knee-high to a milk pail." He read ferociously, and he still speaks in the rolling, rhetorical periods of the late nineteenth century. "As a country boy, I took trips through the hills and brooks of my native town. Nature had poured much of its contents into my thinking. I was deeply moved by poetry. I loved Longfellow and of course the Shakespearean poets." During the winter months, he'd go from house to house, composing songs for his friends. Always a good student, he later received both Bachelor of Arts and Doctor of Divinity degrees.

When Brewster, D.D., moved to Memphis in the twenties, the blues were inescapable, and he heard and enjoyed Bessie Smith, Ma Rainey and Ethel Waters. His idol was

W. C. Handy, and he gradually consolidated a reputation as Handy's opposite number in gospel. East Trigg became famous for its annual pageant plays for which Brewster composed the librettos and all the tunes. As befitted the occasion and his education, the songs were appropriately doctrinal. But what sold them were the irresistible rhythms —Brewster was probably the first to combine the blues and waltz forms in gospel—and gutsy lyrics. "I tend to use the old people's expressions I heard back in Somerville. We had what we used to call *wang-doodling* preachers, hah, hah, I imagine you don't know about them. They would speak in these mournful tones, and it was poetry." So were Brewster's lyrics.

In the late thirties, he auditioned a young choir singer, T. C. Anderson. "I had never heard of a girl with initials for a first name. So I renamed her Q. C. Anderson for Queen Candice of Ethiopia, it's in the Bible." The very naming declared Brewster's black pride. It proved well deserved; by 1941 Queen C. Anderson singing Brewster songs ruled the South. Her voice was high and penetrating, not well suited for recordings, and her few discs with the Brewster Singers disappoint. But in person, "she had no equals."

From the start, Brewster's gospel songs were musical testimonies. No other gospel writer has so definitively rendered the gospel witness' sense of "coming up the rough side of the mountain." His first publication, "I'm Leaning and Depending on the Lord," made Queen C. famous and became part of the Southern speech pattern. (Said one gospel singer about another, "I'm afraid Joe's about gone. They tell me he's really just out here leaning and depending.") Even more compelling was the next Brewster-Anderson hit:

> *I have so much to thank my Jesus for,*
> *Since I've been a soldier out in this holy war,*
> *I count my blessings one by one,*
> *I just see what God has done,*
> *And then I say I thank you Jesus, oh yes I do.*

In the chorus, Queen sang "I thank you Lord, I thank you
Lord, I thank you Jesus, I thank you Lord, I thank you
Lord, you've been so good to me." She became famous
for "thanking Him," and the potent combination of blues
riffs and verbal repetition—dictated apparently by emotional
stress, but actually by Brewster's genius—codified one of
the most striking attributes of the new hard gospel style.

In the mid-forties, Queen introduced Brewster's masterpiece, "Move On Up a Little Higher," in which he collects
and combines some of the richest folk imagery in black
art.

> *Soon as these feet strike Zion,*
> *I'm gonna lay down my heavy burden*
> *Gonna put on my robe in glory,*
> *Gonna shout and tell the story,*
> *I've been coming over hills and mountains*
> *Gonna drink from the crystal fountain.*
> *All God's sons and daughters*
> *Will be drinking that old healing water . . .*
> *I'm going out sight-seeing in Beulah,*
> *Gonna march around God's altar.*
> *Gonna walk and never get tired,*
> *Gonna fly and never falter.*

A very long song—"the pageant plays put me in the habit
of composing tunes that could be sung both slow and fast"
—"Move On Up" proceeds to survey the delights of paradise:

Gonna move on up a little higher, gonna meet the Hebrew
    children.
Gonna move on up a little higher, meet Paul and Silas.
Move on up a little higher, meet the lily of the valley,
Feast with the rose of Sharon,
It will be always howdy howdy, always howdy howdy,
Always howdy, howdy, and never goodbye.

Mahalia Jackson appeared with Queen C. Anderson on a
program and was enthralled. She later recorded "Move

On Up" for Apollo, sold a million copies, and became Gospel's queen with Queen C.'s tune. For many years Mahalia and Thomas Dorsey's old crony Theodore Frye claimed joint authorship; only in the late fifties did she acknowledge Brewster. Having found her niche, Mahalia continued to record Brewster songs of triumph: "Just Over the Hill," "I'm Getting Nearer My Home," "These Are They" and "How I Got Over," all heralding the same good news as "Move On Up." Mahalia was not the only one to sing Brewster's songs. His musical and verbal ideas were plagiarized elsewhere, "but I've never sued. With the racial situation getting so acute, I haven't bothered too much with any publicity."

In the late forties, Brewster began composing songs for Clara Ward and the Ward Singers, at that time the greatest group in gospel. The Wards' biggest hit, "Surely God Is Able," was a Brewster composition. In three years' time, Brewster had written the two biggest gospel single hits, "Move On Up" and "Surely"—quite an accomplishment for a full-time preacher. Like "Move On Up," "Surely" came from the country. "I heard an old country preacher at a ministers' convention, preaching on the subject 'Surely Our God Is Able.' He was a wang-doodler, and he wailed in almost the same tempo and melody I used in 'Surely.'" In later years Brewster told Marion Williams, the lead on "Surely," that her roaring affirmations, "Shore . . . ly, Sho lay," reincarnated the backwoods preacher's.

Brewster's songs were structurally more complex than those of Thomas A. Dorsey. He was the first to compose tunes that commenced "slow and mournful" with melismatic cadenzas reminiscent of Dr. Watts hymns, and then picked up the tempo. The lyrics were filled with Biblical images: "Oh, Brewster," says Robert Anderson, "he's just a Biblical scholar." Many of his song titles—"Treading the Wine Press Alone," "As an Eagle Stirreth Her Nest," "The Wonderful Counselor Is Pleading for Me"—are straight out of the Bible, a scholarly variation of the old spiritual writer's procedure. Others employ Biblical doctrine, like "I'm

Climbing Higher and Higher," which marries the beat of Count Basie to the theology of St. John of the Cross.

First round was regeneration, second round justification,
The third a happy confession, then the Holy Ghost took
    possession.
The next round was great tribulation,
That leads us on to glorification,
Well I'm climbing higher and higher and I won't come
    down.

"These Are They," especially when sung by Mahalia or the Gospel Harmonettes, carried Revelation to the forefront of the freedom movement.

> *These are they from every nation*
> *Who have washed their garments white,*
> *Coming up, coming up through great tribulation*
> *To a land of pure delight.*

"These are they" sounds archaic, but "coming up" brilliantly identifies the "they" as poor black folk. Another lyric, "City Called Jerusalem," resembles Walt Whitman's catalogues of American names. The pleasure here derives from word sounds; once again Brewster made high art of old folk habits.

There are many important cities where the great Apostles
    went,
Rome, Athens, Thessalonica, Antioch and Corinth.
Then John in Revelation when called to come up higher,
Wrote to Ephesus and Smyrna, Pergamos and Thyatira;
Sardis, Philadelphia, Laodicea—a letter around,
But none was like the city John saw coming down.

In the slow-fast tunes, Brewster would begin with a lyric as elaborate as an old hymn, include a mid-chorus in a medium tempo, and a final exultant explosion, the language simplifying as the beat increased. Two Ward Singers hits, "How Far Am I from Canaan" and "Weeping

May Endure for a Night," open with a richly metaphorical verse sung to a lovely, hymnal melody reminiscent of Tindley's "Beams of Heaven," and a middle chorus of summary "doctrinal" nature. But the choruses are the height of simplicity. In the first song, after a verse about traveling in the desert ("I am standing on the Jordan, gazing cross its stormy tide . . .") and a wordy chorus ("How far am I from holy Canaan, land of peace and pure delight . . .") comes an irresistible up-tempo chorus, listed in the sheet music as "Special Chorus: May Be Used For Final Refrain."

> *How far am I from Canaan* [3 times]
> *Where the angels are singing*
> *And the joy-bells are ringing in glory,*
> *How far am I from Canaan.*

The major line switches from chorus to chorus, "I feel so close to Canaan," "Over there we'll live forever," "over there we'll never grow old," etc. Brewster thus allows the congregation's soloist to shine with her mastery of tune and "diction," and, remembering the less verbally dexterous, he composes a simple chorus any choir can pick up.

"Weeping May Endure for a Night" begins in the realm of Dr. Watts, but picks up the tempo with its midway summation:

> *When you spend your years in the Lord's employ,*
> *What you sow in tears, you'll reap in joy.*

Lively if a bit literary; and then makes things extra plain.

> *Weeping may endure for a night,*
> *In God's own time, he'll make it all right.*

After that, hard singing groups can go to town on "He'll make it all right." In such tunes Brewster explores musical possibilities that he was the first, and sometimes the only one, to notice.

He kept turning out songs for the Ward Singers until

the late fifties. In 1959, Queen C. Anderson died, enriched not a penny by Elvis Presley's belated tribute to East Trigg. Her last Brewster hit was "A Sweeter Tomorrow" and her last words were "I'll be dreaming of a sweeter tomorrow." Without her inspiration, Brewster felt little inclination to compose. He kept busy working in the civil rights movement and his own ministers' school. "Most people don't like to think too much when it comes to committing certain expressions to memory. They rely on the same key phrases our grandfathers used. Now I've never believed in all heat and no light. On the other hand, you have all these dry churches with all light and no heat. So I operated minister schools in Chicago and Memphis. I tell the young preachers, our people have changed. It's no longer, Come and get it. You have to go out and *bring* them. I say, 'Out of the Amen Corner onto the Street Corner.' The lambs are still crying for the shepherd."

Brewster became a major political force, and white candidates began wooing him. Governor Frank Clement of Tennessee, whose last request before he died was Dorsey's "Precious Lord," used to stop by East Trigg. "But you can't always bet on these fellows. Clement wanted me to speak for him, but he didn't give me no assurances he'd help us." Brewster dismisses all those cracker politicians who flirt with black preachers as "political comedians." Senator Albert Gore alone won his affection: "the best man I've known in politics." Brewster was devoted to Dr. King; he saw him on the day of the assassination. The older man had fought for like goals all his life. "Back in the forties, when I'd give plays about Jamestown and Nat Turner, the folks would get so fearful. One thing Dr. King did, he removed some of our folks' fear."

And surely Reverend Brewster accomplished something similar with his exclamations of progress to victory: "Surely God is able to carry you through"; "My soul looks back and wonders how I got over"; "Coming up through great tribulation"; "Weeping may endure for a night but joy will come in the morning." Brewster's political boldness and courage, combined with his brilliant development of black folk art, is a thrilling realization of the best impulses in gospel. On the strength of his achievement he should be a culture hero of the first rank. But, as his son, W. H. Brewster, Jr., another gifted preacher and songwriter, said, "My father couldn't be bothered with all those unique parasites scrounging for fame."

At seventy-four, Brewster, sober, dignified, his rich bass-baritone still capable of multisyllabic declaration and gruff, lowdown shouts, expresses the genius and dignity of gospel. Meanwhile Clara Ward and the Ward Singers, the group that conquered America with his tunes, perform in a manner that denies their own history, much less everything Brewster accomplished. With Queen C. and Dr. King gone, Senator Gore retired, and the Wards clowning in the clubs, no wonder "Old Man Brewster" has shifted into an uneasy semi-retirement.

The Clara Ward Singers have one of the most professional routines in show business. They step out demurely, heavily bewigged and rainbow garbed. Their repertoire contains only the best known pop-gospel tunes, every bouncy one culminating in the most flamboyant shout steps imaginable. When Gertrude Ward, Clara's phenomenal mother, defended their behavior, "The Lord told us to go into the highways and hedges as well," to a young militant, his reply was, "You know folks don't come to clubs to get saved. They want to see Negroes make damn fools of themselves." Gospel lovers don't necessarily object to the Wards' appearances in clubs. It's how they do it that hurts—as in the movie *It's Your Thing,* where one stout Ward Singer loses her shoe, deftly picks it up and gets back to business, shouting with the group.

And yet, there was a time when—admittedly with different members—the Ward Singers were the greatest group, together with the Roberta Martin Singers, produced by gospel. And Clara Ward, even today, is an extraordinary soloist. Her admirers range from the old pioneer Georgia

Peach, who told a French reviewer she preferred Clara to Mahalia, all the way to Lady Soul, Aretha Franklin, who grew up copying Clara's style. Both Georgia Peach and Aretha idolized Clara for her hymns: "the only things I like to sing." (Aretha's first gospel records were Clara's best-known hymns, exactly copied note for note.) Ironically, the embodiment of commercialized gospel is only herself when singing and moaning the old Gospel Pearls. The artistic sacrifice has paid off, however, and when criticized, Clara probably shouts all the way to the bank.

In church, Clara used to say, "Behind every great man there stands a great woman. And I don't know where I'd be without my mother, Mrs. Gertrude Mae Murphy Ward." Mother Ward would then get up, flashing a mouth of pearl and gold, and continue emceeing in her unforgettable voice. Years ago she had a goiter removed, and her voice hasn't been right since. It's a great, big, cracked instrument, leaping octaves from word to word. It may start out a loud, shaky baritone and then soar to a gravelly falsetto in an anomalous manner that has inspired scores of party imitations. Clara is right; Mrs. Ward made the Ward Singers. Clara had the talent, but Mrs. Ward had the spunk and drive and determination. Were the two combined, Clara might be the greatest gospel singer of them all. But the spiritual power still belongs to Mama.

Gertrude Ward grew up poor in South Carolina. She was raised on the old Dr. Watts hymns she later taught Clara, and was a devoted mezzo-soprano soloist in the choir. In the twenties she moved to Philadelphia with her husband. Here her daughters Willa and Clara were born. The family was very poor. Gertrude used to stand on corners during the Depression, waiting for white people to pick her up for day work. Often dispossessed, she carried her family to dozens of different homes. ("These old feet," she used to tell church folks, "these feet can remember where there was holes in the shoes. Clara Ward used to walk on cardboard. Glory!" all falsetto exultation and tears.) Then, in 1931, she had a vision telling her to go and sing. This sensational debut was the first of a career of sensations. She walked again the streets of Philadelphia singing

> *Since I gave to Jesus my poor broken heart,*
> *He never has left me alone.*

She returned home and formed a family gospel group, with her little girls accompanying her on piano. The Wards brought Thomas Dorsey and Sallie Martin to Philadelphia. From the start, Clara was the star, banging the piano with long, skinny fingers, and rocking the newer gospel tunes, "On the Jericho Road There's Room for Just Two" and "I'm Gonna Work Until the Day Is Done." Gertrude was a Baptist show-business mother. She kept Clara and Willa in church, and, excepting a brief teen-age marriage, Clara has continued to live with her. In later years Clara confessed to her frustrations as a teen-ager. She loved gospel, but not with the monomaniac dedication of Mrs. Ward.

In 1943 the Ward Singers tore up the National Baptist Convention and became headline attractions in gospel. Mrs. Ward discovered her own gospel route and then wrote a book about it, telling churches how to promote gospel programs. It was a generous gesture, almost enough to cancel the later behavior of the group. In the late forties, Mrs. Ward added new members—Henrietta Waddy, a middle-aged lady from Philadelphia, whose voice resembled the old blues singer Ma Rainey's, and Marion Williams, a Miami teen-ager. Marion proved to be, in another singer's words, "the best singer Miss Ward ever had." During the early days her Florida solos tore up the church. She later led the group's biggest hits, Brewster's "Surely God Is Able" and "Packin' Up." Her voice, ranging from a growling quartet bottom to the airiest, most floating high soprano, became the group's trademark. Through the years they featured other great soloists, among them Martha Bass, a powerful St. Louis contralto obviously inspired by Willie Mae Ford Smith, Frances Steadman, a subtle and evocative near-bass, Baltimore's answer to Roberta Martin, and Kitty Parham, a dynamic soprano shout singer from Trenton, New Jersey. But Marion was the all-purpose singer, unbeatable on lead, and the solid base of the background harmonies.

Marion remembers singing so hard she would develop nervous spells, and holler out for relief during their long car trips. Clara was lazier. She would accompany the group on superb piano, occasionally leading a fast tune like Brewster's "The Old Landmark" or "How I Got Over." But the great moments came when she sang her hymns: "The Day Is Past and Gone," "The Fountain," "Amazing Grace," the very oldest Dr. Watts tunes. At her peak, Clara's voice was an exceptionally beautiful alto, a clearer and firmer version of Aretha's. The voice is no longer so high, but it remains freakishly resonant. Her nasality, almost Middle Eastern in its penetration, makes her a peerless moaner, and her solo records of the hymns "The Day Is Past and Gone," "The Fountain," "At the Cross," and Dorsey's "Precious Lord" were so brilliant in phrasing and so compelling in spirit that she outranked Mahalia Jackson in a newspaper poll as best gospel singer.

The Ward Singers' best records for Savoy combined brilliant soloists, exceptional Brewster material, and Clara's consistently inventive arrangements. Their biggest hit, "Surely," introduced a new waltz rhythm into gospel. From then on, the group became famous for their musical innovations. They were the first gospel group to feature the switch-lead tactics of the shouting quartets; at no time did Clara employ less than four great singers in the group. Meanwhile, the Ward Singers were the acknowledged queens of hymn singing. Clara's solos were complemented by the group's soaring treatments of "When I Wake Up in Glory," "The Old Rugged Cross," and "I Heard the Voice of Jesus." ("Child," Alex Bradford remembers, "The Ward Singers used to do 'I Heard the Voice,' and Marion get to the line, 'I came to Jesus as I was,' she'd play with the words, make those awful faces, and baby, they'd be carrying them out by the forties and fifties.") One record from this period, the old hymn "That Awful Day Will Surely Come," bears the name "Gertrude Ward and Daughters," and is a deeply moving example of South Carolina moaning, with each Ward—Gertrude, Clara, and Willa—singing introspectively to herself. There's never been a group like the Wards. Within the eleven-year period Marion and the rest stayed, the group had more hits, earned more shouts, packed more houses, and charged more money than any group in gospel history.

Singing was only part of their allure. Tired of the old homespun choir robes, Clara began designing fancy outfits of elaborate and, for gospel, peculiar materials. In the mid-fifties, the Wards began sporting wigs that grew more fanciful by the year. In one nightclub experience, Clara and her new girls came on wearing conelike wigs that grazed the ceiling. During the fifties, they stuck to ponytails. It was nothing like later years, but still far-out for gospel. "The Ward Singers were a psychedelic light show," remembers a fan, "and the other groups looked like an old silent movie."

Gertrude and Clara opened the Ward's House of Music, a publishing firm enriched by Reverend Brewster's catalogue. They also turned out souvenir books, the first in gospel, filled with cunningly doctored pictures of the group and the family. Sometimes spirit and publicity worked at cross purposes. In one shot, Clara was shown on her knees. The caption read, "Clara Ward singing out of her soul. 'The Day Is Past and Gone,'" but the photo had been so lightened that Clara looked like an albino child in a nightgown, yowling for her doll.

In the early fifties, the Ward Singers began touring with Reverend C. L. Franklin of Detroit, Aretha's father, and a thrilling preacher and singer. Franklin became a superstar and Clara's constant escort. The two traveled to the Holy Land, necessitating a new souvenir book. "I wish everybody in this church would buy this book," Mrs. Ward used to say. "I wish everybody in America would buy this book." In 1957 Mrs. Ward booked a tour for the Gospel

Train, the eight leading groups in the field. It was the first of many such package tours, and at least one singer, Julius Cheeks, lead of the Sensational Nightingales, calls it his most profitable to date. Of course, all the groups were hot and gospel was at its zenith. But the custodial care of Gertrude Ward was not to be gainsaid.

Then, in 1958, Marion Williams and all the other Ward Singers quit the group. It was well known that the girls received low salaries while Mrs. Ward and Clara divided the group's substantial fees. In addition, Mrs. Ward owned the building where Marion, Frances, and Kitty lived, so the girls wound up paying back part of their earnings to their employer as rent. "It's a sit-down strike," Mrs. Ward told *Jet*, speaking the language of the bewildered capitalist. She began substituting new singers. At least three, Thelma Jackson, Carrie Williams and Jessie Tucker, were first-rate. But without the old singers, the group's popularity nose-dived. Now when the Wards left their massive eight-door limousine, they'd face half-empty churches. Mrs. Ward's old revival ploys—"We want you to lend us your amens"; "Won't you help with the offering? I need fifty dollars, I'm asking for five"—didn't seem to work either.

So in 1961, with much hoopla, the Ward Singers moved into the nightclubs. A big *Jet* story announced Clara's Las Vegas contract guaranteeing her five thousand dollars a week for forty weeks of the year. Other pop-gospel groups tried to follow Clara into the clubs, but without success. In another area, Marion Williams and the Stars of Faith, the ex-Ward Singers, and the Alex Bradford Singers became big European stars in the gospel-song play *Black Nativity*, and Clara wound up on Broadway herself in an ill-starred play by Langston Hughes. After it folded, she returned to the clubs and Disneyland, where the Ward Singers, the cartoons of gospel, joined the wonderful world of Mickey Mouse. The group continues to work steadily, with blazing recent success, in Japan and Europe. While gospel lovers hang their heads in shame, white audiences eat up the Ward routines. Only one other group, the Staple Singers, even remotely achieved the national fame of the Wards. And the Staples, a charming family group who began singing a cleaned-up "down-home style" before switching to folk-rock, have lately moved into soul music. Clara recorded only one gospel album between 1963 and 1970. Her discs included rock arrangements of "Message" tunes like "Zippety Doo-Dah" and "Born Free," perhaps in tribute to Walt Disney, et al. But she never cut a love song, and the group remains identified as gospel.

At first, Clara went into the clubs alone. But eventually Mrs. Ward yielded. Clara had so many extra engagements that both Gertrude and Willa formed their own groups. Gertrude's were a Little League version of Clara's, though at times Mother would make a stab at the churches, carrying good singers and selling her pictures and slides of the Holy Land: "Yes, children, Mother finally made it over." In the mid-sixties one might have seen her on Broadway with her girls, crowned in a black wig with a white streak down the middle. In summer she'd wear a mink coat and —sneakers, as if "these old feet" still remembered.

For, finally, Mrs. Ward is too old to change. With Clara, she moved from Philadelphia to Los Angeles some years ago. ("Walt Disney gave me this chair," she tells Disneyland customers.) She attends all the programs featuring any traveling singer from the old days. When nobody else turns up, Mrs. Ward is there, graciously assuring the artists, "You knew I'd be here." In 1967, Clara suffered a stroke while performing in a nightclub. She survived, and Gertrude began making public announcements about "God's miracle girl." They returned to Philadelphia for a special testimonial program, and when Marion Williams got up to sing "Surely God Is Able," Mrs. Ward ran and jumped and hollered "Sing, sing" as if it were the old days. Then the ladies went back to Las Vegas and Disneyland and the familiar routines.

In 1970 they returned home again for the funeral of Ruth Davis, lead singer of the Davis Sisters and an old friend. Though the night of the wake was sub-freezing weather, the church was packed—more than it had been during Ruth's last years. When Clara and Mrs. Ward walked in wearing massive gold hats, there was a smattering of applause. Out in the halls, somebody said "Clara and Miss Ward are here." His wife replied, "Are they fabulous?" That night, various singers performed and Reverend C. L. Franklin preached. The Wards seemed genuinely moved. During the very first song, when a local choir soloist, Goldwire McLendon, sang "Just to Behold His Face" most beautifully, Clara fell out, hollering long, loud, eminently musical shrieks. Not to be outdone, another ex-Ward Singer, Carrie Williams, fell out a bit later, shrieking magnificent soprano notes two octaves higher than Clara's.

The funeral took place the next morning. Philadelphia waited with bated breath for Mother to overextend herself. Up she came, knock-kneed as ever from the early years of scubbing and hard labor. "Goodbye to my daughter Ruth in the Lord," the voice ruled imperiously, in its proper home, a Philadelphia church. "Ruth isn't singing 'He'll Understand and Say Well Done' any more. Ruth is singing 'All *Hail* . . . the Power of *Jesus'* Name.' " Mother was home free now. Philadelphia had forgotten everything. "You know I'm looking to see Ruth one of these days. It may be somewhere around God's altar, somewhere around God's throne, but you look for me in heaven, God knows—" She paused, smiling, and the audience called back "—I'll be there." Then she quoted Ruth's biggest hit, "Twelve Gates to the City." "You know, Ruth came in by the east gate. I don't know what gate I'm coming in"; and the organist began playing the jazz-rock bridge that always announced "Twelve Gates." The whole church was rocking, and Mrs. Ward started singing, "When we all get to Heaven, what a day of rejoicing that will be." She went to jumping, fell to the ground, was lifted, smiling, ecstatic. Clara got up shouting, the whole church rose up singing, and the aisles were filled with people dancing in the spirit.

Mrs. Ward returned to her seat, accompanied by the lead singer of the Harmonizing Four and the chauffeur for the Nightingales. She remained there, constantly drying her eyes. A bit later, Clara got up to sing "The Day Is Past and Gone," her most famous hymn. She seemed a mite rusty, not nearly so in touch with the old ways as her mother. But she sang well and hummed resonantly. Then she began to shake, and nurses and ushers were enlisted to carry her out. Her voice began to tremble the words of "Father I Stretch My Hand to Thee," but all that came out was "Father," as the prone body was lifted high over the heads of mourning saints, who heard something real and true once more in Clara's voice and cried back to her, "Yes, yes, sing, child . . . call him when you need him, you'll get an answer, he won't fail you . . . call him when you need him." (Clara Ward died in January 1973. See postscript.)

7

Reverend Julius Cheeks and
Reverend Claude Jeter:
The Fathers of Soul

In all the great modern soul singers, one hears echoes of the pioneer gospel shouters. The influences are usually direct and specific: Aretha Franklin sounds like Clara Ward, Wilson Pickett imitates Julius Cheeks, B. B. King resembles Sam McCrary. But vocal styles cannot be copyrighted, and it's a cause of endless frustration for the gospel singers to see the world enrich their disciples while they sing free-will offerings in store-front churches. Two of the key figures in modern quartet are Reverend Claude Jeter, formerly of the Swan Silvertones, and Reverend Julius Cheeks, former lead of the Sensational Nightingales and now director of his own group, the Sensational Knights: any confusion is deliberate. Jeter knows vaguely that his falsetto crooning is duplicated left and right. He lists some imitators: "Well, there's the Temptations and the Inspirations, I mean the Impressions, you can tell I'm not up on blues. In rock and roll, the message is very audible, very sensible, very plain, and it's true. But when I hear the name Jesus in a song, my ears really open."

Cheeks is less casual. He knows that all the hard-shouting tough guys from James Brown to Wilson Pickett couldn't exist "without yours truly, Reverend June Cheeks. When I see them, I say, Hey hey, my man, you owe me some money from that last hit you made mocking me."

Cheeks and Jeter aren't superstars. But any time a rock singer shoots into falsetto—whether he trumpets with the Temptations, the Four Seasons or the latest super group— Jeter has indirectly influenced him. Likewise, when Pickett or Brown work out, it was Julius Cheeks who showed them how to "scream and sweat and cut the fool for the people." The two men originated much of the modern song style broadcast in rock, soul, and country. They remain struggling and poor while their imitators clean up.

Both men speak with authority when they describe the hazards of sticking with gospel. Jeter, the older, is an especially devoted custodian of the gospel tradition. Now in quasi-retirement, he attends all the New York programs, cheering his colleagues with his presence and sympathy. Spotting Ira Tucker and James Walker at Washington Temple, he kids: "I guess I'm too little to be standing with all these stars." The Hummingbirds giggle affectionately, embracing him. He is a tall, light-skinned man of sixty, thin, in contrast to most halfback-sized gospel shouters. On stage his physical manner, all bony fingers pointed at sinners and skinny knees inclined in tribute to "An Old Lady Called Mother," was a Swans trademark. His appearance has always been suave, self-possessed, and, accented by his huge, tinted glasses, a bit weird. Jeter knows he's a special singer and carries himself with consequent dignity. "We've had too much form and fashion on stage. This is a thing where you can only survive by being real. Out of all the people we can fool, we can't fool God. He knows our intentions. So I'd rather fool nobody in the gospel field. If I don't feel the spirit, I won't move. I believe in the soft approach. The Bible tells us, 'If you pray in secret, I'll reward you openly.' I tried to practice that during my career." Jeter likes to shake up a church exhausted by the "hooping and hollering" of other quartets. His strategy is to seductively croon the old Baptist hymns with perfect timing and impeccable falsetto diction. It's a unique style the public loves. "I've never imitated a woman in my falsetto. There's a difference. When some people want to laugh, rather than say I sound like a woman, they'd say I sound like a cat, hah hah." Jeter worked hard to develop a distinctive group sound, and the Swans' ultimate epithet became "sweet-singing."

He was born in Montgomery, Alabama, and, unlike most singers in this book, grew up financially secure. His father was a lawyer and "the only Negro timekeeper" of the TC and R Railroad. Jeter Senior owned a plantation, and the boy's earliest memories were comfortable ones. His father died when he was eight, and though times grew hard, "My mother, Maggie Jeter, bore most of the burden. Now my mother was one of the greatest singers. Man, I couldn't touch her. She used to rock me on her knee: 'Sing for Mommy.' I guess all you say is so odd, my phrasing and time, I picked up from her. Yeah, man, you couldn't beat her with the time." Mrs. Jeter moved her family to Kentucky, where Claude sang in church, graduated high school, and began working in the coal mines of West Virginia, just across the state line, to support her. "It wasn't so bad. You only got paid for what you did. You got so much for a car, each car held six or seven tons. You quit when you got ready."

Since childhood, Jeter had been singing jubilee quartet. "We didn't have none of this modern clowning. The boys stood still and the folks would shout off any kind of thing you were singing about God." In 1938 he formed the Four Harmony Kings with his brother and two other miners. They were later joined by John Myles, another Alabaman mining in West Virginia. Myles is the only remaining member of the original Swans, and the group's current manager. Jeter became celebrated as an all-purpose quartet singer, and even sang briefly with the Dixie Hummingbirds, that other great exponent of quartet harmony. And, up to any demands, the father of falsetto sang bass! The Harmony Kings traveled on weekends from West Virginia to towns like Sylvia and Blueville, North Carolina. Often they'd split twenty cents among them. In the early forties the group was offered a radio broadcast on a 50,000-watt station in Knoxville, Tennessee. To avoid confusion with the Kings of Harmony, they changed their name to the Silvertone Singers. When the Swan Bakery began sponsoring them, their name changed again to the Swan Silvertones. "After we went commercial, every thirteen weeks we got a raise. We stayed five and a half years, and by then we were making pretty good change."

Jeter credits the Swans' smoothness to years of mike training. "For an hour before each broadcast, we'd rehearse mike technique." The Swans became celebrated all over the South for their jumping jubilees and "our touching folk tunes like 'Old Black Joe.'" The gospel era also demanded a hard singer, so Jeter recruited Solomon Womack, a fellow Alabaman singing in Cincinnati. In 1945, the Swans began recording for King. Jeter is not pleased with the forty-five sides the label cut on them. "They only wanted hillbilly style, they didn't care too much for the real gospel." Nevertheless, Jeter's lightly swinging performance of "I Bowed on My Knees and Cried Holy" was a hit for the group. The record juxtaposes Jeter's casual grace with Womack's hard-driving spirit in a style midway between jubilee and modern quartet. The King records, for all Jeter's disapproval, still impress with the beautiful *a cappella* harmonies. Most quartet records of the late forties featured insistent, sixteen-bar blues which gradually induced extraordinary tension. This style was not Jeter's meat, but Womack contributed thrilling performances of "Use Me Lord" and "I've Got a Witness in Heaven," among others. "Poor Womack. He was the best lead I ever had. But he sang himself to death. He'd come out of singing, raining sweat and then go bareheaded in zero-degree weather. We had to turn him loose, and next thing we knew, Womack was dead."

The Swans were by now a name group, but no super-stars. "Often we had to send home for money for our ho-tels. We'd get to programs, the doors be locked, and the promoter split town. You know that part still happens today." In 1951 they moved to Specialty Records. Their first releases featured Jeter, Womack, and the shrill gravelly screams of Reverend Robert Crenshaw, a shouter in the modern bag (though Alan Lomax recorded Crenshaw di-recting a Dr. Watts hymn as an example of the old spiri-tual tradition!). The Swans finally hit the big time with the addition of Paul Owens, formerly of the Hummingbirds and the Nightingales. Ira Tucker calls Paul Owens the fastest-thinking singer he's heard. More than that, he is a brilliant arranger, easily the best in quartet, and an ace at getting a group together. Owens tightened the group's harmonies, modernized their rhythms with an obvious nod to pop music. (Says Owens, "My kind of singers are the Four Freshmen and the Hi-Los.") The Swans' first at-tempts at hard gospel were a bit scattered, but Owens, a master of musical economy, made each moment count. Under his aegis the Swans became a peerless recording group. While Jeter took care of the falsetto hymns, Owens and the group's screamers, Crenshaw and, later, Dewey Young, went to town on "My Rock" and "How I Got Over," tunes that could upset any church.

In 1955, the Swans moved to VeeJay and added a guitarist, Linwood Hargrove, formerly of the Skylarks of Tennessee, and a new hard shouter, Louis Johnson, for-merly of the Spiritualaires of Sumter, South Carolina. Har-grove's tactful and inventive guitar stylings enhanced the Swans' already progressive sound. Johnson's voice, a grav-elly tenor of great beauty, forced Jeter to color his falsetto. "Louis made me add this growl. I'd be switch-leading with him, and I didn't dare get smooth behind his part. I tried to make a little growl and then smooth it over. It ain't re-ally my style, and I don't like it." But the public did, and Jeter's growling falsetto stylings began cropping up in rhythm-and-blues records by all the major groups.

The Swans' two biggest hits from this period exemplify their genius. Their classic rocker, "Mary Don't You Weep," allows Jeter, Owens, and Johnson to romp over beautifully wailed background choruses. While Johnson hollers "Mary" as if she were a naughty child, Jeter rushes in behind and beyond the beat, with wonderful interpolations. One of these, "I'll be a bridge over deep water if you trust in my name," inspired Paul Simon's "Like a Bridge Over Troubled Water." In person, they were quite a trio singing "Mary": Jeter, urbane, urgent, yet removed, those glasses signaling strange messages; Owens, the relaxed pretty-boy crooner who kept even his clapping to a minimal movement; and Johnson, short, stout, clumsy, and troubled by the spirit.

"Saviour Pass Me Not" is the last great Swans record. Johnson sings the first verse with breathy intimacy, but comparatively straight. Then over harmonies marvelously controlled by the dominant background lead of Owens, Jeter comes in, supplementing the simple chorus with glorious ad libs, while Johnson chants the words like a backwoods preacher.

Jeter: Whah, Saviour—
Johnson: It's not any harm to call the name Jesus—
Jeter: Loving loving loving loving loving loving loving lovinglovinglovinglovingloving—
Johnson: It's not any harm to call the man—
Jeter: *Hmmm-mmm—*
Johnson: This is what I want him to do for me—
Jeter: *Hmmm—*
Johnson: I just want the man to hear—
Jeter: Whah hear my oh Lord humble—
Johnson: When the devil try to turn me around—
Jeter: Hear my hum-m-m-m-ble cry . . .

In the mid-sixties Jeter quit the Swans. He was tired of the highway and the struggle. Years of ad-libbing had conditioned him for the ministry, and he was ordained in the Church of Holiness Science (!) of Detroit. The Swans continue to sing, though only Myles and Johnson remain of those Jeter trained. Since he left, they've featured two imitations, Carl Davis and James Lewis, who copy his intonation and phrasing with surprising accuracy. He has recorded as a soloist and gives occasional revivals. "One of my old singers, Reverend P. L. Perkins, offered me one thousand dollars for a week's revival. But his church is in Clarksdale, Mississippi, and I don't like it down there. Anyway we never made the most down South nohow." He lives in Harlem, a few doors down from the Hotel Cecil, once New York's headquarters for gospel singers, where he lived for years. His new place is clean and homey, with felt strips reading "What Is Home Without Mother" and "Jesus Saves" pasted on the walls. He still drives a fine car with "Rev. C. J." on the door. "I've kept my voice because I didn't believe in exerting myself. I let the other fellow kill himself. Just say, I was never a *selfish* singer." When he leaves the house, he whistles his favorite tune, "What A Friend We Have in Jesus," while greeting the assorted neighborhood junkies and prostitutes who knew him mainly as sometime manager of the Cecil. "What's new, Jeter," they ask. "Nothing new, nothing good, just thank God for life up here with these heathens and muggers."

Julius Cheeks is Claude Jeter's polar opposite. Where Jeter is urbane, relaxed, a sweet singer, Cheeks epitomizes the hard gospel shouter, a gorgeous baritone splintered into hoarseness as if to validate Jeter's strategy of "letting the other fellow kill himself." He is medium-sized, solidly built, and seen up close he astonishes one with the tiny eyes and protruding cheekbones of his American Indian ancestors. Cheeks is all nervous energy, "just ate up with soul," a bundle of contradictions. On one hand, he's the original clown. "I was the first to cut the fool . . . do what the people wanted." The clowning that got him thrown out of some churches is now a universally accepted phenomenon, the trademark of a dozen quartet leads and soul singers who came up under him. And a few of his routines are

corny and embarrassing; in some ways, he did set it up for
the charlatans who clutter quartet. Yet this same Cheeks,
"a country boy from his heart," all during the fifties spoke
up against segregation, the only major gospel singer besides Dorothy Love to do so. Cheeks is a clown—and an
artist. In his presence, the soul power vibrates a direct,
compact, melancholy energy—"When I'm not singing, I'm
cracking jokes—" but the sting-ray eyes are winsome and
watery. Despite his macho manner, one knows Cheeks
is putty inside. "I sit home sometimes and play my old
records. I just cry, it'll make you cry, you know."

Cheeks grew up the poorest, least educated man in this
book. He was born in Spartanburg, South Carolina, Ira
Tucker's home, in 1929, four years after his idol Tucker.
There were thirteen kids and a widowed mother they called
Big Chick. "It were bad, man. We didn't have a clock, we
told time by the sun. We didn't eat right, we lived off fat-
back and molasses. All us kids worked in the cotton fields,
and Mama would whip me every day. I'd looked for it, it
was signed. When I was eight, she'd tell me, You take one
row of cotton, I'll take another. If I catch you, I'll hit you.
But she kept us straight. It was embarrassing for a police
to come down our road because people lived among themselves." Mrs. Cheeks was powerful enough to raise thirteen children, but too defeated to aspire to anything else.
"Mama never wanted for much. When I began hitting, I'd
go home and say, 'What you want, Big Chick?' 'What you
want to give me?' I'd give her forty-five or fifty dollars.
'You don't mean to give me all this money.' Sam Cooke
might be with me, and he run his hand in his pocket and
give her twenty-five or thirty dollars. She'd go off crying."

In 1954, when Cheeks preached his first sermon in New
York, he flew Big Chick in. "It was her first visit up here.
The sermon went over good. Everybody in the place was
shouting but her. So when it was over, somebody asked
her, 'Miss Cheeks, didn't you like the sermon?' She said,
'He's a chip off the block, and the block don't fall too much
from the chip. Go ahead further, son.' " Powerful and in-

dependent to the end, Mrs. Cheeks raised her grandchildren as she'd brought up her own. When they were grown, "She just died on us. I'll never forget the wind blowing so hard when we buried her. Like you got a whip on you."

Because the family was poor, Cheeks had to quit school after the second grade. "I can just about write my name. No, I can't read the Bible, but I played it smart. I bought me a recorded Bible in 1953 with a deck of records from *A* to *Z*. I just listen. I listened to it so much till I like to went crazy. Sometimes I come home at two in the morning and listen to my Bible, and sometime next day, it dawned on me, 'June, you ain't been to bed.'" He was a hard-working, ambitious child and only Big Chick's strict command made him suppress his rage at the white kids who'd ride to school and shout from their buses, "'Hey, you with the cotton sack on your back. Hey, you nigger,' and wasn't anything you could do about it." Even as a boy, he identified himself with the outcasts who wouldn't buckle down and deny themselves as Big Chick had. "I used to go hear this blues singer, Blind Boy Fuller, man, it would be swinging. When I was twelve, I went to work in a shanty car. That's where all the poor, broke hobos used to stay in the Depression. They hired me out as a water boy. They gave me a lot of schoolin', the black men and Mr. Spencer, the white manager. They treated me good, ain't nothin' wrong with men who can't make it down there."

The family next door had a radio, and every Sunday he'd hear his favorite spiritual groups, the Dixie Hummingbirds, the Fairfield Four, the Soul Stirrers. He joined a local group, the Baronets, whose patched overalls belied their name. "I was wearing patches on my overalls one night in 1946 when we sang with the Nightingales and Archie Brownlee's Blind Boys. Man, we turned it out so bad, the next day Barney Parks, the Nightingales' manager, came for me. I worked in a filling station up the street. It was so cold, when he came up, I was shooting water up the car, and it was falling piercing ice on my head. My man came up, gave me ten dollars and told me to meet him in Charleston that night." Parks, an ex-Hummingbird, knew a good singer when he heard one. Cheeks's lusty baritone sounded straight off the cotton fields. Under Parks's supervision the boy became a master of harmony and showmanship. "Our manager made us get up at eight or nine and we'd rehearse till lunchtime. Man, it was like gettin' out there plowin'. We'd hang a broom from the ceiling like a mike, and we sang all around it. After lunch, we'd get right back into rehearsal."

The Nightingales were a gifted group; other members included the ubiquitous Paul Owens, Jo Jo Wallace, their current guitarist, Carl Coates, long their bass and now married to Dorothy Love, and Howard Carroll, later to become the great guitarist for the Hummingbirds. At the center was Cheeks, the hardest worker in quartet history. Back then, Archie Brownlee was king of the road with his bloodcurdling shrieks and his sixteen-bar-blues tributes to Mother: "Mother Don't Worry if Your Child Should Go to War," "Keep Your Lamp Trimmed and Burning Till Your Child Comes Home." Cheeks went Brownlee one step better. "I was the first to run up aisles and shake folks' hands. Man, I cut the fool so bad, old Archie started saying, 'Don't nobody ever give me any trouble but June Cheeks. That's the only trouble I have, that's the *baddest* nigger on the road.'"

(By 1959, the Gales were on top, and the two groups shared equal billing on a New Orleans program. "Archie came out of the hospital. He was so thin I didn't think he'd be able to sing. But he wailed like he usually do. Then he must have known, cause when they leave the stage, he ran back and told the people

> *I'm gonna leave you in the hands of the Lord,*
> *I'm gonna leave you in the hands of the Lord.*
> *Just like a mother told her child*
> *Just the day before she died,*
> *I'm gonna leave you in the hands of the Lord.*

Man, I woke up in the dressing room. That's the first and only time I ever fell out. Man, that Archie Brownlee was *tough.*" Archie died that same year.)

Cheeks butchered his voice night after night; the Gales "worked ourselves to death," but the group made no money. "We was in Miami, and after paying our hotel, we wound up with fifty cents apiece. I just went and threw mine as far as it could go into the Atlantic." To support his wife and child, he joined the Soul Stirrers for two years. He only recorded with them once, but his singing helped transform the group. "I was the one caused Sam Cooke to sing hard. I gave him his first shout. We was working in the San Francisco City Auditorium. Sam used to stand real pretty on stage. I pushed him, and he fell off the stage. People thought he was happy. I said, 'Move, man,' and the two of us fell into the audience. We were doing 'How Far Am I from Canaan?' and things just came together." Cooke became his "main man." Years later, when Sam made it big, he acknowledged Cheeks's influence. "The first five-hundred-dollar bill I ever had, Sam gave it to me. All these singers now, Wilson Pickett, they'll give me a few pennies. When I hear their records, I know where they get it from. They know it too. But Sam's the only one treated me right."

In the early fifties, Cheeks returned to the Gales. Now everything clicked. The group had eight hit records in a row, all on Don Robey's Peacock label. Their guitarist, Jo Jo Wallace, affected a sky-high pompadour and a hop-skip-jump choreography; Jo Jo, now a saved minister, remembers "I was Chuck Berry and Little Richard and Jo Jo rolled up in one." The group's harmonies were unique. Jo Jo's high, skinny tenor, all slurs and off-notes, combined sinuously with Carl Coates's soft, rolling bass "boom-de-de-boom-booms." The group could holler, but their sound was basically clean and introspective, in pleasing contrast to Cheeks's relentlessly hard lead. "Man, everyone, Tucker included, had to start working once we hit the scene."

He was also actively attacking the enemies of "our people," while more timid groups would sing about "doors
slammed in your face," and "stumbling blocks in your
way." Even on top, Cheeks was just another nigger to the
crackers. "In 1956, we was riding, when they announced
Jackie Robinson had hit a home run. I got out the car and
did the war dance. The state patrolman called up five cars
and said, 'Listen, nigger, pull over.' The Swans were behind us, they pulled over to help us. 'Hey nigger, anybody
stop you?' This cracker held the gun barrel in his hand.
'You better get the hell out this goddamn highway. Boy,
where you from?' 'Philly.' 'Shut up.' They made me do
everything, 'Get out the car, sit down, get up, do this.' I
knew what they wanted. Couldn't be no win with five or
six guys there, so what they said do, I did it."

Cheeks was clown and country, but he was also a gifted
writer and arranger. Each Nightingales disc contained
something new. When most quartets coasted on guitar and
drum accompaniment, Cheeks added pianos. On "See How
They Done My Lord" and "Somewhere to Lay My Head"
he developed new tempos, allowing him to stretch out and
ad-lib in the roughest development yet of the style sweet-
voiced R. H. Harris created in the thirties. Even his ad libs
were innovative. On the group's great hit, "To The End,"
he interspersed chuckles and exclamations between the
choruses. One phrase, *"Let's get together,"* was brand new
for gospel records, and is probably Cheeks's contribution
to sixties folklore.

Two of the most beautiful records, "Burying Ground"
and "Standing at the Judgment," exemplify the Gales'
combination of old and new. "Burying Ground" is a simple ring shout:

*I wonder can you hear (cancha hear, cancha hear, can-
    cha hear?) the church bell toning [three times]*
Way over yonder in the new burying ground.

Cheeks's baritone is resonant and exceptionally beautiful.
The Gales sing high and loud, rising to a piercing plateau

of "way over yonders" while Cheeks enumerates all those gone: "I've got a mother, I've got a father." Midway though the list, Jo Jo changes the key on "yonder," and the shrill background becomes deeply moving. To some, the climax is a lot of yelling, but as Cheeks gracefully drops from a screamed "way over yonder" to a husky final "in the new burying ground," he's summoned up any poor Southerner's last trip. It's chilling and satisfying and almost consoling.

"Standing at the Judgment" also employs a simple chorus:

> *O look at the people [three times]*
> *Standing at the judgment about to be tried.*

This time Cheeks's approach is downright relaxed. The group employs a bit of echo, enhancing their down-homey, Dr. Watts-styled harmonies. Between choruses, "I believe I see my father, mother, etc.," Cheeks ad-libs, "Wait a minute," another gospel first. The song ends with the group repeating in mid-register, "Standing in the judgment, they got to be tried," while Cheeks preach-chants a sermonette about the 144,000 John saw. The disc ends with Cheeks and the group harmonizing, more softly with each line, until we have an ideal four-part harmony, barely above a whisper. If Cheeks was a clown and a terror on the floor, he was a superb musician in the recording studio.

He was also temperamental and quick to anger. In 1960, he left the Gales and went into semi-retirement. But he couldn't stay away, and he formed the Sensational Knights. The group's early tours seemed to bring out his worst. The man who fought segregation all through the fifties became a walking travesty. His group developed a routine wherein the little tenor leaped into the arms of the mighty bass. When Cheeks bore down on the hard numbers, his pianist and wife of the moment would rise to her feet, dancing up and down the piano, banging notes with her elbows, sometimes stabbing keys with her shoes. The

golden baritone was completely shot, loud but without tone
or texture. To those who had seen Cheeks strong, these
performances were heartbreaking.

In the mid-sixties, he began to restore himself. The
voice stayed the same, but the spirit dominated. "I can't
sing like white folks. If that sounds bad in their ears, I
don't care. Folks come up to me and say, 'Boy, your voice
is so raggedy.' I don't mind, that's *me*. They don't know
the times I left doctors' offices hearing, 'Don't sing for a
week,' and me going to a program." He recorded the old
hymn "The Last Mile of the Way" in a thrilling medium
tempo while his Knights harmonized beautifully behind his
rasping "Wait on me, wait on me, hah hah, somewhere
around God's throne." Cheeks chuckled with absolute self-
confidence, feeling his help coming on.

In person, "to liven the routine," he'd call the names
of states and ad-lib funny extra comments. "Anybody here
from Georgia? You're looking good. Anybody here from
Mississippi? Nobody want to own up, well I'd be ashamed
of it too. How about—Philadelphia? Aw—you didn't come
from no Philadelphia. What about South Carolina? I'm
from South Carolina, I stay *from* South Carolina." It's soul
humor, but it always makes its point. And Cheeks tells
the truth: this most rural of quartet leads hates the South.
"I go down home right now and look at my sisters and
brothers and I wonder. I got two brothers who been overseas four years in the war, and they go back and don't
make nothin'. Let's face it, you know what they're gonna
do to you. I got a sister got a trailer home, and another
brother with every kind of credit card. But for me, it isn't
there." To signify his hatred of the South, Cheeks has left
instructions that his body not be carried below the Four-
teenth Street Bridge in Baltimore.

During his heyday on the road, Cheeks "had myself a
time" and he still likes his liquor. Somewhat chastened by
three marriages, he's settled down to a peaceful sedentary
existence in Baltimore. His new wife is a businesswoman,

practical and generally unsympathetic to the gospel highway and the sacrifices it demands. She has little patience with his down-home faith in the Lord making a way
out of no way: "June tells me I don't know what religion
is." He travels occasionally, usually with the Clouds of Joy.
The Mighty, Mighty Clouds are the leading quartet—hard-
driving young men who filled the position Cheeks vacated
when he quit the Gales. "Had I stayed, there'd never been
any Clouds of Joy. My man at Peacock would have told
them we got a June Cheeks." The Clouds work in an elaborate, predictable routine that especially shouts the
women—they sport the tightest form-fitting pants in quartet
—but turns off many older groups. Recently they recorded
a salute to Cheeks and the Nightingales, redoing the older
group's biggest hits and coming off a weak second. Still,
it was a terrific tribute to Cheeks, and he's grateful. "The
Clouds took time out to salute me, and their lead, Joe
Ligon, still come up to me: 'Pastor, give me some numbers
for my next album.' He's got the voice but I got it upstairs."
To make Cheeks's influence on soul complete, Soul Brother
Number Two, Wilson Pickett, duplicates his every vocal
and physical trait. Even his dance steps are parodies of
Cheeks's shouts, with muscular arms flapping in the air.
One guesses that if Pickett could have his way, he'd be
another June Cheeks; when he recently joined the Clouds
of Joy for a guest appearance, the number he sang was
Cheeks's "New Burying Ground."

Cheeks remains his own man, the same who tossed his
last fifty cents into the Atlantic. In 1970 he cut the maudlin
"Just Crying," in which a curious passerby stops at a
chapel where a little girl is being "funeralized." All the
mourners can do is keep "just crying, just crying," etc.
The ghoulish narrator then follows the family to the graveyard, where he joins them "just crying, just crying." The
record is the kind of hillbilly extravagance always dear to
the hearts of black and white Southerners. It put Cheeks
back on the road, and it shouts a few sentimental souls.

But, I tell him, for an artist of his caliber it's demeaning, backward, corny. "Man, you say that's corny. That's corny, that little song that has the people shouting, that's corny? Man, I'll drink to that."

Since gospel singers excel at making something out of nothing, Julius Cheeks turned his last years into one long attempt to convert decline to ascent, collapse to comeback. After a near-fatal bout of illness, he recorded an album with his sister, Maggie Jeter, and her children, one of whom, Genobia Jeter, had an exceptionally powerful voice. As a witness to God's mercy, Cheeks described the doctor stepping out of his hospital room and informing his relatives, "The boy is dead." Whether the family's subsequent shouts were for real or for show, Cheeks' urge to capitalize on his mortality chilled a listener. When at last, in 1981, he died, his burial in Newark was an occasion for many of his old quartet buddies—among them Claude Jeter, Dewey Young, and Jo Jo Wallace—to salute the hardest lead singer of all, and wonder, to a man, that he'd lasted so long.

8

"Bessie Can Moan and Move a Mountain"

Bessie Griffin's dilemma is simple and hopeless: she's too good a singer. Thirty years ago, singers began announcing that she could outsing Mahalia Jackson, and Bessie has never lived it down. Her contralto is huge and lustrous, worthy of comparison with Bessie Smith's or Mahalia's, but successors to great singers seldom make it. So, forced to follow in Mahalia's footsteps, Bessie has known nothing but trouble. Her whole life sounds like one long blues, but Bessie won't sing devil's music. Instead, she moans with terrifying power. Just when the bad times seem to overwhelm her, a new Bessie appears, strident, aggressive, a bit evil. "They make things so hard for me, those jealous-hearted singers, but I gets up anyhow and sings. I know I'm black and I'm beautiful, and the Lord's gonna bless, and if they don't watch out, I'll tear up their program." Everything she says is true. Bessie is dark and pretty in a girlish way, fat yet shapely. ("I still keep a thirty-eight waistline. My husband tells me, 'Baby I'm gonna buy you some fine pants. You can wear them better than some of those out

here, fat and all.'") And she gets through almost every
time. Because the cynicism and paranoia dissolve in wordless moans. Because all Bessie's long, unprofitable exposure
to nightclub and TV audiences has commercialized her
only in the world. In church, performing any old hymn,
Bessie is the moaningest singer alive. As one old singer in
Los Angeles said, "Bessie can moan and move a mountain."

Bessie's moans are blues preceded and transcended. Like
Mahalia, she was raised in New Orleans, but unlike Gospel's queen, Bessie paid little attention to worldly music
while coming up. Or perhaps the world was there anyhow
and she naturally leaned toward church singing. She was
born Arlette B. Broil, the daughter of Enoch Broil, a sani-
tation worker, and Victoria Walker Broil. "My mother
was what we call Creole. On the plantation, she only spoke
a broken French. She was companion to this white girl,
Arlette Cox, that's where I got my name." Her father
drank, but her mother belonged to a small Baptist church.
"My mother was one great moaner. When the preacher
would be preachin', she'd rest him up to catch his wind by
moaning

> *When you see me crying, Lord Lord Lord,*
> *It ain't nothin' but my trainfare home.*

Rev used to say, 'Shut up, Vick, you'll make me preach
myself to death.'" This good lady died while Bessie was
young, and she was raised by her "grandmother," Lucy
Narcisse, actually her mother's cousin.* She remembers
riding ponies with "eye-talian" neighbors, and being
mocked by black and white for her name. "They used to
say:

* Lucy's relative, Louis B. Narcisse, went the route of many New
Orleans Creoles, from Baptist to Spiritualist, a fascinating infusion
of the Mojo, gris-gris world of New Orleans voodoo with Pentecostal
fire. He is now King Louis Narcisse, a Spiritualist luminary in Oakland.

> *Arlette, I let me go,*
> *I bite me toe*

or

> *Arlette, I let*
> *The shivelette*

or just old black Arlette. They kept misusing my name until I named myself Bessie. The B. was just there, doing nothing, so I turned it round to Bessie A. Broil."

Bessie's grandmother sounds like a Sanctified Mrs. Portnoy. A great church singer, she was an autocrat at home. "She used to tell me, 'I'm gonna spit on this stove, and if you're not back by the time the spit dries, you'll get a whupping.'" Mrs. Narcisse worked in a pecan factory, and she expected the child to wash her outsized garments, the family laundry, and the red brick steps. She'd express her affection by telling Bessie to buckle down or she'd wind up a seamstress. "I'd tell her I won't be a seamstress, I'm gonna be a songstress." It was hard going, and Bessie used to console herself over the tubs and steps by singing "Soon I Will Be Done with the Troubles of the World" or

> *I wish I had died when I was young,*
> *I wouldn't have this race to run,*
> *All my trials will soon be over*

for which her grandmother beat her. Bessie was clearly bright and tough. "I was never no dummy in school, they started me in the third grade." She exhibited other kinds of brightness, too, by stashing extra sheets under the house while doing the laundry or singing back to her grandmother; after all no parent wants to be called a slavemaster. In church, when her grandmother led the congregation in "God Be with You Till We Meet Again":

> *Till we meet, till we meet, till we meet*
> *At Jesus' feet (at Jesus' feet)*

Bessie would chime in, "His cheesy feet," for which she didn't receive a holy kiss. During the Depression, she'd line up at the welfare office to pick up butter, eggs, and powdered milk. "I used to fake a faint, and all the people say, Let that little girl through, the sun's got her. So I'd be first on line, get my stuff, and come home skipping."

Like everyone else in gospel, Bessie began singing at a very early age, learning the old Dr. Watts hymns—"Amazing Grace," "The Day Is Past and Gone," "I Heard The Voice of Jesus"—that Lucy Narcisse loved. Blues was forbidden at home, but New Orleans streets vibrated with blue notes, even if not especially in church. "This old country preacher Blind Frank came up for a revival in a horse and buggy, and somebody stole his reins. He was so depressed, he got up in church and sang

> *I didn't come here walking,*
> *Neither on no train,*
> *But I came in my horse and buggy,*
> *Lord, somebody done stole my reins."*

And what Bessie is singing here is pure twelve-bar blues. On records she heard the very popular Reverend Gates, who used to preach sermons on the titles of popular blues: "Tight Like That," "Shake That Thing," "Pay Your Policy Keeper." (This habit still obtains. Bessie's pastor in Los Angeles recently preached a sermon on "Who's Making Love to Your Old Lady While You're Out Making Love?") The other record Bessie remembers was Mahalia Jackson's "God Shall Wipe All Tears Away." After school the kids would play Mahalia's disc on the jukeboxes, and even then Bessie had no trouble hitting the rich, heavy contralto notes.

By the early forties, Bessie was a great soloist in a city of gospel queens. Singing with conviction was a habit Lucy Narcisse had drummed into her. "She'd tell me shouting's all right, but when you shout make sure you're not playing, because if you're not sincere, you might break your neck.

Do what the spirit of God leads you to do." Once, at a friend's funeral, Bessie sang "I'm Bound for Canaan Land," and the spirit led her to jump out of the balcony. When she came to, she rose without a scratch—confirmation of the spirit's wisdom and protection. Twice, the power of Bessie's singing literally killed people. Once, in New Orleans, she wailed "I Want to Rest," and laid one lady to rest. Another time, in Texas, she sang "Just Over the Hill," and a lady went over. "I didn't pay it no mind, because people were screaming and carrying on so. Later they told me she had a heart condition and they'd poured cold water over her, and it brought on the seizure. I never got over it."

For ten years Bessie sang with a female quartet, the Southern Harps. Now as Ira Tucker, R. H. Harris, and Claude Jeter can testify, *a cappella* quartet was a hard and frustrating vocation. Bessie's quartet, patterned on male groups, with women singing tenor, baritone, and bass parts, had all the regular quartet troubles and more. On the strength of their radio broadcasts they'd travel from hamlet to water hole, usually earning enough to stay in one hotel room, all four sleeping in the same bed. But, except for "Baby Helen," the littlest and youngest, the Southern Harps were built like cellos. "We'd lie crossways, and you know our leader, Alberta Johnson, weighed over three hundred pounds. So when she'd be pressing too much on the rest of us, somebody'd say, 'O.K., everybody ready, one, two, three, shift.'" A typical hard-time incident has become Bessie's favorite anecdote for television appearances. "We were driving in Mississippi on these maypop tires, you know what maypop tires is, may pop any moment. It was real late and our car was stopped by this cracker sheriff. He ask the boy who's driving, 'Where you taking these girls?' He told him we were gospel singers. So the cracker says, 'Oh good, I just loves to hear niggers sing. Wake 'em up, girl.' So I tell them, 'Wake up, Alberta, wake up, Helen, wake up, Lucille, this man wants to hear us sing.' 'Oh shoot,' says Lucille, 'go back to sleep.' 'You bet-

ter wake up, he's got a *gun.*'" And what did the Harps
sing? "What a Friend We Have in Jesus."

Bessie made a few mediocre records in the late forties,
but gradually her house-wrecking abilities came to national
attention. In 1951, Mahalia Jackson invited her to sing at
her anniversary at Chicago's gigantic Coliseum. Bessie
drove North with her husband-to-be, Spencer Jackson (her
first marriage to Willie Griffin ended after two years), and
the car crashed en route. Her friends had chipped in to buy
a white velvet robe with black satin fringes, and as soon as
she hit Chicago, the robe was stolen. "Spencer knew I was
discouraged and nervous. So the night before the program,
he took me to the Coliseum, walked me all around the
building, stood me on the stage, and told me, 'You look
around, cause, girl, tomorrow you're really gonna be *out
there.*'" The next night, on an all-star program before
42,000 fans in the New Jerusalem of gospel music, the awkward New Orleans girl stole the show. She sang the old
hymn "Come Ye Disconsolate," and Reverend Brewster's
"How I Got Over." Mahalia, the Dixie Hummingbirds,
Rosetta Tharpe, couldn't do a thing afterward. If Bessie
hadn't proved herself the champ that evening, she was
clearly a leading contender. Mahalia seemed delighted
with her compatriot's success; she dubbed Bessie "The
Black Patti" and showered her with qualified praise. "She
told me, You're a great singer but you're not ever gonna
get anywhere because you're too easy and you're too soft."
For though Bessie can get evil and, provoked by demons,
work like one, she's not a fighter. Mahalia, the ingenious
black capitalist, had purchased real estate, flower shops,
beauty parlors with her early earnings. Bessie had neither
the luck nor the financial skill.

Like most female gospel singers, including at times even
Mahalia, Bessie is often shy and nervous. Considering the
risks and pitfalls, who wouldn't be? Anyhow, in 1953, she
returned to the security of a group, this time not a quartet
but a female gospel group, the Caravans. The group was
founded by Albertina Walker, a former lead singer for

Robert Anderson's group. Robert Anderson was the top male soloist in Chicago, with a deep, husky voice, and he read a lyric with the amazing grace of his teacher, Roberta Martin. Albertina absorbed Anderson's style and went on to form her own group from ex-Anderson singers. In later years the Caravans featured a good dozen name talents, and from 1958 to 1966 were the most successful gospel group on the road. But the glory came years after Bessie had left. While she sang lead, the group knew only hard times. "We used to sleep all day, not to be hungry." Albertina Walker is an impressive soloist, but she's also content to rest in the background. From the start she let other singers work for her. So, every night, Bessie would wail a sixteen-bar "Baptist blues" that told her story as precisely as any blues:

I've been blessed and I've been brought up by the Lord,
I've been blessed and I've been brought up by the Lord.
Since my mother died and left me,
I don't have no one to help me,
Thank God, I've been blessed, yeah,
    and I've been brought up by the Lord.

On her record of the song, Bessie ends with a raspy, hoarse yell, "Hey-hey-hey-hey, by the Lord," then drops an octave to the richest contralto tones, "Sho' nuff, by the Lord." She often cracks at such moments, and the effect is, as Wordsworth said, "too deep for tears." Such solos with the Caravans won Bessie the respect of everyone on the road. But again, no money. "I had one pair of patent-leather shoes, and my feet was tapping the ground. The Caravans used to be so embarrassed, there my shoes'd be crooked over and I was out there singing and shouting, sweating like a dog. In Cleveland, somebody threw those shoes away, the group must have been ashamed, and Spencer had to go out, buy me some new ones." That's all very funny, if one doesn't remember that the barefoot girl with cheek was one of the best black singers in America.

Bessie stayed with the Vans about a year and then moved to Chicago, situating herself in one seedy hotel after another. Gospel singers tend to settle on one hotel in any given town. These hotels are usually cheap, stuffy, and wide open. Pimps, prostitutes, dealers, and addicts are their neighbors; no hotel is marked "sanctified" except for the various Father Divine missions. In Chicago, impoverished gospel singers hung out at the Lake Ridge Hotel. No cooking was allowed, but occasionally Bessie would fix beans, rice, and garlic on her hot plate. "Bessie's cooking," would sound through the halls, and her room would be packed. "Are you cooking?" the manager might roar, distinguishing the reek of garlic from the sweet smells of grass and whiskey. "No," Bessie would say, flashing her most innocent girlish smile, hiding the hot plate under her bed.

All this time, Bessie was tearing up Chicago churches, consolidating her reputation as the city's finest soloist. But, as singers say, "Home folk never pay their own." The traveling singers got the bread, Bessie the glory and the beans and rice. By the mid-fifties, Bessie's style had matured—and it has remained essentially the same. She is not an overwhelming stylist; the excitement she manufactures depends on vocal power and spiritual depth. Her diction is impeccable, among the best in gospel, and on clear days her contralto sails gracefully through almost three octaves, all natural; most gospel singers supplement their wide ranges with falsetto. As a singer, she is what she first was, a Baptist moaner and a quartet lead. Borrowing an old quartet theme, she used to introduce herself in song:

> *Good evening, how do you do,*
> *I'm Bessie Griffin and I come to sing to you.*

Her forte is the old hymns. If you listen to her Decca records of "It's Real" or "The Day Is Past and Gone," or her Savoy performances of "He Lives" or "Come Ye Disconsolate," you'll hear Bessie's basic arrangement; she seldom veers from a given approach. The one thing records always miss is the passion. One disc alone, "Too Close to Heaven," recorded before a shrieking congregation of Memphis saints, and fellow singers, captures Bessie's spirit; only live recordings can.

In church or out, she has always been prodigiously, even foolishly, generous with her talent. She'll cook for the crowd, sing for them too. (Not surprisingly, clever Chicago singers began using her arrangements and copying her special habit of repeating key words, sometimes past the requirements of emotion or good sense.) Even now, in Los Angeles, she holds simulated church services in her home. Recently a friend called her long distance. The man's father had died, and he wanted Bessie to sing "The Day Is Past and Gone" cross-continental. Fortunately some singers were in the house, and one accompanied her on piano. Bessie sang as if she were in church, and wound up getting everyone happy, including herself.

"I still sing all those old songs, it's all how I feel. If I'm in a real blue mood, I'll sing really blue songs like 'Nobody But You Lord,' or maybe I'll just moan 'It's Getting Late in the Evening,' something that *keeps* me in this blue mood till I get out of it. And then when I'm sick, I'll reach back to the old 'Beams of Heaven,' skip the verse, and go right into

I do not know how long it will be,
Or what the future holds for me.

I'd just be feeling I may die tomorrow but I'll keep singing anyhow. You see, that's why I never know what I'm gonna do in church. I need to be free, I don't even like to be dressed tight so I'll be self-conscious when I move. Folks come up and ask me, 'Bessie, you gonna sing this tonight?' even Spencer, and I have to tell him, 'Baby, you know better than to ask me that. Maybe it won't be the song the people want to hear, but it's got to be something that will satisfy me.' "

Bessie left Chicago in 1955. For about a year, she toured with Reverend W. Herbert Brewster, Jr., the son of gospel's most brilliant songwriter. Brewster, Jr., is an excellent

songwriter too, and a powerful preacher. In admiration he
dubbed her "Good Queen Bess." But Mahalia was still the
Queen of Gospel, and at the tour's end, Bessie's earnings
were far from regal. She moved back to New Orleans,
working both as a soloist and disc jockey. This double
strength earned her the title "Queen of the South," without
any change in her estate. Then, in 1959, Bumps Blackwell,
a gifted record producer who had initially promoted such
ex-gospel luminaries as Sam Cooke and Little Richard, conceived *Portraits in Bronze.* Adapted from Langston
Hughes's *Sweet Flypaper of Life,* this was the first gospel
musical. It starred, of course, Bessie, accompanied by a
local quintet, the Gospel Pearls. Most of the supporting
talent, including the Pearls, left much to be desired, but
Bessie's lead singing made things right.

Portraits signaled the first move of gospel into clubs and
coffeehouses. Naturally, church folk had fits—though their
benign neglect had placed Bessie in the position, to begin
with. The production was pop-gospel—"We didn't know
how people would react to us shouting 'Jesus' so we'd sing
'My Saviour' or 'Master' "—yet Bessie always threw in a
few down-home gospel numbers. If the drunks wanted
"Saints," she'd make them sit through "The Old Rugged
Cross." *Portraits in Bronze* packed them in. "We had Steve
McQueen, Hedy Lamarr, Peter Lawford, Bette Davis came
to see me in Chicago. Baby, we had a time."

On the strength of *Portraits,* Bessie got a flock of TV
dates and some national club work. She was, out of nowhere, a gospel celebrity. But she learned quickly that exposure isn't always profitable. She had to do a lot of free-
bees, and even in *Portraits,* she worked on a percentage of
the gate. Most of the big TV programs pay union scale, so
Bessie might appear with Dinah Shore or Danny Kaye
before fifty million Americans and take home $350. She's
had a couple of good paydays, the TV show "Operation
Entertainment," and a one-nighter at Disneyland. But the big
TV and club money eludes her. Though Bessie was the first
to appear in clubs, Clara Ward had effectively sewn

up Las Vegas with some more of the Baptist cunning that placed Clara and Mahalia on their respective thrones. Bessie had a revenge of sorts. A Ward Singer died after a club performance, and Bessie performed "The Day Is Past and Gone" at her funeral. "The people shouted so bad they say Dorothy looked up from her coffin to see what was happening." Once again, Bessie had sung herself proud, but Clara and Mother Ward still owned Las Vegas.

Bessie's TV appearances seldom show her at her best. She is not preeminently a rhythm singer, but she's always saddled with some pop-gospel jump tune. Occasionally she'll sing a real gospel hymn, and the difference is a revelation. Other times, one remembers the extravagant leaps and growls. After an athletic performance on the Pat Boone show (!), George Jessel observed, "That girl doesn't have a tiger in her tank, she's got a kangaroo in her tank." Now in church, Mahalia skipped, crawled, and leapt with the best of them. But her TV appearances were carefully calculated to exude dignity and high seriousness. Bessie too often appears a laughingstock. No help, either, is the patronizing manner of TV talk hosts. "Bessie, you're such a nice *girl,* you're such a sweet *girl,*" fatuously babbles Woody Woodbury, though Bessie is manifestly no girl.

Bessie made a rare visit to New York following an appearance at a campaign dinner for Mayor Carl Stokes of Cleveland. She stopped off with Linda Hopkins, the "Baby Helen" of the Southern Harps. Linda is a good pop singer in the Dinah Washington vein who makes a respectable living as the Borscht Belt's Queen of the Blues. Despite her move out into the world, Linda's first loyalty is to church music. She is constantly evoking or bestowing "Gawd's blessings," and in her fascination with old gospel ways seemed more the gospel trouper than old Bess.

Linda lives in Lenox Terrace, Harlem's first luxury complex. Her home is decorated in the ubiquitous French Provincial, with everything under plastic except for a large, lumpy, comfortable chair. To a guest sprawled out on the down-home seat, Linda recalled, "Bessie Griffin . . . that woman sang . . . Lord, letmetellyou. She'd get up, start moaning, raise her hands up in the air, *mmmm!* Never heard nothing like it."

Bessie seemed bored. "But we sure had it rough in the Harps." Linda talked about house wrecking; Bessie remembered the hungry days. "You remember the time we stopped off in Bogalusa? The promoter had promised to feed us and didn't have nothin'. You remember she had a yardful of chickens, so soon as she left the house, I told youall if you kill me a chicken, I'll cook it. Child, that no-good chicken made us so *sick* . . ." Linda laughed. "But you got to give one thing to old Alberta, she kept us together." "That's right, she'd tell us, 'Girls, we're out here, and it's all for one and one for all! If a fellow wants to take a girl to dinner, tell him he have to take us *all*. Or if he don't have enough money, tell him to buy some meat and bread, and we'll do the cooking.'"

"Lawd, Bessie, the Lawd has blessed us," said Linda. "Every time I went home, Alberta take me aside and say, 'Helen, I'm proud of you and Bessie too.'" The flood of nostalgia made Linda teary and grateful, but Bessie had lived with the memories too long. For her, the anecdotes merely proved that times could be worse.

The next day Bessie, Linda, and Linda's "play mother," Mrs. Conley, drove out to a small Connecticut town where Linda was booked on a package. They were greeted at the door by the theater manager, a comedienne, and the Magid Triplets, three plump, dimpled teen-agers of twenty-six. Everyone knows Linda, and they all rushed to embrace her. "I want you to meet my friend, Bessie, you know the gospel singer Bessie Griffin." "Oh yes," said the manager, "like Mahalia Jackson." Bessie smiled and said, "Pleased to meet you."

Such bookings offer little glamour, but they keep Linda working, and that night she delighted a hall packed with Jewish War Veterans. She closed with "Saints" and yelled out, "You're enjoying yourself, darlins, some of you must be Baptists." "Yes I am, I'm a Baptist," hollered Bessie, hugely enjoying herself. But afterwards, backstage, Bessie was in a blue funk. "You people in show business *cooperate*," she commented after the Magid Triplets had bounced in to compliment Linda. "But the gospel singers make it so hard. Even when I lived in New Orleans, when they came to town, I'd fix food for them and I'd pick them up by car. When I'd go to their home town, I'd get no invite." Linda and Mrs. Conley sympathized. "It's a terrible thing."

"And what hurt me so bad is that some singers don't even tell where I am when people want to book me. I've had folks to tell me they've asked *everyone* where I was, and they all know, because they've all stopped by, sang and *shouted* in my home." The three ladies looked into the wall-length mirror, not at each other. "Yet God blesses. You can feel so blue, you understand why folks takes the pills to sleep and drinks to kill the day. But I'm going on, anyhow. Cause, remember, the old folks used to get together and they'd sing, 'My witness is in heaven and my record is on high' "—Bessie moans the first line. As she repeats it, Linda chimes in singing tenor and Mrs. Conley unleashes a thunderous contralto bottom. "I guess we better leave that alone," says Bessie as Linda and Mrs. Conley begin hollering out, about to have a shout service in the Waterbury Chamber of Commerce.

9

Professor Alex Bradford:
"The Singing Rage"

One doesn't quite know how to take Professor Alex Bradford. When he cavorts around the stage, his oversized,
bottom-heavy face bouncing under a high-fringed fore-
head, he seems part bulldog, part capon. Bradford is
lowdown, "real," completely himself. But what a complex
self! One moment his voice is the huge, husky instrument
of a field worker, the next, dappled with falsetto, it's the
countertenor of the academy. In his flamboyant robes,
Bradford is Gospel's Little Richard, letting it all hang out.
"When we first went to Floville, Georgia, we were wearing black robes, each fellow had a different-colored pastel
stole. Child, those country women died laughing, they
thought it was dresses." Then Bradford gets worldly on
you, throwing around a large vocabulary—"I'm praising a
magnanimous Saviour," "I know music, I can tell catatonic
from a simple basic"—and one feels like shouting, Come
off it, Bradford, who are you fooling? "I want to record
all kinds of music, and I mean all kinds. And I'm definitely
a night person, like Sinatra. I can't record at day." Is this
the same man who wrote "I'm Too Close to Heaven and

I Can't Turn Around"? But of course. Bradford will fool
you, come on campy, and leave you deeply moved. As a
lady in Detroit said, "That man can do the most ridiculous things, but I want to tell you, Professor can sing, do
you hear me?"

There's something mythic about Bradford; like Chau-
cer's Pardonner, he seems a weird admixture of sinner and
saint, or, more curious, a sinner more trustworthy than
some naïve saint. He's been involved with worldly music
almost all his life; when he was four, he began singing and
dancing in vaudeville. In later years, he has helped spawn
a crop of Newark gospel singers (Dionne and DeeDee
Warwick, the Sweet Inspirations, C. and the Shells, Judy
Clay), some of whom became pop superstars. He capti-
vated the Beatles in Liverpool and the Kinks in Sydney.
Bradford really has been everywhere, and there aren't too
many show biz secrets he doesn't feel privy to. Yet he is
also a gospel singer "from his heart." When he makes distinctions between other singers, he separates the trained
from the "soil" singers. And though, in his time, Bradford's male soprano could soar to A above high C, and
though he's recorded "I've Got to Be Me" and "The Impossible Dream," he calls his singing *earth. I prefer the
soil singers because I'm from the soil." When his old colleague Dorothy Love appears on a program with him, she
says, "There's our old friend Alec. He say he from Chicago, but he's from Bessemer, Alabama," and Alex waves
his hand as if to say, Go away, come again.

As a performer, Bradford is a born star, the cynosure of
all eyes. He's also a great pianist, organist, choir director,
group arranger, and composer. As a musician, his records
are among the most carefully produced in gospel. Bradford has written more standards than any gospel writer of
his generation. He's also written songs for friends in
rhythm and blues—"Ray Charles told me I was his ideal as
a gospel singer, and if I ever wanted to send him a song,
all I'd have to do is announce my name and he'd give it
first preference." Ray Charles learned much from the

young Bradford; so did Little Richard and Sam Cooke. Meanwhile his compositions for LaVern Baker in the late fifties may have been the first marriage of gospel and pop sounds in the pre-soul era.

Gospel singers are notoriously precocious, but all his life Bradford has apparently been the way he is today. The shmoolike build came later, though the face was always oddly elongated, and all the earliest publicity shots show huge eyes glowing past rapture. In other words, Bradford has always been a performer: "I'm always on stage, baby." Like every other good singer, he came up the hard way. He's got as much testimony as any man, and that's why "I don't care where I shout, before the Queen of England makes no difference." He was born in Bessemer and raised during the worst days of the Depression. His father was an ore miner, a hard-working, soft-spoken Southern Baptist father. But his mother, Olivia Bradford Spain, was something else. "My mother did just about everything. She was a great cook, she sewed well, she was a hairdresser, used to do hair at twenty-five cents a head, and in later years she became an insurance agent and a supervisor." One of Bradford's sisters won a Marian Anderson contest; his half-brother is a welfare supervisor in Brooklyn. In Alabama, Mrs. Bradford was a great and famous lady, and she had big ambitions for her son.

As a boy, Bradford quickly learned to make do. When no food was available, out went the trusty slingshot. "Sure I can remember every boy having a slingshot or b.b. gun, and at evening we'd chase birds—swallows, blackbirds. Bring them home in a flour-sack bag, our mothers would be *glad* to see them. We'd serve them with the earth mostly, you know, greens, beans, sweet potatoes. We didn't go hungry." Like many Southern towns, Bessemer had no *de facto* segregation. "Our backyards joined, the Negroes lived on one street and the whites on the other, and the alley where the refuse was left was the dividing line. But as kids we used to play together. And I'll tell you something, whites and blacks down South are just about the

same in things they like and in things they like to do. They
believe in going to church on Sunday morning and they
believe in you go to yours and they go to theirs. But aside
from public assembly, they got along fine on all other issues. When we were sick, I've seen the Fitzpatricks who
were our neighbors and the Smallings, they'd bring soup
and flowers and cry over the dead just like they were their
own. The white people beat their children just like the
colored people beat theirs, they insisted you respect people
who were respecta*bulle*. And I should say there's no difference in poor people, white or colored."

Olivia Bradford's son got his fair share of breaks. As
a small boy, he began taking dance and also music
lessons from Martha Belle Hall, a jazz pianist who Duke Ellington once claimed could play "Sophisticated Lady" as
well as he. "Martha also used to tutor the choir and she'd
slip in a blue note and a boogie-woogie beat even then."
From the start, Bradford was torn between the world and
the church. He made his debut in vaudeville at four. But
there was a Sanctified couple who lived in a shotgun house
down the alley. He played guitar, she tambourined and
prophesied. They sold barbecue at a penny a bone, which
brought in all the neighborhood kids. Then, at night, their
musical services enlivened the neighborhood. Bradford
joined the Holiness church at six, though his mother
wouldn't let him stay.

He was surrounded by the purest forms of country
blues and gospel. "Every night, Ol' Man Joe Horn would
come by singing. I think he was scared of the dark, and he
loved music and he loved his woman and he used to come
home singing 'Oh babe, you don't mean your bull cow no
good' "—and Bradford sings the line like no country blues
singer alive.

There were also quartets. "And happily the best of them.
The Blue Jays, the fathers of quartet, came out of Alabama. Three of them lived in Bessemer, two in Birmingham, and one out in the mining town, Mulger. Silas Steele,
their lead, lived crosstown. And Little Turner, who used

to sing lead with those bad Kings of Harmony, he lived down the alley from me. And there were the Swan Silvertones, Claude Jeter and his brothers. I went to school with Jeter's nephews and nieces." Bradford's right—he was surrounded by the best quartets of the thirties. But he always veered toward gospel music because of its fire, its flamboyance, its musicianship.

All of these were personified for him by Prophet Jones. "Prophet Jones started in Bessemer. He was the first man I saw to play piano with his feet. He started in Spiritualist, and wore these fabulous robes. He inspired *all* the young people around." Prophet Jones later switched to the Church of God in Christ and then founded Triumph the King of Christ Universal Dominion Kingdom of God and Temple of Christ, International Fellowship. For a while, he owned Detroit, though with the seasons he has been overtaken by scandals. Yet, in his day, "I saw women throw their mink coats down for Prophet Jones to walk over." Bradford was doubly inspired, and he's become not only a great pianist à la Jones, but also something of a prophet himself. "I was staying at Albertina Walker's house back in 1965 when the Caravans were really swinging. And this picture came into my head. Cassietta, the darkest in the group, began to glow brighter than Johneron, the lightest. Then I got the vibrations, in three weeks she'd be gone. I told Tina to watch out, she'd go through a period of unproductiveness. Three weeks later, Tina called me up crying, 'Prophet, is this the prophet?' And I've done this many times, and I can call on many witnesses."

Every year a local producer, A. G. Gaston, of Booker T. Washington Enterprises, presented "America Back to God Day." "They used to hold it in the white ball park, Legion Field, and people used to come from hundreds of miles with their chairs on trucks, just to sit on the turf because the grandstands be so packed." Here Bradford saw the great gospel pioneers at their toughest. "There was Georgia Lee Stafford, we called her the Songbird of the South. Now to tell you the truth, she was the one who in-

spired me to sing those high soprano notes. And there was
Arizona Dranes, the blind Sanctified lady. She'd sing 'Thy
Servant's Prayer' and crackers and niggers be shouting
everywhere." Mahalia Jackson came every year, and Bradford remembers best her duets "He'll Understand" and "I
Can Put My Trust In Jesus," with Mahalia singing contralto and her pianist, James Lee, singing soprano! And,
greatest of all, Reverend Brewster's singer, Queen C. Anderson. "My God, how that woman could sing. She could
take any hymn, it wasn't the *tim bruh* of her voice. You
know she never made records that meant anything, but
she was a standup singer. She was beautiful, she wove a
spell. She was a great phraser, and she was quite—to the
point. Everything was done right—" he snaps his fingers—
"as you say now, *right on.*" Bradford's tones become rev-
erent as he calls her great hits: "How I Got Over," "Move
On Up a Little Higher"—and deep, deep pause—"I'm
Leaning . . . and Depending on the Lord," shaking his
head as if he still can't stand to remember all that power.
These were magnificent singers with massive, idiosyncratic
personalities. Even more than Prophet Jones, they instructed Bradford in the ways of gospel showmanship.

Bradford formed his own group, the Bradfordettes. To
distinguish them from other groups, he developed a style
of choreography he'd swiped from show business—"My
sister was Minnie the Moocher." Their gestures were
hardly subtle. "When we sang 'run,' we ran, when we
sang 'fly,' we'd flap our arms. We believed in making things
come alive, sort of like the deaf do today." But Bradford
executed his ideas so well that before long, Mahalia Jackson and Roberta Martin had taken him under their wings.
Bradford was the Bessemer *wunderkind*—until he had the
most serious run-in of his life.

Previously he'd had only amicable relations with white
folks. "But when I was twelve or thirteen I decided to go
to work in the local drug and sundry store. There was a
cracker and he was kin to the sheriff some sort of way, you
know nepotism, they always hire their cousins, and he

must have been sixth assistant to the assistant sheriff and he was going with the waitress in the place. Now the owner had told me to wash the windows every morning. I came in and had to stand on the counter, they didn't have no ladders and of course Mary asked me to get down, they didn't want me washing the window, 'I'm telling you not to wash them.' Later Mrs. Haggerty came in and chewed Mary out about it. Mary was in tears by the time her old assistant-sheriff boyfriend came in and he saw her crying and she told him that this nigger had went to the boss on her. So he came downstairs in the kitchen where I was washing dishes and started questioning me. First question he asked me, 'Have you lived here all your life, boy?' and I said 'Practically.' And he said, 'Practically, listen at this nigger use practically, where you learn a word like practically?' 'Well, I go to school every day and I'm the head of my class and I've been to New York and Detroit.' 'Well, no wonder you're so sassy to these white women around here.' I said, 'What white women? You mean Kitty, Annabelle, Janine?' 'Oooh, you're calling white women by their first names, you really think you're smart—' and that's when I found out he was a cracker and really after me for some reason. I was washing dishes and he didn't know in the sink I had one hand on the cleaver and the other hand on the butcher knife, and if he came near me he was going to get death right *there*. But my cousin Charlotte saw what was happening and immediately called Mrs. Haggerty and Mrs. Haggerty was Johnny on the spot —and, of course, thereupon lies why I had to leave Alabama. My mother just wouldn't be content with me staying there any longer."

His mother shipped him to New York, where he directed his own group, the Bronx Gospelaires. When he returned to Alabama, she enrolled him in private school. For a while Bradford taught school himself—thus the "Professor" title—while toying with the idea of singing blues. Yet, always with his eye on the main chance, he managed to become an ordained minister in three churches (he's now a lay minister in two others). During his Army service, he would entertain at camp shows. "I'd sing 'Drifting Blues,' 'How Long,' 'Trouble in Mind.' My idols were Peetie Wheatstraw, Gatemouth Moore, and Eddie 'Cleanhead' Vinson." On weekends Bradford moonlighted as an ordained minister in Mother Hargrove Bishop Universal Spiritual Church of Birmingham, Alabama, having a penchant for colorful, proud, sanctified *grandes dames.*

Immediately after the war, Bradford moved to Chicago. To support his first wife, he did all kinds of manual labor —on railroads, in foundries and factories. He eventually chucked these jobs for music. "I had solidly made up my mind I'd go out for blues till I came to Chicago and started to working for the church on the corner. They would pay me eight dollars a week. There was this tavern next door, Red's Tavern. I got a job there, paying eighty-five dollars a week. So whenever I got mad at the deacons for not paying me my eight dollars, I went right back to the tavern." For all his talent, he had a hard time making his mark in Chicago. "Roberta Martin and Mahalia owned Chicago. I remember when Bert introduced me—" and his voice becomes all phony gentility—" 'Little Alec Bradford is with us, and we know him, and we want Chicago to hear him,' smiling one of her beautiful, deceitful smiles. So I got up, and they'd never heard a man make all those high soprano notes before. Baby, they were carrying folks out *bodily.*"

Chicago loved him but he found the presence of the old masters oppressive. "Everybody was little somebody to Roberta and Mahalia." (Deloris Barrett Campbell says, "The other night Mahalia introduced me, 'And here's our little Deloris. That girl has a voice just like a rose, it opens up, we just love to hear our little Deloris.' And there I was, looking like Big Maybelle.") "They kept you under that tradition thing, you're always little this, and that's why I left Chicago, I couldn't stand anymore of that little. And as long as Mahalia and Roberta were gonna live, they were gonna rule the roost."

At the time, Sallie Martin was living in California, but

upon her return, the two became fast friends. "Sallie wasn't like this. She'd take you from place to place, she'd stake you, she'd loan you some money. I'm not only speaking of me—Raymond Rasberry, Robert Anderson, James Cleveland, any other singers who needed a break, Miss Martin knew you couldn't afford it, she'd lock arms with you." To Bradford, Sallie is the greatest, bad voice and all, because of her unconquerable spirit. "She is really the undisputed queen, and she has manners and behavior like a queen, she believes in giving to subjects and helping subjects. But don't get me wrong, she's not regal, very modest. You can always get something to eat. In all her success, four o'clock in the morning is not too late to knock on her door, and it might be me or anybody from down South, and Miss Martin will try to get them some place to stay. . . . Only one thing, if you wanted to eat breakfast with her, you had to get up at six o'clock. She had a favorite restaurant in any town she was appearing in, and you had to be there at six-thirty. No such thing as she giving you two or three dollars to eat at ten or eleven, you had to eat when she ate or you didn't eat." Bradford loves to mimic Sallie. He'll get up like her, start singing "I hoid the voice," then holler *"owww,"* twist to the side, "of Jesus say," get out his handkerchief, wave it in the air, "Come unto me and rest," and collapse laughing on his chair. But though he knows all the anecdotes about Sallie, his respect for her is obvious. "She's an astute disciplinarian woman —and I love her." And whenever Bradford himself gets in the spirit, he'll also holler out *"owww,"* and waddie through the spasm twists.

During the early fifties, Bradford traveled and recorded with several groups. But he had more luck turning out lyrical ballads like "Since I Met Jesus" and "Let God Abide" for Roberta Martin. In 1954, he formed the first all-male gospel group, the Bradford Specials. Their unusual garb and falsetto harmonies puzzled the South, and on one tour, the eight men earned barely enough to purchase two bushels of peaches off which they survived till they reached Chicago. Then Specialty issued Bradford's version of his own composition "Too Close to Heaven."

> *I'm too close to my journey's end,*
> *Too close to turn back in a world of sin,*
> *I wouldn't take nothing for my journey right now,*
> *Just got to make it to heaven somehow.*
> *I'm too close, almost reached my goal.*
> *Too close to finally saving my soul,*
> *I'm too close to heaven, and I won't turn around,*
> *I promised the Lord, I wouldn't turn around.*

The song sold over a million copies and established Bradford as the "Singing Rage of the Gospel Age." His huge, rough voice shook listeners, but what turned America on most was the Bradford Specials choreography. "I'm too close," Bradford would sing, answered by the resonant tenor of Little Joe Jackson, the group's spark plug. Then the two men would gracefully swirl off together, while the other Specials would similarly dip in unison. When Bradford sang "He'll Wash You Whiter Than Snow" (a disc he recorded with Sallie Martin), he let out all the stops. "With outstretched arms, he'll completely just take you in—" and he'd practically fall back to be caught up by the spirit, or at least by superb muscle control. Next, "washing," he'd rub the folds of his robe together. One of his less tasty lyrics, "Carrying the Cross for My Boss" (sample line—"I work for Holy Ghost Incorporated"), involved the transformation of a microphone into a cross, borne valiantly by the group as they stared stage right while the organ crunched out a torrid mambo beat.

During this period, the Bradford Specials made a lot of money—as much as $3,100 in one day—but squandered it on clothes, good times, fair-weather friends. By the early sixties things had slowed down considerably. Then "the Lord blessed me with *Black Nativity*." This gospel musical, based on some Langston Hughes verse, suffered from a meager script and minimal direction. But its leading performers, Marion Williams and Bradford, were the most versatile, quick-thinking stylists in gospel. Marion had sung for years with Clara Ward, Bradford's idol: "Marion and Clara, they were electrifying together." Marion herself is a Sanctified country woman, and she went along with Bradford in being an "earth" singer. Beyond that, they were drastically dissimilar personal types. The first act of *B.N.* included gospel versions of traditional Christmas songs. Marion's arrangements were more imaginative than Bradford's; likewise her supporting group, the Stars of Faith, all ex-Ward Singers, were superior to Bradford's group. But in the second act, a simulated gospel meeting, Bradford's showmanship and fluency found more familiar territory. He could preach and charm—Marion is not verbally talented—and the two stars split the honors more equally.

Black Nativity fared moderately well in New York, but its European tour galvanized the continent. "We're the biggest thing since *Porgy and Bess*," Bradford wired his friends, while ordering thousands of copies of "Too Close to Heaven." In the mid-sixties, Bradford carried his own company to Australia. His featured female vocalist, Madeleine Bell, has since situated in England, where she is much in demand for session work (Madeleine's churchy backups can be heard on Rolling Stones and Joe Cocker discs). Bradford flourished in the more free-spirited European capitals. He began sporting a floor-length cape and sunglasses; "I see Bradford's really doing his thing overseas," fans started saying, while slapping palms.

In recent years, he has devoted most of his time to directing the Greater Abyssinian Baptist Choir of Newark, New Jersey. He sings occasionally, sometimes with a group, usually accompanied only by his wife, Alberta Carter Bradford. For two years he toured in another musical, *Don't Bother Me, I Can't Cope,* in which his preacher role owed more to Flip Wilson than to Mother Hargrove. "I want to be an all-around singer. I'd love musical comedy, I'm too late for opera. I want to sing 'I've Got to Be Me' and also be the embodiment of earth." He re-

cently appeared at City Center in *Black Alice,* a production conceived by Vinnette Carroll, who directed *B.N.* Miss
Carroll wittily cast him as Father William. "Vinnette
wanted me to raise a shout on 'You are old, Father William' "—and to demonstrate he rocks the chorus, ending
in an orgiastic Sallie Martin *"owww."* He has also appeared with his Bradford Singers—only one of whom,
Charles Campbell, sang with the original group—in a college production of *Dark of the Moon.* "We do this mock
hillbilly tune

> *O the angels laid him away,*
> *Yes the angels laid him away* (*away*),
> *They laid him away in the cold, cold clay,*
> *The angels laid him away.*

The stage is pitch black, and the light comes on showing
this scraggly-haired blond boy playing his guitar, and then
the Bradford Singers doing this hillbilly tune—" Bradford
can't speak for laughter.

Bradford wants to branch out, sing blues and pop, do a
Tom Jones, as he says. But one suspects his deepest impulses are all religious. He's learned how to make money
out of the church, through choir direction if not professional singing. "I know Nixon doesn't love us, but I say,
as long as he leaves the Negro churches alone, I'll be all
right." As this would suggest, Bradford is no political acti-
vist. He felt bad when Dr. Martin Luther King was assas-
sinated ("I do believe if some white man had said something cute, I'd have cut him in a minute") but Bradford
reserves his anger for the music scene. He's the dedicated
composer when he says, "I think it's terrible they still play
Chopin when they got as much people out here with music
in their souls as Chopin who have no chance. Why we
must keep enriching the estates and libraries of these people who are long gone and dead, and they've got children
who'll never be heard, it's *wrong,* the system is *radical,*
I'm terribly against it, I'm *militant.*" Then, in case anyone

doubted it, "That's one of the few things I'm militant about."

Bradford knows people talk about him—he couldn't care less. "I pay them no mind. Sure I drink, the rabbi drinks, everybody drinks. It's a better thing than shooting dope, *I* think. There's some folk who like both of them. I think in this world, people ought to do what they want to do." That's what he said in 1950, and his philosophy is unchanged. In fact, Bradford is unchanged. Singers are always counting him out—"Bradford's lost it—" and he always proves them wrong. He can still sing rhythmic shouts and hymns with the best of them. So, even if he goes through an hour of embarrassing routines, he somehow manages to reach back, sing an old standard like Dorsey's "Today," and change the mood completely. At his peak he can evoke a spirit of almost scary proportions; for the moment one can believe Bradford as a mystic and a prophet. "It's pretty warm in here," he'll say. "Jeremiah told me it's like fire shut up in the bones." Now all the hip, pop phrasing disappears, and he moans like a King of Harmony:

The devil's getting angry because he's lost my soul.

At the very least, Bradford's soul is his own.

Bradford's last gospel musical, *Your Arms Too Short to Box with God,* occasioned a final pyrrhic victory. While almost devoid of plot or catchy tunes, it became a hit, thanks largely to the performances of Delores Hall, William Hardy, and Jennifer Holiday. But Bradford fell out with the director, Vinnette Carroll, and took his grievances to the *New York Times.* Once again, he was engaged in warfare with a determined woman, shades of Mahalia Jackson or Roberta Martin. But he was no longer "Little Alex," claiming his share of gospel turf. The world was—at last, as always—too much for him, and in the midst of his legal woes, he collapsed from a stroke. He lingered a few weeks— those who knew him felt he was too vivid a figure to die at fifty-one—but finally his overwhelming spirit gave out.

10

"I Won't Let Go of My Faith": Dorothy Love Coates

The great eyes express rage and pain. "Sometimes I think of the problems of the world in general, and my race in particular, and all I can say is how much longer must we suffer?" When Dorothy Love sings, she seems to be suffering for every man. A tall, handsome woman, her body contorts with agony, leaps with joy, seems almost an autonomous agent, performing in response to her words, cueing the audience's responses. Dorothy's voice is not great. A shabby contralto, frayed at the edges, it still encompasses a range from deep contralto to vigorous falsetto —the vocal answer to her skips and leaps. What Dorothy doesn't know about phrasing and swing can't be learned; a gifted songwriter, perhaps the only one attuned to political realities, she is actress, playwright, and audience in one. Were gospel to be more publicly acclaimed, she might have the stature of a Billie Holliday or a Judy Garland. Instead, for thousands of black people, she is *the* message singer, the one they can trust.

Because Dorothy, the inspired show-woman, "won't play. I have to give them the truth, wake 'em up to the mess going down. The pressure's so bad now, people are dying from heart attacks and strokes every day. We've sold our souls for a few pennies, and we turn against the very folk who still try to live right. That's why I love the hippies, because they don't fall for the materialist trap." She tackles all comers, white ("Our Governor Wallace, child, he's so confused he can't even see right, and as for Governor Maddox, church, he's *just pitiful*"); and black ("They've got folks going around saying if you love your brother, you're an Uncle Tom"). Everyone knows she lives the life, so she's earned the right to defend those by the wayside. "We're always picking on the addict and the drunk. They never advertise those other addicts. If you're gonna persecute one for what he does, you ought to get them all. We got some lying addicts, can't get through a day without telling a lie on somebody. We've got some church-going addicts, but going to church will not get you into heaven . . . just trying to straighten you out. And we got some home-wrecking addicts. They say if I can't have peace in my home, I'm sure gonna make hell out of yours." Audiences holler with laughter, leaping out of seats to wave approval. Dot looks down on them, compassionate, grim, and witty: "I'm gonna step on all your toes tonight."

Dorothy's history reflects the shifts in self-awareness of three generations: "my mother's, my own, and now my children's." She was born Dorothy McGriff in Birmingham fifty-odd years ago, and still lives there. "Why not? I've stayed in the North. It's the same everywhere, if you look like me." Most other singers have migrated, and now sport fancy clothes and wigs. Dorothy dresses with simple taste, and her hairdo has remained the same for years. She's always been this way. As a child, when the neighborhood youngsters would get together for amateur nights, singing the hits of Duke Ellington and Lil Green, Dorothy would appear in her homemade robe singing "God's Gonna Separate the Wheat from the Tares." She was already a special presence, alert, earthy, but morally committed, a mini-prophet, a child of the Old Landmark.

At that time, Birmingham was a center for gospel music. Like her childhood friend Alex Bradford, Dot grew up following the gospel pioneers, Queen C. Anderson, Georgia Lee Stafford (the "Songbird of the South"), and J. William Blevins, a former concert baritone and the first black singer on Birmingham radio. In store-front churches she could hear Mahalia or Sallie Martin or Roberta Martin, "the greatest lady we've had in gospel." Rebert Harris' singing helped lift her from her sickbed. "I became a stone gospel bird. I used to stay up all night banging that beat-up old piano. I'd keep the neighbors up and we'd all rejoice."

Her home experiences were "the same old thing." Her minister father left home, lured by Northern prospects, when she was six. Shortly after, the McGriffs were divorced. Mrs. Lillar McGriff never married again. "My mother was a beautiful woman, she could have had all kinds of men. But she kept her home *clean* for her children. When Mama died, we stood around pleading, 'Mama, don't die, please don't die.' But she knew best, she wasn't a happy woman, not after my father left her." She was, however, a Sanctified Baptist and a lady. She kept her family together, formed a youth group, the Royal Travelers, and in her favorite child, Dorothy, instilled a religious sense inseparable from the suffering that determined it. There was no reason for Dorothy to sing the other kids' blues—her gospel contained its own blues. In the months after her mother's death, Dorothy would tell church audiences Mrs. McGriff's story; afterwards, during her testimony song, "Lord You've Been Good to Me," she'd ask the women, "When your husband walked off and left you, didn't God bring you from a mighty long way?" Somehow, what could have been vulgar and indiscreet became a grand gesture, as if Lillar McGriff's advice to "take it all to Jesus, what leaves the heart reaches the heart" could withstand the most public intimacy.

Dorothy had to quit high school to work "all the standard Negro jobs," such as scrubbing floors for white people ("I still look in on some of the old ones"), clerking in

laundries and dry cleaning stores. Her first husband, Willie
Love, sang lead with the powerful Fairfield Four. The marriage didn't last long. By the late forties, Dorothy was a
popular soloist singing other singers' hits. She felt inhibited
in this role and began ad-libbing extra choruses—the pre-
liminary step to becoming her own composer. Since the
early forties she had been singing with the Original Gospel
Harmonettes, Birmingham's top group. The Harmonettes
—soprano Vera Kolb, mezzo-soprano Mildred Miller Howard, contraltos Odessa Edwards and Willie Mae Newberry,
pianist Evelyn Starks—were middle-class girls, some of them
schoolteachers, and they never quite related to the urgency
of Dorothy's message. Their support was dignified and
technically fine. Mildred was a tough second lead, and
Odessa's sermonettes wrecked houses. But Dorothy's fierce
need to express herself in the most individual manner only
confounded the group. "Girl," they told her, "you're ahead
of your time." If Dorothy had been living in Chicago or
Philadelphia, a large colony of gospel singers could have
encouraged her. In Birmingham, a city of solid, foursquare
gospel, she had to make her own way.

During a period when every choir singer sang gospel
with undiluted spirit, Dorothy's dedication surpassed the
rest. "On nights, I'd sing and sing for the people, days I'd
work for the white man." Eventually, as mentioned earlier,
she collapsed with pneumonia shortly before her first child
was born. "They broadcast bulletins on my sickness over
the radio, calling for prayers, and to this day, some folks
think I lost a lung." She didn't, but her daughter Cassandra
was born afflicted with cerebral palsy and epilepsy. Soon
after, the Harmonettes received an RCA Victor contract,
but Dorothy couldn't make the gig. Instead she traveled
North, seeking medical help for her child. (Today Cassandra is a competent young woman, thanks to her mother's
and grandmother's care.) By her early twenties Dorothy
had experienced enough bad times to defeat anyone. Divorced from her husband, penniless and vocally weakened

by her illness, she kept going sustained only by her family
and the idea of gospel; ultimately the two became syn-
onymous. "I get worried very often," she'd tell North-
erners, "and I call my mother. She told me, 'You go on
. . . and sing your song. . . . We're telling God, and *God
is fighting our battles.*' "

In 1951, Art Rupp signed the Harmonettes to Specialty,
and Dorothy rejoined them. Their first releases, "I'm
Sealed" and "Get Away Jordan," established the group's
image as dignified accompanists to a spiritual dynamo.
When singing "Get Away Jordan," Dorothy moved in sav-
agely graceful leaps—"They'd never seen a woman work
like that before." All over the country, young women and
men began moving like Dorothy, who had extended the
bounds of emotional expression from vocal to physical contortions, allowing the vocally weak but athletically gifted
a new opportunity to shine. "Get Away Jordan" also included her original verse:

> *When my feet get cold, my eyes shut,*
> *Body been chilled by the hands of death,*
> *Tongue glued to the roof of my mouth,*
> *Hands, they're folded across my breast.*
> *You don't have to worry about the way I felt,*
> *God almighty done told me he'd be right there.*

The lyrics recast traditional images in a new context; typically, the song made a lot of money for many artists, including the white Statesmen Quartet, but not for Dorothy.
After that she began composing her own material outright.
Her first tune, "(He may not come when you want him
but) He's Right on Time," is a gospel standard. Subsequent
compositions, "You Must Be Born Again" and "That's
Enough," were even more popular. These were no simple-
minded repetitions of clichés. Guitarist Jo Jo Wallace says,
"You take Dot's lyrics, she's saying something in every
line." The most popular, "That's Enough," in its mixture
of paranoia and self-assurance was the story of Dot's life:

There's always somebody talking about me,
Really I don't mind.
They're trying to block and stop my progress,
Most of the time.
The mean things you say don't make me feel bad,
I can't miss a friend I've never had,
I've got Jesus and that's enough.

By 1958, when the Harmonettes retired, they were second only to the Ward Singers in popularity. The power of Dorothy's personality was the key to their success. Audiences couldn't forget the tall young woman who worked so hard, vocally and physically, and who invariably concluded her performances seated, her legs shivering uncontrollably beneath her choir robe. Her presence was scarifying; she could roll her eyes and bring a church to its feet, reach for a Bible and have grown men fall out.

Only when she quit the road did her fellows realize what they'd lost. It wasn't her talent, though they all borrowed from it, but her soul. Everyone who came in contact with her recognized the goodness. Dorothy engenders a special loyalty in her colleagues.

In the late fifties, she employed as pianist Joe Washington, a Chicago disciple of Roberta Martin. Joe was a sweet-natured, skinny, nervous boy, not manly, and disposed toward the bottle. His problems were easily analyzed: "Dorothy, I used to cuss the Lord why he took my mother and left my no-good father." Dorothy straightened him, respecting where others had ridiculed. "I'll always love Dorothy," he used to say. "She knows if she ever needs help, I can be anywhere, even in Europe. I'll be there." In the sixties, Joe toured as accompanist with *Black Nativity*. After the play closed, he retreated to Newark boarding-houses, earning a few dollars by directing store-front choirs. Occasionally Marion Williams, formerly the female lead in *Nativity*, got him work accompanying her, "I just love Marion, she's never made me a promise she didn't keep." But there was no steady money, and he kept drinking;

he became ill and he swelled to almost twice his normal size. He always sought out the Harmonettes when they sang in Newark, filling in as organist when they needed one. Dorothy remained his one hope that "We'll all live again." Once, backstage at the Apollo Theatre, he entered her dressing room. "Dot, the doorman downstairs just told me this was the first gospel program he remembers where folks didn't drink and carry on. My eyes filled with tears." In September 1969, he suddenly, gratuitously rejoined the Harmonettes. "That boy played like I never heard nobody play. He must have known. There were times we had to stop driving, Joe be breathing so heavy." Finally he couldn't function, and the Harmonettes left him with Mildred Howard's aunt. One day Dorothy recognized things were hopeless. "I got him to the hospital. He kept saying, 'You won't leave me, dear, you won't leave me.' And I told him, 'No, dear, have I ever left you?'" That night he died. Without Dot, Joe might have ended up a drag queen in the gutter. He knew the object of his devotion, and to the end she didn't fail him.

During her retirement from 1959 to 1961, Dorothy married Carl Coates, bass singer and manager for the Nightingales; their child, Carletta, is a bright, lively youngster who sometimes plays tambourine on Harmonettes recording sessions. Dorothy had always been race-conscious, but the civil rights movement fired her imagination like nothing since she'd first heard gospel. She began working with Martin Luther King, marching down Birmingham streets, and sleeping in jail. Now when she sang in church, her moans were very specific. Not merely was this "a mean old trouble land," it was a place where "our children can't go to decent schools," and women like her mother grew middle-aged at thirty.

In 1961, Dot reorganized the Harmonettes, retaining Mildred Howard and Willie Mae Newberry Garth, adding soprano Cleo Kennedy, and Dorothy's younger sister, Lillian McGriff, as contralto. The group regained their popularity with Dot's compositions, "Come On in the House,"

Some get happy they run, others speak in an unknown
*   tongue,*
Some cry out in a spiritual trance,
Have you ever seen the saints do a holy dance?

a musical depiction of gospel itself, and "I Won't Let Go
of My Faith":

Old Satan is busy stirring up wrath,
Gathering stones to block my path.
Enemies inflicting all the hurt they can,
Throwing their rocks and hiding their hands.
If you dig one ditch you better dig two,
The trap you set just might be for you.
He put it in my heart, you can't change me,
My soul's on fire, and the world can't harm me.

Nothing docile about this faith; it darts armed and ready
before its enemies. Dorothy's biggest recent hit, a solo,
"Lord You've Been Good to Me," is simpler than her
usual lyrics, but her hums and shouts speak volumes. "I
know you brought me from a mighty long way," she sings,
as hundreds of hands wave in the air, identifying with the
testimony.

Dorothy claims she is not a recording artist, but her best
records indicate otherwise. Raggedy the voice may be, but
its texture is vibrant and supple, meshing hums, grunts,
falsetto whoops, chuckles, hollers and moans. In up-tempo
shouts, like "I Won't Let Go," she invariably finds the right
words and syllables to turn limp lines swinging. In my
favorite, "How Much More of Life's Burdens Must We
Bear?"

Through many dangers, toils and snares, already come.
I'll hold to my faith and depend on your grace
Till the battle is fought and the victory won.
But oh, how much more, oh Lord I just want to know,
How much more of life's burdens must we bear?

the word "bear" is reset into three syllables, the last rising
to an ecstatic "Yeah-eah," topped by the subsequent "oh
lordy, you *know,* you know how much *more"*—a *cri de
coeur* one imagines accompanied by angry fist-waving. As
the song ends, Dorothy repeats the questions with a force
that resolves itself in the final "must we bear?"—a graceful
relaxation of tension, at once humble and determined. To
these ears, that vocal grace symbolizes Dorothy's musical
and personal integrity.

After Odessa Edwards retired from the original Harmonettes, Dorothy became the group's narrator. In her new
role, she appears as preacher, reporter, and counselor. She
will begin by reminding the people of her home. "The Lord
has blessed our going out and our coming in. He's blessed
our sitting in, too." She details employment statistics down
South, the number of black shopgirls in Kresge's, and
clerks in the city bank. Then she gets into her message
about hostility in all corners. After years of struggle, she's
witnessed enough to say, "You take your route, I'll take
mine, but we're still graveyard travelers." The religious
support she offers en route is never ostrich-headed. "They
have a saying now, Pray and then get off your knees and
hustle." From her, the advice becomes news from home.

She talks about social conditions, about deserted wives,
unemployed fathers, sons dying in Vietnam for rights denied them at home. She sees reasons for racial unrest all
over. She crouched on the floor during the 1967 Newark
riots, "which wound up, like always, with colored folks
killed."

She fights on church grounds too. Recently a Philadelphia promoter placed her last on a long, exhausting program. Adding insult to injury, he then demanded she cut
her performance to fifteen minutes, telling her anyone
could get a message through in that time. Dorothy likes
to stretch out in her performances, gradually building to
an emotional climax. The promoter's directions were too
much for her. "He says I can get my message through in

fifteen minutes," she told the crowd. "Well, Jesus Christ came down through forty-two generations, hung on a rugged cross, suffered, bled, and died for your sins and mine." The crowd yelled "Amen" to the familiar litany. Dorothy turned angrily: "That was two thousand years ago, and some folks *still* ain't got the message." *"Read, girl"*; "Help yourself, Dot," the crowd roared.

Despite all her dedication, Dorothy is often angry and bitter. While most singers continue to rearrange old tunes, she turns out wonderful new songs on every album. "I feel like I'm feeding the entire gospel field. They all take my songs or my sayings. And then these promoters bitch about paying me 1960 prices." She mentions a New York promoter. "That Negro wanted me to come up from Birmingham, carrying six people, and pay me two hundred and fifty dollars." With all strikes against her, Dorothy always tears up, and the other professionals are jealous. At a TV taping, the Southern white producers swarmed around her, to the chagrin of some other singers. "I told them, Don't bother about me. The white man don't love any of us. When he quits making his change off me, he'll drop me in a minute." Sometimes she burns over the acclaim soul singers get while gospel singers starve; "They take a simple gospel beat, change the words, and the world goes wild." But she couldn't possibly switch over. "Sure, those singers get more money, but there's some money so dirty you hate to touch it."

Dorothy's been betrayed so often that "Don't nothing frighten me more today than people. People. They don't feel any more." Yet she obviously comes alive before an audience, entering the church with a frown, but smiling in spite of herself at the applause and adulation. "I guess singers like me, we're only happy when we sing." When she skips through an audience, she can discover her own need for the music reflected in their faces. Though her extravagant gestures could be called erotic, she considers them pantomimic, transcending sexual barriers, and many quartet leads learn from her timing and stage presence, acknowledging her implicit summons to sing with the body. The daughter of all the hard-working, defeated Baptist mothers is finally more artist than matriarch, living most vividly in her music, the incarnation of gospel to both sexes. Rebert Harris says, "Dot's the only one still out on the road keeping this thing alive."

She sees her image as a poor black asserting herself against all odds—a weak voice, an inconsistent group, a limited instrumental accompaniment ("these quartets with their electric guitars and basses and drums will make you sound like a *tin whistle*"), financial insecurity—yet somehow always getting through to the people. "I want them to think, If she can make it with that raggedy voice, we can too." They all listen to her message: whom Dorothy doesn't shout, she enlightens, but her real message is dramatized almost subliminally by her presence. Audiences expect her to be hoarse; one fan told me, "The worse Dot sounds, the better I like it."

Catch her in private, and she's usually tired. Yet she's always carrying someone to the doctor or taking her kids to museums and shows. Dot's energy and endurance, like her suspicion and anger, reflect her roots. One imagines her another Shirley Chisholm, though she may reach the masses even more with her mixture of earthy wisdom and old-time religion. "Everything I see takes me back to my Bible. Man thinks he's so grand and great. He's taken everything out of the earth and made money on it, the rubber, the oil, the diamonds, he put his own claim on them. But whatever man possesses, he got it from God's earth. Like General Tire. Mr. General Tire can say it's his, but the rubber came out of the trees, it's just a stone fact. Behind everything man's done to make his own empire, he's created his own jungle which he himself can't control. Man'll steal and lie. The one thing he can't stand is the truth. Like these gospel singers today. When the whole country's collapsing, they go out telling these ungodly, shameless, Mother Goose lies. But that's all right. I'm gonna wait on my change, and that's a *fact*."

PART THREE

THE
HOLINESS
CHURCH

11

The Holiness Church

The sidewalk preacher confronts a jeering crowd of winos, prostitutes, and workmen: "I belong to a Sanctified church. Not a *cranktified* church, I say a Sanctified church." He needs the apology. For though the Holiness church is palpably there in black ghettos, with many blocks containing at least one store-front church, it's also unutterably strange. Even in the kaleidoscopic world of the ghetto, the Holiness church maintains a discrete and at times impenetrable mystique. It may be the blackest of institutions, but for millions of black Americans, it's a fantasy world beyond their ken. "To me, it's like going to a movie," says one practical nurse. "They just *amazing.*" The lady is Baptist born and reared, and has done her fair share of shouting in her time, but Holiness worship is still something else. The ritual, the spirit, the very physical manner—as saints say, "I started to walk and I had a *new* walk"—are all unfamiliar to her. Likewise the Sanctified sound is very special. Once, on the TV show "Soul," the celebrated soul saxophonist King Curtis supported Marion Williams in the old Christmas song "When Was Jesus Born?" Miss Williams is a great Sanctified singer, and her rhythms are fiery and complex. Yet soul music is supposedly founded on the gospel beat; the "soul clap" is pure Pentecostal. For all this, Curtis could scarcely keep up with Marion, as he interpolated old Coasters riffs and staccato scale descents.

The Holiness church is a world unto itself. Its branches are myriad; schisms proliferate as in the days of the Gnostics and Manicheans. The Pentecostal church, the Church of God in Christ (abbreviated C.O.G.I.C.), the Church of God Apostolic, the Church of Holiness Science, the Fire Baptized Holiness Church, as well as literally thousands of smaller churches (some claiming no more than a half dozen members), may differ on theological doctrine: Should converts be baptized by fire or water? Who comes first—the Father, the Son, or the Trinity? Can women preach? But finally they all come together as the churches where "neither form nor fashion" prevails, the houses where "Let go and let God" is the motto. In the 1890s, America was swept by a Latter Rain Movement aimed to irrigate the dry bones in the churches. White and black Pentecostal congregations sprang up all over America, especially wherever the people were poor and depressed. Because the Holiness people jumped, shouted, danced, and fell out for Jesus, because, in a word, they acted "crazy," they became a national laughingstock, the Holy Rollers of fable and cliché.

Yet the intense concentration and missionary efforts of Holiness people has paid off. They have introduced a whole new religious concept into American theology, "saved, sanctified, and filled with the Holy Ghost." "Saved" means commitment; "sanctified" means change in life style; "filled with the Holy Ghost," the third and most arduous last step, means spirit possession. To signal this "going out of self," the Holiness people emphasize glossolalia, more commonly known as speaking in tongues, a fluent kind of gibberish filled with Hebraic-sounding syllables. At least twenty million Americans have had long and deep exposure to Holiness. There are easily as many white

Sanctified as black, and their behavior may be even more frenzied; some whites are so "deep" they'll take up snakes and drink poison while in the spirit. But the Holiness church, like most of America, remains segregated. Occasionally a big-name white evangelist, like the late Reverend A. A. Allen, will perform before integrated audiences, accompanied by a predominantly black choir, but Allen was an exception. The Pentecostal people in Sweden, Italy, Holland, and Australia (to mention but four countries where Holiness thrives) have no more knowledge of gospel music than their Catholic brothers. But they do understand the spirit. "I can't stand to see the Puerto Rican [sic] Sanctified folk," says one singer. "You talk about deep—" shaking his head.

In all black Holiness churches, song and dance make up a great portion of the service. This is true whether one attends a large church like Brooklyn's Washington Temple C.O.G.I.C., which seats 2,500 people, or small, wondrously named congregations like Philadelphia's Greater Zion C.O.G.I.C., Atlanta's Highway and Hedges Fire Baptized (from Jesus' admonition to "go into the highway and hedges as well"), Chicago's Widow's Mite Holiness ("If you cannot give a hundred, you can give a widow's mite"), or St. Louis' Lively Stone Church of God Apostolic ("the one lively stone in the building"). Jesus said, When a few are gathered in my name, there I shall be. He also promised to be a husband for the widow and a father for the orphan. And so, in all these churches, and thousands like them, a few widows and orphans gather each Sunday to "lift up the name" of the one who saw them through the week.

The music attracts one first. Much of it is older than the gospel songs Dorsey and his confrères began composing in the twenties. Some Sanctified songs are as anonymous as spirituals; others were written by pioneers in the Holiness movement. As everyone knows, the Holiness churches were the first to employ musical instruments, formerly banned as the devil's tools. The most famous New Orleans tune, "When the Saints Go Marching In," was originally a Sanctified shout, celebrating the "saints," the ones who have followed Jesus all the way. Most of the old Holiness tunes are similarly simple and repetitive. The musical interest lies almost solely in the rhythms—Sanctified handclapping is a miracle of rhythmic complexity—and the glorious voices. The subject matter is invariably joyous. "This is the Church of God in Christ" is a musical definition of the church's qualities. Other songs, like "Sunshine Always Follows Rain," carry Tindley's "Storm Is Passing Over" to a happy conclusion. But the most affecting are the songs of personal victory.

> *He brought me out all right,*
> *He brought me out all right,*
> *Brought me out of darkness*
> *And into the sunlight,*
> *Yes he brought me out all right.*

The cynical impulse is to change the adjective to "all wrong." But the poor people singing the song know what they're shouting about.

Not that the optimism can't seem a bit strained. Recently the great gospel pioneer Robert Anderson joined Deloris Barrett Campbell at her husband's store-front church. Myrtle Scott, a legendary Chicago soloist and their former co-worker in the Roberta Martin Singers, was leading the congregation in the old Sanctified shout,

> *Oh I'm a millionaire, yes I'm a millionaire,*
> *My father's rich in houses and lands,*
> *And I'm his heir,*
> *That makes me a multi-multi-multi-millionaire.*

"Girl," said Anderson to Deloris, "you know I ain't gonna sing that lie. Me with a dollar in my pocket singing I'm a multi-multi-multi-millionaire."

The archetypal Holiness song is a slow chant usually sung as the service begins, or else when the spirit has

erupted in an outburst of frenetic shouts. Its words are
simple, almost nonverbal:

Yes! Yes! Yes! Yes! Yes, Ye-h-e-ess! Oh ye-he-hess!

Sometimes the saints will add:

Send the rain, Lord, send the rain, send the rain,
The latter rain.

Thank you Lord, thank you Lord, thank you Lord,
Thank you Lord, thank you Lord.

You've been so good, you've been so good, you've been so
good,
Lord, you've been so good, you've been so good.

Invariably hands clap beautifully to a nonexistent beat,
both applauding and invoking the spirit. There is nothing
in American religion so intense and fervent as this chant,
and no more moving moment in public life. To go into a
Holiness church when the spirit's high, and the world's im-
purities are cast out into the streets from whence they
came, to hear the saints assenting, is to believe that music
can transport one to "higher ground." To be caught up
in "Holy Ghost fire" is to sing along:

> *God is not dead, he's yet alive,*
> *I can feel him in my hands,*
> *I can feel him in my feet,*
> *I can feel him all over me.*

"If you sing with spirit, the Lord never fails to stop by,"
says one saint. Her daughter, a college student, adds,
"When you're in a Sanctified church, you just can't doubt
God. I'll leave him outside, but you know, in church, he's
just *there*."

Most of the larger Sanctified churches depend on the
personal charisma and showmanship of their ministers.
There are some great shouting preachers in these taber-
nacles, but perhaps the most moving services occur in the

smaller churches where, ideally, each member is a minister. Some saints shy away from the bigger churches, either out of pique with preachers—"I'm serving Jesus, not Daddy Grace"—or dissatisfaction with bourgeois forms—"The Sanctified churches are getting as bad as the Baptists. It won't be long before you'll be afraid to say Amen." Others choose the small churches because they are friendlier, more open. The makeup of the big Holiness churches can be surprisingly heterogeneous, including middle-class professionals—Faith Temple's Youth Choir includes students at Juilliard and Bronx High School of Science. But storefront members are usually illiterates, often scared into meek submission before more educated blacks. Economically they are the most deprived, many on welfare, most of the women domestics or factory workers. Ridiculed and parodied by outsiders, these saints have cultivated a microcosm of fellowship and affection. A typical small-church service may include, beside the preacher, a half dozen males, among them a guitarist who may be a paid outsider, about thirty-five women, and fifty children. The church "mothers" are just that, and the numerous children are treated as belonging to all. This outpouring of love translates and expands the conventional family structures; as one young saint said, "I may not have had a father, but I've had many mothers."

The vibrations of community are so strong that saints can enter the spirit of things in whatever Holiness church they visit. Despite the apparent chaos, a cohesive bond is formed by the very presence of saints worshiping together. As the service begins, each member prays for himself "in his own way." There is seldom specific request; rather, the general forms, "Ease my troublin' mind," "Come into our hearts, Lord," "Move these things that's troubling me," "We need you in our homes, Jesus," subsume personal griefs. After prayer come the testimonials. The atmosphere of communal love envelops and inspires the poor suffering witnesses for Jesus. Men and women, outcasts in rented rooms, scared inarticulate by street jargon, become verbal firebrands. On and on they speak, silent all week, but now superbly fluent. One often sees some tiny, battered woman rise timidly and pour forth an almost reflexive stream of praise, nonstop:

> Giving honor to God and all the saints, I'm glad to say this evening, I'm saved, sanctified, and hallelujah [she twists to the side] filled with the marvelous Holy Ghost. I'm thankin' God for looking over me and my children one more week, for keeping Satan away, for stepping in when I needed him most. Truly . . . God's beenmyall inallforwithouthimtodaychildrenIcouldn'thavemadeit thusfar. *Truly* . . . I'velearnedifGodbeforyou, he'smore thanthewholeworldagainstyouandthere'srealityinservinga trueandlivingGod. *Truly* . . . hisGraceissufficientandall thedaysofmyappointedtimeIintendtostretchoutonhisgood- nessandwaittillmychangecomes. I'm asking you to pray much for me, cause I'm still a motherless child standing in the need of prayer. Amen, glory to God, thank the Lord.

After she sits down, she remains in the spirit, punctuating the testimony of the next witness with cries of "Glory, lift him up, my my my, what a wonderful Saviour." Testimonies can be admixtures of conventional Biblical imagery: "He delivered Daniel, I know he'll deliver me"; private fantasy: "Last night, children, I waded out in grace knee-deep"; and autobiographical experience. Among the most affecting are testimonies of ex-drug addicts. One young man testified, weeping, "I thank God for doing what the doctors couldn't do. For saving me from my dope habit. No hospital could do nothing for me. They'd given up on me, the doctor walked away and shook his head, but I've learned to trust God and know ain't nothin' too hard for *my* God." I remember the testimony of a lady whose only son had been killed in Vietnam. "Folks tell me to cuss God because I've lost my boy. I know that ain't nothin' but the devil putting stumblin' blocks in my way. I'm gonna be like Job and say, Yea though he slay me, yet shall I trust him." That's religion.

After the testifying, there'll be preaching and singing. And if it's a good service, and "If it's Holiness, it's supposed to be good church," folks will get happy. Each man shouts in his own way, with his own steps. Younger members may throw in a little Boogaloo or Funky Chicken, or go the street one better, and come up with brand-new twists and turns. If the spirit's high, some saints so gifted may indulge in healing, "laying on of hands" and prophesying. The members leave with a spiritual high that must sustain them through six bad days. Church is very simply a glorious experience; when the spiritual says "Every day will Sunday," Sunday means lowdown church, not mere rest and recreation.

A stranger, white or black, attending the service will find the outbursts savage and mindless, the atmosphere dense with repressed sexuality (and in some white rural communities, the population explodes nine months after the annual revival). The saints know otherwise. These are their rituals. Religion is truly their all in all, so why not cheer for Jesus as others holler for Hank Aaron? When the spirit is so intense, why not run, crawl, dance? And when it gets all over you, then "fall out," let yourself be "knocked out by the Holy Ghost."

What must be emphatically stressed is that the saints come "ready." Holiness is a way of life, and most of them have been preparing for Sunday all week. Some churches operate like well-organized resorts in which every free moment is accounted for. Choir rehearsals, church outings, club meetings, healing, prayer and testimonial services can occupy the saints each night of the week. Meanwhile, as the song says, saints live the life at home. They pray all over their houses—"Some of my best prayers," says Alex Bradford, "I get through on the toilet." (Shades of Martin Luther.) Most of the saints I've spoken to think nothing of speaking in tongues outside church. They'll do it at home, and occasionally on the bus or subway, one sees somebody cry, "Thank you Jesus, *shandalahaya*." Almost anywhere one can see some saint quiver and extend a hand, palm perpendicular to arm, which moves in the rapid, counterclockwise motion saints employ in answer to the spirit's prompting.

A large body of Holiness literature, put out by white Evangelical outfits and the all-black Church of God in Christ Convention, instructs one in the rites and dogma of sanctification. "Holiness is like going to college," says Evangelist Willie Mae Ford Smith. "You need to become educated in God's ways." Sallie Martin says, "Reading? That's all I do . . . I just thank Gawd for giving me strong eyes to read." Though the talk of gospel singers is a perpetual joy, the Holiness literature is, sadly, no treasure house of vivid, charged folklore. One suspects the publications are a bourgeois trapping, curiously contrary to the anti-intellectual bias of the earlier saints:

You can go to the college, you can go to the school,
But if you haven't got religion, youse an educated fool.

The very considerable wisdom of the saints clearly doesn't come from books. The young saint could have said, Many mothers, many teachers.

It boggles the mind to imagine the millions of Americans caught up in the Holiness mystique. Sanctified faith is predicated on mystery ("I can't see the Lord, but I can *feel* him"), on inspired intuition, and vision bordering on hallucination. The Sanctified superstars lure their faithful with more theatrical stuff: One celebrated bishop, supported by wires, flies over his congregation in a "foretaste of glory"; Prophet Jones interrupts a sermon with a message the spirit gave him especially for Sister Believer; Dorothy Norwood peeks under chairs and carpets "searching" for Jesus; Professor Herman Stevens sings a falsetto note three octaves above middle C, leaps from the altar and zooms around Faith Temple before returning to mike and song, without missing a beat or changing a key. But compared to the wonder of saints worshiping together, all this is so much showmanship.

The fancy choir robes, the trick lighting, the giant organs and grand pianos of the big churches provide a pretty overwhelming spectacle. But the sheer human drama of a small congregation, saints dressed simply, almost in defiance of "dressed-up" churches, doesn't depend on external trappings. Another mystery—through sheer effort, willpower, soul, if you will, they call into being a community of saints in which testimonies converge and complement each other, so the apparent babble becomes harmonious praise, the week's fasting and praying is rewarded, and persuaded by the aura of love, saints can sing

> *You can't make me doubt him,*
> *Because I know too much about him.*

Such faith is too energetic to be dismissed as defeatist and quietist. If it's an escape, it's also a difficult, demanding change in life style. To that extent, Holiness resembles more recent black radical movements. Similarly, many abandon Holiness simply because they can't stand so much "living close." Yet the sweetness of being saved is hard to forget: a WLIB disc jockey calls his partner over; "Reggie, you remember the days back at Washington Temple?" and Reggie breathes deeply, "Oh, yes," just like the saints do. Indeed, one of black gospel's unheralded "charismatic" gifts is this gift of self-parody. Saints, ex-saints, and gospel lovers in general, Baptist, Methodist or agnostic, casually employ church talk in worldly context. Some say "Yes Lord" and "Thank You Jesus" on the most secular occasions; a good meal, a winning numbers ticket, an itch well scratched. Some express their delight in open-eyed shouts. Deloris Barrett Campbell recalls visiting one celebrated singer on the occasion of her divorce. "She told me, 'Well, girl, I'm free of him at last,' and we locked arms and just danced all across the room. Then she turns to me and says, 'Thank God for Jesus, but you know I still love that man.'" One singer, bored by a long solo, yells out, "Sing, sister, sing for Jesus, cause you sure ain't singin' for *me*."

Because the ghetto forces one to be ironic and irreverent, even the deepest saints retain an earthy humor that saves Sanctified faith from the sentimental excesses of white Evangelism. (An interesting topic for sociological investigation: Is white Holiness characterized by similar self-parody?) Perhaps because the streets are never more than a church door away, the saints are seldom naïve about the world. The fully saved live lives of almost total abstinence: no makeup, no fancy clothes, very few pleasures of the flesh. But many others, less continent, call themselves saved. Of course, there are always swindling preachers who seduce their female followers. But most immediately striking about many of the larger Holiness churches is the inordinate number of male and female homosexuals. As one singer bluntly put it, "There's more sissies and bull daggers in the Sanctified churches, and they all think they're the only ones going to Heaven."

Gospel music, and especially the Holiness church, attracts many homosexuals and lesbians. Now bisexuality is much more common, or at least more public, among poor blacks and Puerto Ricans than among middle-class whites. Since gospel is theatrical, and theater is the paradigm for much of the gay life, gospel has a special allure for gays. Finally, the enshrinement of Mother must take its toll. I. F. Stone once observed that the black mother raising her children right with all strikes against her is the true American hero. Cheap psychology won't work here; mother-worship is justified (even Malcolm X said he'd kill the man who'd insult his mother). However forced by circumstance to be tough and strict—all gospel singers remember how their mothers used to thrash them—the mothers inculcate a nagging sense of obligation in their offspring. The annual watch-night services of the black Baptist and Holiness churches can degenerate into orgies of guilt over mother-mistreatment. Many gospel hits capitalize on this emotion. From the Pilgrim Travelers' "Mother Bowed and Prayed for Me" (1948) to Archie Brownlee's "I'm Gonna Leave You in the Hands of the Lord" (1958):

Sometimes I get to wondering
Did I treat my darling mother right?
Mother used to groan early in the morning
And Mother used to moan very late at night

to the Consolers' "Waiting for My Child" ("If I only knew what town my child was in, I'd be there on the early morning train,/ Lord no matter what the crime, you know this child is mine") and Shirley Caesar's "Don't Drive Your Mama Away" ("If you drive her away, you're gonna need her someday"), tributes to Mother's goodness and reminders of children's ingratitude always reach the guilt-stricken record buyer.

This alone can't explain the number of homosexuals in the Sanctified churches. "They're naturally emotional," says one member of Faith Temple, "so they come where they know they can be themselves." The extremer ones gravitate to churches where anything goes. When there, they are among the wildest participants. Once, at the Apollo Theatre, a young man wiggled in conspicuously, greeted his cohorts, "Hi, Miss Thing, Hello, Mr. Lucy," and then loudly pronounced during the film, "Child, that's what I should have been, a priest, so I could wear my skirts *for days.*" Yet when the gospel concert began, the spirit found him a ready target. While Marion Williams sang "The Lord Will Take You in His Arms," the boy collapsed in sobs and shrieks of "Thank You Jesus," and it took three ushers to carry him out. The frenzy may be a form of camping, and no doubt many a "sissy shouts to be seen." But this man was out cold. Meanwhile the young woman three seats down from him, her hair cropped close, contorted in spiritual agony as the Gospel Clefs sang "Father Open Our Eyes."

And who are better witnesses that "If God be for you, he's more than the whole world against you"? The more glamorous black gays can move elsewhere, into soul music or fashion or hustling, and those left in gospel are seldom as beautiful. To be poor, black and noticeably strange in a community where deviance is both casually accepted and cruelly derided, that's a bundle of crosses. One female singer is at her best when betrayed by her girlfriends, giving her a reason to "take it to Jesus" and to wail with the ferocity of old country women calling on the only man they can trust.

For, finally, the gospel homosexuals are poor blacks in pretty much the same straits as the straighter saints. One singer understates: "I know half my troubles come from being black." The Holiness church is not yet political enough to see that sinner and saint are victims together. Rather, it says with the spiritual, "When all God's children get together/ Won't that be a time, what a time, what a time." And whether impelled by guilt or inspired by prophecy, all the members have something to shout about; "He included *me*."

The Holiness church is abundant with paradoxes. There are numerous swindling preachers, many of whom owe their survival to the numbers racket; when a follower of Bishop Crookedheart testifies, "Thanks to Bishop's prayers, hallelujah, the Lord blessed me with five hundred dollars," the implicit message credits the Mafia as much as Mary's Baby. Corruption mingles with sanctification, reaction cedes to energy. And the church keeps marching on. There are more great singers and musicians in the Holiness church than anywhere else. The combination of evangelical fervor and musical sophistication has produced the most brilliant modern gospel singers (even a staunch Baptist like Mahalia Jackson was raised next door to a Holiness church). From Clarence Cobbs's First Church of Deliverance Choir in the thirties to the Edwin Hawkins Singers in 1970, the church has always found a way of holding and attracting its youth, by providing the most swinging musical institutions in sight.

Yet, in time, many choir members backslide, cross over, go out into the world. The faithful few, "the Lord's despised few," remain the same battered, broken, born-again

saints. Like Sallie Martin, they seem heartened by the
world's contempt. So a gospel singer will often appeal to
his audience: "I'm not ashamed to say I got saved in a
Sanctified church. A lot of folk ain't particular about Holiness, but I had a praying mother and no matter what the
world may say—" growling like a preacher—"she told me
to hold out to the end." He knows full well the response.
Saints will holler out, "That's all right," "Justify her," and
that great answer to the whole world's scorn: "Sing. Sing
anyhow."

12

The Traveling Saints

If you're saved and a singer, your options are pretty well defined. You can stay in the church, guaranteed an appreciative if impoverished audience, or you can go out into the highways and hedges, spreading the word to audiences who couldn't care less about Jesus. In other words, you're either a "consecrated singer" or an "entertainer." But since Sanctified music is worldly to begin with, these distinctions get a bit abstract. For example, the greatest pioneer Sanctified singers, Sister Rosetta Tharpe and Evangelist Willie Mae Ford Smith, took divergent routes. Rosetta entered show business, sang in clubs and theaters, broadcast the dangers of venereal disease, invented pop gospel, became a household name and the archetypal cheerful gospel singer, everybody's sister—until Mahalia came along as America's great black mother. Until recently, Willie Mae Ford Smith had cut three records in her life. Yet her church performances are legendary, and no other gospel singer has inspired so many great soloists. Both would have made great blues singers. In fact, Rosetta cut a few blues sides, to her eternal disgrace in the church. Willie Mae admits if she hadn't gotten saved, she would

probably have done the same. For both come out of an era
when blues was the living force in black music, and with
years and experience, both view gospel as one saved step
away from blues. "There's something about the gospel
blues that's so deep the world can't stand it," says Rosetta.
And Willie Mae says succinctly, "The gospel song is the
Christian blues. I'm like the blues singer, when something's
rubbing me wrong, I sing out of my soul to settle me
down."

They couldn't be more different, these two great singers.
Look, for example, at Rosetta's cover photo on her Savoy
album, "Precious Memories." Rosetta's dyed red hair
gleams a golden coronal over a large face, a huge toothy
grin, an abundance of ostrich feathers, an evening-
gowned knee supporting a brown-and-gold guitar over
which the lady leans. It may smack of rent parties and
honky-tonks, but the photo is also almost naïvely country,
indeed country and western. ("They want me for the
Grand Ole Opry. I'll be the first colored girl they've had—"
and she once cut a disc with Red Foley.) She's been to all
the dens of iniquity, but when she introduces her old
swing-band hit, "Bring Back Those Happy Days," she carries her listeners back to Cotton Plant, Arkansas. "I remember when I was a girl, how much love we had. Why, I
used to be busy all day, carrying Aunt Lucy and Aunt Jane
some po'k chops. You can't get them fresh no more, now
they put them in the deep freeze and *embalm* them for
months and months. Seems to me, church, the sweetness
has gone out of the land." Rosetta is a mistress of mala-
propisms: accusations become "acturations"; she attempts
the contemporary by crying "Lord give us peace in
Korea." She once appeared as m.c. of "TV Gospel Time."
Deloris Barrett was guest soloist, and Rosetta kept introducing her as "nationally known gospel singer, Deloris
Brown." That mistake was corrected, but the program
closed with my favorite Tharpe-ism. "This is your own Sister Rosetta Tharpe asking you to tune in next week for another program of your *favorable* gospel music."

If you see Willie Mae Ford Smith at the Gospel Singers Convention, which she directs with Thomas Dorsey and Sallie Martin, you'd never guess this is the lady many veterans rank above Mahalia Jackson. She stands at the door, collecting dollar tickets with smiling humility. She wears the standard white nurses' outfit, sensible shoes, and horn-rimmed glasses. There's nothing glamorous about the lady; she couldn't be more saved. The visual difference between her and Rosetta is astonishing. Yet Willie Mae, the typical evangelist, is also more lucid, less rural, finally more regal than Rosetta. Generalizations are not easy in the Holiness church.

Rosetta Tharpe has always been a creature of shifting moods, but lately her nature is decidedly darkened and saddened. "Your sister's going through some hard times now, brother, Mama's gone." She's still the gregarious hostess: "Boy, what you doin', not comin' over here for some good soul food?" and she still knows enough low-down stories about celebrities to entertain the dourest sinner: "Lord, what I didn't learn in the clubs, I found out about in the church." But the raucousness has mellowed since her mother, Katie Bell Nubin, died two years ago. Mother Bell was one of the old-time saints, the kind who will shout any church by standing up and croak-chanting their testimony. Mother Bell could do more than that, and her voice was firm and abrasive till death.

As long as Mother Bell was around, Rosetta couldn't stray too far. The old lady would seat herself by the piano, pluck her mandolin, and sing the old-timey shouts, "Be Ready When the Bridegroom Comes," "The Miami, Florida Storm." She lived for singing and Jesus; if you asked her about speaking in tongues, she'd tell you, "Lord yes. The Holy Ghost, that's my company-keeper." A few years ago Dizzy Gillespie accompanied her on an album, Mother Bell changing her style not a hair. She remained healthy till eighty-nine. "Then one day, Mama called me to her. 'Rosetta, you're so good, you're so kind.' I say, 'Mama, what's the matter?' 'I'm feelin' cold right now, and it sounds to me like Count Basie's playing in the next room.' 'Oh, you poor thing, that's just the angels getting you ready.' She got up and left, and I went down on my knees. And the spirit gave me a message, 'Let the Lord's will be done,' so I got up, went into the rest room to wash my face. And the next thing I knew, Mama had her stroke."

Rosetta is a bundle of energy, always singing, cooking, or exercising. While her husband plays the Pilgrim Jubilees' swinging "Won't It Be Wonderful There," she prances about, kicking her leg up to chin level. "I'm fifty. I know I don't look it," she says. The age varies, the formula never. She's perpetually announcing a change of fortune: "It's my big comeback, I'm hot like I used to be—but I don't like to brag." Is her self-parody unwitting? Not at all; Rosetta can always laugh at herself. "Back then when the people were real," she'll tell a church, "I ain't gonna tell you when, I'm not gonna tell you how *old* I am, back there in thirty-eight, thirty-nine, that's all you need to know." She lives in one of a series of newly built attached homes that stretch out for blocks, scrupulously clean, as if Philadelphia needs evidence that blacks don't lower property values. Rosetta's home, with its rose-trellised doorway, its wall-to-wall mirrors, its semi-circular bed, is officially "fabulous." But Rosetta laughs at it too, pointing to the soldiers on the wallpaper: "They're coming to get me."

"Someday I'm gonna write the story of my life, the people will cry and cry. I've been robbed, cheated, married three times, but God is so good—" and Rosetta flashes her pinched, supersweet smile, letting out a characteristic "Oh yes." The life has certainly been varied. She was born in Cotton Plant, Arkansas, a tiny hamlet known as the birthplace of whiz kids (Cotton Plant students are always winning state debating contests). Rosetta was a precocious child, walking and talking before she was one. By six, she had mastered the guitar and, traveling with her mother to Holiness conventions, would shout the people with two very sad, very adult songs, "The Day Is Past and Gone" and "I Looked Down the Line." The last is her master-piece, a magnificent gospel blues about the sinner's pursuit of God. Katie Bell was a traveling missionary, and mother and daughter eventually wound up in Chicago. The Holi-ness church by then was filled with remarkable talents. One of them was the blind pianist, Arizona Dranes, who used to regale Alex Bradford in Birmingham. Rosetta heard her in St. Louis singing in a gritty whine, "The Storm Is Passing Over," her diction impeccable, almost affected, and her piano pure ragtime. Sister Dranes influenced many young singers, especially Madame Ernestine B. Washing-ton, Rosetta's old chum from Arkansas, who moved to Brooklyn, became the "Songbird of the East," and married Bishop F. D. Washington of the Temple. Rosetta's voice was a bit smoother, but Dranes's fervor and diction obvi-ously influenced her. Baby Rosetta heard men and women with guitars, harmonicas, mandolins, jews-harps, and trumpets. And though her guitar is her trademark, Rosetta will tell you, "I don't think those good guitarists, Brother Willie Eason, Utah Smith and all, are copying off me. They been around long as I. Why, we got some musicians in our church can cut all of us out here." One singing dulceolaist, Washington Phillips, recorded a lovely sixteen-bar blues, "Denomination Blues," in 1927.

You can go to the college, you can go to the school,
If you haven't got religion, youse an educated fool,
And that's all, that's all,
We've got to have religion now, I tell you that's all.

Eleven years later, Rosetta recorded the tune with Lucky Millinder's band.

Rosetta's church style was more secular than the other saints'. She could pick blues guitar like a Memphis Minnie. Her song style was filled with blues inversions, and a res-onating vibrato (she calls it "vibrater"). She bent her notes like a horn player, and syncopated in swing band manner. Above all, she had showmanship. Grinning, joking, camp-ing, a million spiritual laughs, Rosetta was obvious star material. And, starting in 1938, she scored as no gospel singer has done since.

Her first Decca records featured Rosetta and guitar alone. They included Thomas Dorsey's "Rock Me," "I Looked Down the Line," "That's All," and her famous novelty, "This Train."

> *This train don't pull no jokers,*
> *No whiskey drinkers, no cigar smokers,*
> *Because this train's a clean train, this train.*

The blues riffs on guitar and Rosetta's sprightly girlish voice made the records the biggest gospel hits of the thirties. Almost at once she joined forces with the big bands of Cab Calloway, Lucky Millinder, and even Benny Goodman. She carried gospel into the Cotton Club and Café Society Downtown. Shrewdly noticing that white people couldn't dig the deeper tunes, Rosetta stuck to the up-tempo spirituals she rearranged: "Didn't It Rain," "Down By the Riverside," "Up Above My Head I Hear Music in the Air." Meanwhile she didn't neglect the saints. For them she recorded Dorsey's "Precious Lord," the Tindley hymns "Stand By Me" and "Beams of Heaven," and Lucie Campbell's "End of My Journey." In 1939 *Life* ran a feature story on Rosetta's moving the saints on Sunday and entertaining the big spenders on Monday.

During the war years, Rosetta and the Golden Gate Quartet were the only black religious singers on V-Discs. She toured widely with gifted quartets, especially her favorites, the Dixie Hummingbirds—"Tucker's my baby, he sing just like me—" and Tucker did learn a lot from Rosetta's free, witty, and deliberately stylized approach. She's famous for rapid-fire repetitions, "Nononononono," sung up and down the scale; Tucker one-ups her by changing voice in mid-riff. In 1944, Rosetta began recording with the boogie-woogie pianist Sammy Price. Their first disc, "Strange Things Happening Every Day," a typical Tharpe novelty, hit the race-record top ten, a feat she repeated several times. (According to the *Billboard* charts, only the Five Blind Boys, the Bells of Joy, and the Edwin Hawkins Singers have duplicated her chart success, and in all instances, only once.) In 1945, Alan Lomax produced a program on V.D., selecting the country singer Roy Acuff and Rosetta as the folk entertainers the masses trusted the most. (One imagines all kinds of obscene verses to "This Train", suitable to Lomax's theme.)

In 1946, Rosetta joined forces with Marie Knight, a Sanctified shouter from Newark. Madame Marie Knight, as she came to be known, was prettier and younger than Rosetta ("Marie's three years younger than me," Rosetta deliberates. "She always were three years younger than me.") She had one of those magnificent contraltos like Mahalia, Bessie Griffin, or Willie Mae Ford Smith. But, though she sang with fervor and shouted with awe-inspiring control, Madame Marie wound up resembling a pop singer. Her plain and unstylized approach proved a perfect foil to Rosetta's flamboyance. Their first record, "Up Above My Head," hit the *Billboard* race charts. Their skillful counterpoint and witty interaction "tickled" the church crowd and won them engagements at the Howard Theatre and the Blue Angel. Rosetta was the queen. She traveled with Marie and various quartets. In 1951, she married Russell Morrison, ex-manager of the Ink Spots, in an outdoor gospel wedding with 25,000 paying guests.

Then, dark day and cursed, Rosetta and Marie cut some blues. The two split up, and Marie began a long, singularly unprofitable career as a blues shouter, her voice, glorious in what had always seemed its proper metier, now going to waste. Rosetta didn't dig blues and she returned to the church. But her engagements fell off, her records stopped selling, she became *persona non grata* in the Sanctified church. It wasn't merely that she had "sold out"; it was that *she* had sold out. If Sister would do you like that, who, the saints wondered, could you trust? "I'm still *me*," Rosetta replied, "I'm back. The Lord said he'd forgive you seven times seventy times a day", but the church was stingier. So she went off to Europe, singing for almost a year on gigs arranged by Hugues Panassié, France's famous rear-guard jazz critic. "Shoot, I didn't do worse than the rest of them. Ernestine cut a jazz record" (in 1946, Madame Washington cut two discs with the New Orleans musician Bunk Johnson) and "Mahalia's out there singing with Duke Ellington." Not blues, however, and not in nightclubs. Rosetta was, to put it kindly, ahead of her times.

Yet she loves gospel best. In 1960, she appeared at the Apollo Theatre with the two leading gospel acts, the Caravans and James Cleveland, stealing the show both times. By now her voice had lowered an octave, and she chanted more than she sang. It made no difference. One night she came out in tailored street clothes, in worldly contrast to the billowy robes of the Caravans. She romped through "This Train," hitting fancy riffs, holding her guitar notes while making silly faces as if to say, Well, my, my, think of that. In her own words, she "cut the fool." Then she got serious with Dorsey's "Peace in the Valley," one of her gospel classics. The phrasing was inspired, and when she began ad-libbing on the line, "I'll be changed from the creature that I am," she had truck drivers rolling in the aisles. Rosetta cut some steps herself, after judiciously removing her guitar. The audience was screaming for more when the m.c. brought Katie Bell Nubin on stage, wearing a long black dress that made the Caravans seem Jezebels. Sweating profusely, Rosetta sat at the piano, cued her mother, and Mother Bell hollered, "There Was No Room at the Hotel." Rosetta is nothing if not a trouper.

Sister is no longer a household name. But she still travels in Europe ("Last time, I went with Muddy Waters. He say he wouldn't sing behind me because I made that 'Troubled in Mind' and 'Lonesome Road,' and he think I can outdo him. I tell him, 'Go ahead, boy, I ain't studying about no blues.' Lord we had a time"), and turned up at the Newport Folk Festival in 1967 ("I showed those children how you can play anything in gospel: blues, jazz, country and hillbilly"), garbed in unfolksy mink. She's even back on records now, and her first two Savoy LPs are splendid. One earned a Grammy nomination: "It's wonderful, but I don't like to brag."

However, the church provides her steady income. Russell Morrison is a crafty manager, and he has developed a route made up of small country towns where big-name singers never appear and where Rosetta's old records are still fondly remembered. "I sing way out in the country, out in Florida and Arkansas and Georgia. That's where they got that good, fresh food, right out of the ground. And the people are just so sweet to me. You know, they tell me, 'Rosetta, you singing better than ever.' I tell them my age, they don't believe me." It's not good money every night, but Rosetta's booked solid, and since she travels alone and provides her own music, she winds up one of the biggest earners in the church. Sure, it's a bit like singing in backwoods bars after headlining the Apollo. But Rosetta prefers it down-home and country. "I'm not particular about cities, I don't want no cities. Give me the country where the people are *real*."

In some ways Rosetta is singing better and deeper now than ever before. "I don't know, it's that seasoning, life'll give it to you. I just sing and the tears roll down my cheeks, and looks like the people shout everywhere. They even shouting off 'This Train.' You know I'm out here alone now, since Mama's gone, and I'll sing 'Mother left me standing out on the highway, wondering which way to go.' Oh yes." A few months ago, on a rainy afternoon, a subdued Rosetta sat musing on old times. Marie Knight, now a telephone operator in Brooklyn, had just called to tell her Ernestine Washington was in the hospital. This in turn reminded her of Mother Bell's funeral, and how "Ernestine Washington sang so pretty. But the one who tore up was that Marion Williams. That child got happy and started singing Mama's song, '99½ Won't Do,' all out into the street. The folks hollered and carried on like we had revival." It rained that day too—and Rosetta's momentary transport swings back to melancholy. "I just love those good gospel singers. I just sit and look at them, and I can

really feel what they're singing, how they have to struggle
and don't get nothing. I just look at them and I cry."

As a request, she demonstrates how she sings "I Looked
Down the Line." "If the spirit's high, I reach back and
sing the old verses

I went to the graveyard to see how far I was from God.
But the grave looked so sad and lonesome, sad and lone-
some, sad and lonesome,
The grave looked so sad and lonesome
To see how far I was from God."

Rosetta's voice sounds mighty sad and lonesome, but she
knows what she's doing. "Right then, I look all serious and
I sing, 'Then I cried to the Lord, Lord have mercy—' " and
she presses the words with fearful urgency. "That's when
the folks start screaming. We call that a Sister Fluke number," Rosetta grins, "for Sanctified folks who like to shout."
I ask her if she has theatrical ambitions. "Just give this old
girl a chance," she says, smiling.

Willie Mae Ford Smith is the greatest of the "anointed
singers," the ones who live by the spirit and sing to save
souls. Such singers carry themselves with a quality of dignity and religious privacy, as if they're always aware of
some special spiritual soundings. Willie Mae has taught
singers to croon and belt all the fatigue out of the stalest
hymns. In her grace and drama, she made gospel almost a
physical vocation. "I always did have emotional gestures.
You just move with the feeling, you sway with the feelings.
I'll sing with my hands, with my feet—when I got saved,
my feet got saved too—I believe we should use everything
we got." Other singers got rich following the route she
set up, but at eighty-one, Willie Mae lives in a senior citi-
zens' home and still regards herself as poor. "That's how
it always is for pioneers. The pathfinder usually gets some
rough, downtrodden weeds for his reward. That's all right,
I'm singing for Jesus. Anyway, I wasn't particular. There
was so much you had to do to get on wax. I sing for reality,

not for formality, and not for financial gain. I need money, I need money *bad*, but there's some money so dirty you hate to touch it."

As head of the Soloists Bureau of Dorsey's Gospel Convention, it was her task to demonstrate the appropriate style and delivery for the newer songs. She's a born teacher, warm and sympathetic to her students. A tall woman, with huge doe eyes and a massive bosom, she's pretty in a way one immediately recognizes as "churchy." Less eccentric than Sallie with her "skip-dip" or Mahalia with her "snake-hips," Willie Mae is evangelist, Sunday School teacher, "cultured" neo-concert singer, and gutsy blues shouter, rolled up in one. In the Sanctified church, they call her "Mother Smith," and she's that, too.

She was born in Rolling Fork, Mississippi, and raised in Memphis. "There were fourteen children. We were so poor our coats did double time as our blankets. We sometimes slept four in the bed, but we had so much happiness, so much love, so much fun. My father was a deacon, and now I can see he just kept us singing to keep from thinking." A railroad brakeman, Ford moved his family to St. Louis when Willie was twelve. Mrs. Ford opened a restaurant, and the girl quit school in the eighth grade to help run it. The Ford home was devoutly Baptist but "I sang everything I could sing, blues, reels, you name it, when Mama wasn't around." Ford formed a family quartet, and in 1922 the Ford Sisters crashed the National Baptist Convention with their arrangements of "Ezekiel Saw the Wheel" and "I'm in His Care." A few years later, after the sisters married, Willie Mae decided to sing alone. She had a high soprano and was contemplating a career in classical music when, in 1926, at a Baptist Convention, she heard Madame Artelia Hutchins of Detroit. "My God, how she sang 'Careless Soul, Why Do You Linger?' Now she wasn't too emotional, I was the one. When I knew anything, I was gone like a light, and she'd keep on anyhow. I knew then I had to be a gospel singer." She married a man with a general hauling business, and during the thirties she began traveling to supplement their income. A diplomatic organizer, she became a force in Baptist politics; for seventeen years acting as directress of the Education Department of the National Baptist Convention.

Inspired by Dorsey and Sallie Martin, she organized a St. Louis chapter. From the mid-thirties on, her solo recitals became a highlight of their Conventions, and for many years she has headed the Soloists Bureau. "If I wasn't the first to sing free, as long as the spirit told me, I don't know who was. I didn't hear anybody sing with a beat before me, either, not gospel *solo*." Each year, she instructed the singers gathered together in the new gospel style. Like a Sunday-school teacher, she began with kid stuff. To demonstrate that slurs and note bending fit any tunes, she performed many standard hymns, revised, rephrased, reconceived into whole new numbers. "I took 'Jesus Loves Me,' 'Throw Out the Lifeline,' songs they all thought was nothing. I told them it isn't the music or the words, it's the way you demonstrate it. I used strategy. I told them it's better to leave it alone, if you don't feel it so, just leave it to the kindergarten children. But you know, we're all just grownup children, and Jesus loves us too. If you just think about it, there's a whole lot of meaning in those simple songs." With Roberta Martin accompanying her, Willie Mae's approach galvanized the Conventions. "They went home, all over America, singing my arrangements like they were brand-new tunes." She sang that hoary old hymn "What a Friend We Have in Jesus" at a California convention and people threw hats and handbags out of the balconies. Even Roberta Martin picked up on "What a Friend," making it her best-known solo. She published the new arrangement, adding in small letters "as sung by Willie Mae Ford Smith of St. Louis," but Willie Mae didn't see a cent of royalties.

With her background and musical tastes, it was natural for Willie Mae to resemble Bessie Smith. (In fact, Thomas A. Dorsey feels the young Willie Mae could have surpassed Bessie.) In 1937 she tore up the Baptist Con-

vention with her own composition, "If You Just Keep
Still," a triumph of the gospel idiom. A sixteen-bar blues,
it opens with a depiction of Joshua in battle array, "a
sword in his right hand, a dagger by his side." As always,
Willie makes it plain for her followers, and the song moves
in a typical gospel leap to a "Christian blues" testimony.

> Sometimes I want to be in company,
> Then again Lord I want to be alone,
> When enemies press me hard,
> And confusion's all in my home.
> Sometimes I stand with folded arms,
> And the tears Lord come running down.
> Lord you said you'd fight my battles,
> If I just keep still.

The next step might have been blues, but in 1939, Willie
Mae joined the Church of God Apostolic ("We baptize in
the name of Jesus, period, not the Trinity"). "You know
I used to love to party, to dance and to sing. Count Basie,
Bessie Smith, Cab Calloway. Before I got saved, I used to
have a ball. I imagine I'd have gone into blues myself. It's
just, when I got saved, nothing interested me but serving
God. I'm not condemning anybody, it just wasn't for me."

By then, her style was set. Seductive croons would clash
with preacher roars. (Says Alex Bradford, "She'd weave a
spell, like a Morgana King, she'd just sing all in and around
a note.") Before each song, Willie Mae would "talk it up,"
setting the pace for the sermonettes gospel singers now
employ. Between her explications of the text and the demands of the spirit, Willie Mae could easily get a two-hour
concert out of ten songs, many years before John Coltrane
popularized the fifteen-minute solo.

Willie Mae had voice, spirit, and gumption. Excepting
Sallie, she was probably the first really hard-traveling singer.
Even Mahalia came later; when Willie Mae first heard her,
she was still selling her home-brewed ointments and
powders. "She often told me, 'Willie Mae, I'm gonna leave
this beauty shop, I wanna be like you.' I had her and Pro-

fessor Dorsey to my church, back in 1940. I liked her right
off, she was more like me, a mover and a go-getter." While
Sallie ripped it up with her skip-dip, and Mahalia provoked
the spirit with her "belly-dancing," Willie Mae relied on a
subtly induced sense of mystery. She was saved, sanctified,
and filled with the Holy Ghost, an ordained Evangelist, and
she let it show. "When I'm overcome, I lay hands on folk.
The Lord just anoints me while I'm singing. He didn't give
me the gifts of prophecy or healing, but he gave me a story
and a song. That's why I love to sing 'Blessed Assurance,'
because this is my story, I've got a song, just praising my
Saviour—" her voice is barely above a whisper—"and it's
all the day long." Those who attended her programs consider them some of the deepest experiences of their lives.
Showmanship didn't pertain here; she was a singing mes-
senger. "I never could go along with those folk who say I
shouted so and so many. When folk shout, I give it all to
God. I carry on for his honor. If they do it out of the message, then I'm grateful. . . . If God doesn't stand up, if
he isn't glorified, then I just don't do."

Like every gospel pioneer, Willie Mae sang for pennies.
She'd hold revivals and barely earn room and board, much
less carfare, "but I was happy because souls were blessed."
She gave generously of her talent. Unlike Mahalia touring
with Dorsey, Sallie busy with Martin and Morris publications, and the Roberta Martin Singers out selling Martin
Studio sheet music, she was obligated to no publisher. She
performed anybody's tunes, among them her pianist Abe
Windom's "Canaan," a gospel standard based "on an old
Scotch melody" (!) On her travels, she instructed and inspired a generation of soloists. While the group leaders
obviously benefited from their protégés' performances,
Willie Mae's impulses seemed genuinely altruistic. Her
pupils make up an honor roll of gospel talent. In 1938, she
traveled to Washington and performed at a Women's Club
tea. Edna Gallmon, the pastor's daughter, heard her sing
"What a Friend." Edna had planned a career in semiclassical music: "I was going to sing 'Trees,' but Willie Mae

performed with such *finesse,* I was inspired to be like her." Edna's voice was as lovely and petite as her miniature four feet eleven size (in later years she ballooned, but back then, they called her "The Sweetheart of the Potomac"). She obviously couldn't shout like Willie Mae. But her strong vibrato and intricate note bending were talented "mockings" of an older woman.

In Chicago, Willie Mae inspired another legend—Myrtle Scott. (The inspiration was more than musical. Both Edna and Myrtle followed Willie Mae into the Sanctified church.) Myrtle recorded only two sides with the Roberta Martin Singers, but many Chicagoans consider her their greatest singer. A beautiful jet-black woman, her approach is subdued and subtle, the softer side of Willie Mae. But . . . "If you don't watch out, Myrt'll make you hurt yourself." She stays out of sight during the year, except for a very rare program. Deloris Barrett says, "The church is always packed. Myrt gets up and sings one song, that's all. But the people can't stand it. She'll pick up her money, wave them goodbye, and the folks will be shouting like they didn't have no sense."

There were other great protégés. In St. Louis, Willie Mae trained Martha Bass, who later traveled with the Ward Singers during their golden period. In Huntington, West Virginia, she championed Goldia Haynes, a short, stout woman who combined Arizona Dranes's razor-sharp intensity with Willie Mae's control. But her most successful student was Brother Joe May. During the early forties, the young tenor would visit her after work in a chemical plant. The boy adored her, "So I carried him with me to New York and California." By 1950, his spectacular volume earned him the title "The Thunderbolt of the Middle West." His first discs, "Search Me Lord," "Old Ship of Zion," and "He'll Understand," were great performances. They were also note-for-note copies of Willie Mae's arrangements. Joe May had plenty of Pentecostal power on his own, but to some fans he was nothing but a poor man's Willie Mae. America didn't know this, and Willie Mae decided there was no need to record, what with Joe May making a fortune off her style.

So she shifted to Evangelical work. She still holds occasional revivals and performs annually at the anniversaries of her musical offspring. The voice is still mellow, though obviously not the instrument of twenty-five years ago. She seldom goes to programs any more. Two of her favorite singers, Queen C. Anderson and Edna Cooke, are dead. Her favorite groups, the Ward Singers and the Martin Singers have long split up, though she still admires their former leads, Marion Williams and Deloris Barrett Campbell. Most of the other singers strike her as copycats. "They're just suckers, suckin' up. It's like a smorgasbord, after you eat up all the salads, you got no place to put the meat. The thing that's gonna stick to your ribs, you pass it by." Sallie used almost the same metaphor, and like that other consecrated singer, Willie still tells the young, "Be original, be yourself."

Mahalia and Joe May became famous in a belting style Willie Mae introduced. She is not bitter. "I know who stepped in my way, I'm not calling any names. But God wouldn't have allowed it if he didn't want it that way." She has accepted the frustrations and gratuitous insults by almost doing away with ego. Others are not so lucky: "You got singers who think God is nobody, God's the giver and I'm the controller. We need to forget our little puny selves. Now everybody wants to be the mogul, the big star. But juggle the letters around and you got rats instead of stars." Stardom is nowhere—Mother Smith's obsession is soul saving. "I'd be willing to give my life to prove Jesus didn't *play*. He died that we might have freedom and peace, let's get him in the front and center of our will."

Almost fifty years a saint, Willie Mae's whole outlook is Pentecostal. Were she not so saved, she wouldn't have stirred so many churches. But she might also have fought harder, accepted less, become another Mahalia or Clara Ward. Her rewards are purely spiritual, and in the long run, they've proved good enough. She visited her old friend, Roberta Martin, during her last, fatal illness. Bert, of course, had all the business sense Willie Mae never bothered to cultivate. "We hadn't seen each other in years, and I didn't know she was so sick. But we had a very beautiful talk about heaven and getting ready to make this exit. She was quite encouraged about her soul. Yes, we talked about 'What a Friend,' and taking it all to Him. She became very excited and said, 'Why didn't you tell me before now about Holiness?' I had, so many times, but I guess it didn't sink in before. When I left, she said, 'Don't make it so long next time.' "

Willie Mae and Rosetta, so different, are both children of their church. Rosetta enjoys "mocking" Sanctified preachers: "I can holler like a man, tear up too," and most of her repertoire comes out of C.O.G.I.C. songbooks. A big leaner on nostalgia, she likes to sing "Bring Back Those Happy Days":

We healed the sick, we cared for the poor,
And we even raised the dead
We greeted each other with a holy kiss,
Lord bring back those happy days.

Conversely, Willie Mae believes in moving forward spiritually. So her speech is studded with images of process and education. For her, there's no nostalgia for simpler country days. "Religion's like school. With Holiness, you graduate to go to college. When I was converted, I consented there was a height. But I sought a higher height. That's how I found Holiness. I moved from one degree of God's blessing and power, and I found it's just sweeter as you go along." (Rosetta Tharpe died in October 1973. See postscript.)

13

The Crown Prince of Gospel:
James Cleveland

The sixth annual Gospel Singers Workshop Convention was a smashing success. Ten thousand gospel lovers attended, and, unlike the followers of Thomas A. Dorsey and R. H. Harris, the majority of these folk were young, very young, half under twenty. In the obligatory ecumenical gesture, the Workshop spotlighted a white group, J. D. Summers and the Stamps Quartet. But the headline attraction, the presiding genius, father and mother of the convention, was Reverend, Professor, the Crown Prince of Gospel, James Cleveland.

Cleveland, a heavy-set, garrulous man, oversaw everything with bulbous cow eyes. His gruff, unpretty voice—"they call me the Louis Armstrong of gospel—" functioned as imperiously as Gertrude Ward's or Sallie Martin's. Cleveland incarnated the Convention. All the young choir musicians with their way-out arrangements, their jazzy pianos and soul organs, owed their origins to Cleveland. His work had revolutionized the gospel sound, enabling them all to extend gospel's boundaries far beyond the limits of the Baptist hymnal. Now the choirs convened, singing his songs and arrangements, their leads echoing his semi-pop vocals. The man obviously loved them all. Naturally emotional, he shouted when the spirit ran high, encouraging the strong-voiced youths whose energy recalled his own. He also kept matters professional, limiting each choir to an allotted time span. "You got ten minutes," he told them, "so if you have to shout, shout in two." When his latest creation, the Southern California Community Choir, broke the Cleveland auditorium up, he tried to control them. But too many folk were shouting for even his mighty arms to contain. He wound up shouting along with them.

James likes to identify himself as "part Baptist, part Sanctified." He is the most important figure in modern gospel because he so exactly mediates between the two churches. Born in 1932, he came in at the tail end of gospel's second generation. He's old enough to have seen the greatest pioneers sing their hearts out, and he learned from all of them. Like his protégée Aretha Franklin, his style is a composite of other singers. He learned the essentials—how to build tension musically and emotionally. He added a gruff voice dappled with falsetto, resembling a more virile Bradford. The voice is loud and strong, and its very lack of conventional beauty makes it soulful. In the day of Ray Charles or James Brown, when voices are supposed to sound fractured and hard-pressed, Cleveland's harshness is exactly right. And meshing the eclectic phrasing and the raucous tones into a beautiful musical whole is Cleveland's sensational piano, the most influential since his idol Roberta Martin's. When he brought in the strong, clanking chords, the heavy pedal alternating with the limp, lyric right hand, he provoked dozens of vocalists to sing well. Until he realized the best accompaniment for the Cleveland chords was the Cleveland voice.

He was raised in Chicago. His parents were poor and his father worked on WPA projects. But "things were never *that* bad," the struggles weren't horror stories, and his parents always encouraged his musical career. He was a boy soprano at Pilgrim Baptist Church, whose minister of music was Thomas A. Dorsey. He was spellbound by Roberta Martin's piano. "My folks being just plain, every day people, we couldn't afford a piano. So I used to practice each night right there on the windowsill. I took those wedges and crevices and made me black and white keys. And, baby, I played just like Roberta. By the time I was in high school, I was some jazz pianist." There was a girl in the choir, Imogene Greene, a year younger, and when they were thirteen and twelve respectively, he introduced her singing Dorsey's "When the Gates Swing Open," while he played behind her. "My beautiful boy soprano just went haywire on me when my voice changed," so he employed others, like Imogene, to demonstrate his ideas. She later developed a sensuous, husky contralto, the sexiest in gospel, and had hit records with three groups—the Davis Sisters, the Caravans, and the Gospel All Stars—all the songs composed by "my brother in Christ, James Cleveland."

He wanted to sing anyhow. His idol among female singers was the legendary Myrtle Scott, of the Roberta Martin Singers. Cleveland also patterned himself after Eugene Smith, the group's narrator, manager, and baritone. Smith's voice wasn't lustrous either, but his irrepressible energy and spirit were dynamite in church. When happy, he'd bang podiums and stomp his feet, shaking the flimsier storefronts. Cleveland liked Smith's fervor. He also imitated another ex-Martin Singer, Robert Anderson. Anderson's husky, resonant baritone and immaculate phrasing inspired his nickname "the Bing Crosby of gospel." Anderson remembers, "When I used to sing, people would sit so still you could hear a pin drop." He could do more than croon; when he got into his magnificent composition "Prayer Changes Things," or his theme, "Something Within Me," he was a preeminent house wrecker. But it was his ballad capacities that inspired Cleveland to marry Anderson crooning and Smith flamboyance. Louis Armstrong taught the boy to sing beautifully with a homely voice, and the Queen of the Blues, Dinah Washington, clued him to the possible integration of gospel and blues sounds. After all, Dinah once sang lead with Sallie Martin, and years later told a *Down Beat* interviewer that her favorite gospel singer was Roberta Martin. For Cleveland, everything close to home fitted.

"James always did love the music," says a fellow Chicago singer. "But I can remember when folks paid him no mind. He'd just go to everybody, begging them to let him sing on their programs. Remember, we had some singers back then. The folks weren't particular about that boy. *Hmmm,* he was so skinny then, he'd go begging us all for food off our plate. It wasn't nothing to see James anywhere, out there hustling. But it paid off, didn't it?" In 1950, two Roberta Martin Singers, Norsalus McKissick and Bessie Folk, formed their own trio, the Gospelaires, with James as pianist and occasional third lead. The group was sensational, if short-lived, and the teen-age Cleveland had effectively become a Martin Singer. In the mid-fifties, he began composing tunes for Roberta. "I was so happy to have Bert record my material, I'd sell her stuff for a few dollars." His best tunes from the period, "Stand By Me," or "Saved," or "He's Using Me," show obvious debts to Dorsey and Bradford. They are simple and insistent, unlike the elaborate metaphysics of Reverend Brewster. What's new is the sheer funkiness. Cleveland took blues riffs for granted. His songs had more lilt than those of the other Chicago composers; they were lowdown, driving, and easy to learn. Likewise his arrangements of old spirituals, "It's Me O Lord," "Every Time I Feel the Spirit," "Old Time Religion" and "Walk in Jerusalem," were both rocking and stylized, virtually unrecognizable, thanks to the funky riffs he'd tack on the ending:

> *So I can walk, so I can talk,*
> *So I can sing, so I can shout,*
> *In Jerusalem just like John.*

Cleveland and Clara Ward were probably the best arrangers of the mid-fifties. Both benefited from being second-generation gospel children. Their parents struggled to bring the secular sound into gospel; they coasted from there.

In the mid-fifties, James joined the Caravans, who were led by the wonderful contralto Albertina Walker. Tina, always shy and modest, "a lazy singer," lets her other gifted singers star, and the group has produced a good dozen recording acts. Tina herself came out of Robert Anderson's group, and her phrasing, her special "yodel," a rolled note almost as elaborate as Sam Cooke's, still echo Anderson. Since Cleveland credited the same ancestry, the musical marriage was a happy one. As always, he was a great catalyst for a group. "James's arrangements will make you sing," says Tina. The ladies who sang while he stayed with the Vans, Cassietta George, Dorothy Norwood, Inez Andrews, Tina, and Imogene Greene, all learned something about pushing and plugging from the man. A typical Cleveland achievement was the Caravans' hit recording "The Solid Rock." James narrated the hymn in his hoarse, cracked, roughly epicene voice, while the Caravans sang in unison with great feeling. The contrast between their fervor and James's relaxed, consoling words, "We want you to be *encouraged* in knowing all other ground is sinking sand," was a gospel drama in itself. When James left his piano to lead the ladies in "The Old Time Religion," demonstrating the lines like a Dorothy Love or an Alex Bradford:

> *Give me that old time religion,*
> *Gets in your feet and makes you shout sometime*

he was Eugene Smith all over again, but a few inches taller and several pounds heavier. In the first Caravans studio pictures, James is skinny and glowing, all eyes. By the time he left, he had sprouted a moustache and a bulky, solid frame which in later years made him resemble a football halfback.

James got a reputation as a musical prodigy of uncertain temperament. He kept leaving and rejoining the Caravans, and he stayed briefly with some other groups, the Meditation Singers of Detroit and The Gospel All Stars of Brooklyn, N.Y. With the All Stars he recorded some good records, assisted by ever faithful Imogene Greene, who cut a classic record of Cleveland's "Every Now and Then" with the Brooklyn ladies. His best disc of the period, "Lord Remember Me," is a soft, intense vocal reminiscent of Robert Anderson. The song was then thirty years old, but he slowed it down to a virtually beatless ballad filled with poignant ad libs: "I'm a motherless child, Lord remember me." Imogene softly answered him in the background. Years later this sort of verbal echo became predictable melodrama, but then it was fresh and sweet and really suggested a communion between the two. Cleveland also cut Ray Charles's "Hallelujah I Love Her So" in 1959, an early acknowledgment by gospel singers that two could play at the same game. Another All Stars recording was the old spiritual "Meeting Tonight," with Cleveland contributing the solid, driving piano and narration: "We used to go to a meeting a long time ago, and being children, we'd ask, Mother, Mother, where are we going? and Mother would look down at us with compassion in her eye and say . . ."; then the patronizing Sunday-school teacher's voice is replaced by medium-soft growls, "We're gonna have a meeting," and the All Stars' high-pitched bluesy wailing, "Meeting tonight."

Cleveland became the architect of the strong, pushing gospel sound. Singers began revering him—"James has the worst voice I know and he does more with it than anyone else out there—" but he kept floundering from group to group. His hippest was the Gospel Chimes, a Chicago group featuring Dorothy Norwood and later the ubiquitous Imogene, as well as three strong-voiced young men, Lee Charles (now a soul singer), Claude Timmons (the best group tenor in gospel) and Jessy Dixon. Jessy and James sang alike, they both phrased in a modern, quasi-pop manner on ballads and roared and leaped like possessed men on shouts. Both men moonlighted as choir leaders, and the harmonies they arranged for the Chimes mediated between 1950s gospel groups and the nascent choir sounds. James burst forth more dramatically than ever. With the Chimes, he developed a routine he still employs. After singing a song soulfully and medium tempo, he'll turn around and say, "You know we belong to a Sanctified church. And if we were home, we'd probably sing it like this," and go into a rocking Holiness shout.

James's physical image became as stylized and distinctive as his singing. When moved by something, the spirit, a well-phrased line, a high note by any of the male sopranos he likes to feature, he'll rub his head and make a pained face, moaning "Ooooh." It's a spirited, orgasmic kind of pain, and if it continues, he'll bang his feet like old Gene Smith. When he shouts, he tends to turn in position, take a few backward steps, then kick forth with Holy Ghost abandon. As he became the leading figure in gospel, a whole slew of singers and preachers began dancing and moaning and rubbing like him. Since shouting is supposedly a release of self, such imitation proved the sincerest, most unconscious flattery.

In 1960, Cleveland simultaneously ushered in the decade and the modern gospel sound. He recorded a Soul Stirrers tune, "The Love of God," with a progressive Detroit choir, the Voices of Tabernacle. The Voices were the most musically disciplined gospel choir ever. Their director, Charles Craig, was as experienced as Cleveland; their pianist, Herbert Pickard was formerly the accompanist for Dorothy Love. The song itself was a pedestrian pop ballad; Cleveland crooned, and the Voices made like the Mormon Tabernacle Choir. But apparently the discipline and Cleveland's spirit were what gospel needed. "The Love of God" was a smash hit, and he became, after years of struggling, a major gospel attraction.

The choir directors began copying his weird time signatures. The back-home choruses used to hymns and Dorsey retired from the spotlight, and young peoples' choirs that could keep up with Cleveland's changes became the rage. James returned to the Apollo with the Gospel All Stars in spring 1960. He had never been so intense or worked so hard. When the disc jockey Fred Barr said, "Faith is a wonderful thing. James came here with the flu, but he's been able to sing anyhow," James rushed to the mike, hollering "The Love of God" with an emphatic power the record barely suggested. The last night, Albertina and the Caravans, then the top group in gospel, stopped by. James began testifying, "God's a wonder worker. When I look back sixteen years ago . . . I went to a church one night, I wasn't nothing but a poor boy wearing tennis sneakers. I'm glad Albertina's here because she knows what I'm talking about." It was a rare moment in gospel, the two great artists getting happy together over their journey thus far. As Cleveland called her name, Tina began chuckling to herself, what saints call the holy laugh, oh yes she knew.

Cleveland signed with Savoy Records. His first releases with the All Stars and the Chimes sold respectably. Then Fred Mendelsohn, Savoy's artist and repertoire man, decided to combine James with the Angelic Choir of Nutley, New Jersey, a moderately gifted local choir that needed a hit. Cleveland by now had his own group, the Cleveland Singers, featuring on organ Billy Preston, a child prodigy who played the boy W. C. Handy in *St. Louis Blues,* and later went on to stints with Ray Charles and the Beatles. On his second album with the Angelic Choir, Cleveland featured Billy playing "How Great Thou Art" while he himself recited the words with a relaxed fervor that left the congregation in fits. He had found his proper groove. Preaching, chanting, singing, he dominated everything, aware of the tough musical demands of his arrangements, yet constantly responsive to the emotional requirements of the moment. The choir left much to be desired, but Cleveland orchestrated things so brilliantly that the first three albums (he's recorded ten with them by now) really are the best documents of church services on record.

In that second album, he leads the choir on the old hymn
"Remember Me." His introduction cites the thief on the
cross. "I love God today because when they looked in the
grave He wasn't there, and that makes me know He's all
right." The choir sings the chorus softly, then James steps
in, singing the verse of "Father I Stretch My Hands to
Thee." He solos with immense passion. His very first word,
"Father," is so dramatic that he moans in falsetto,
"Whoooh," then softly growls, "Thank God" and continues:

> Fa-a-ather . . . whoo, thank God . . . Father, I *stretch*
> [again the spirit's too much for him] yes . . . *suh* . . .
> my *hands* (thank God), I stretch my hand to thee,
> *hmmmmmm*, no other help, *Whah!* no other help, O
> thank you Jesus [modest, almost apologetic] no other
> help I know, O thank you Jesus, O thank you Jesus, O
> thank you Jesus.

> And the reason I call you like this, cause if thou . . .
> aw, if thou withdraw . . . somebody know what I'm
> singing about, thy *self a*way . . . away from me, thank
> you Jesus, I don't know where, I don't know where, I
> don't know where, I don't know where, I don'tknow-
> whereIdon'tknowwhere, *whoo*, Thank God . . .

By now, Billy Preston's played the tune, but spirit or no,
Cleveland captures the underside of the beat and makes it
home safe, "I don't know where I'd go." Then he begins
reciting, the heartbreakingly fervent chanting replaced by
matter-of-fact preaching, "You ought to hear me sometimes, late at the midnight hour, I get out of bed on my
knees, and real quietly I say . . ." and he starts whispering, "Remember Me O Lord," while the choir sings softly.
The control is as awesome as the passion.

Cleveland's third album with the Angelic Choir made
gospel history. The title selection, "Peace Be Still," was, of
all things, an eighteenth-century madrigal filled with archaic diction and imagery:

Master, the tempest is raging,
The billows are tossing high.
The sky is o'ershadowed with blackness,
No shelter or hope is nigh.
Carest thou not that we perish?
How can thou lie asleep?
When it seems each moment is threatening
A grave in the angry deep.

Cleveland solos the verse, and his initial "Master" is a
stabbing growl that translates madrigal into gospel shout.
After the verse, he chants "Get up Jesus because," and
the choir sings:

The winds and the waves shall obey thy will
Peace be still, peace be still,
Whether the wrath of the storm-tossed sea
Or demons or men or whatever it be.
No water can swallow the ship where lies
The master of ocean and earth and skies.
They all shall sweetly obey thy will,
Peace, peace be still.

Each line moves progressively higher, till "The master of
ocean and earth and sky" booms a solid octave over "the
winds and the waves." It's a lovely tune—the choir hits
their notes, and Cleveland is commanding, as always.
None of these reasons fully explains the record's success.
"Peace Be Still" has sold over 800,000 albums to an exclusively black gospel audience. No record ever, neither Bing
Crosby's "White Christmas" nor the Beatles' "Abbey
Road," has so blanketed its market. With "Peace Be Still,"
Cleveland became the most important gospel figure since
Mahalia Jackson. His next hit with the Angelic Choir was
an old gospel hymn, "Stood on the Banks of Jordan," once
featured by his old idol, Myrtle Scott. The record begins
in mid-spirit with Cleveland softly grunting, "Lord help us
tonight," while members of the audience shout, scream,
and holy-laugh "Mymymy."

In gospel, where five thousand copies confers hit status, virtually all Cleveland releases sell at least 25,000 albums. "Savoy's recorded me every which way." In the eighties alone he has cut hits with the Charles Fold Singers of Cincinnati; the Salem Inspirational Choir of Omaha, and the Southern California Choir; facilitated the comebacks of Albertina Walker and Cassietta George of the Caravans, and even recorded brilliantly with an L.A. quartet, the Gospel Cavaliers. He cut two sermons, "God Is Not Dead" and "God's Promise," and three albums of solos. "I'm no soloist," he always apologizes, but some of his best performances are the solo verses between choir choruses. The first album of solos was dedicated to his mother. After performing her favorite hymn, "It's Real," he collapsed in tears. Savoy's Fred Mendelsohn remembers, "We just left him alone. He kept crying for half an hour. If you listen carefully on the record, you can hear him start."

Cleveland found himself in a new position now. With all his other groups, he'd been catalyst, architect, promoter, not to mention arranger and accompanist, but essentially the *éminence grise*. Now he was the star, and for once he had to do all the singing. His backgrounds were uniformly superior. As a contrast to his husky baritone, he employs male sopranos. Not since the era of the castrati have there been such high-voiced male chorales. Roger Roberts was the group's mascot for years with his boyish, Sanctified showmanship and his Fs above high C; Ms. Cleo Kennedy now sings coloratura for the group. Odessa McCastle, alto, Clyde Moultry, baritone, and the pianist, Charles Barnett (baritone or mezzo-soprano, depending on the harmonic demands), have stayed with James for over five years. The other singers come and go; briefly he featured a Spanish-American Pentecostal, Gene Viale, in gospel's first gesture of integration. As should be clear, such supporting artists are compelling novelties. The major responsibility belongs to James, and he leads at least 80 percent of the selections.

At his most authoritative, in the mid-sixties, Cleveland developed a routine that left them rolling in the aisles. He has a standard patter he affixes to most of his tunes, no matter which tempo:

> *He'll pick you up, turn you around,*
> *Place your feet on higher ground.*
> *It's no secret what God can do,*
> *He'll bless your neighbor, then bless you too.*
> *One day I woke up, I had no food on my table,*
> *But the God I serve, I know he's able.*

(The latter couplet earned him the title "Knife and Fork King" in some cynical quarters.) He rearranged "Peace Be Still" so that the group would moan "Peace" precisely before and after each rhyme. The voice, the beat, the high harmonies, the words, all worked together to set houses up. Then he'd say, "I'd like all the witness, the sure-nuff born-again Christians to get up and shake my hands," and start rocking a triumphant shout, "To the Utmost Jesus Saves" or "Give Me Two Wings to Veil My Face." One time in Boston, I saw sixty people shaking hands and dancing, dancing and shaking hands, shaking hands between steps, as Cleveland roared over them like a latter-day Daddy Grace.

He was absolute ruler of gospel. *Ebony* wrote an article about his successes, his sensational contract with Savoy guaranteeing him over $20,000 a year, his extravagant home "filled with things I went right downtown and picked out myself," including a Czechoslovakian crystal chandelier, rooms luminescent with red wallpaper, and closets packed with one hundred suits, fifty pairs of shoes and a Persian lamb overcoat ("I had it made by the best furrier in Chicago"). He cut the wretched "Without a Song" in a pop-gospel style that briefly hit *Billboard*'s Hot 100. He even headlined Paris' Olympia Theatre where they billed him "Papa James Cleveland," like a gospel pope.

But Europe didn't accept him well. "I'm really not this kind of singer," he said, while his co-star, Miss Liza Minnelli, belted out her strained imitations of Mama. "Without a Song" left them cold, and the male sopranos' "Lord's Prayer" provoked a flood of titters. Cleveland returned home to discover his musical imitators lording it over their respective turfs. His protégé Jessy Dixon was being set up as "Crown Prince in Succession" by promoters unwilling to pay Cleveland's high fees (up to two thousand dollars). New choir directors like Dixon and Mattie Moss Clark and J. C. White and, most especially, Edwin Hawkins, began turning out progressive arrangements and compositions. Cleveland was frankly tired. Obviously never turned on by the Angelic Choir, he cut several releases with them that were downright mediocre.

"That's all right," Dorothy Love said. She too has been derided for her shot, shabby voice, and people are always laying bets that her fantastic drive will exhaust itself. "Just give James some new inspiration. You're talking about a dedicated artist there. Why, if James lost it all today, that mansion and those bank accounts, he'd be out there tomorrow finding some church choir to play for." In 1969 he helped organize the Southern California Community Choir, a disciplined and adventurous group. Their president is Annette May, daughter of Brother Joe May, the "Thunderbolt of the Middle West," the musical son of Willie Mae Ford Smith and the most powerful male soloist in a day when gospel singers had the greatest voices in America. His favorite modern singers are the O'Neal Twins, two gargantuan baritones from Willie Mae Ford Smith's St. Louis. The blend of progressive musicians and foursquare gospel veterans has always incited his imagination. His albums with the choir and the Gospel Girls (Annette May and two other choir soloists) are his best in years. Once again, he's breaking the 50,000 mark with his releases.

And then there's the Gospel Singers Workshop Convention. Cleveland is in charge and obviously delighted to be surrounded by the brightest young gospel musicians. "Some of them knock me, I know that, but they know I opened the doors for them." When he arrives anywhere, at the Convention, at his programs, sometimes even at church, the audience rises for him. He smiles, thrilled and a bit awkward before the acclaim—no Alex Bradford he. In Philadelphia, when disc jockey Mary Mason calls the saints gathered in the old Metropolitan Opera building to rise, he looks sheepishly, happily out at them. He speaks in the cracked, rasping manner, both fluent and stumbling, that still suggests uncertainty and even modesty. "And now America's greatest choir, the fabulous Victory Choral Ensemble." What a gracious, self-effacing introduction from the Crown Prince.

Cleveland can out-sing Ray Charles and the rest of the pop competition just as Marion Williams, Dorothy Love, Bessie Griffin, and Deloris Barrett Campbell can beat all their peers in blues. But for all his obvious affection for worldly music ("I like singers who tell a story. Joe Simon's my man"), one can't imagine Cleveland in pop. He's a gospel baby, still the delivery boy for Mahalia and the pupil of Roberta Martin and the teen-age worshipper of Myrtle Scott and Robert Anderson and the accompanist for Norsalus McKissick and Albertina Walker and the trainer of Aretha Franklin. He appeared recently on Della Reese's TV program singing "God Bless America" and proving once more that conventional entertainment is not his metier. Even in church, his showmanship, compounded of routines and gimmicks, can bomb—which is why singers always say he's dropping out—unless he's inspired. Then everything works. "There's something that happens when the saints of God get together," he said once at the Apollo Theatre, and even his old rival Alex Bradford felt the vibrations, waving his hands slowly to acknowledge the spirit.

Cleveland is the soul man, the first to really wed gospel and pop. Give him his Roberta Martin chords and he'll meet the world halfway. In spring 1970, he performed before a group of black militant students at Berkeley. Cleveland himself sports an Afro hair style but has always retreated from political involvement (witness "God Bless America"). Today, however, he knew his audience. As he accompanied himself with thunderous, mildly atonal chords, he told the kids, "We have an old saying in our church. We wonder if you'd help us with it. We say Amen. Can you say Amen? . . . That's it. Can you say it again? . . . Can you say it again? *Right on!*"

14

"I've Been Way Out on the Stormy Raging Sea": Marion Williams

Ooooh, *oooh* . . . *Whah,* mmm-*hmm,* Lord . . . We take so *much* for granted. We think we're out here on our *own,* we don't *know* we've got a God above, waking us *up* in the morning—child . . . *Whah,* let your feet land on your side of the *bed,* you ought to thank him for that . . . Yes Lord . . . uh huh . . . then when I feel I got the . . . activity of my limbs . . . *hah* . . . I say Thank you Lord, thank you Lord, thank you Lord . . . hmmm . . . *hey* . . . when I walk down the street, let me tell you, and I see . . . somebody that's blind . . . let me tell you, I wipe out the corner of my eyes, looks good, hah . . . thank the Lord for my *sight* . . . Thank you Lord, I thank you, thank you Lord . . . oooh-*oooh,* my, my . . . then when I can open my big mouth . . . and I can talk awhile and I can sing aloud . . . *whoa,* cause we got so many out here can't even *talk* . . . sure nuff . . . I say thank you Lord . . . hey, hey . . . thank you Lord for all you've done for me.

Marion Williams will testify anywhere. She spoke these words in a Boston church after singing "How I Got Over."

Each phrase attached itself to the beat that pulsed from her to the piano to the hand-clapping saints and back again to Marion. Her style is to respond to the moment, giving of herself as "God gives it to me." So she defines and reconciles her twin dispositions, for she is both a modest saint, saved, sanctified and filled with the Holy Ghost, and an overwhelming showman who has delighted audiences in Europe, Africa, and dozens of American colleges. The two impulses, retiring and flamboyant, aren't always balanced, but when spirit and style converge, the result is unparalleled. Marion is simply the most lyrical and imaginative singer gospel has produced. When she's right, she seems to move effortlessly into improvised musical structures where the most special demands of time, melody, and phrasing arise out of the moment. Each "spirit-filled" performance proposes a new arrangement, each exactly suited to itself, and demonstrably different from the one before. (As with some great *a cappella* quartets, the actual lyrical procedure assumes a musical interest comparable to the most lustrous and coherent jazz improvisations.)

Hers is thrilling musicianship, but it expresses a *gospel* talent, formed from the grit and mire of gospel soil. Which is why some recent attempts to wed her style to the psychedelic tropes of folk-rock usually backfire. Marion can relate to anyone's suffering, but trouble for her is spelled bills, racism, and back-stabbing colleagues, not metaphysical *angst*. If she's saved to the utmost, she's also as worldly as any other gospel singer. And that means pretty worldly. She's a fat sweet-faced woman whose physical graces belie her size. When she sings, she may strut, run, Suzy-Q, sashay, sit, or kneel, and she can sing softly in a way that evokes erotic goose-bumps. "The folks always said I sing sexy." She's out to save whom she can, but "I live in this world too, this is my home." So she'll tell a young friend suddenly enriched, "Don't hold on to that change, child. When you're dead, you're *done*. Your features will turn to ashes and your fine clothes will decay off your body—spend that money!"

In her travels she's received some spectacular notices. "You know how I feel when I read that stuff? Like a real fool." She seldom volunteers the success of a program; "It was nice," she says. Someone else must mention the four standing ovations. If people shout, she doesn't say she tore up; rather, "The Lord really blessed." So that night in Boston was very special as she testified, broadcasting in words what her singing usually implies. The wordless moans and song-chants effectively turned her testimony, abetted by the driving beat, into a new song.

Thank the Lord . . . he's done so *much* for me . . . Marion's got a lot to be *thankful* for . . . God has brought me from a long way . . . when I think about it, the time that I used to work in a laundry from sunup to sundown . . . *good* God almighty . . . when I look down from where God has brought me from . . . I say thank you Lord, hey, *hey,* good God almighty, thank you Jesus . . . Then God brought me from there . . . heh heh . . . and I went to Phila*del*phia to visit my sister . . . then I went to hear the *Ward* Singers . . . *hah,* they called me to sing that night . . . *hmmm,* when I got through Miss Ward and Clara was right there, children, saying Marion we want you . . . hah . . . Lord have mercy . . . this little barefeet girl come from Florida . . . oooh Lord . . . this *known* group, *nationally* known group wanted me to sing with them . . . yeah, I didn't tell them right there I would . . . I said, you know we get big sometimes, hah, try to be grand . . . I'll let you know . . . it was a year after that, I wrote them, I said yeah I think I want to join you . . . and they came to Florida to get me.

Marion was born in Miami in 1927. Her father was a West Indian who worked as a butcher during the week and gave music lessons on weekends. Her mother was a South Carolina saint. "You would have loved my mother. I can't speak well, never could, but my mother . . . child, you

talk about a prayer warrior, what you say. She used to go
from fence to fence, spreading the good news. She kept
me saved, I didn't go to the movies till I was nineteen."
Williams died when Marion was nine. "After that, we were
poor as Job's turkey. I quit school in the ninth grade to
help support my mother." Mrs. Williams was a diabetic
who eventually had both legs amputated. Marion worked
as a maid and child nurse. Her hands are still lye-wrinkled
from working in a laundry "from sunup to sundown. I
didn't see the sun for days at a time."

On weekends, she sang in church and street-corner revivals. On those streets she heard all the indigenous sounds
of the Miami ghetto—blues, calypso, and gospel. By her
teens, she was the queen of Miami soloists. Her beautiful
high soprano distinguished her from the other shouters.
But Marion could drop from falsetto into "that Sanctified
twine. We all got it, Rosetta, Ernestine Washington, it's
just in the church." If Marion had any inspirations outside
of the church, they were the great traveling quartets. "The
Kings of Harmony. Boy, they were some bad men to hit a
stage. I tell you, their arrangements were something else.
And you talk about singing a Dr. Watts hymn." All the
early quartets swear by the Kings; less known are Marion's
other early favorites, the Smith Jubilee Singers. "Professor
Smith could just sing for me. I was so taken that I followed
them to their hotel after the program." She laughs. "I
didn't mean no dirt, I just had to see them close, they were
that tough." (Smith's wife Genessee was another Willie
Mae Ford Smith protégée. Smith himself trained many
great quartet singers, including James Walker, the second
lead of the Dixie Hummingbirds.)

Marion had offers from the start to sing everything from
opera to blues. But her great ambition was to become a
traveling gospel singer. Clara and Gertrude Ward instantly
recognized her potential. Marion, in turn, stood in awe of
the Wards. "Clara could sing a hymn better than anyone
out there, and just tear up that piano."

God stuck with me through *that* . . . yes Lord . . . let
me tell you, it wasn't easy always . . . but I stayed there
eleven years . . . God blessed me there, every hit record they had, I was *leading* on . . . *Hah, whoa!*

At once she established herself as the group's star. Initially she sold the Wards with her Miami solos, Dorsey's
"What Could I Do" and "Live the Life I Sing About,"
and her immense, irresistible smile: "I'm not much as a
singer but the folks always liked to see me smile. Fred Barr,
a disc jockey in New York, was the first to call me 'Miss
Personality.'" In 1948 the Ward Singers began recording
for Savoy. "My records never sounded right to me. I was
always nervous or hoarse." Her first record, Brewster's
"How Far Am I from Canaan," was a solo. The phrasing
is subtle and poignant, the voice a bit sharp and piercing.
"Canaan" was better in person—"I used to have to sing it
three times a day—" and the legend goes that benchloads
of saints would fall out during the performance. The number that turned everyone around was another Brewster
tune, "Surely God Is Able." "I begged Clara to let me cut
that. Finally she gave me a verse on the record." That
verse made the record, and "Surely" made the Ward
Singers.

There's never been a gospel hit like "Surely God Is
Able." Sung to a waltz tempo, combining testimony and
affirmation, it could stir any church audience. After Clara's
introductory verse, Marion would come in, syncopating:

> *Don't you know God is able, he's able, he's able,*
> *God is able.*
> *He'll be your friend when you're friendless,*
> *He's a mother for the motherless,*
> *He's a father for the fatherless.*
> *He's your joy when you're in sorrow,*
> *He's your hope for tomorrow.*
> *When you come down to the Jordan,*
> *He'll be there to bear your burden.*
> *He's gonna step down before you,*

In the judgment, he's got to know you.
Well surely, surely, surely, surely
He's able to carry you through.

Marion's "Surelys" were the most terrifying blast out of
gospel in the fifties. "We came to Chicago, and nothing
seemed to move the people. Then I sang 'Surely,' and I
guess the Lord must have touched me. I started running,
hollering 'Surely.' One lady threw her pocketbook at me
and fell out, and a moment later, there were ten others.
After that, you couldn't get a seat at our programs."
"Surely" may be the biggest shout number of all time.
Night after night, Marion wailed the tune, and others
equally as hard.

Her versatility helped make the group the biggest draws
in gospel. "I liked the way Marion hit all those high notes
in the background, and then came in with that heavy quartet lead," says one singer. Two of her best records with the
Ward Singers, "Take Your Burdens to the Lord" and "I
Know It Was the Lord," are sublime marriages of gospel
and quartet. Marion makes her high notes, but rumbles
down to a gravelly preacher voice in her own extra verse
to Tindley's "Burdens."

You trust him in the midnight,
You trust him in the day,
Friends may talk about you, but trust God anyway,
In the midnight hour, the sweat is on your brow,
You sometimes feel discouraged, but trust God anyhow.

In true country style, Marion scatters her blue notes everywhere, on first, last, and middle words; her reading of "anyway" and "anyhow," squalled from the furthest reaches
of her throat, is seraphic funk. On "I Know It Was the
Lord," her survey of God's peripatetic powers

> *Who do you think was in the furnace door*
> *With Shadrach, Meshach, and Abednego,*
> *Who took the heat from out of the flame,*
> *I know it was the Lord, praise his holy name.*

ends with the answer, "Jesus," sung in a floating, high falsetto that gave one Baltimore fan a nervous rash.

Marion's invention and showmanship were complemented by a special sense of humor. When, for example, she sang "Surely," she sometimes sat on people's laps. "I never used my full weight, so people always were surprised how light I seemed." It takes some discipline to sing that hard, while people are fainting all about one, and still control one's thigh muscles! During "Weeping May Endure for a Night," another Brewster composition, she might solo for fifteen minutes. Jessy Dixon remembers, "Marion used to just hold this note and walk down the aisle, all round the church. The people would be crawling the walls." In 1957, she cut her second-biggest hit, "Packin' Up." The song has plenty of high notes and low growls, but everyone remembers best Marion's demonstrations of packing up. "Most folks didn't mind if I took their pocketbooks and coats. But one lady just kept struggling with me: 'You ain't gonna take my stuff, you Ward Singer!'" Another time, in Charleston, Marion packed up a man's briefcase and a pistol fell out. "I guess he felt like watching as well as praying."

In 1958, Marion left the Ward Singers, having given them eleven years of spiritual labor. "I used to work so hard I got nervous spells. Sometimes when we'd be riding, I'd just holler and yell. That's why I don't like making so many high notes, they'll go to your head." But as everyone on the road knew, Marion and the other Ward Singers —Frances Steadman, Kitty Parham, and Henrietta Waddy —were on salary. No group ever made money like the Wards, and the bulk went to the family. So Marion and the others split and formed their own group, the Stars of Faith. Nine years later, Marion rejoined the Wards for a night. Clara had just recovered from her stroke, and Gertrude and Clara came to testify at a Philadelphia church. Mama Ward called all the ex-Ward Singers to the altar. Clara began playing "Surely" and Marion sang. Philadelphia shouted as it hadn't shouted in years. Mother Ward ran up to Marion, beating her on the back. The spirit might have been too much for her, or maybe she was deploring ten years without her favorite disciple. Marion remains loyal to the group. When someone complains that they grew rich off her singing, she says "That's all right. If it wasn't for Gertrude Ward, I'd be taking care of somebody's children, and singing on Sundays. And," nodding emphatically, "Miss Ward's got spirit, that old South Carolina way about her, even if they do carry on in the clubs."

> So I went on . . . formed the Stars of Faith . . . took them under my wing . . . then I heard from somebody . . . let me tell you what *God* can do . . . God can put you *on people's minds* . . . aw, yeah . . . he know how to work miracles . . . yessuh . . . he *know* what to do . . . and I got with Mr. Kramer . . . and he wanted me to sing solos then . . . and I said you take me, you take my group . . . and through Mr. Kramer, we went with Barbara Griner and Michael Santangelo into *Black Nativity* . . . you know we had a time . . . we toured Europe for three years, and we thanked God for that. . . .

The first years with the Stars of Faith were very hard. None of them had Gertrude Ward's managerial capacities; in the wings, Clara and Mama would smile, "I told you so." Marion composed a few good songs based on old Sanctified shouts, like "Holy Ghost Don't Leave Me" and "We Shall Be Changed," but she is no Brewster. Her arrangements beautifully explored the possibilities of female harmony. But the one thing the people wanted, she refused to do—"I'm not gonna kill myself like I did with the Wards—" and she let the other singers, the handsome, leaping shouter Kitty Parham, and Frances Steadman, a tasteful and inventive contralto, do the deeper numbers. It didn't work. "Listen," said another female singer, "when Marion was with Clara, I never knew a woman to sing with so much soul. But this stuff here ain't nothin' but jivin'."

Then, in 1961, Marion "met Jesus again. I'd strayed while I'd been with the Ward Singers. I felt what I was singing, but I didn't live right. Now I'm living to live again, and I just believe God's gonna bless me." Gary Kramer, a musical scholar and producer, decided she had the greatest native musical talent he'd encountered in black music. Inspired by her imaginative Christmas album, he commissioned *Black Nativity,* a gospel musical with script by Langston Hughes. Barbara Griner and Michael Santangelo later took over the production. With *Black Nativity,* Marion was back swinging. Her rocking arrangement of Christmas carols and spirituals became the show's trademark. In its first few weeks off Broadway, Marion, the Stars of Faith, and Alex Bradford sang harder than they had in years. "Alex and I wasn't doing much in church. We knew this was our big chance, and we'd better sing."

In act one, Marion wailed the old spiritual "No Room at the Hotel" in a down-home, bluesy manner that convinced Frances Steadman "if Marion ever sang blues, she'd beat everyone." Her face would contort with the agony of childbirth; it was almost too much feeling for downtowners to absorb, so the big hit of the night was "When Was Jesus Born," in which Marion asked the Stars of Faith, "Was it January, February, March, April, May," etc., up to "September, October, November, the twenty-fifth day of December, the last month of the year." She still had her old Ward Singer ponytail that lashed the wind symmetrically as she turned from Frances to Kitty for an answer. The song was a showstopper, though its essential silliness alarmed some fans. They feared Marion could slide too easily into the "clowning" bag. The second act, a straight gospel concert, featured Marion on "Packin' Up" alone. Though *Black Nativity* carried her all over Europe, it scarcely expanded her repertoire.

The church came to her rescue. All during the trips to Europe, Marion remained a saved witness. "Some of them might be doing everything they're old enough to do," says Frances Steadman, "but Marion stays in her room, read-

ing her Bible or singing." The gospel fans began joking,
"They tell me that child lives in the Lord." From group
singing, Marion turned increasingly to solos. Her musical
imagination had reached a pitch where no group, not even
the Stars, could keep up with her. And the more saved she
got, the more unpredictable became her improvisations. In
church, Marion sang solo with the fire of Ward Singers
days. The two songs that fit her mood best were "It's Real"
and a revived "Live the Life I Sing About in My Song."
The first described her spiritual progress:

> *When at last by faith I touched him,*
> *Then like sparks from smitten steel,*
> *Just so quickly salvation reached me,*
> *And bless God today, I know it's real.*

Not even Clara Ward could read a hymn lyric so eloquently, and phrase "just so quickly" with such uncanny,
split-second precision. "Live the Life I Sing About," Dorsey's great gospel blues, suited Marion's new stance as a
singing evangelist. "I can't go to church, shout all day Sunday," Marion sings, then throws in the old country expression "slip around . . . and get drunk and raise *hell* all day
Monday." Back in Florida, "folks had fits when I'd holler
out hell," and for very different reasons, so did the world.

> Mmmm . . . *hmmm,* mymymy . . . and then I went
> on, and God blessed me with my home, and I thank him
> for that . . . It may not be what you think it should be
> . . . but I thank God that he gave it to me . . . I got a
> roof over my head, thank you Lord . . . I'm not *brag-
> gin'*, children, just thankin' God. . . .

Marion sits in her small, close-fitting living room in the
long quarter of attached homes where Rosetta Tharpe and
Frances Steadman also live. The furniture is French Provincial modern, quite fancy and securely under plastic. "I
notice white folks like things plain. But that ain't my style.
If you knew where I came from, a little two-room shack,
child, you'd know why I thank God for my home."

Oooh *Lord* . . . then I thought about it . . . I think I better get out here on my own . . . different ones had been telling me, Marion *why* don't you sing solo . . . you know I don't like for nobody to rush me into nothin' . . . I like to take my *time*, think about it . . . yes Lord . . . aaah . . . but . . . hah hah, when this one was pressing me on *this* side . . . and this one piercing me on *that* . . . *whoa*, that let me help me make up my *mind*, sure nuff . . . thank you Lord . . . I started singing for myself. . . .

In 1965, Marion and the Stars of Faith parted company. (Led by Frances Steadman, the group still travels a good quarter of the year in Europe.) She returned to Europe for an unsuccessful tour in a new play and came back penniless when her mother died. "I felt so bad my mother dying and me so far away. But you know, at the funeral, this lady got up and told me and my sister and brother not to grieve, because my mother had lived the life. And it came to me then my mother had finally made it in—you don't know what I'm talkin' about. I felt so good I started singin' Mama's favorite song, 'O Jesus Let Me Ride.' It was like a revival, we had *good* church. Baby, I shouted at my mother's funeral." With all that spirit, Marion had no trouble adjusting to her new role as soloist. If anything, her naturally stubborn spirit, rendered suspicious by years of group singing, began to relax. "I know I'm nicer because I don't have so many worries. I'd rather drink muddy water and sleep in a hollow log than sing with another group of women."

She gave her first solo concert at Yale and quickly proved she was the old Marion. In "Don't Forget the Family Prayer" she called Yale students to the altar, creating an instant happening. Then she asked a church lady to walk hand in hand with her as she sang "When you gather in the evening, don't forget the family prayer." The lady got happy and started waving her hand. Marion held her all the tighter, while the college kids clapped fervently but ponderously behind her. During a rocking calypso-tempoed

"Even Me," she Suzy-Q'd over to an open Bible, flicking the gold-embossed pages to her syncopated beat. She closed with "The Day Is Past and Gone." After a wailed first verse, she invited her young son to come to the podium. "This is my son Robin and he say Mommy you haven't introduced me." Then after the people had applauded the grinning, embarrassed child, she went back into the mood, moaning about nights of death and laying our garments by.

Marion knows hundreds of obscure old songs. But like every gospel singer performing for white people, from Mahalia to the Ward and Staple Singers, she feels obliged to sing the pop spirituals, "Didn't It Rain," "Hold On," "Whole World," and "Michael Row The Boat Ashore," though always in a new and interesting way. "We Shall Overcome," for example, she returns to its gospel source, by singing

> Overcome (*maybe you ain't never heard it like this*),
> Overcome (*this is the way I sing it*)
> *We shall overcome some day*

to a driving church rock. Then she slows the pace to a nonmeter hymn, singing "We'll walk hand in hand," so demonstrating with a white member of the audience. In 1966, she toured Africa, and on some trips she wound up with a miniature United Nations—Chinese, Nigerians, and Egyptians—overcoming with her. Obviously, in a black church Marion can't do all that. She tells this story. "When I got to Kenya, I began walking with the consul there. He was from the South and not too sweet about colored folk. I started singing 'We'll walk hand in hand' and I could feel his hand slipping. So I took it, placed it under my arm real firm, and said, 'We'll walk hand in hand *today*.' Church, he was stuck!" By the time she's back to the beat, the church is up.

Sometimes Marion's showmanship gets a bit overpowering, so it was a revelation to see her sing "Precious Lord" the week after King's assassination. Explaining the song, she ad-libbed, "I imagine Dr. King thought as he was standing over that balcony, 'At the river, Lord, I'll stand.' " The word "Lord" was the saddest, bluest note I've heard. As she sang it, Marion clapped her hands decisively and stalked three or four steps toward the altar's edge. It was an old-time preacher's stride, almost masculine—no Ward Singer strut but a physical response that transcended gender or generation.

For a while Marion seemed to be winning the war and losing the peace. She tore up European jazz festivals and then stayed out of work for months. Without a hit record, she found church sponsors slow to pay. In disgust with one promoter, she spoke for all the swindled artists by singing "Touch Not My Anointed, Do My Children No Harm." Unlike other singers, she refused to go for percentages. "If they won't pay my money, shame on them. I'd rather sit home than go through that mess again."

Lately matters have improved. She's made some fine solo records with more style than her Ward Singers' discs, but with comparable spirit. In an album saluting Thomas A. Dorsey, she follows Dorsey's spoken testimony with an eloquent "Precious Lord" that begins with a melancholy lyricism suitable to Dorsey's tale. But she subtly changes her vocal coloration, complicating and expanding the mood. Virtually every syllable heightens the tension: She sings the line "When my life is almost gone" and underlines the "al" in "almost" with a confluence of emotions: anger, terror, determination. Then she ad libs "I don't want you to leave me there, this is what I want you to do for me," and having reached the point where Dorsey's testimony has become hers, hollers a raucous "Lord, hear my call" that no longer pertains to a miserable man bereft of wife and child, but to anybody confronting her own extinction. Although Marion can still rock and syncopate with the verve that inspired Little Richard and the Isley Brothers, her best recent records have been slower tunes. Her version of "The Day Is Past and Gone" matches that

of Clara Ward, but while her old boss phrased the climactic
line,

> *Though death may soon disrobe us all*
> *(interpolating "Oh children") of what we now possess,*

with limber, youthful grace, she reads it with an old-time
preacher's authority; she growls out "death" three times,
then lightens her voice for a lyrical summing up: the dynamic
shift reflects the catharsis. In another mood, the equally som-
ber "It's Getting Late in the Evening" shows her witty and
determined: After she wails "Every time you see me crying, that's my train fare home," she enumerates her troubles,
"not one time, not two times, but every time" and limns her
consolation—"my fare, my fare, train fare," appending a
fighting chuckle before reaching a confident "home, whoo-
hoo."

Also notable are her a cappella solos: e.g., Blind Willie
Johnson's "Motherless Children" (without knowing his 1927
recording, she echoes his rhythmic force), "Anyhow," "Poor
Pilgrim of Sorrow," "Precious Memories," etc. In these she
manages to evoke Dr. Watts's congregational singing while
blocking out sound patterns, sculpting the silent spaces
around her chanted words. She fits so well into this style that
her own expansive manner, with its constant surprises,
becomes a logical culmination of years of introspective country moaning. "Those country people can moan those Dr.
Watts hymns and make each note go right through you." Her
variations are more personal and sensuous than her predecessors'; but her aim is the same. They all believe that with
the deepest gospel hymns, each note should count as if it were
one's last.

**Marion makes her living singing in colleges. She doesn't
change her approach too much, though a square crowd
tends to get a square's repertoire. So it was a pleasure to
see her sing in New York's Bryant Park in one of the summer 1974 season of noonday concerts. There was an affectionate audience of black gospel fans and midtown office**

people on lunch breaks. And it is a mark of something that the two groups responded in very similar ways: The whites enjoyed the hymns "Blessed Assurance" and "Amazing Grace" quite as much as the blacks. Though they didn't shout, they showed no awkwardness when some stout fans exhibited very public displays of emotion. One could walk through the crowd and see a young white man rocking while a middle-aged black woman three feet away lifted her arms and contorted her face, in the time-honored manner of acknowledging "that's my story too." In the midst of "Precious Lord," Marion decided to "open the doors of the church," and a black minister made an uninspiring altar call. While a group of kindergarten students scampered about, thirty people, black and white, came up to shake Marion's hand. I doubt any expected to be saved—the blacks had gone that route, while the whites were no Jesus freaks. It was merely a sign that the communal vibrations of gospel are now public property, and that Marion is their most universally appealing vehicle.

Marion's ability to incorporate the best traditional approaches in a uniquely personal way, her vocal range from growl to whisper, from big-mama holler to little-girl trill, should impress anybody. But ours may not be an age of soloists. "That's all right. As long as I can pay my bills, I ain't studying about stardom. I just thank God I'm not struggling in the church," and she tells the standard horror stories, made current by the week. As she moves into the world of pop music, she's anything but astonished. "Most of what they're doing, key changes and way-out beats, the Kings of Harmony was doing when I was a girl." They tell her the gospel's too rough for the masses, but gospel mannerisms have filtered into every form of music. "Anything I hear, jazz, soul, rock, they got some gospel snuck up in them somewhere. Black people been singing 'Amazing Grace' for years. Nobody sings it like us, and then Judy Collins goes and has the hit." She doesn't need militants to perceive all this as an insidious form of racism. "You know I can't understand it. They used to call us crazy and clowns and Holy Rollers, and now all these white children are carryin' on worse than we ever did, and everybody's hogtied like it was something new. I'm looking for them to start speaking in tongues next."

One time I phoned Marion to congratulate her on a fine concert. I asked her to sing "Prayer Changes Things." "God knows if anybody knows that, I do," she said, and obliged. Usually she sings it up-tempo, but this time she slowed it to the grinding, insistent beat of the old quartets. When she came to the lines, "I've traveled through sorrow's valley, so many times my poor heart's been made to bleed/ By some friends whom I thought were with me/ Through disappointment I was knocked down to my knees, but I rose with faith and grace," she hollered out "Hey yes Lord," and throughout the rest of the song, she kept interpolating "heys" and "yes Lords." "I know prayer changes things, I've been way out . . . yes Lord . . . on the stormy . . . yes Lord . . . raging sea." After a moment's pause to collect herself, she said, "Yes Lord, if you don't bless me again, you've blessed me enough," clearly addressing someone other than her caller. Then she remembered me: "You know I'm not worried about hard times. I've been way out on the stormy raging sea, and God delivered me every time. That's just your lot if you're singing the gospel. Your way's never gonna be too easy. But do you know . . . I'd go through it all over again and still thank him for my journey." Then she *hmmm*ed to herself.

15

The Young Singers

Gospel now claims its fourth and fifth generations. The young saints today are a very different lot from Marion Williams and James Cleveland. Most of them are financially secure. Many attend college; high school graduation is taken for granted. The girls are secretaries, not domestics, the men aim for white-collar jobs, not factory work. For the past few years, these young people have been cultivating a whole new gospel sound. Their musical sources include jazz, soul, and white rock, as much as they do the old Gospel Pearls. They are young, devout, and lively, they like the gospel fire and community. The testimonies don't sway them—"I simply haven't paid those kind of dues," said one —and the old groups and quartets leave them cold. For the first time, gospel has acquired its own generation gap.

With all their musical sophistication, it was inevitable that some young saints would hit the pop charts. Every major group tried, but the hit was "O Happy Day" recorded by a previously unknown Sanctified choir from Oakland. The choir's leader, Edwin Hawkins, is the best-known Sanctified musician in pop. But within gospel the representative artists include Shirley Caesar and Jessy Dixon. Both typi-

fied a new era of gospel music. Each was hip, educated
—former college students—and saved. Both came up in
Holiness, inspired by the great gospel pioneers. But they refuse to consolidate other people's gains. "Anything that's
dead should be buried," says Shirley, and Jessy is known
among Chicago choirs as "Mr. Progressive." One understands
their frustration. For the first time the gospel sound is no
longer too ferocious for popular consumption. A generation
of young soul singers without their showmanship, spirit,
or sex appeal has cleaned up with gospel hand-me-downs.
Shirley and Jessy won't sell out. She's never sung a secular tune in her life excepting "My Lindy Lou" in grammar
school. Jessy sang ballads in a Houston club but hated the
work. Gospel satisfies them almost completely. But both
admit Satan's hellhounds are loose today, and the devil's
temptations never dangled so luxuriously before young saints'
eyes.

"They've got a saying going around that God is dead.
But if that's so, just answer me three questions: Who killed
him? Who was the undertaker? And why wasn't I notified,
because I'm his child and he's my father?" Shirley Caesar
comes on very strong. Where others build their fire gradually, Shirley blazes forth, happily frenetic from get-go.
As if the Holy Ghost were a puppeteer, she jerks up and
down, a marionette for Jesus. She is small and pretty and
gifted with great muscular control ("I can do any kind of
exercise you want to see"). When she dances, her limbs
assume an oddly pliable rigidity, her characteristic shouting posture, while her feet move at a sensational clip, barely
hitting the ground. One time with the Caravans, she livened
a dull service by coming on shouting. "I try to act dignified
but it just ain't in my system. You see I've got the Holy
Ghost, church, I feel like dancing right now," and she did,
even before singing. Such spirit makes her the idol of some
saints. But others are less impressed. "Shirley's got a good
voice," said one, "but she's too durn fidgety. She makes me
nervous."

Shirley has always been a fighter, and her pugnacious spirit asserts itself in all her performances. Her career is a model of sheer energy and spunk. When she joined the Caravans, she was a cute teen-age copy of Dorothy Love, little more than a group mascot. The group's leads, Albertina Walker and Inez Andrews, were ten years older and more professional. Both had immense contraltos, dramatic phrasing, and considerable dignity. "No, I didn't have a big voice, but I guess if you just sing with *virtue,* that virtue will carry you through." And like a sanctified Sammy Glick, Shirley overtook her superiors. In the early days, Shirley might open the program, but the spotlight was on Tina and Inez. Tina, a "flat-footed singer," used to sing "Lord Keep Me Day By Day," seldom moving from her mike position; sometimes facing the audience only in profile, she would squall the words, "I want to live, oh yes I do, oh yes I do, YEAH," so mightily other singers would fall out. Shirley sometimes pulled a Mama Ward and hit her: "She sang so well I just wanted to beat her." The Caravans' star then was Inez, whom they called the High Priestess. She looks the part. A coffee-colored woman with high Indian cheekbones and an intense, almost drugged stare, she can sing higher natural notes than anyone on the road. Tina said, "The rest of us sang awhile, but the folks really wanted to hear Inez whistle." Shirley would help her singing, "I've Been Running for Jesus a Long Time, I'm Not Tired Yet," proving her conviction by running up and down hundreds of aisles. She'd shout for sure, but the house only went up when Inez came in, screaming D over high C.

But youth and virtue triumphed. Group members came and left; only Shirley held fast. The older women grew tired, but Shirley always seemed itching to run. "I'm like Reverend Franklin, I believe in shooting for the moon, so if I fall somewhere, I'm still on higher ground." By the end, Shirley dominated the group and closed the program. As she says, "It was pitiful how the people shouted."

If Shirley seems aggressive, events have made her so. She was born forty-six years ago in Durham, North Carolina, one of twelve children. Her father, Big Jim Caesar, sang with the Just Come Four, and was known as a great Carolina quartet lead. One morning, when Shirley was twelve, she found him lying dead. She often tells how she was left fatherless with "an invalid mother," relying on the testimony as a kind of pep pill to revive her, if nobody else. "I told the Lord, I may be fatherless but I'll go." Taking Jesus as a father for the orphan, she joined the church. She was saved, but clearly no goody-goody. "I didn't know about sin, but I was a fighter, always a fighter." To support her mother, she began traveling under the name "Baby Shirley." At that time, she'd note-bend and moan like Clara Ward and "yodel" like Sam Cooke. Her gumption won her a small following in the Carolinas, but, as she was still in school, she could only perform on weekends. "From the age of fourteen to eighteen, I was out on my own. I used to have to wait in bus terminals all night long, coming from my programs. My mother allowed me to buy a cherry Coke and a hamburger. I'd sleep on the bus. Once I got home, Mama would have a baloney sandwich ready and she'd allow me seven cents for milk. I'd give the rest to her, then I'd be off to school." (One of her fellow students, James Herndon, later joined the Caravans as accompanist and later recorded duets with Delores Washington, the Vans' former soprano.)

In the mid-fifties, Shirley joined forces with Leroy Johnson, a one-legged gospel preacher. For a while they performed on a local TV show in Portsmouth, Virginia, for which *they* had to pay the station. On June 3, 1955, they were en route to Bennettsville, South Carolina, just outside of Columbia. They stopped at a little gas station for Cokes. Exhausted by hours of driving, Shirley's pianist yawned. "You tired, boy?" a white attendant asked. "Uh huh," was the reply. The attendant saw red. "Call me sir, nigger," he said, and started beating him. The boy ran out, and the owner and attendants dashed after him, crying, "Let's kill them all." They beat one member of the entourage with a hammer, and he still bears the scars. The other men and women began running to town. Shirley had been sleeping but the commotion awakened her. "Feet, do your duty," she said to herself, "don't fail me now." Another woman was hit in the back by a bottle, but Shirley managed to make it unharmed. "They picked me up crying in an empty lot in Bennettsville." When they called the cops, they'd "gone fishing." This is Shirley's other horror story, after her father's death, to remind her that "the Lord has brought me from a mighty long way."

Shirley studied for two years at North Carolina State College, a Negro school, majoring in business education. She had always dreamed of joining a professional group, and in 1958 quit stenography to join the Caravans. The group was very hot, thanks to Inez' songs and sermons. But Shirley could preach too. In 1961 she recorded a sermonette, "Hallelujah 'Tis Done," and turned the Apollo Theatre upside down. "I remember," she ad-libbed, "when I was on trial for murder, but the Lord brought me out." Naturally, she spoke figuratively—"I knew I was guilty of killing many souls with a lie or unkind thought—" but such metaphors will make anyone notorious. Tina told Shirley that night, "Girl you found your song." She'd also found a new career as preacher. Shirley became an Evangelist, and supported herself with revivals during the group's vacations.

She returned to the group, each time spiritually refreshed and alerted. The ten-year advantage began to show. While the other Vans would walk off stage, Shirley would still be shouting or whomping her tambourine. She began to acquire her own special style. Her singing is filled with blue notes and slurs, her legacy from Big Jim Caesar. She also likes to achieve rhythmic effects by repeating consonants— "running in the midmidmid midmid midnight hour—" a habit she picked up from Ira Tucker. More unusual were her intense nasality, the "yeahs" squalled high or ad-libbed low, the heavy breathing of an old country preacher. And Shirley's physical charm helped too. One roguish singer told her, "Girl, if you work in the bed like you move on the floor, you'd be something else." "Loose your hold, Satan," Shirley joked, by now a past mistress at dodging wolves. When she sang "Comfort Me," she campily embraced herself, and young men would come up to her after service: "Shirley, come on and comfort me."

"Running for Jesus" was succeeded by "Sweeping Through the City," a song with very similar beat and movements. The song was Shirley's first hit on records. Though the sweeping usually shouted the people, Shirley would sometimes slow things down and wail in old country fashion,

> *I'm gonna view that holy city,*
> *Where my captain's gone on before.*
> *I'm gonna sit down by the banks of the river,*
> *And I won't be back no more.*

That was the old way the saints remembered, and to heighten the familiarity, Shirley would sit in some old saint's lap. Then she'd speed up tempos and sweep around, occasionally hugging the "sweetly saved."

The great thing about the Caravans was their teamwork. They knew each other so intimately that they could easily predict each other's improvisations. So, if Cassietta George hollered "I'm gonna be all right, I'm gonna be all right," Delores Washington would echo her phrasing, note for note, an octave higher, while Shirley might rush in, "Here, Cassietta, let me tell it, some day-yeah." The Caravans were the hippest ladies in gospel. They cultivated their own slang, a compact of gospel idioms and song lines, but deployed with secular irony. "I went through that house like a dose of Groton Salts" meant someone had torn up as wickedly as the Salts; "You talk about flowery beds of ease" meant someone was coasting; "The stick is still sweeping" meant Shirley had no worries. In hip manner, they'd praise something with "It's bad, it's terrible, it's something else." While in other groups, one encountered several distinct personalities, the Caravans resembled each other in style, dress, and attitude. Not surprisingly, the union of witty, combative egos eventually failed. In 1966 Shirley quit the group, and three months later, everyone but Albertina had flown.

Shirley went back to evangelical work. "My ministry's much more dynamic than my singing, believe it or not." Preaching around titles both substantial—"Choose Ye This Day Whom Ye Shall Serve"—and obscure—"Go Take a Bath—" she earned more money her first months out than in her long stint with the Vans. When she preaches, she sometimes lays hands on the mourners' heads. "They just pass out like flies, one by one. I give God the glory." She began cutting records under her own name, supported by various choirs. "Everyone's getting on the choir bandwagon, and I don't intend to be left behind."

Shirley's first LP on her own, "I'll Go," remains her best. The title selection is an old hymn, and Shirley solos with a subtle eloquence often absent in her more rambunctious shouts. The note-bending is almost worthy of an Edna Gallmon Cooke, and the conviction is beyond question. A fascinating selection on this same LP, "Choose Ye This Day," is sermonette, song-chant, and aesthetic document in one. Shirley recounts how she composed the tune. "The ink in my pen ran out, the devil got in it." Martin Luther threw an inkpot at the devil; Shirley simply "reached over and got my pencil, glory to God." Her lyrics catalogue everyone in need of salvation, from butcher to policeman. When the postman knocks at her door, she decides, "That postman needs to be born again. I said to myself, 'Go tell the postman what he must do,'" then she ad-libs, "wait a minute, the other day I saw the President on TV:

> *Tell the President too,*
> *Tell the Governor,*
> *The Internal Revenue,*
> *Choose ye this day whom ye shall serve."*

The very hip Young People's Choir of the Institutional Church of God in Christ supports her on this LP, and their emphatic "Chooses" would terrify any sinner. They perform two tunes without her. One, "Stretch Out," became a gospel hit. Its rhythms were free and complex, pointing the way to the progressive sounds of Dixon and Hawkins, though any saint could pick up the beat and message. It was natural for our rhythmic *wunderkind* to wail with the choir, but the album's big hit was a real sleeper, an *a cappella* hymn, "Oh Peter Don't Be Afraid," sung in the down-home fashion of the Young People's parents. As in "I'll Go," Shirley sang with delicacy and poignance, proving that a fine country singer lurked behind all that frenzy.

Suddenly Shirley had a whole new personality. She was the young lady who sang the old way. To signal her return to her roots, she moved from Chicago back to Durham. "Saints, I sing the old-timey hymns because I've come up the rough side of the mountain, and I'm glad about it. You know, when you go up the smooth way, you can fall and slide to the pit. Now when you come up the rough side, you always got a few twigs or branches to hold your fall." Shirley already had the young people; now she made a calculated move for the old. She recorded "Don't Drive Your Mama Away," a ten-minute sermonette, with a St. Louis choir. This is the plaintive story of a mother with two sons. One goes wrong and leaves home. The other is conventionally good. He zooms through college, marries well, and earns a lot of money. His socialite wife grows tired of Mama's old-fogy ways, and eventually they send her to an old age home. Then, just as the bourgeois son drives off with his mother, he is stopped by "that no-good son" who claims his Mama, while singing the old hymn

I'm a stranger, don't drive me away,
If you drive me away, you're gonna need me some day,
I'm a stranger, don't drive me away.

It's a touching story, even if it resembles Dorothy Norwood's "The Denied Mother." "When my mother heard 'Mama,' she told me, You're going to get a gold record off that one, and a trophy too." Shirley got both. "Mama" outsold every other gospel disc released in 1969. "I went to a store in Washington, and they sold three hundred records in one hour, but I give God the glory."

Shirley now travels with her own group, the Shirley Caesar Singers, in a spanking-clean trailer bus. The group is hard-working and, shades of Big Jim Caesar, more quartet than gospel in flavor. Her repertoire is evenly divided between old and new. Her sister, Anne, joins her for a duet, "Stranger on the Road," a contemporary ballad without any reference to God or Jesus. And there's always "Peter" for the congregation to join in on, or "Mama," if Shirley has enough time. But the stick is still "Sweeping."

Shirley faces the eager saints. "Folks are talking about black power and white power, but nothing can make me doubt the power of God. Now, saints, if you know that you know that you know that you know that you're born again, if the Lord's really done something for you, I want you to come up and shake my hand—" and immediately she begins "God Is Not Dead." The saints are shouting even before they can touch their idol. A minute later she begins the working part of "Sweeping." As the girls yell out, "In the city," she romps through the halls and auditoriums. She often says, "I don't work so hard any more. I'm not particular about folks shouting, I like to see them cry. A few boohoos will do me," but she remains the same Shirley. And the people want it that way. One night at Washington Temple, she left a good dozen people shouting. The m.c. came on: "Let's give a big hand for that bundle of dynamite, Evangelist Shirley Caesar." As the people applauded, the spirit encored, and a whole new flock were up honoring Shirley—"And, believe me, I've sung much better." Virtue will out.

Merely by lasting, Evangelist Caesar ceased to be "Baby Shirley." Her 1982 wedding to Bishop Harold Williams, a major figure in her denomination, was held in Durham with all the participants dressed in antebellum outfits, a regal occasion for the diminutive gospel queen. (Along with the elaborate trappings, there were soulful touches: e.g., bride and groom saluted each other in song.) Likewise other talented members of Shirley's generation must now be accounted seasoned pros. Among the most respected is Evangelist Rosie Wallace Brown, a woman with a lovely face and body enough for all The Supremes, minister of Philadelphia's First Church of Love, Faith, and Deliverance. Rosie's compositions, piano and vocal stylings reflect the post-Cleveland changes, but her dignity and bearing demand comparison with the saints of old. No other singer under fifty can match her grittily focused soprano or approximate her powerful presence. Rosie first sang in the Thelma Davis Specials, along with Jacqui Verdell, who later sang lead with Thelma's group, the Davis Sisters. She was a mature stylist at sixteen, and Aretha Franklin's delivery has Jacqui stamped all over it; after years of dabbling at pop music, Jacqui has committed herself exclusively to gospel.

Unlike other forms of black music where changes may severely define and delimit an era, all the gospel changes received institutional support. The sanctified churches leapt into the late twentieth century with sacred sounds as innovative as their earliest music. Having heard conservatory chorales execute the harmonies of Bach or Brahms, young musicians decided that their homefolk should do no less, but to the familiar gospel rhythm. In time, that too was altered: Where once they had idolized Roberta Martin or Curtis Dublin, young pianists now swore by Art Tatum or Herbie Hancock. As augmented and diminished chords became commonplace, it seemed not impossible that moans and slurs would be relegated to the Amen Corner. Simply by sounding the way they did, the younger artists made the old-timers seem dated: It was predictable that young people who swooned to the intricate five-part harmonies of the Clark Sisters found male quartets banal and retrograde.

Yet the newer gospel remained true to its roots because it was so firmly embedded in its traditional settings, particularly the Church of God in Christ. And, as if hearkening back to the origins of gospel—a song service held around some ramshackle family altar—virtually every new act was a family group. They had all attended the annual C.O.G.I.C. conventions as kids, many of them were pastor's children who had grown up in church. "I can't lose my roots," said one. "The Gospel is *me;* you don't lose yourself." If now they shouted to music that baffled the older saints, they were still shouting, anointed with zeal, and claiming both holy ghost *and* fire.

The first to click was Andraé Crouch. Andraé and his sister Sandra were raised in Los Angeles. Their father pastored Christ Memorial C.O.G.I.C. Bishop Crouch was an old-time gospel warrior; Mrs. Crouch was not. Andraé once recalled that when his father would moan and groan, his mother would whisper demurely, "It's too *loud.*" Honoring his parents, Andraé developed a middle way although, as always in gospel, mother had the most influence.

In the early sixties, he formed the COGICs, a group in the tradition of the Gospel Clefs in which his slight but fervent baritone was one of several colors. When his musician Billy Preston and several singers switched fields, Crouch formed Andraé Crouch and the Disciples, a male group built around his crooning vocals, ballad compositions, and soul music arrangements. In the mid-sixties, he was discovered by white Pentecostal evangelists and signed a record contract with Light, a white religious label. The late sixties produced the twin movements of Jesus freakery and charismatic revival: Crouch fit securely into both. He adopted the hip, street-smart language and the informal wardrobe of the ex-junkies and switched-on saints who comprised his new audience. His biggest hits, "I Don't Know Why Jesus Loved Me" and "Through It All," combined traditional messages with melodies redolent of pop music. Though his quivering baritone could hardly be termed soulful, he became a model exponent of new-breed gospel. He could shout a black crowd with his arsenal of sanctified tactics, but he could also arouse the more restrained members of the Full Gospel Businessmen's Convention; where his father's generation had sung the old "Yes" chant, he brought in the charismatic anthem "Hallelujah."

Ultimately he trod too thin a line. He recorded an elaborately produced soul album with frank lyrics: One song described the gay waifs who hustled on Hollywood Boulevard. This move upset the saints. "I'm not singing rock and roll," he swore: The only rock he knew was the Solid Rock; the only roll, the one on which his name was signed. His sister, Sandra, helped rescue him. Returning to Christ Memorial, she directed and recorded her father's choir; once again, the name Crouch topped the gospel charts, this time with an album that sounded traditionally churchy: the hit selection "He's Worthy" was a transparent echo of the old hymn "Revive Us Again."

Another California family became the new gospel royalty. The Hawkins children—among them Edwin, Walter, Lynette, and Daniel—were raised in Newark; as children they idolized the Ward Singers and the Davis Sisters. By 1968, Edwin had become the pianist and director of the Northern California C.O.G.I.C. Youth Choir. The youngsters cut a vanity album which they sold at church conventions. The record was a happy blend of amateurism—the room sound was both cheap and spacious—and ambition; the music was loaded with foreign influences from bossa nova to soul jazz. When released by a major label, it was retitled "Oh Happy Day" and the group's name changed to the Edwin Hawkins Singers. Although "Oh Happy Day" was easily the biggest gospel hit of all time, they didn't stay lucky. The choir, reduced to seven family members, wound up appearing in Las Vegas and at New York's Continental Baths.

As the saints say, "God's always got a ram in the bush." Once again, Church saved them. Edwin's brother, Walter, had married the choir's soprano Tramaine Davis and become pastor of the Love Center C.O.G.I.C. in Berkeley. Thanks to Andraé Crouch, its choir recorded live—once again under primitive conditions, with Walter preaching, Tramaine soloing, and Edwin on piano. The "Love Alive" album featured two powerful vocals by Tramaine, "Changed" and "Going Up Yonder"; the latter sounded like a 1940s attempt at Tin Pan Alley calypso: The Hawkins's would not suppress their eclecticism. With "Love Alive," Walter Hawkins and the Hawkins Family became the biggest draws in gospel. Tramaine, an astonishingly beautiful woman—the first gospel star who could pass for a Paris model—now records on her own; as a soloist, she sounds surprisingly bluesy and raucous: Her earlier work had revealed a Broadway light soprano. Edwin and Walter Hawkins have inaugurated a gospel workshop; in keeping with Edwin's theatrical bent, they offer courses in the dramatic arts.

By all odds, the most musically extravagant family was also the most church-based. The Clark Sisters were the daughters of Mattie Moss Clark, the pre-eminent choral director of The C.O.G.I.C.'s National Convention. In addition, Mattie served for years as director, soloist, and composer for the Southwest Michigan Choir, one of the few successful choirs James Cleveland did *not* conduct. She has always favored melodies that evoke high church anthems, while insisting on the rollicking fervor identified with sanctification.*

Mattie's daughter Elbertina "Twinkie" Clark became a star keyboardist at C.O.G.I.C. conventions. After studying at Howard, Twinkie rejoined her sisters for a series of albums that made them the first significant female gospel singing group in two decades. The Clarks touch all bases: Their harmonies are complex, their rhythms dizzying, but their showmanship and preaching are conventional to the point of reaction. (Shortly after the group proclaimed a special ministry to homosexuals and lesbians, their record "You Bring Out the Sunshine" became a surprise hit in gay discos.)

The versatile Twinkie devastates other musicians with her facility. "One time in church," a Philadelphian recalls, "Twinkie caught my eye, winked, and made this outta sight chord without even looking down. I wanted to go up and hit the girl." Her organ provides the ballast for the Clark Sisters' harmonies. In choir style, she likes to stagger parts, imposing and super-imposing voices over each other. But because the voices are few and similar, she can achieve instrument effects impossible in choral

---

*Her equally talented brother, Bill Moss, represents an opposing tendency in gospel music. He is a slim, wily-looking man who usually sports sun glasses. Spinning out bluesy arpeggios on electric piano and synthesizer, he presides·over a family quartet, the star of whom is his wife, Essie. A modest vocalist but an extraordinary personality, Essie Moss sweeps through churches by reciting her precious memories—"God helped me raise all my children, saints, I know he's been good."

situations. So in a song like "Name It, Claim It," her sisters Karen and Dorinda can vocally doodle in counterpoint to each other and their three sisters. The syllables flow like scat sounds or unknown tongues. In fact, the Clarks occasionally sing in tongues: affixed to such highly mannered styles, the tongues reveal them "in the spirit" but scarcely "out of self."

Detroit singers enjoy vocal contortions that make Stevie Wonder sound restrained. In a tune like "Is My Living in Vain," each sister distorts in her own way: "Is my living in vaie-ee-yae-ee-yae-ee-ain?" one wonders; her sister adds, "Is my singing in vai-ee-yae-ee-oh-whoah-ah-yae-ee-yain." In the song's second verse, "Am I wasting my time" gets an atypical gospel rhyme, "Can the clock be unwind?" (sic), and two others ripped from the old landmark: "Have I let my light shine? Have I made ninety-nine?" (100's the goal). The chorus begins with a prim, schoolmarmish reply: "No, no, no, of course not." But within a few measures, the "no no nos" break loose; Karen ad libs "no no nonono," and a bar later, the group repeats her patter; then she double-times "nono"s. The aural information is almost on overload. You'd think the Clarks couldn't disentangle themselves, but it takes only one Twinkie modulation and they are harmonizing as decorously as a five-part ensemble in the Howard University Choir.

The gargantuan Twinkie sits calmly at her organ, while the slim Dorinda acts as group spokesperson. She comes on with her Aunt Essie's flash. She rebukes the sinners by revising their idioms. "I'm an addict—I'm addicted to God's word; I'm *hooked* too . . . I'm hooked to something I can't turna loose . . . I'm tripping too . . . instead of tripping on LSD, I take trips with GOD, and he takes me higher . . . and he lights my fire." Soon Karen and Dorinda are racing through the audience, chanting out the familiar pieties while the sisters on stage sing counterpoint and countermeasure. Their stick is called "Hallelujah"; and it summons up Handel and storefront churches, much as their work encapsulates a century of black religious song.

Male family groups tend predictably to echo traditional quartet. But while the Williams Brothers, younger siblings of Huey Williams of the Jackson Southernaires, perform in a style that merges introspective Mississippi moaning, close harmony, and typical soul-gospel devices. A Detroit group, the Winans, are closer to Andraé Crouch's kind of singing, although their father still prefers "the real *hard* quartet."

Important new singers include Vanessa Bell Armstrong, Richard White, and Douglas Miller, all of whom came up under Mattie Moss Clark. Armstrong, a short squat woman, the mother of several children, sings in a manner that fuses C.O.G-.I.C. extravagance and the Baptist moans of her sister Detroiter, Aretha Franklin. Reverend Richard "Mr. Clean" White has the vocal power of a 1980s Joe May. His sermons and compositions favor new versions of old tropes, "The Handle's on the Inside" or "Jesus Dropped the Charges." Douglas Miller, who has a B.A. in sociology, possesses a husky resonant baritone. Besides wailing chants like "When I See Jesus, Amen" in a style that recalls his childhood idols the Davis Sisters, he is an exceptional arranger. In "Pass Me Not," he takes a relaxed approach while his choir, the young people of Dallas's Trueway C.O.G.I.C., juxtapose and intermingle their parts, as if a children's round had turned dissonant. Halfway through "Power," he pulls back and lets the chorus sing *a cappella*; then he allows replies from a synthesizer programmed to sound like a horn section. By playing the old habits off the new technology, he makes the machine seem downright folkloric. Miller benefits from two precocious keyboard men: twenty-year-old Arthur Dyer ("That brother can sit down and play Mozart, and turn around and kill you with stone gospel," says Miller) and twenty-four-year-old Gary Henry, a Newark native who moonlights as producer for artists like Grand Master Flash and LaToya Jackson. The only untrained musician in the band, Miller has evolved his own method: "I want my stuff to be progressively traditional . . . orchestrated so you really feel *church* in it."

A similar slant animates several other musicians. Thomas Whitfield, a dazzling technician, is gospel's Art Tatum, but his work always bears the influence of Detroit's Tabernacle Apostolic Church where twenty-five years ago James Cleveland ushered in the modern choir sound. Ricky Grundy, the twenty-one-year-old pianist for Los Angeles' Pentecostal Community Choir, composed the rousing "Call Him Up," which segues from high church chords to a syncopated chorus, "I can't stop . . . praising his name; I just can't stop . . . praising his name," that conjoins the disco with the storefront church. James Perry, a twenty-six-year-old Newark pianist, listens to Art Tatum and Bud Powell but despite his training, he feels that "technique . . . [and/or] time signatures don't have much bearing on gospel . . . It's still a strictly feeling situation." Perry's colleague Milt Biggham sings and performs "from my Now experience," but when he romps through his composition "Prayer Will Fix It Every Time," with Newark's Revival Temple C.O.G.I.C., you remember that he began touring with his mother, Sister Christine Sykes, in the backwoods of Georgia. Like the jazz musicians, David Murray (raised in a Berkeley C.O.G.I.C.) and the Chicago Art Ensemble (whose leader, Lester Bowie, is Martha Bass's son-in-law), these men rely on their musical heritage to provide launching pad and safe harbor for their experimentation. As James Cleveland's acolyte Jessy Dixon once said, "The more I get into this thing, the deeper it takes me."

PART FOUR

———————

THE
GOSPEL
LIFE

16

"You May Never Go to Prison"

You may never go to prison, you may never go to jail.
When that awful hour comes, you'll need somebody to go
your bail.

The greatest gospel singers were Depression children. "We
never had nothing but a hard way to go," they'll say, and
in memory their childhoods seem bleak existences divided
between hard work and church. At twelve years old,
Julius Cheeks picked cotton in South Carolina, Marion
Williams scrubbed floors in Florida, Dorothy Love washed
dishes in Alabama. The trouble wasn't limited to the
South. One singer was raised in New Jersey as a ward of
the state. When she was twelve, she learned that her real
mother had been killed by her father. Years later, she sang,
in her most thrilling performance, "There's a man going
around taking names./ One day he took my mother's name
and he left my heart in pain,/ I don't know what I'd do
without the Lord," investing the gospel clichés with a terrifying accuracy. No wonder gospel at first seems one way
out of poverty and violence, or that most singers start out
innocent and dedicated, thrilled to be traveling and able

to send a few pennies home. But inevitably the road hardens them into a bitter, suspicious lot, "trusting Jesus, that's all." At best, the road rewards them with a comfortable living. More often it leaves them broke, sick, and disillusioned. Year after year, the gospel highway seems both the toughest and most dangerous route in show business.

Every group has been a witness, no matter how old or successful. One Ward Singer, knocking them cold in Las Vegas, collapsed and died of pneumonia. Ira Tucker's idol, Norman "Crip" Harris, lead singer for the old Norfolk Jubilee Quartet, was murdered two years ago in Harlem by robbers; to compound the horror, the aged Harris was completely blind. Quartet's greatest alumnus, Sam Cooke, was slain in a seedy, back-room brawl. Jimmy Outler, his successor in the Soul Stirrers, developed a ferocious temper on the road. Ultimately he pulled a knife on someone and was accidentally killed in the struggle. One of Gospel's major losses was the death of Ruth "Baby Sis" Davis of the Davis Sisters. Ruth was the hardest female belter in gospel, "scared of no man" when it came to squalling. At home she'd enthrall friends with her blues, and all the singers insist she could have been another Dinah Washington or Big Maybelle. She certainly looked the part of a hard blues shouter. When in good health, she loomed like a football halfback, her hair cropped in a fifties d.a. In private, she was retiring, basically innocent and vulnerable, a tomboy who never grew up. She looked powerful enough for all the hardest singing and partying the road could offer. She wasn't. When she died, a victim of high blood pressure, diabetes, liver and kidney trouble, she was as small as the young Shirley Caesar. Typically, this epitome of the hard gospel life died in the bosom of her family. "Ruth took sick around Christmas," her sister Alfreda recalls. "We asked her to go to the hospital but she said, 'Let me stay with you and the children for New Year, cause I know when I go to that place, I won't be coming back.'" The Davis Sisters had not worked much during those months, and Mary Mason, the local d.j. who spoke at Ruth's funeral, observed that Ruth hadn't seen such a packed church in years. Said one gospel singer, "If Baby Sis, strong as she was, couldn't stand it, I know this life will kill me; I'm staying home."

A few gospel publishers and promoters have made fortunes, but for most of the singers, gospel pays like unskilled labor. Gospel promoters are notoriously crooked. Their excuses always sound plausible—small crowds, high costs of promotion, competition with other events. The singers simply know "an honest payday is rare stuff." Sometimes the promoter doesn't pay them at all, and frequently he settles for an amount less than the contracted fee. "But what can we do?" says Dorothy Love. "Most of us don't have the means to sue. Plus, if we did, we'd stay in court." They are prepared to bitch with promoters over fees no higher than they were fifteen years ago. As in the late sixties, a big-name group with a recent hit record still earns a thousand dollars on a good Sunday program, while their weeknight services usually average two hundred and fifty dollars. So, in addition to singing, most groups hawk their records and pictures at programs. For a few extra pennies, singers who shouted congregations ten minutes ago must mill among the departing crowds, selling their wares like street vendors.

Even more demeaning are the "free-will" offerings and the "percentage" programs. At a free-will program, instead of admission, an offering is taken up. Professional singers of the highest caliber must sit patiently through long glib spiels as the minister-promoters ask for "donations to help support this wonderful program, the Lord will bless you." Sometimes the singers themselves carry tambourines, like beggars. One gospel singer said pungently, "I'd rather eat doo-doo than go back to the free-will programs." A percentage program means that the group gets a fixed part of the take, but no guaranteed fee. It's not so humiliating, but it's frequently as unrewarding. For example, the Dixie Hummingbirds sang recently in Rahway, New Jersey. On a 60–40 percentage of a three-hundred-dollar house, each man wound up with a whopping thirty dollars.

A few singers beat the system. James Cleveland charges as high as nine thousand dollars a program, and Shirley Caesar cleans up in revivals, where congregations offer most freely to support the diminutive Evangelist. The smaller the act, the better. The Consolers, a husband-and-wife team from Florida, sing duets, with Brother Sullivan Pugh on guitar and lead and his devout wife Iola singing harmony. Their simple country approach stresses such sturdy virtues as humility ("If I'm Too High, Lord Bring Me Down"); kindliness ("Give Me My Flowers While I'm Still Living"); and mother love ("I'm Waiting for My Child to Come Home," "Every Christian Mother Surely Prayed for Her Child"), and made them among the biggest gospel record sellers after Cleveland, with all profits going into the family. Ministers like Reverend C. L. Franklin and Reverend Cleophus Robinson have grown wealthy from their record sales and advances—Robinson, for one, is a whiz at recording deals—and the love offerings of their congregations. When he was healthy, the Thunderbolt of the Middle West, Brother Joe May, earned enough in Southern hamlets to send six children through college.

But these are extreme instances. The average big-name group works eight or nine months a year, averaging about four thousand dollars a month. With five or six members to a group (most consider the car their seventh split), a group singer is lucky to earn six thousand dollars on the road. By the time he takes it home to his wife and children, he winds up as poor as any of his neighbors.

If anything, it's getting worse for the gospel singers. The groups are being supplanted in public favor by the choirs. But choirs come cheap, and most choir singers are happy to get their travel expenses paid. Whatever fee is left over goes to the choir director or preacher. (The Edwin Hawkins Singers reportedly earn salaries, but as gospel singers say, they're in "the other field.") Most of the choir singers want to travel like the idols they grew up imitating. Apparently it's worth it for them to pay their own way so they can go back to Brooklyn or St. Louis or Chicago and tell their friends about the towns they visited and the famous choirs they out-shouted. Very few of these choristers seem to realize the extent of their victimization. So no matter what branch of gospel—soloist, group, quartet, or choir— the singers wind up swindled. "The white man robbed me all my life," says Dorothy Love, "and now the black man's doing it. They all treat us like dogs and puppies, like we didn't have no sense." There's no room for sentiment in such a brutal world. "Let me move the people and earn my money" is all a gospel singer wants. That's not greedy; it's eminently practical and, under the circumstances, even modest.

The violent deaths of the Soul Stirrers suggest the dangers of gospel traveling. From the days of the T.O.B.A. ("Tough On Black Artists," singers used to quip) circuit, black show business has been difficult. After paying assorted arrangers, managers, tailors and beauticians, few soul singers wind up rich. But compared to the gospel warriors, their life is truly a flowery bed of ease. In order to save money, the gospel singers travel by car. The cars are usually brand new and expensive to signal a group's progress. (The Consolers' anniversary book of 1964 contains two pictures captioned: "The Consolers' first car, a 1956 Oldsmobile. The Consolers' second car, a 1950 Cadillac.") But they are seldom paid for, and long hours of traveling by car are exhausting. Sometimes the singers don't even use their elaborate air-conditioning for fear of catching cold. In winter they run the risk of icy, slippery roads. (A few years ago, an accident killed the Swanee Quintet's bass guitarist and left J. J. Farley, manager of the ill-starred Soul Stirrers, severely crippled.) Singers think nothing of traveling hundreds of miles for a program and leaving immediately after. Marion Williams was so conditioned by Ward Singers' traveling that she recently drove from Philadelphia to Cleveland for a college concert of twenty-five songs and left an hour later. Indeed, as long as they get paid, the singers accept this constant flux as a working condition. But the strain invariably tells. It's almost impossible to sing with spirit when one arrives exhausted: "Baby, I stays tired."

When they've time enough to stop over, gospel singers usually rest at hotels. Until recently, each big city ghetto had two or three hotels where gospel singers hung out. Lately they have begun moving downtown, where very little is changed but the skin color. Whether he stays in Harlem or downtown, the gospel singer in New York will sleep in a small, stuffy room furnished with a drooping bed and a few pieces of Danish-Japanese modern. The halls stink of cheap cooking and marijuana, the bathrooms aren't always clean. His fellow guests are junkies and pimps, prostitutes and transvestites of both sexes, as well as that great silent majority of hotel dwellers who lead lives regulated by whiskey and television. Things may be a bit better downtown. The Violinaires' manager says, "Shoot, I ain't going back to the ———. You get out your car, some brother comes up—'Hey man, let me take your suitcase to your room—' and you never see it again." Recently one such hotel lost its telephone, making their private world even more off limits.

"How-be-ever," the corruption and discomfort remain the same uptown or down. Some singers drink—why not? But the bad whiskey they drink has killed a few. The food isn't much better. The cheap soul food available in restaurants is usually clotted with grease. The fatty hog's innards —chitterlings, pigs' tails, snouts, lips, "everything but the oink"—that produced generations of high blood pressure when cooked lovingly can't do better when served in greasy spoons. The gravy owes more to flour than meat drippings, the rice is soggy, the corn bread seldom fresh. The soft drinks, sodas and lemonades are sweet unto syrup, helping along any incipient diabetes. Like most of the leftovers poor people make do with, soul food isn't very healthy, and many singers wind up on diets, forbidden to eat pork, starches, and hot seasonings, the staples of soul cuisine.

To a man, they'll tell you food was better when they were young. "We ate out of the earth," says Alex Bradford. Rosetta Tharpe's classic line is "Now they put the pork chops in the freezer and embalm them for months and months." If the gospel singer eats the cheap white food available in the snack spas that fill America's Times Squares, he gets a mess of grease, stale ingredients, and liquid gas. He's probably best off eating the church suppers served after programs.

According to legend, gospel singers have special friends in every town. As professional entertainers they do not want for admirers. But there's a hard, practical reason for the promiscuity. The quartet singers need their women to help pay their hotel bills, cook for them, and treat them nice. Since most are family men, the eighty or ninety dollars they clean up on the road would make them candidates for welfare if gospel groupies didn't come to their rescue. Things are less easy for the female gospel singer—the sexual double standard brands her a "whore" if she entertains protectors—which may explain why she often seems so tough and wary. The gay singers have their camp followers too, though admiration seems the main currency exchanged here.

The gospel groupies are a special phenomenon, long predating the willowy nymphets who comfort rock musicians. Like their pop analogues, they usually share a deep love and knowledge of the music, enabling the singers to talk shop, taking their listeners' knowledge and sympathy for granted. Sometimes the groupies show up at programs, expecting to be treated as celebrities themselves. At the Apollo Theatre's gospel concerts, they may sit in the first three rows where they're known as "the cheering section." In churches, they parade in grandly, ignoring the ticket taker, assuming their arrival guarantees free admission. In order to sell their favorites, the groupies may shout, scream, or fall out. One gospel singer remarks, "Those quartets ain't saying nothing, they just have their women shouting

for them." Likewise a quartet lead will say, "Dig those
sissies shouting for their choir." The groupies, for all their
generosity and devotion, are a mixed blessing.

The gospel life wears almost everybody down. Amaz-
ingly, most groups stay together for years, unlike the pop
supergroups that last an album and a half. This despite the
years of close traveling and the natural jealousies and sus-
picions of performers. Sometimes a group's manager, who
is usually a member doubling as booking agent, may swin-
dle his group. Or a lead singer may resent splitting equally
with his background musicians. Yet the singers tolerate an
awful lot in the name of group harmony. As a result, all
the older singers instinctively feel for each other, as if all
their horror stories were the same gospel blues.

Which, of course, in some ways, they are. And this may
explain why lyrics that to white listeners seem abstract and
corny are charged with specific, resonant meaning. If the
gospel world is dreadful, it merely reflects the inescapable
conditions of black life. At home or traveling, the poor
gospel singer is always in or near some kind of danger.
Coming out of church, Myrtle Jackson was shot by a
sniper. A former Davis Sister burned to death after un-
wittingly lighting a match near some spilled kerosene. One
of Bessie Griffin's pianists was a missing person for weeks
till Chicago police found her corpse in the oven of a deserted tenement. Nobody is immune: "We ain't no strangers to trouble." Take Mother Marion Williams, as they
call her in the Holiness church. In the last few months,
she sang at the funeral of an old fan stabbed to death; a
good friend's nephew died of an overdose of heroin; a
former co-worker's brother was killed in a gangland slay-
ing. In the family of that Baptist saint Dorothy Love Coates,
an in-law accidentally shot himself to death; a few years
earlier Dorothy's aunt had been killed by her husband.
Not to mention all the friends of both ladies who lost sons
and brothers in Vietnam. When even the holiest are sur-

rounded by such violence, a gospel saying like "We're here today and gone today" sounds like stone fact.

Gospel music is dismissed as escapism, but the singers are as worldly as any in show business. The gospel scene makes the escapades of most rock singers seem what they are: privileged child's play. "I've seen it all," says each professional gospel singer, and as far as the underside of America goes, he's probably right. The ugliness and paranoia of the gospel world infect all those who are part of it. Compare Diana Ross and Aretha Franklin. Diana grew up poor and, like everyone else, attended a gospel church. But she was never caught up in the music. Her whole image and manner is little girl, innocent, mildly perverse, in the daintiest, most antiseptic way. Aretha, daughter of the church, a traveling soloist at fourteen, seems weighted with anger and insecurity. There's a lot of piety in gospel but very few Pollyannas. Even Mahalia Jackson, so humble and optimistic on the Ed Sullivan Show, liked to tell a congregation, "My Bible tells me don't put your trust in man, chu'ch, because man will betray you."

17

"Turn Your Radio On"

Turn your radio on and listen to the music in the air.
Turn your radio on and listen to the glory that we share.
Turn your radio on and listen to the music in the air.
Get in touch with God!
Turn your radio on.

The gospel disc jockey is a powerful figure. In most towns his program provides the only public exposure for gospel music outside the church. Denied access to any other public media, gospel singers depend on the jocks to advertise their programs, spin their records, and create a demand for their appearance. Many pop stars survive comfortably without airplay. In gospel, only a few groups have the contacts to book themselves steadily without some assistance from the disc jockeys. In most instances, the d.j. extracts a price for his services. Usually he expects groups to come cheap and perform on programs he promotes. Sometimes he quits spinning their records after the concert, and once again the singers lose out.

There are gospel d.j.s in every city with a sizable black population. Their number varies and has declined steadily in recent years. As a result, some of the jocks are running scared, lording it not quite so magisterially over the singers. When waters run calm, gospel d.j.s are a friendly lot and extraordinarily garrulous. As they keep telling you, their mission is to lift the spirits of "the sick and shut-in," as well as the factory workers who rise to "Morning Spirituals," the maids who clean by the "Gospel Train," the hospital orderlies and cooks who send in requests for "Spirituals at Sundown." When they're not lifting spirits with folksy chatter, the jocks are hustling their sponsors' products. At a tortoise's pace, they advertise the triumvirate of gospel commercials—discount furniture stores, cosmetics, and funeral parlors. They're all matter-of-fact business about the furniture stores, impressing the listener with his folly if he doesn't drop everything and rush to Friendly Fannie's for the sale of the century, "with a special bonus for Gospel Corner listeners only." Cosmetics and laxatives get a more low-keyed approach. One recorded commercial features three witnesses for an "old-favorite family laxative." To heighten the folksy, after each unidentified testimony the announcer may ask "Natchez, Mississippi?" or "Newark, New Jersey?" Naturally all sections of the country are represented in an all-American bowel movement. Or the disc jockey himself may extol the wonders of some product. "I know about Down Home Cold Tablets," he may say, "because they brought me out," as if the pills were anointed. Funeral ads invariably include an organ recording (Maceo Woods's "Amazing Grace" being especially popular for such purposes) over which the d.j. drones in appropriate tones a message about mortality, consideration, and caskets for all sizes, needs, and family budgets, "limousines graciously provided."

If the ad content dismays, the follow-ups get downright insulting. We are not given the telephone number to call merely once or twice. "Call 111–1000. Remember, friends, for quick, dependable service, it's 111–1000, 111–1000. That's right, Mama, 111–1000. I've been there and seen it for myself, 111–1000." With all these ads, it's not uncommon for a gospel program to be 60 percent commercials. But gospel fans are so hungry for their music that they withstand every abuse. And in a vicious circle, the higher the program rating, the longer the commercials. Some big programs now feature ads for national products like Coca-Cola and Jell-O in addition to Nadinola Skin Cream and the Unity Funeral Parlor.

Another kind of advertisement is crassly religious, to the point of self-parody. "Look who's coming to Brooklyn, Charleston, Tampa, Detroit," the tapes exalt. "It's that dynamic servant of God, Brother Lucifer." Upon which Brother Lucifer comes on breathily, directing the listening "children" to meet him at such and such a time for a special blessing service. Some of the superstar evangelists tape fifteen-minute programs, highlighted by dramatic testimonies to God's power to cure illness and raise money. The preachers then run through the tired litany of giving God the glory—"I'm just his agent—" while implying, "Deal with me for a hot line to the throne." A few are black, but a surprising number are southern whites. The most famous was Reverend A. A. Allen of Miracle Valley, Arizona, the last of the red-hot healers. Allen died recently of alcoholism, leaving a good dozen drawling disciples to continue the work "in Brother Allen's name." Every night on New York's WWRL the extremes of white Pentecostal evangelism, Brother Al and Reverend David Epley, can be heard. Brother Al, "God's 'umble servant," always begins in mid-hysteria. He never lets up, weeping, screaming, dropping into tongues, all because of the world's dreadful conditions. In good Southern tradition, he's an ex-ball player ("but I'd rather pitch for Jesus"), obviously if not defiantly illiterate ("I don't like all this mawdern, social gospel"), and a champion of Mother ("Any mother's all right with me"). While Brother Al usually leaves his listeners exhausted, Reverend Epley is quietly epicene. Even when he heals, prophesies, and speaks in tongues, his tone resembles those whispering poetry readers of 1930s radio. After a dose of Brother Al and Reverend Epley, even the worst gospel d.j.s sound good.

Most jocks love the music. Some, like Brother Thurman Ruth, former lead and manager of the Selah Jubilee Singers, or Sonny Mitchell, former guitarist for the Soul Stirrers, are old gospel pros. A few double as ministers, choir singers, or loyal church workers. Their salaries aren't large. A top d.j. earns no more than three hundred dollars a week. Most supplement their incomes by promoting programs. Joe Bostic runs a record distribution service which sells discs wholesale and retail, and in the late sixties had purchased the New York gospel market. Not surprisingly, the bulk of his program consists of records he distributes. The late Brother Henderson, who once ruled the Los Angeles gospel market, owned his own record company, Proverb, and Californians were treated to more Proverb discs in a week than graced the rest of America in a year.

The d.j.'s approach is always folksy and familiar. While a record is played, he may cry out "Sing" or "That's all right," and sometimes call for an encore. He knows his audience well: "All right, children, stop shouting, I've got a commercial for you." A few jocks get happy on the air, conveniently between commercials. It's odd and patronizing, but the audiences seem to like it. They send in requests dedicated to mothers, aunts, pastors, and friends. They call in to report missing children and pets, to inform the d.j.s of church programs and revivals. All the big d.j.s receive touching letters from the old and sick. About 10 percent of Joe Bostic's mail includes requests for assistance with welfare or plumbing problems. Some jocks, like Bostic, Pauline Wells Lewis in Baltimore, and Mary Holt in Cleveland, are actively involved in community work. On many sepia stations, the most community-minded people are the gospel d.j.s. For all this, they are virtually apolitical. Bostic's son, Joe Bostic, Jr., a youthful man in his late thirties, has organized Youth for Christ, a group composed of young choir singers in the New York-New Jersey-

Connecticut area. Youth for Christ's political content is negligible. Their leader's political personality can be gauged by his remarks during the Watts riots. "Thank God, Gospel Train riders were brought up right. We know this isn't the answer."

The dean of gospel disc jockeys is Joe Bostic, Sr. An ex-sports writer, long active in Brooklyn Democratic Party politics, Bostic began his "Gospel Train" in the late forties. In 1950, he joined forces with Buddy Franklin, a young political journalist who has since become one of the few gospel experts. Their first joint venture was a Carnegie Hall concert starring Mahalia Jackson. Since then Bostic, assisted by Franklin, has taken gospel to Newport, the Coliseum, and Madison Square Garden. He helped develop the current choir craze, distributing several choirs on his own label, Holy Hour. His origins in journalism are always evident; his radio persona is part social worker, part political analyst, part college lecturer. The middle-class manner scarcely prepares one for the earthy music he plays. Yet, when he needs to, Bostic can sock it to his listeners, whether selling Busch's Jewelers ("every diamond is a prize") or a food campaign he organized for the impoverished migrant workers in Mississippi. His program was the most profitable on his station, and often featured three ads for every record played (and was cancelled in 1973).

Few other gospel d.j.s exude Bostic's confidence, though Louise Williams, self-proclaimed "Gospel Queen" of Philadelphia, speaks like a graduate of a 1920 school for elocution. Most older d.j.s, especially in the South, sound less professional and consequently more real. The younger the d.j., the whiter the sound. These d.j.s can jive-rhyme one moment and be pointedly serious the next. In a day's time, they may be humble-folksy for gospel, pompously correct for news, and superfly hip for soul.

Most jocks have favorite artists, usually the ones scheduled to appear on their forthcoming programs. As a result, depending on the jock's whim, a song can be a "monster" in Miami and unknown in Philadelphia. This uncoordi-

nated approach leads to a healthy variety in record programming—Joe Bostic's ten records an hour were never
Mary Mason's—but it also severely limits gospel sales. Obviously, only small specialty outfits with tiny budgets and
minimal promotion can bother with such a market. The
enterprising capitalists who live off gospel are usually white,
but they share much in common with the jocks they service—most particularly the distrust of the singers.

In the mid-forties, Private Cecil Gant's "I Wonder," released on a small, independent label (as distinguished
from the "major" labels like Victor, Columbia, Decca, Capitol), sold over a million copies to an all-black audience.
Dozens of small companies sprouted up aimed exclusively
at the "race" market. By that time, gospel was a genre
with a fifteen-year history and scores of professional singers itching to record. A few artists opened the field. Sister
Rosetta Tharpe was queen then, and every small company
found a singing guitarist who resembled her. After an era
of jubilee quartet, the early Soul Stirrers hits on Aladdin
helped develop a market for the many hard gospel quartets
who imitated them. In 1948, the St. Paul's Church Choir,
directed by Professor J. Earle Hines (and featuring Sallie
Martin), overwhelmed the market with "God Be With
You," ushering in a series of choir records only distantly
related to the "shouting preacher" discs of Prophet Michaux and Reverend Gates. Within a five-year period,
gospel produced several smash hits: Rosetta's "Up Above
My Head" and "Strange Things Happening Every Day"
(Decca); Mahalia's "Move On Up" and "Even Me"
(Apollo); The Ward Singers' "Surely God Is Able" (Sa-
voy) and "How I Got Over" (Gotham); The Roberta
Martin Singers' "Only a Look" and "Old Ship of Zion"
(Apollo); the Angelic Gospel Singers' "Touch Me Lord
Jesus" (Gotham); and the Trumpeteers' "Milky White
Way" (Score). By 1950, even big companies like Victor
and Columbia were releasing gospel records.

Except for the St. Paul Choir on Capitol, and Rosetta on Decca, the gospel market belonged to the newer independents. Savoy, Apollo, Gotham, Chess, Manor, Aladdin, Specialty were headed by small-time entrepreneurs of great shrewdness, all of them white, who, operating out of two-room offices, managed to earn much on small investments. Only one major gospel outfit, Peacock, has been black owned (though black producers include Milt Biggham, John Harley, John Daniels, and Thomas Whitfield), and significantly Peacock originated in Houston, not New York, or Los Angeles. Attuned to the South, Peacock had always specialized in quartet records. In the early fifties, their biggest hits, the Bells of Joy's "Let's Talk About Jesus" and the Five Blind Boys' "Our Father," hit the *Billboard* "race" charts. As late as 1970 another quartet tribute to Mother, "Too Late," by the Jackson Southernaires, reportedly sold over 100,000 albums. Continuing an old tradition of Mom-and-Pop-store entrepeneurship, newer gospel firms include such obscure names as Gospearl, Atlanta International, Malaco, and Church Door.

Some gospel entrepreneurs became walking legends. Leonard Chess, the founder of Chess and of Chicago's all-black WVON, was a record lover whose death in 1970 was widely mourned by Chicagoans. But the embodiment of the gospel capitalist was Herman Lubinsky, the legendary, infamous owner of Savoy Records. Mr. Lubinsky, a former Navy radio operator, managed a Newark record shop in the thirties. The only gospel singers he sold then were the Selah Jubilees, the Georgia Peach, and Rosetta. In 1939 he formed Savoy, and three years later recorded his first gospel act, the Kings of Harmony. In the late forties, he spread out in gospel and blues. His jazz line was equally illustrious, and included classic performances by Charlie Parker, Milt Jackson, and Bud Powell.

In the late fifties, Lubinsky acquired a new a. and r. man, Ozzie Cadena, who helped him with Savoy's first gospel albums. Cadena always worked at Rudy Van Gelder's technically astonishing recording studio, and the sound on those old Savoy albums still transcends any current gospel releases. Virtually every Savoy album produced by Cadena was a masterpiece; he is, with Art Rupp of Specialty (producer of classic discs by the Harmonettes, Pilgrim Travelers, Soul Stirrers, Alex Bradford, and Joe May), probably the most gifted producer in gospel history. Cadena's successor at Savoy, Fred Mendelsohn, originally worked for the company in the early fifties, and has had a long, honorable career in blues, where he helped discover the greatest modern shouter, Big Maybelle. Under Cadena and Mendelsohn, Savoy developed the finest catalogue in gospel, including work by the Ward Singers, Davis Sisters, Roberta Martin Singers, Caravans, Gospel Harmonettes, Clara Ward, Marion Williams, Rosetta Tharpe, Bessie Griffin, Alex Bradford, Robert Anderson—the list is endless. In a choir era, their choir hits blanket the market. Their biggest seller, James Cleveland, rules gospel and frequently sells 50,000 LPs per release.

Savoy was first situated in a misshapen factory-warehouse in Newark. The offices were defiantly old-fashioned, their walls congested with pictures of the kind exhibited in outdoor art shows. In the several floors above, rooms filled with old Savoy records; below, a small office staff headed by Fred Mendelsohn who single-handedly produced and promoted all Savoy discs.

At the heart of it all stands Herman Lubinsky, a veteran of nearly forty years, whose energies remain undiminished. He is extremely patriotic: "Stephen Decatur, a great statesman, said 'My country right or wrong.' That's what I believe." He is proud of his accomplishments, and indeed, very few executives have inaugurated the recording careers of so many gifted artists. He speaks affectionately of his customers. "I always say I make records for the man with the dinner pail and the lady over the washtub." When one of his choirs performs his favorite song, "Nearer My God to Thee," he bursts into tears. As he grows older, he delights in recounting the same anecdotes about his long career, dating back to the Irish and Italians he fought as a kid. He likes to tell "snappy" stories about the record business, but is always scrupulously polite before "a real lady," such as Miss Roberta Martin, whom he dubbed the Helen Hayes of gospel. (Lubinsky died in 1973.)

Except for a rare smash like Cleveland's "Peace Be Still" or the Ward Singers' "Surely" and "Packin' Up," Savoy has never really broken the Southern market, though it rules the East and West. The South belongs primarily to Nashboro, a Nashville-based company started by Ernie Young, who owned a large record store and a huge mail-order business. For over twenty years "Ernie's Record Mart" has broadcast over WLAC, a 50,000-watt station that reportedly reaches 65 percent of the black population. Naturally the program's bulk is made up of Nashboro records, offered at special rates to mail-order customers. Until lately these were poorly recorded discs by country-oriented singers like the Swanee Quintet, Madame Edna Gallmon Cooke, Brother Joe May, and the Consolers. Thanks to WLAC, Nashboro artists who are virtually unknown in the North outsell their most famous colleagues. The Angelic Gospel Singers, a simple, down-homey act whose approach hasn't changed in twenty years, are seldom played in New York or Chicago. But single after single, they outsell every female group in the field. Edna Gallmon Cooke's sermonettes, "Stop, Gambler," "The Mule Talked," and "Seven Steps to Hell," still sell steadily seven years after her death.

In recent years Nashboro has assimilated the slick technology that makes Nashville "Music City." They have built an imposing sixteen-track recording studio, Woodland, and signed the more hip acts like Dorothy Love, Alex Bradford, and several modern choirs, while dropping country quartets and soloists by the dozen. Nashboro albums were formerly an insult to eye and ear. Their biggest seller by the Consolers had a typical Nashboro title "Heartwarming Spirituals," the cover a red heart on a white background; a characteristic album liner note referred to "Edna known to many as Madame Cooke." Now the company features color photos back and front. The sound is improved too, and is at times juiced up by Woodland's Moog Synthesizer, a far cry from the Radio Four's guitar.

The prominent figure here was Shannon Williams, a forty-three-year-old white Southerner. Shannon speaks the molasses-coated drawl of the old South. But he is a flashily modern dresser who hates hillbilly music and loves only blues and gospel. It wasn't always so. "I started working in Ernie's mail-order office ten years ago. I used to dearly despise gospel music. These boys would come in from Vanderbilt asking for records by C. L. Franklin. I thought they were plumb crazy. Now I love it." Shannon is the only gospel producer extant who comes from a Holiness church, albeit a white one, so he's wise in the ways of gospel hysteria. He attended Lee College, a fundamentalist school in Cleveland, Tennessee, where emotional outbursts were the norm. Every night, prayer services were held in the dormitory halls, and he remembers picking his way around the bodies of young students slain by the spirit. He himself never fell out, though "I've seen too many healings not to believe in all this."

Shannon's favorite artists are the young choirs. He likes their volume and flamboyance. "Now these choirs will do something to me. My breath gets short, I can see myself letting go." Still, he's more convinced of the reality of the white Pentecostal's faith. What he likes about the black gospel life style—its humor, irreverence, self-parody, and sheer exhibitionism—is absent in the superstraight world of white Holiness. But he's long out of that scene. "I went back to Lee last year, and do you know? Those children were playing Simon and Garfunkel. I was shocked." He wears an elaborate pink-and-purple silk shirt, topped by an elflike jumper vest bearing the initials of his favorite choir, the Twenty-first Century Singers.

The gospel singers depend on the record companies and jocks, but they don't trust them. "You'll never get an honest statement from a record company," they tell you. "I know my records are hits and they wind up saying I owe them money." As for the modern d.j.s, "They just play choirs because choirs come cheap. I can tell you one thing. They definitely don't help the cause of the groups." In the long run, nobody prospers. The unimaginatively programmed shows get canceled, the singers lose their one outlet of exposure. Meanwhile, soul radio is booming with decadent versions of the joyful noises gospel invented.

David said the word of God was sweeter than honey,
But so many gospel singers give it all up for money,
I'm glad I've got the master on my side.
                                        —BROTHER JOE MAY

During the fifties, the leading rhythm-and-blues artists approached gospel as comparative outsiders. The major blues singer, B. B. King, never sang gospel professionally, though his early idol was Sam McCrary, the sensational tenor lead for the Fairfield Four. King's vocal lines are more elaborate and dramatic than those of the laconic early blues singers; McCrary's quartet stylings provide the difference. Similarly Ray Charles, the first man to sing secular words to a gospel beat, never sang the real thing. He began his recording career as a warmed-over Nat King Cole before assimilating the anguished cries of the Five Blind Boys and Alex Bradford. After Charles's innovative style revolutionized pop music, ambitious young singers began to leave the church en masse. By 1970, almost every important soul star could claim gospel origins. Many recorded with popular gospel groups: Sam Cooke, Johnnie Taylor (the Soul Stirrers), Lou Rawls (the Pilgrim Travelers), Wilson Pickett (the Violinaires), Roscoe Robinson (the Five Blind Boys), Judy Clay, Cissy Houston (the Drinkard Singers whose manager's daughters, Dionne and DeeDee Warwick, are both pop stars), Laura Lee Rundless (the Meditation Singers, who also produced Della Reese), David Ruffin (the Dixie Nightingales), to name a few. The walking incarnation of soul, Aretha Franklin,

"Lady Soul" herself, is the most gospel-influenced singer of all.

Aretha tells *Time* reporters, "My heart is still there in gospel music. It never left." James Cleveland explains it another way: "Everything Aretha does is gospel." It's not merely her singing. When she dances across a stage, she's shouting pure and simple, no pretense at the Bump or Funky Chicken. Her frowning demeanor, her incredible facial contortions, her very presence on stage, evoke the gospel manner. When all else fails, she goes back to the gospel roots. After a couple of moderate sellers she returned to the top ten with "Don't Play That Song Again," an old Ben E. King tune distinguished by piano riffs, front and center, that dated back past Clara Ward or Cleveland, her obvious inspirations, to none other than Roberta Martin.

Aretha grew up in church. In some ways her father, Reverend C. L. Franklin, is the real superstar in the family. He came out of the Mississippi cotton fields to assume pastorates in Memphis and Buffalo before he moved to Detroit and the 4,500-member New Bethel Baptist Church. Franklin may not be the best, but he's the most famous preacher in the gospel circuit. "The Man with the Million-Dollar Voice" commanded four thousand dollars a sermon in the early fifties. Occasionally he'd sing in a huge, thrilling baritone; years later, Joe Ligon of the Mighty, Mighty Clouds of Joy became road champ mimicking the Franklin roars. Despite her father's success, Aretha was not a happy child. Her mother deserted the four Franklin children when she was six. In her early years, Frances Steadman and Marion Williams of the Ward Singers used to help mother her, "show her how to take care of herself." But she was always moody and retiring. Her idol was Clara Ward, Franklin's long-time friend; when she saw Clara ecstatically throw her hat at the coffin after singing "Peace in the Valley" at a relative's funeral, she decided to sing too. In 1956, the fourteen-year-old Aretha cut her first records "live" in New Bethel. They included Clara's best known hymns, "The Day Is Past and Gone," "The Fountain," and "Precious Lord," all sung exactly as Clara would, complete with moans and ad-libbed "good Lords." Her most successful disc from this period was "Never Grow Old." When the young Aretha wailed "We'll never grow old Old OLD," her voice lifted to a thrilling high note while New Bethel gasped and hollered its approval.

In 1960 she switched to pop singing with a generous contract from Columbia Records. On her first album, she cut what some consider her best pop vocal, "Are You Sure?" a neo-gospel show tune in which the phrasing is superior Clara Ward. Her beautiful voice and stylized vocals impressed all the critics, but for years her records didn't sell. She played seedy jazz clubs, singing show tunes and ballads, trying to wed Barbra Streisand to Clara Ward and not succeeding. In 1966 she left Columbia owing the label $70,000 in advances, and considered by most rock critics in their charming argot, "just another spade chick singer." Jerry Wexler of Atlantic thought otherwise. "I took her to church," Wexler says, "sat her down at the piano, let her be herself." The result was an unprecedented series of million-sellers.

Aretha is the most successful gospel-based vocalist of our time. Yet one often feels she's not happy in blues. Many of her performances are tired, melodramatic, and extravagant, perhaps because the pop idiom seldom provides sufficient inspiration for her. Most of her biggest hits remind one of other gospel singers. "Respect" is Jacqui Verdell all over, especially in the soaring "RESPECT." In "I Never Loved a Man," she scoops menacingly like Mavis Staples; in "Satisfaction," she syncopates in falsetto like Marion Williams. The Clara Ward moan is always at the core; the physical manner increasingly resembles Mahalia's. But then, after a series of much-publicized personal scandals, Aretha told Mahalia, "I'm gonna make a record and tell Jesus I cannot bear these burdens alone." On a TV show, after a series of lackluster performances, she sat down at the piano, began "Precious Lord," and found herself happy on camera. "I'm strong in my religion," she ad-libbed; "I wish other people knew Him like I do," and she began screaming "Jesus" while her father bobbed his head approvingly in the background. Happy or sad, Aretha is a gospel child. She cuts her best recent pop with Billy Preston, Cleveland's former organist, and stars in Las Vegas with Albertina Walker and the Caravans. "I'm looking for Aretha to come back one of these days," says a friend. "She won't be happy till she does."

Next to the Edwin Hawkins Singers of "Happy Day" fame, the most influential gospel group in folk-rock are the Staple Singers. Well-known critics have called them the best and most inventive of the gospel groups. In truth, they are an appealing novelty, if not the stuff of gospel legends. Though they're best known for their hit, "I'll Take You There," an odd mix of soul and bubble-gum music, in another era, their blend of down-home, neo-hillbilly harmonies, a simple blues guitar, and an understated pulsation made for some great records. (The down-home school of gospel is now represented by the Consolers and Bill Moss and the Celestials, an Alabama family group; sadly, the most gifted of all, Brother and Sister Quince, the National Gospel Twins of Delray Beach, Florida, are seldom recorded.)

The genius of the Staples is their father, Roebuck Staples. He learned guitar on the plantation in his native Mississippi, copying the blues licks of Barbecue Bob and Big Bill Broonzy. In the forties, he moved to Chicago with his wife and children. The Staple kids, Cleotha, Purvis, Mavis, and Yvonne, are all beautiful, and Staples is a handsome man several shades darker than his children; together they make an arresting impression. While working in the Armour meat factory, he set up a family quartet with the youngest daughter, Mavis, singing bass. They worked awhile around Chicago with little success. In 1957 they cut the hymn "Uncloudy Day" with Mavis singing a deep, erotic lead. "Uncloudy Day" was a smash, and the Staples followed up with several excellent records: "Too Close," a solo by Roebuck, who sings Alex Bradford's classic in a thin, winsome voice punctuated by beautiful guitar comments; "Pray On," a frantic rhythm shout with Mavis belting like her idols Dorothy Love and Ruth Davis; "Will the Circle Be Unbroken?" an old country hymn sung to the same arrangement popularized by the hillbilly Carter Family in the thirties; and "Somebody Saved Me," in which the family sings together in harmonies enhanced by Cleotha's tense, skinny tenor. The Staples were the novelty sensation of the late fifties. Roebuck, the shrewdest manager since Gertrude Ward, had them booked with the most professional groups. Though his guitar and arrangements made the Staples sound, the pressure to perform in person fell on Mavis. To Chicagoans she was one of many fine young singers; but Roebuck was clearly out to produce another Aretha. As so often with gospel's third generation, the inspiration came from above and behind.

In the early sixties the Staples signed with Gary Kramer, the gifted manager who also created *Black Nativity*. Via Kramer, they moved to Riverside Records and a series of "folk-gospel" albums. The white folk establishment adored them. They appeared at all the major folk festivals and were the first black artists to record Bob Dylan's tunes (Dylan for years touted Mavis as his favorite soul vocalist). When Riverside folded, they signed with Epic and cut two hits, "Why?" a protest number reminiscent of old Pilgrim Travelers chants, and "For What It's Worth," the Buffalo Springfield tune. As a result, they began appearing with major rock acts. For a while they were one of the few black acts to tour the Fillmore circuit. But the rock world rarely sticks with its token black darlings. Purvis, who admits, "We got the old man to turn around and do all this new stuff," retired from the group, and went into management and production. The first group he signed

was the Emotions, another Chicago child gospel group:
"I'm getting them while they're still young." He had
grounds for bitterness. At least two rhythm-and-blues hits,
"Chain of Fools" by Aretha and the Sweet Inspirations
(and a very Stapley guitar) and "Freedom Train" by their
buddies Gladys Knight and the Pips, were shot through
with Staples harmonies.

Eventually the Staples joined the competition. They
signed with Stax Records, a Memphis soul company. They
cut a series of folk-rock message tunes with little success.
Finally Mavis switched to pop, as Chicago had been pre-
dicting for a decade. Her wide-ranging contralto has
proved a notable addition to the soul vocalists, though her
two albums without the family support seem nervous and
tentative; a potentially great soloist remains a group singer.
The Staples briefly tried to straddle both fences, keeping
their gospel identification even as Mavis rode the soul
charts. It was a hard trick to manage. On Thanksgiving
Day, 1969, they made a rare gospel appearance in Philadelphia, where Mavis' latest ballad was a smash hit. They
went back to the same routine that had sustained them
for years. Mavis shook hands on "Help Me Jesus" and
groaned with suffering on "Tell Heaven I'm Coming
Home One Day." Philadelphia remained very still. The
girls walked off stage shyly and obviously hurt. But Roebuck wouldn't give up. "Listen, church, you have to look
out for yourself," he said strumming the guitar. "Don't
nobody want to go to heaven more than I do, children,
but we got to live down here too." The message was clear,
but no "Amens" resounded. Finally Roebuck brought
Mavis back to sing "Precious Lord." I've seldom seen her
work harder. She was all over the audience, crying, roaring, running. Four ladies screamed, the least such effort
deserved, but the rest of the church remained very still.
The applause was barely polite as Cleotha led the en-
tranced Mavis out.

Despite their pop status, the Staples retain their gospel
loyalties and are hurt by those singers who accuse them of

merely switching for the money. ("We're still a *message* group," they insist somewhat disingenuously.) And though they have made a lot of money, other gospel singers who move are seldom as lucky.

Their apparent sell-outs are more properly trades, one black show-business insecurity for another. While Aretha and some others may be millionaires, dozens of singers struggle along in pop for the same few pennies they earned in gospel. The Davis Sisters' Jacqui Verdell stepped out the same year Aretha did; twenty years later, she remains unknown. There are other girls who might match Aretha. Lois Snead of the Dorothy Norwood Singers has some of the sweetness and the twang; "Big" Liz Dargan, a stout young woman of Ruth Davis vocal proportions, could be overwhelming in blues; with her nerve, there's no telling what Shirley Caesar might do. To some, the most promising singer of all in the late fifties was Sondra Peyton. At fifteen, while Aretha was mimicking Clara Ward, Sondra was featured with the Ward Singers and tearing the Apollo Theatre up each performance. But her Sanctified grandmother kept her home. Except for a brief tour in *Black Nativity,* Sondra had no professional career and died young. What could have been the finest soul vocalist of her generation went the way of other gospel legends: "You should have heard that child, you talk about Aretha. . . ."

Jessy Dixon might easily become a pop idol, combining the appeal of Sly Stone and Marvin Gaye. Willie Rogers could continue the Soul Stirrers tradition in pop. If recorded right, Johnny Jones of the Swanee Quintet would have no peers among falsetto soul stylists. But, finally, why should any of them move? Without promotion and management, they'll languish and fade. At least, in gospel, singing can carry you through. In pop, the disillusioned singers say money is all. If you're an Aretha, with Clara and C. L. Franklin and Columbia and Atlantic behind you, fine. Otherwise, Billie Holliday was right: "Then that's got shall get, them that's not shall lose."

18

A Weekend with the Campbells, 1969

"And then we being *blood* sisters, I always say that gives our harmony a special edge." Deloris Barrett Campbell and her sisters, Billie Greenbey and Rhodessa Porter, call themselves the Barrett Sisters. Their harmony is special, probably the best in female gospel. It converges around Deloris' huge soprano, a voice of operatic scale fitted to its owner's Wagnerian frame. Billie and Rhodessa are much more petite, and their voices are uncanny fractions of their sister's. Rhodessa sings the coloratura notes of Deloris' youth; Billie's soft, skinny, placid alto predicts the downward tendency of Deloris' mature voice. Sometimes, to regale Chicago with their versatility, they sing "Climb Every Mountain" and "Born Free," sounding to some like Gospel's Lennon Sisters. But cotton candy turns to grits and greens when the sisters bear down on their hard numbers. Deloris is a legendary house wrecker, though it's Billie and Rhodessa who fall out. When happy, "Lois" may holler out "Yessir" or "Praise him, children"; more likely she just keeps on singing while her trim, middle-class sisters "go ahead and shout."

The Barrett Sisters typify the struggles of all gospel

groups. Talent notwithstanding, their commercial success is slight. All three work at other jobs, Billie as a secretary, Rhodessa in a bank, and Deloris, "doing the only thing I can do," sings for a local funeral parlor. Similarly while Rhodessa's husband is a supervisor at the Ford Motor Plant, and Billie's husband deals in paints, the poorest off is Lois' husband, Frank Campbell, a minister and tailor, of great dedication and talent, but little luck in either line. Not that Chicago doesn't know and love their Barrett Sisters. Each year the ladies sing at Democratic Party campaigns, and Thomas A. Dorsey chose them as the stars of his 1970 musicale.

Chicago especially loves Deloris of the fabulous voice —Marion Williams says, "That girl can make a song so sweet you want to eat it"—and charming presence. People always request that she sing at their funerals. Even at a party, an old lady accosted her: "If the Lord calls me before we meet again, I want you to sing 'God Is So Wonderful' for me." Lois has been moving them for almost thirty years. When she was still in her teens, Roberta Martin heard her, trained her, turned her into the lead vocalist of the Martin Singers. During the war years, traveling on special clergymen's passes, Deloris and the Martins made the best money of their lives. It was an exhilarating time. The young Martin Singers—Deloris, Bessie Folk, Norsalus McKissick, Robert Anderson, Willie Webb, Eugene Smith —all superb soloists, were spreading the gospel sound with a spirit and fire uncontaminated by the professionalism of later days. Deloris recalls the house wrecking, but also the fun. "Willie Webb used to have us in stitches. We'd be performing, trying to get deep in the spirit, and Webb start whispering, 'Sing mustard greens,' 'Sing turnip greens.'" In the early fifties, Lois married Frank Campbell. Though she continued to record and sing locally with the Martins, she seldom left Chicago after that. She remained close to Roberta, who was unfailingly generous to the Barrett Sisters, accompanying them on their records and in person. Sallie Martin and Mahalia also showered her with

Ruth Davis, New York, 1957.
Photograph by Lloyd Yearwood

The Clark Sisters. *Top row*: Jackie Clark, Mattie Moss Clark, Twinkie Clark. *Bottom row*: Dorinda Clark, Denise Clark, Karen Clark.

Dorothy Love Coates, New York, 1970.
Photograph by Stephen Paley

James Cleveland, New York, 1970.
Photograph by Stephen Paley

The Caravans, New York, 1957. *Left to right:* Dorothy Norwood, Johneron Davis, Albertina Walker, Inez Andrews.
Photograph by Lloyd Yearwood

Deloris Barrett and the Barrett Sisters, Chicago, 1968. *Left to right:* Rhodessa Porter, Deloris Barrett Campbell, Billie Greenbey.
Photograph by Shannon Williams

The Swan Silvertones, New York, 1965. *Top row, left to right:* Louis Johnson, William Connor, Paul Owens. *Bottom row, left to right:* Linwood Hargrove (guitarist), Claude Jeter, John Myles.

R. H. Harris, Chicago, 1954.

Black Nativity: Marion Williams and Alex Bradford, New York, 1961.

Shirley Caesar running with member of audience, St. Louis, 1970.

Photograph Courtesy of Hob Records

James Cleveland, Shirley Caesar. Andraé Crouch and others on tour in Jerusalem.

The Hawkins Family. *From left*: Daniel, Feddie, Tramaine, Carol, Walter, Lynette, Joel, Edwin.

compliments. "But Mahalia kept telling me I'm gonna make it, and I'm long past grown. I'm tired of waiting." Often her teen-age buddy, Dinah Washington, would call her and jokingly advise her to switch to blues. "She told me, 'Girl, you'll tear up out here.'" With four kids, she was sorely tempted.

In a beautiful reversal, she was held to the gospel plow by her father, Lonnie Barrett, Sr. Mr. Barrett was a "stone Baptist," a native of Hickory, Mississippi, who divided life between hard work and prayer. He was an early and eager unionist, one of Chicago's oldest members of the National Bricklayers Union. He died while working, at seventy-eight. Frank Campbell remembers, "My father-in-law was the real old school. If he'd meet you, first thing he'd say would be 'Are you married, son? Are you a Christian? Where do you live? Do you like my daughters? They're fine girls.'"

Barrett built the ranch house he bequeathed to the Campbells. As a result, Deloris lives in the same neighborhood as her wealthier sisters. Chicago's South Side is studded with lovely homes, vacated by terrified whites and now homogeneously spotless. It's a far cry from the slum rot of her childhood, from the cluttered apartment with its family altar around which she did her first singing. Deloris knew the worst of Depression ghetto life. "As kids, we used to sleep in the same bed. I lost some of my brothers and sisters to the tuberculosis. I believe they got it from sleeping together, and to this day, I don't like my children sleeping too close." Gangs are infiltrating even her fine neighborhood, and she often sings at funerals of members of the Black P. Stone Nation, Chicago's biggest gang complex, "and let me tell you, their kiss of death is something else."

Lately Deloris has been overwhelmed by tragedies. Her mother died after a long, wearying decline ("Mama wasn't too confused. She just say to the man on television, she wasn't cooking anymore, Deloris did it now"). Then her father dropped dead on the job, and a few months later

"Miss Martin's death like to kill me." Early in 1970, high blood pressure sent her to the hospital, and under doctors' orders, she began to lose weight. Six months later, her fourteen-year-old daughter died of hepatitis. The work in gospel has been slow. She had a great gig in San Francisco, performing to a crowd of three thousand, but the next night in Los Angeles, she sang to fifty saints. "Thank goodness for the funerals." I volunteer that funeral singing must be a great emotional strain. "It is. I always cry. I just think about my mother and father. But then again, I like giving people a release. So many say my singing really brings their suffering *out*. And," defending her sure thing, "I guess even if gospel's slowing, there's always gonna be funerals." Which is to say that Deloris hasn't escaped her childhood after all.

The July Fourth weekend kept Deloris busy. Friday morning she spent cleaning the house and worrying about her children. The oldest, Frankie, is fresh out of high school and jobless. Of the three girls, Sue, Roberta and Mary, only Roberta had a job—as companion to a dying old lady. While the girls watched the noonday soap operas and Frankie sang his Nat King Cole imitations in the shower, Deloris planned her shopping at the massive Jewel Market. Naturally, the store was jammed with customers. Most of the remaining food looked inedible. Deloris apologized for the chopped steaks, expensive and overloaded with fat. "Usually I buy my meats in the white stores." Fans and friends stopped her. "Didn't I see you on 'Jubilee Showcase'? My, you have a pretty voice." It was two hours before she returned home, having spent forty dollars on food for the weekend.

Late in the afternoon, Billie and Rhodessa joined her, and the various families and assorted children drove out to the country. Despite a cold, rainy July Fourth, the picnic was a success. It was a mini-vacation for the kids, who camped out, but Deloris had to return to Chicago for two funerals. So Saturday night found her back home and exhausted. We sat around the kitchen table, nibbling at the sweet-potato pie Jewel bakes for its ghetto customers.

Then enters the wildest outfit, all black-leathered skin-tight suit, blinding ascot, heavy tilted cap and shades. It's Frank Campbell, gray-haired, forty-nine-year-old Baptist minister, but manifestly no square. Frank is a good-natured fop by inclination and also as advertisement for his tailoring service. His outfits are striking: "A Frank Campbell original" say the labels, but because Frank will only work with the best materials, his profit margin is slight. Likewise, he's the least charlatan gospel preacher I've encountered, and that doesn't hoist up the family account either. Oddly enough, the Frank who affects the fop outdoors is anything but flamboyant in church. "I get emotional but I'm not what you call a shouting preacher. I believe in giving a message, sort of like a lecture."

There's so much sincerity and dedication in his approach that, during her last illness, Roberta Martin deserted a huge Baptist church and worshiped in his store-front. To Deloris, Miss Martin is still Miss Martin; Frank refers to her as Bert. But they weren't always so tight. "I was once so mad with Bert I wouldn't speak to her. That's when Lois was singing 'Wonderful' and tearing up everywhere. She begged Bert to record it, but she was so narrow she wouldn't let her, just because she didn't own the publishing. So Sam Cooke went along with Lois' song and made a mint. It took me awhile to forgive Bert that." But the early hostility cemented the friendship, and Frank was a pallbearer at Roberta Martin's funeral.

This past week, the predominantly white Pentecostal Businessman's Convention convened at the Conrad Hilton. One afternoon, Deloris sang at the services of Katherine Kuhlman, a healer whose gifted finger-tapping automatically lays white matrons in the aisles. Frank attended every day, and he is delighted by the fellowship he encountered. He urges me to come to his church tomorrow to hear the testimonies of three born-again white people, praising God and speaking in tongues. Deloris, good Baptist daughter of Lonnie Barrett, is immediately suspicious. She doesn't like Frank's speaking in tongues. Lately some Baptists have begun the practice, but to her it smacks of mumbo-jumbo witchcraft. "I was taught you need an interpreter, otherwise it's just een-nah-la-ha-ya—" she mocks the tongue talkers—"just a lot of mess don't nobody understand." Frank disagrees.

Beersheba Baptist Church is a good half-hour's trip down the newly built, piously named Dr. Martin Luther King Drive. By the time Deloris arrives, service has begun. The church, like all store-fronts, is not prepossessing on the outside. Indeed, the minister's name is faded into an *ampb,* much like the dim print on Frank's tailor shop that turns his name into *Fra Ca pbe.* But inside, Frank's style greets the eye announced by long, polished wood paneling that makes the store-front seem cathedral-sized. It's summer and a holiday, so the church is not filled. There are a few young men, several women, mostly middle-aged, and three old deacons seated beneath the altar. Frank stands to the side, and seated on the altar proper are three white guests, fellow veterans of the Pentecostal Businessman's Convention.

As Deloris enters, an old deacon leads the congregation in the old Dr. Watts "long meter" hymn: "Before this time, another year, I may be dead and gone." The voices curve, tremble, and soar in a black Baptist wail two hundred years old. To this listener, Dr. Watts hymns are still the most moving kind of gospel. To Deloris they are reminders of Lonnie Barrett, Sr., and she sits, eyes closed, touched by the congregation's off-key, heartfelt singing. Then the choir enters, ten women and two men, including the Campbells' son, Frankie, in church despite himself. They sing "Yield Not to Temptation," the song with which Deloris and the Martin Singers swept America in the forties. From her seat she leads them, throwing out lusty soprano notes.

At the piano one notices Myrtle Scott, Chicago's "Sweet Singer of Zion." She is a striking jet-black woman, her features and manner totally anomalous. Her head is a bit tilted, as if she's listening to more than fills the room. Jessy Dixon says, "I hate to use the word bewitched" but it suits Myrtle. One senses immediately the power, diminished only slightly by years of illness and poverty. Lately Myrtle has started singing again, and like her old boss, Roberta Martin, she worships at Beersheba. However, Myrtle is Sanctified or at least "on my way, trying to walk soft before him. That's not easy, walking soft." Today she attends everything, perceives in a daffy, almost unconcious way, frequently dabbing her eyes, then smiling privately.

Frank gets up to speak about his experience with tongues. Myrtle talks back to him, too soft for him to hear, but then, she's really speaking to herself. "I've been fighting against the spirit," Frank testifies. ("I know where you are," says Myrtle.) "But I learned I had to yield God everything, the use of *all* my members." ("Give it to him.") "And this week, something came to me, while I was on the phone, hah, hallelujah—" he skips back, then recovers himself. "I can't explain it, but it was the most wonderful outpouring of God's love." ("It's real, you can't explain it but it's real.") "And I'm so filled with the spirit this morning. I just have to thank God for everything." ("That's it, for everything you did for me.")

Frank calls on the choir's key soloist, Ella Moore, to lead them in prayer. Ella, a pretty, light-skinned woman, walks humbly to the podium. Her life has been terrible. Among many tragedies, her oldest son was falsely accused of murder, and another son was killed a few years ago by a hit-and-run driver. "But God gave me a little girl in his place—" and the child sits beaming up at Mommy. Ella's eyes shut firmly, as she continues to praise God. "We haven't served you always but you loved us right on, we don't live the way we should but you love us right on." "Right on, right on!" The Panther slogan is revived in a new kind of litany. Ella clearly feels the spirit quickening, for she removes her glasses in expectation. When she finishes, she heads back to her seat. But what is this? Suddenly her body snaps to, and she begins speaking in tongues, this foursquare, lipsticked Baptist. And the tongues come forth with a fantastic fury, the equal of a possessed Brazilian Corybant's. Her alto plunges to a harsh bass, and she hollers gibberish with a ferocious intensity that turned into song would make her the scariest singer alive. Then she runs down the aisle, begins jumping and screaming, while the older male choir member sheepishly, smilingly guards her in her frenzy. One of the white men goes up to her, lays hands on the frantic woman, and gives forth his own tongue in a voice with one-fifth her resonance and one-tenth her fervor.

When she has calmed down and is no longer a spectacle for the bemused children, Frank introduces his visitors. Three are spirit-filled, but there is one Jewish friend in the audience who loves gospel music and isn't even saved. First to speak is a Methodist bishop from Buffalo. A genial, middle-aged man rises, grinning like an insurance salesman. "Oh, my Jewish friend, I have the most wonderful news, you too can be saved!" Perhaps seeing that his smiling address meets an irritated glare, he turns to the other benighted souls, deprived of the marvelous Holy Ghost. One thing, he insists, the Holy Ghost cannot be induced. You can't hurry tongues, but when they come, don't stop them. He's an obvious pro even before a black Baptist crowd, and they're sorry to see him leave for the airport. Before he goes, he hugs and kisses his cohorts and Frank, holy hugs, holy kisses.

Next to speak is a white nun in street clothes, one of 40,000 Catholic Pentecostals. She works as guidance counselor at a black college, and so her first line attempts hip—"I feel high on God—" scarcely the expression for mothers scared of junkies and contemptuous of hippies. In a sweet-natured, friendly way, the nun talks of her own seduction by the devils of sophistication. "The white

churches get too mental," she tells the congregation. "Stay
like you are, friends. Stay simple, don't be sophisticated."
Ella Moore, now revived, her child on her lap, grins appreciatively. The nun continues, describing her healing
experience. Katherine Kuhlman merely touched her and
she fell back. "It's nothing to be scared of. It's almost comical. We're just like matchsticks in the wind. God can
blow us down like matchsticks. But," she smiles, "he blows
us back." Ella, a witness, rocks her daughter. Yes, the
nun went all the way this week, became a Holy Roller herself. "I was laying on a couch and a brother laid hands
on me, and my whole body twitched and trembled in the
spirit. I didn't even know what was happening." The deacon who led "Before This Time Another Year" snores.

Now comes the offering. Usually on the first Sunday,
the church raises a monthly offering for its minister. But
with typical generosity, Frank donates his money this week
to the Southern Baptist who laid hands on Ella and will
address them in a little while. In the meantime, Deloris
gets up for a solo. She sings "His Eye Is on the Sparrow,"
whispering as she leaves her seat, "I'm so hoarse." There's
no evidence of hoarseness. She sings most of the song in
the soft, sweet manner Marion Williams finds good
enough to eat, but when she sings "I sing because I'm
happy, I sing because I'm free," the word "free" is a D
over high C that fills the room, followed by a raucous
squall that charmingly parodies the operatic pretensions.
When she finishes, Myrtle Scott comes in from the back
of the church, pocketbook in hand, and, remaining in Lois'
key, sings "I'm a Child of the King." True, the voice is
hardened and shaky, but the authority is terrific. Even the
white saints lift their hands in praise, and with great
aplomb, Myrtle picks up the beat and sings

I'm a millionaire, I'm a millionaire,
My father's rich in houses and lands and I'm his heir,
That makes me a multi-multi-multi-millionaire.

If the service ended now, everyone could leave satisfied.

But first we must hear from a Southern Baptist. Like his
Methodist crony, he first addresses himself to the other
white. "Oh, my Jewish friend, I'm so glad to see you. You
know one way you can tell a Christian, they always love
the Jews." The ploy doesn't serve, so he tries another. "You
know God loves the Jews. That's why he won't let the
Arabs and Russians take Israel away. No sir. Those
heathens will be so badly destroyed it'll take six months to
count all the slain. The God of Israel is a mighty God."
He's bubbling over with glee, sure that his Jewish friend
will begin speaking in tongues on the spot, glorified by
the prospect of six months to count the slain in Sinai. But
a radical glare meets his eyes, and only an anxious Deloris prevents the kind of outburst Beersheba couldn't tolerate.

The preacher's testimony is sincere and long-winded. All
the deacons are snoring as he tells of his troubles in Texas.
"I love the Nig-groes, but seems like my own turned against
me for loving God's children." When his congregations tol-
erated his "Nig-gro-loving," they couldn't abide their
pastor lying prone before the altar. "Lord, I prayed, show
me the way. Don't seem a place for me anywhere." Myrtle
and Ella grin responsively, but the other members seem
a bit irritated.

So he gives them some livelier salvation. "The Lord
blessed me with many gifts this week. Why, we had a
visitor from Turkey and couldn't nobody get through to
him. But the Lord blessed me, and I started talking Turkey to him, and that brother was saved." The Lord also
gave him the gift of lengthening legs. After pleading for
a subject, he finally persuades one old mother to limp forward. As the congregation, including Deloris, prays, he
lays hands on her. And even the old deacon wakes up in
time to say, "Dear Christian friends, the two legs are the
same now," as the old lady hollers the victory.

The young preacher is delighted. He makes the final
appeal in his slow, drawling Texan way.

"Dear friends, don't look at me as a white Southern Baptist. Look at me as a child of God." Now his aim is clear: he wants these old Baptists to get like Ella. "You know, when my four boys gets in the bathtub, the water runs over. That's what tongues are like, the spirit just overflows." Contrary to the Methodist bishop who said tongues couldn't be planned or prompted, he believes in tongue-talking by imitation. "Just follow me," he says. "Let the bath water rise in you. Get up on your feet, all you who want this glorious overflowing." Everyone rises but the unsaved one, dizzied by all these visceral metaphors . . . and someone else, Deloris glaring angry Lonnie Barrett's daughter's eyes at Frank. "Oh, get up," says the Texan. "The preacher's wife shouldn't be left out." And with a minister's wife's diplomacy, Deloris stands up too.

The tongue-talking really doesn't work, even though he lays hands on almost everyone in church. So he tries another tack, *singing* in tongues. Again he asks everyone to imitate him. "First we're all gonna sing 'Amazing Grace.' I know you know 'Amazing Grace,' every Baptist knows that song. Then we're gonna sing 'Thank You Lord' to the same tune. And then we're gonna sing it in tongues." And what a sad spectacle it is to see the deepest, most important of all black Baptist tunes so massacred. Thirty people, average age near fifty, are singing their favorite hymn, trying to duplicate the Hebraic-sounding syllables that roll out of the Texan's throat—singing "Amazing Grace" in nonsense syllables and hoping it's an unknown tongue!

Finally the service is over. The minister hugs everyone he can. He notices Deloris is a bit shy, so he comes to her. "You want to speak, don't you?" Lois smiles uncertainly. "Just talk like me," he says, as he lays hands on her throat, and commences to speak. Lois imitates him. "See, you're coming close!" But later, in a cab, Lois is an angry, hardline Baptist. "I could have fooled him just so easy if I wanted. I could have said anything." Frank sits behind her, a bit embarrassed. Even he was not prepared for the Texan's performance, but he consoles himself with his spiritual gifts. "I tell you, Frank, you just can't have anyone in your pulpit. Shoot, singing 'Amazing Grace' in tongues."

Deloris is home that night very late, fagged out by two funerals. Did the people shout? "Oh, yes," she says in a breathy but matter of-fact way. Late Sunday night, all the Chicago church choirs broadcast. Tonight they're going to announce a big "anniversary" scheduled for tomorrow, featuring "as honored guest, Deloris Barrett and the Barrett Sisters." Frankie comes in, sporting a white version of his father's spectacular outfit of last night. The Spiritualist minister tells his listeners over the air, "I love you. All of you. I got some men out there shooting dice. I want you to know I love you. I got some girls out here walking the streets. I love you." Frankie yawns. "Man sounds like Moms Mabley," he says and retires for the night.

It seems Chicago's best choirs are Spiritualist. As Clarence Cobbs's First Church of Deliverance bursts forth, Lois wakes up. "They're singing this evening. Sing, children!" Then she flicks the dial, and the choir from Bishop Anderson's church swings the latest rock-and-roll dance beat to the words of "Blessed Assurance." "That's all they're singing, these young folk. Rock and roll in gospel. It's hard to keep up with them." (The next night, predictably, the Barrett Sisters stole the show from the young choirs.) When the services end, Lois and Frank retire in a Sunday-night routine familiar to two generations of Chicagoans. The best gospel singer left in Chicago goes downstairs to a basement apartment, to a bedroom with ceilings barely six feet high. She earned enough tonight for the weekend food bills. All Frank's earnings went to the Southern Baptist. "And you know folks stop me on the street and ask me for money. They think because your name is known, you're rich."

EPILOGUE:

"Looked Down the Line and I Wondered" (1971)

The prognosis for gospel is never optimistic. Audiences stay poor, crowds dwindle, the world remains unsympathetic though ready to adapt gospel's most attractive qualities for its own ends. Yet in the last few years, spurred by the progressive choir arrangements, the "Peace Be Stills" and "Happy Days," young people have begun following gospel in larger numbers than ever. At a big gospel concert one sees Afro walking with blond wig, dashikis next to satin and sequins; an old mother hollers, "Thank You Jesus," her children cry, "Right on!" The young people's sound is defiantly middle class and cleaned up. Their music may be innovative—although how progressive is it to sing "Must Jesus Bear the Cross Alone" to the tune of "Auld Lang Syne"?—but it lacks the deep-down "sure nuff" heart's truth guts and spirit of earlier gospel.

Lately ghetto residents have begun to acquire a public voice, usually one that confounds and agitates their white listeners. The language and rhythms are all familiar to gospel followers. The ghetto mother at a City Council meeting speaks a church rap. Her manner—gutsy, rhetorical, emphatic—takes tone and idiom for granted. This is the only speech style she knows, and she employs it without self-consciousness. The average viewer seeing her on television might appreciate only some of her slang and miss completely how her shifts in tone and facial expression convey specific meanings. A gospel fan can spot her immediately as a church type. Not that anything about her behavior is unique to the gospel church; it is simply that the church alone has allowed such free public use of common habits of discourse. Chances are the ghetto mother has heard Dorothy Love Coates. For years, Mahalia Jackson kept trying to tell America something; the most important thing was her very telling. Mahalia and Dinah Washington—the protégée of Sallie Martin, remember—were the only soul forces out there, speaking with the drive and impetus of church and street.

Today, of course, the soul manner is *de rigueur* for black entertainers. Operatic sopranos cook sweet-potato pie for *The New York Times;* Senator Edward Brooke tells *Ebony,* "I'm a Soul Brother Too." Cultural nationalists who ignored gospel and blues when roots weren't fashionable are suddenly soul-music champions. Soul mannerisms have become common currency for negotiating the continued betrayal of the black poor, yet the singers are still accused of being Uncle Toms—alas, with some cause. For years, New York amateurs participated in a contest sponsored by Aunt Jemima Cake Flour. A cynic can't improve on the Aunt Jemima Gospel Contest. More to the point, the dismal track record of gospel preachers on most community issues is legendary. Even now, their attempts to accommodate the current politics can prove disastrous. The St. Louis preacher-singer Reverend Cleophus Robinson discusses civil rights on his television program in noncommittal statements—"As for the issue of racism, the roots lie within both groups—" guaranteed to offend nobody. He continues, "You can bring in a crowd talking about civil rights, and you can bring them in talking about . . . psychology, and . . . police brutality, but the only thing that keeps them in is Jesus." Now Reverend Robinson, whose

vocal cords seem controlled by a triumvirate of Rosetta
Tharpe, Mahalia, and Brother Joe May, is here borrowing
Dorothy Love's rhetoric and, not knowing what to do,
mangling it. But with such sentiments broadcast on television, gospel's image is bound to suffer. Or take Reverend
Lawrence Roberts' sermonette with the Angelic Choir in
which he tells of a praying mother who sends her son to
college, humble and neat. He returns cheeky, irreverent
and sloppy, implicitly Black Panther. Naturally the Lord
makes a way and the mother's prayers bring her radical
son back to Jesus and a razor. Again, the gospel lover is
embarrassed. Worst of all, Reverend J. H. Jackson, the
head of the National Baptist Convention, occasionally attacks black radicals in addresses to the John Birch Society.

Yet all during the fifties, when nobody in rhythm and
blues and very few in pop music even bothered to discuss
civil rights, Dorothy Love and Reverend June Cheeks never
forgot the conditions back home. Not until artists like Nina
Simone appeared had any black entertainers laid matters
so squarely on the line as Dot and June. In 1958, with her
"That's Enough" and his "To the End" among the biggest
hits in gospel, they were clearly king and queen of the gospel highway. And they spoke about lynchings and bombed
schools and segregated facilities. Other gospel singers may
not be so blunt, but their singing is always filled with the
stuff of their lives. What other music so expresses these
bedrock responses? Blues seldom travels to the graveyard,
while much of gospel is about the imminent danger of
death: "We're here today and gone today," "Death may
soon disrobe us all of what we now possess." Rock and
soul may talk about love trouble but they dodge the deeper issues
of betrayal and distrust basic to gospel. Gospel is simply the only
music sung by people in terrible conditions *about* those conditions, in an attempt to get out of them.

Every gospel singer, from the thorough-going conserva-
tives like Sallie Martin to the progressives like Cheeks and
Dot Love, is filled with black anger. If they exhibit no special loyalty to any current vanguard group, neither do the

black masses. They all disagree with black separatists, but
then so do the Panthers. Some choirs like the Victory
Choral Ensemble of Philadelphia have begun sporting dun-
garee suits like the Panthers and Reverend Jesse Jackson's
Operation Breadbasket workers. Even the super-elegant
Clouds of Joy did the Panther clothes bit one Sunday,
ostensibly to "show their sympathy with the poor," though
also to confound their imitators: "Let's see them follow
that." Black pride and black power are easily assimilated in
gospel, a music exclusively by and for blacks, to begin
with. A New Jersey choir had a mild hit with a tune reminiscent of "Twist and Shout" and a lyric subverting the
old "White is right" cliché:

> If you're white, that doesn't make you right,
> And if you're black, you don't have to stay back,
> Just spread a little sunshine, make somebody glad.

That may seem like naïve social consciousness, but it
complements the soul protest songs like "Say It Loud, I'm
Black and I'm Proud," "We're a Winner," "War, What Is
It Good For," "Ball of Confusion," or "Message from a
Black Man" ("No matter how hard you try, you can't stop
me now"). Anyway, black pride in gospel is as old as the
hymn "I'm a Child of the King." Reverend Brewster exhibited black gospel pride back in the thirties when he
named Q. C. Anderson after Queen Candice of Ethiopia.
In the forties, quartets sang "No Segregation in Heaven"
and eulogized Roosevelt, "the poor man's friend," for helping black people.

Gospel reflects the conditions and consciousness of its
audience, no more, no less. That may not be politically progressive, but until recently what music has done as much?
Already rock, the music of the counterculture, has turned
from its defiantly subversive image and replaced it with
neo-hillbilly paeans to the good life retired in the country;
Bob Dylan has disowned "It's All Right, Ma, I'm Only
Bleeding" but Dorothy Love still stands by "How Much
More of Life's Burdens Must We Bear." Gospel's audience

can still turn nowhere else for such free and passionate expression of their deepest needs, fears, and resentments. For them, rock and soul can't compete. Willie Mae Ford Smith says, "What I've got is better than liquor, it's better than a shot. Cause when the world's through, they've got a hangover. But when I'm done, I've got 'Precious Memories.' "

Gospel's final justification is not social but artistic, and it lives in the work of its best singers. Gospel is their life but it's also their art, and one's mind draws back in amazement at the creative genius that sustains them so long for so little reward. Gospel will continue; no matter what the world says, it'll be where its people are. But the great gospel witnesses will not come again. Conditions have changed too much. Despite their varying levels of consciousness, none of the young people require good gospel; the world has enough other options. The old singers understand that they symbolize another era. One says, "My Bible tells me your younger generation is always wiser . . . and weaker. Let's face it, mother wit can carry you just so far." Yet mother wit can be refined by years of hard living and singing into a very special wisdom. The older singers still know everything about moving an audience. "All right, we're has-beens," says a singer edged out of prominence by the choirs, "but we're good has-beens. Better a good has-been than a bad never-was."

The old singers are so seasoned and tested, "deepened in the spirit," that their every note seems to answer to a compelling, mysterious force unlike anything in modern music. But then, they all go back to a time when gospel wasn't merely entertainment but "everything we needed, our all in all." Mahalia Jackson says, "Somebody singing blues is crying out of a pit. I'm singing out of the joy of my salvation." Dorothy Love says, more glumly, "Gospel's saved my life and many more. If we didn't have this assurance, baby, I hate to think. . . ." R. H. Harris stuck with the music because "It had a tendency to lighten my burdens and give me an easy day. Put it this way, it kept the avenue of friendliness open to me." And Marion Williams speaks for all the testimony singers: "Child, I've had some singing days. I'm not talking about making money. I'm talking about singing to *express* myself. You know that's a *blessing*."

POSTSCRIPT

Gospel singers like to quote the biblical passage "the race is not to the swift, nor the battle to the strong, neither yet bread to the wise, . . . nor yet favor to men of skill; but time and chance happeneth to them all." In the past few years, time has removed some of the major gospel singers—the three most famous, Mahalia Jackson, Clara Ward and Rosetta Tharpe, in the course of two years. Chance meanwhile has rewarded some old pros with the change in image and fortune they've waited upon (as in the spiritual line "All of my appointed time, I'm gonna wait till my change comes"), while others have worked less than ever, though their talents are undiminished. Pretentious choral arrangements and sapless gospel-rock hybrids have snatched their prizes, but down-home gospel has made a surprising comeback. The combination of time and chance, as inchoate and unpredictable as life itself, bespeaks the organic nature of gospel folklore. Time displaced the old gospel sound; chance may run back and fetch its survivors. Even so, chance placed Mahalia, Clara and Rosetta above their peers; time cut short their domination; and chance blesses us with enough great singers to keep alive the gospel these women symbolized in other bad times.

To paraphrase Thoreau, gospel singers lead lives of deep suspicion, nurturing their secrets like money that may be stolen any minute. None of them, especially Mahalia Jackson, was meant to live her life in public. Yet in her last years, Mahalia's marriages, divorces, remarriages and consequent breakdowns made her a laughing stock; the church folk now had a handle on the woman who had moved up too high, the queen was now down again with her subjects. Mahalia's private disposition was honest, earthy, a bit vulgar. But the world knew her as a religious zealot; the image might fit devout Willie Mae Ford Smith or contentious Sallie Martin. It was not natural to her, and when it crumbled so publicly, physical collapse was the predictable result. In the world, a natural sympathy and respect for her image attended Mahalia in her decline. But before church audiences, a peculiar tug of war obtained, as if Mahalia and the people had replaced affection with contempt, familiarity with suspicion. Not that she didn't work to rekindle old memories. At one church program, she tried to rouse a lethargic congregation by descending to her knees, but she lacked the strength to rise up. Ushers came to her rescue while her friends wondered at the showmanly risk; even now, the queen knew "my folks think you ain't done nothing if you haven't shouted them."

In the late sixties, the old warrior came onstage, uncertain of the support behind or before her. Her old pianist, Mildred Falls, suffered for years from arthritis and eventually retired. Her successors, Gwendolyn Cooper and Edward Robinson, were good modern musicians, but it took an old-timer like Mildred or James Lee (the male soprano who sang duets with Mahalia in the mid-forties) to create the simple blues ambience that best fulfilled her urge to testify. She was once again "truly out here on my own." When the spirit fell around her, there was no longer the sympathetic encouragement of Mildred's chords to push her in and guide her out.

As business and personal problems began to overwhelm her, she turned once more to the old testimony tunes; one remembered the time she used a divorce decision as a public excuse for singing "How I Got Over." But such songs couldn't contain the number and complexity of Mahalia's worries. So what had been, despite all its eccentricities, a free-form *style* became increasingly incoherent. The characteristic swoops from croon to roar now seemed to answer no need but emotional release. Mahalia's spirited if dotty nonsequiturs had always made dramatic sense. Now the emotional mood of any next moment seemed unpredictable, "Start when you feel like, finish when you can." Gospel songs may not have been the most appropriate vehicles for expressing Mahalia's feelings, but the queen and her followers knew no others. Granting the physical weakness, the failure of Mahalia's late art was, in some ways, the failure of the form itself.

In the fall of 1971, she made plans for a European tour and the final purchase of a Chicago synagogue she would transform into the Mahalia Jackson temple for all peoples. Here, she told reporters, "everybody can come and enjoy this . . . uh . . . wonderful . . . joy." Before leaving, she appeared on Flip Wilson's show, singing "Just a Closer Walk With Thee." She looked fine, streamlined enough to accentuate her small waist and rollicking hips. In fact, she strutted more sensuously than usual, appeared happy with the rhythm and message, and at one moment, seemed to be snapping her fingers or at least caressing them with worldly intent. The camera flashed briefly on an elegant black woman of uncertain age clapping very modestly, as if to say, "well, it's one of us, so why not." It was, of course, Sallie Martin. The two old friends having met earlier, Mahalia had suggested that Flip allow Sallie her moment on national television. (It is Miss Martin's dream to return for a full appearance.) Certainly Mahalia's gesture and Sallie's cool response were complicated by years of friendly rivalry.

After this special treat for gospel lovers, Mahalia flew to Europe but returned almost immediately, gravely ill. There had been so many close calls for the queen that her friends ignored this last illness. She rallied briefly and became tangled in problems of talmudic complexity involving the purchase of the Mahalia temple. The jumbled events sent her back to the hospital with heart trouble, this time in critical condition. Some old friends stopped by, more would have had there been time. (The singer Mahalia once called "the best there is," Willie Mae Ford Smith, had come during an earlier illness. "Halie said, 'Well see, I've sent for you, I paid your ticket.' I told her I was glad to come and I'd come again whenever she needed me, I'd raise the money somehow.") Instead, in early January 1972, *Jet* announced on its front cover: "World Famous Gospel Singer Dies Alone." The last word was also the final insult; if Mahalia was not to die in peace, she might have been spared this ultimate invasion of privacy.

Two funerals took place, the first in Chicago, the second in her hometown, New Orleans, where she was buried. The night before the funeral, her church, Greater Salem Baptist, ran a wake in which a steady stream of singers addressed the stern-faced corpse, the troubled face not even relaxed in death. Sallie Martin spoke, "You know when I first knew Mahlia, lots of churches wouldn't take her in. But I didn't do like that. I've always believed in lending a hand . . . to help somebody. I'm gonna sing for you Mr. Dorsey's song 'It Doesn't Cost Very Much.'" Suddenly she spasmed to the side. "Hey, hey," Eddie Robinson called, "that's Sallie Martin, you can't beat a trouper," though one doubted if Sallie was out to beat anyone. Another old rival, Clara Ward, sang at the wake; although it was her protégée, Aretha Franklin, who sang at the funeral. After her mother, Gertrude, chanted Tindley's "The Storm Is Passing Over," Clara sang the great Philadelphia composer's "Beams of Heaven," moaning and growling

"I do not know how long it will be
Or what the future holds for me."

Was the point to tear up in a final battle of queens? Whatever, Clara sang beautifully. She returned to her seat,
walked a few steps, then tore off her mink wrap and tossed
it at Mahalia's coffin. She had already suffered two strokes
and was to die a year later. Clara's flamboyant gesture
called attention to her wealth and her song. It was in keeping with the Wards' record of showmanship, but it seemed
a more private statement from Clara to Mahalia, beyond
words but fully comprehensible to those who knew them.

The Chicago funeral was a national occasion. It was
held at the huge Aerie Crown Theatre and excerpts appeared on the evening news programs. To protect themselves from the January lakefront cold, and perhaps to assert their own regality, scores of fine singers paraded past
the open casket, garbed in swank furs, minks for Mahalia.
Many dignitaries spoke—Mayor Daley, Ella Fitzgerald.
Sammy Davis, Jr., performing one of his earliest errands
for Richard Nixon, relayed the President's condolences.
But it was not the knock-down going home service gospel
singers expected. Of the many elegant mourners, few were
called to sing.

As a feeble recognition of Mahalia's origins, the program
listed solos by three singers—J. Robert Bradley, Robert Anderson and Aretha Franklin—and comments by Sallie Martin and Thomas A. Dorsey. Dorsey, as always, was equa-
ble and unruffled. He recited a brief poem, "just a piece of
doggerel I composed this morning," and returned to his
seat. Sallie Martin wasn't so easily assuaged. "See this girl
calls me up and says, 'We want you to say a few words,
Miss Martin.' I told her, 'I'm sorry, darlin', I'm a singer
not a talker'. She comes around with 'Well, I'm telling you
like it was given to me' and I say, 'I'm telling you like it
is.'" So Sallie relinquished her time to Deloris Barrett
Campbell who sang a brief solo while Sallie called out encouragement.

Robert Anderson, Mahalia's old buddy, sang "Move On Up a Little Higher," accompanied by Mildred Falls, now so weak from arthritis that she had to be supported to and from the piano. The spirit had no chance to sweep the auditorium; the dignitaries kept interfering. But then J. Robert Bradley strode to the mike. Despite his years of vocal training and obvious resemblance to Paul Robeson, Bradley knows the exigencies of gospel theatre. He cued his pianist, and, building his fire precisely, allowed the musician a long, melodramatic introduction. He sang "I'll Fly Away," all three verses, paying tribute to Mahalia and his colleagues. Sallie Martin leapt from her seat, "Sing, Bradley. Always said he could sing our gospel. Just wanted to be a concert singer too bad, but . . . hey," and she stopped commenting and began praising. Mahalia's first husband, an old invalid in a wheel chair, started to cry. Deloris Barrett Campbell patted his hand. Seeing James Lee tremble, she hollered, "Hold on, James." Then the meaning of Bradley's song hit her. "I know what you're singing about," she cried. "Living to fly away, sure nuff, sure nuff, sure nuff," and she jumped with each "sure nuff" more impassioned than I've ever seen her.

Bradley ended the song, paused for a moment, then turned to the mike, "I don't care who you are, white or black, red or yellow. I want you to shake your neighbor's hand and say 'I love you.'" The resulting pandemonium was close to the emotional catharsis a gospel singer's funeral deserves.

It ended with Aretha Franklin, simply dressed and beautiful, singing "Precious Lord." She sang it as always with traces of Clara Ward. Gertrude Ward leapt to her feet, moved by the family phrasing, even if represented by an outsider. When Aretha's name was announced, people began applauding, not a customary funeral response. Sallie Martin was beside herself, "Worst thing I ever heard . . . a night-club singer at a gospel singer's funeral." But the long dry service had only exhausted Thomas A. Dorsey. While Sallie Martin was grumbling and Aretha Franklin was killing them loudly with his song, the old man nodded and snored.*

Brother Joe May, the next to go, had often sung with Mahalia, and once shared a New Orleans stage in a double coronation. Years earlier, Joe May and his mentor Willie Mae Ford Smith had presented Mahalia in St. Louis, "giving her," Mother Smith says, "the first thousand-dollar fee that girl ever saw." Joe May was the only man who could share a stage with these ladies. His immense bluesy tenor prompted Willie Mae to dub him "The Thunderbolt of the Middle West." He learned other things from his "mama," how to strut and sashay ("Joe used to help me sing 'Give Me Wings Lord' and we'd fly away together") to a sanctified beat, how to move from whisper to roar and back again within a four-bar phrase. Joe May's first hits were all songs Willie Mae had taught him, and he veered only slightly from her interpretations; on these records, her adopted daughter Bertha Smith accompanies him on piano. Willie Mae was not embittered. "He was my Joe baby, and he knew how to stir me, no doubt about it. And he never got too big to forget me. Back when he was making all that money, he'd still come up after a program and say, 'Mama when you pass, I want you to leave me your know-how.'"

From Mahalia, Joe May derived her characteristic slurs

---

* The New Orleans funeral was more spirited. Its high point came from another New Orleans native, Bessie Griffin, the one singer constantly cited as Mahalia's source of terror. Bessie sang "Move On Up a Little Higher" until dozens of people fell out. "I don't know how many, 'cause they had to take me out too." Bessie had proved, finally and for good, that she was the queen's match. But once again the artistic triumph was only good for rhetorical purposes; her career was not elevated. And a month after Mahalia's death, half a dozen others had already been crowned the world's greatest gospel singer. With predictable hubris, Cleophus Robinson rushed out an album entitled "Cleophus Robinson: The World's Greatest Gospel Singer Sings the Beloved Songs of Mahalia Jackson." Like a young Sallie Martin, Dorothy Love Coates could only observe the multiple coronations with scorn. "They say they're ready to fill her shoes . . . but most of them won't be able to walk out the door."

and bent notes and a disposition more bluesy than Willie
Mae's. His own contribution was an aggressive, riotous
manner. He was an immense man, but like his female idols,
his physical width narrowed to sharply defined facial features, muscular cheeks and a luminous gaze. In the spirit,
he'd dash down aisles, dragging an altar Bible on his back,
to signify his cross and staff of redemption. He would approximate Sallie Martin's sternness, but tickle audiences
with it: "No more table grace these days. Hmmm. Maybe
that's why we got so much colic."

During the fifties, with a series of brilliant Specialty recordings, Joe May was the king of gospel singers. He
earned enough money to build a home in East St. Louis
and send five children through college. In the late fifties,
he moved to Nashboro Records. Whether because his
repertoire now shifted from Dorsey compositions to revised
folk spirituals, or because Nashboro's strength lay south of
the Mason-Dixon line, but the thunderbolt of the Middle
West now became a southern mainstay. He cultivated a
route of backwoods churches where gigs were frequent but
modest. Borrowing his origins from Specialty Records he
announced himself as "Brother Joe May of Hollywood,
California." The provinces responded with Brother Joe
May days, banquets and scholarships, even making a hit
out of his folksy admonition to liars, "Walk On, Talk On":

> *You wake up in the morning, get in the street,*
> *Talk about me to the people you meet,*
> *You don't know but you pretend,*
> *To sum it all up, it's the lying end.*
> *If you were the right sort, I'd never squawk.*
> *But a big-mouthed person just loves to talk.*
> *Anybody's business around town,*
> *You lie from sun-up till the sun goes down.*
> *You better watch yourself about what you say*
> *Get ready for a test on Judgment Day.*
> *I've seen them come, I've seen them go,*
> *I've even seen the hearses back up to their door.*

In the mid-sixties, Joe May toured Europe with Marion Williams' company of *Black Nativity,* but the national recognition granted his peers eluded him. He returned to the South, suffered a stroke, recuperated, went back traveling, somewhat diminished in strength but with a new novelty hit ("Don't Let the Devil Ride"). When Mahalia died, he was touring and unable to return for her funeral. It was too late to revive their old rivalry; while Mahalia's sisters mourned her in their minks, Brother Joe was busy supporting his family. He persisted in his travels despite the apparent collapse; after a disastrous Knoxville concert he begged the people's forgiveness, he'd do better next time. The voice rallied briefly, the spirit stayed firm, but the body gave up in June. Joe May suffered a stroke in Thomasville, Georgia, and became the only great gospel singer to die on the road.

He was buried in his hometown, East St. Louis. In their grief, the family turned as always to Willie Mae Ford Smith. "I never thought I'd be saying good-bye to my child." Recently, she has begun to receive some recognition: she sang at the 1972 Newport Jazz Festival and has recorded two albums for Nashboro. "Even Joe's label and he didn't live to see it." Willie Mae couldn't afford the trip from St. Louis to Chicago for Mahalia's funeral, but she made it to Joe's. "I sang 'Peace in the Valley' for him. The man worked every day God gave him . . . now *he's* at peace."

Clara Ward too kept working to the end. In recent years, what with Aretha acknowledging her stylistic debts and the market for pure gospel expanding, she found herself able to include in her secular repertoire the only songs she enjoyed performing, the hymns. "I let the rest of them carry on with that boom-de-de-boom-boom mess, you know I'll live and die a hymn singer." The group, fashionably slim and Afroed, danced as arbitrarily as ever; once on TV they cut a shout step in Flip Wilson's jive Church of What's Happening. What was happening was show business, and

Clara affected bewilderment at the choruses of insulted
gospel lovers. She, at least, could always tell a dime-store
marble from a gospel pearl.

After years of commercial recordings she cut a series
of gospel tunes for Nashboro. They ranged from group
to choir to solo, and were all of some merit. But after one
session, Nashboro's producer Shannon Williams dismissed
everyone from the studio but Clara and an organist. Seated
at the piano, eyes stabbed shut, chin jutting out as ballast
for all that nasal fervor, she sang three hymns, "Beams of
Heaven," "The Name Jesus" and "The Last Mile of the
Way." They were certainly her deepest recordings since
1958 when Marion Williams and the others had quit her.
And now, without even Gertrude Ward around to build
the fire, Clara seemed to be absolutely serious, fully on
her own. At the end of the last song, she sang "When I've
gone," paused to laugh, then ended, "the last mile of the
way." The holy laugh is from that diaphragmatic root
where moans originate. It's the lustiest chuckle I've heard
and Clara's finest individual sound in years. Afterward she
apologized to Shannon Williams, "I don't know what made
me do that. God knows, I haven't enjoyed a record session
like this in years."

Who could explain the split in Clara, the consummate
hymn singer and the cynical showman? Perhaps the
chuckle was her defiant laugh at all her critics, "You can
spot me but you can't stop me." Clara, the product of poor
Philadelphians, had as much invested in the Tindley hymns
of her childhood as the home folk she so often embarrassed and exploited. So after her last illness, when she
rallied enough to sit at the piano, her mother requested
"How I Got Over," Clara's biggest record hit. But that
testimony belonged better to Marion Williams and Mahalia
Jackson, women who had scrubbed floors and carted laundry at the same age Clara had been shouting the parish-
ioners at Tindley's church. Clara's solace lay in her
beginnings. "Mama, the song I want to sing is

When the storms of life are raging
Stand by me."

"Church," said Mrs. Ward later, "Clara sang as never before." This Tindley hymn like "The Last Mile of the Way" is not a testimony tune; its situation is that of a mourner planning her last trip. It reduced Clara's situation and her art to its essentials. Not a musical sermon nor a blues testimony, Clara Ward's last number was a plea for mercy.

She died in January 1973, almost a year after Mahalia. The indefatigable Gertrude Ward made even death an event. If two funerals had speeded Mahalia home, her daughter would also leave here twice. The people might have criticized Clara, but she knew her daughter as a "praying child," and so she scheduled two funerals, a "Service of Triumph" in Philadelphia and a "Going Home Service of Praise and Thanksgiving" in Los Angeles. No expense was spared, no extravagant effect ignored. "I won't give my child . . . the world's greatest gospel singer . . . a pitiful funeral. Clara gave me everything I wanted. I'm saying 'thank you Clara.' " First she accompanied her daughter's coffin to Philadelphia, selecting for the occasion the old Metropolitan Opera House where but six months earlier Clara had wailed "If Jesus leads me, I'll make it home some day." The Met was packed the morning of the funeral and the performing cast was all-star. Old Mary Johnson Davis, for whom Clara played piano thirty years earlier, sang the obligatory "Precious Lord," and Aretha Franklin, still echoing her inspiration, sang Clara's greatest hymn, "The Day Is Past and Gone." Alex Bradford saluted his favorite singer, "The choir's getting smaller down here. Used to be twenty or thirty, looked around the other day and found only two or three. Clara, I want you to know I'm too close to heaven to turn around."

But the most stirring moments came from two Philadelphians. Rosie Wallace, with the build and spirit of an old-timer, led the mass choir in "When I Wake Up In

Glory," proving herself the finest gospel singer under forty. Then Kitty Parham romped through Marion Williams' tune "We Shall Be Changed:"

> *"Changed from mortal to immortality*
> *In the twinkling of an eye."*

The old Bible words and the sanctified syncopations propelled Mrs. Ward out of her seat. She scooted down the aisles, shaking hands with mourners, turning a funeral into a revival. Kitty was now beside her in the audience, and Mother Ward blissfully beat her ex-singer's shoulder blades as if to say, "I can't take much more but you better not stop." Hundreds of people started shouting with Kitty while Mrs. Ward wept, fainted, rose glassy-eyed, shouted the victory, skipped, squealed, fell conspicuously silent, reminding Philadelphia that she was not only a mother but a Ward.

She returned to Los Angeles, still charged with that administrative spirit that preoccupies us at times of mourning. Marion Williams had been touring California colleges at the time of the Philadelphia funeral, but was now able to support "the woman who made me. I called Miss Ward up and told her not to worry. I'd stay right there and cook and clean for her." She did even more. The Los Angeles service was not as spirited as Philadelphia's. If this was a gospel program, it was of the semiprofessional sort until Mrs. Ward signaled for the phonograph to play the Wards' standard "Surely God Is Able." The twenty-five-year-old Clara sang her verse in an unearthly double denial of time, with a sweetness of tone and spirit she hadn't shown in years. Then where Marion's part occurs on the record, out she stepped, large as life, continuing the song in the present. As once again, her best singer strutted down the aisles, hollering her "surelys," Mrs. Ward could recall the group's finest hours. "Children," she informed Philadelphia friends, "the Ward Singers was . . . clinging."

After that, she stayed mostly by herself. She occasionally toured with the new Ward Singers, reminding folk "before there was a Clara Ward, I was telling dying men and women it's a God somewhere." Whenever singers or friends would visit, she'd insist on taking them to the cemetary where Clara lay buried "with all the stars." She outlived her daughter by a decade.

Rosetta Tharpe may have died the most miserably, for the others departed like royalty, but her passing was scarcely noticed. Thirty years ago when Mahalia and Joe May were snuggling under Willie Mae Ford Smith's wing, Mahalia selling her home-brewed beauty potions and Joe May punching the time clock at Monsanto Chemical, while Clara Ward was trailing her mother to singers' conventions, bunking with preachers' families, Rosetta was riding the race record charts with spirituals, packing stadiums with saints and ballrooms with sinners. Rosetta's image and celebrity were of another quality than Mahalia's, but in her time, she was something of a household name herself. From the mid-fifties on, Rosetta's career had degenerated to annual tours of southern churches, usually sharing the program with quartets like the Dixie Hummingbirds and Sensational Nightingales, with occasional trips to France and Catskill mountain resorts.

By then, she was an unembarrassed hustler, selling records, perfumes and nylons, advising country women how to trap city men, tickling audiences with a double meaning or two—as her husband fiddled with her electric guitar wires, she'd say, "Come on, Daddy, plug me in"—playfully alluding to her reputation as a backslider. The death of her mother removed her greatest spiritual resource, and for the last decade of her life, I doubt if she added a single new number to her repertoire. No matter, the songs had become second nature to her. The husky contralto bore slight resemblance to the sprightly, girlish voice of earlier years, but the style and guitar technique were unchanged, and to this listener, the melancholy of her gospel blues— "I Looked Down the Line," "Precious Lord," "Stand by Me," "Peace in the Valley" and "Precious Memories"—

deepened with time. Inverting her energies, she de-emphasized entertainment and settled on a combination of nostalgia, sanctified evangelism and melodrama, sure to stir any audience too mature to condemn her for the past. (Though one record album note with unconscious irony described her career as "a sellout, in every sense of the word.")

In the fall of 1970, she toured Europe with a package of blues singers. One night onstage, she complained of a sudden, deep chill. She was rushed back to Philadelphia, suffering from a stroke. The effects were bad. Her speech was distorted, sometimes clear, sometimes palsied. Her leg bothered her severely and was eventually amputated, though the nerve endings continued to pain her. For a year she stayed home, while her husband traveled with the Dixie Hummingbirds, taking up collected offerings for his sick wife. Rosetta's will power and energy remained strong. She continued to entertain friends, cooking as always ("Isn't it good? isn't it tender? Don't you know your sister can outcook ol' big mama, you know what's her name? More greens?") and joking with the same low-down frankness (to Bessie Griffin, "Girl, I ain't heard from you or Ma - ha - lee - a for years. What you mean, I ain't been nowhere, right here. Shoot, I maybe can't talk good but I can get you *told*"). She slept a lot, practiced walking on her artificial leg, played with her poodle, told off-color jokes to some friends, but reserved her deepest confidences for her closest friend of all, Mrs. Ira Tucker ("Louise, that's my sister").

In 1972 and early 1973, she managed a couple of tours with the Nightingales. Dressed in night-club gowns, she'd walk onstage, supported by crutches, then sit down, strum a few chords, "It's good . . . to be here in the land of the living." Discretion had never been her virtue, and like Mahalia, she didn't shun from telling the people her business. "The doctor . . . says I might lose this leg too . . . but I told him, long as God give me strength, I'll lie on my back and play my guitar." Her speech was garbled and her reflexes slightly off. So her timing, once flawless if not metronomic, became as scattered and arbitrary as that of Mahalia, Joe May or any gospel blues singer. Though her speaking was impaired, her singing wasn't; impediments weren't noticeable, and the indirect phrasing complemented the guitar. For now, even if she had never scrubbed floors, she was truly a testimony singer, of the sort who may shift musical gears from bar to bar in answer to the promptings of memory and the spirit. But even as her soul looked back in wonder, it also looked ahead in fear. Rosetta's "Precious Memories" could tear you up with its evocations of "precious father and loving mother who fly across the lonesome years." But you didn't leave her concerts with her sense of mourning for the dead or gratitude for her survival. Rosetta was scared—"Pray for me, children, I don't want to die." It was the most basic fear of all. I have never seen it incorporated into art the way Rosetta did. Literary artists treat their fear with a range of technical devices from irony to humor. Rosetta was either more naïve or honest; she made it plain she was singing on borrowed time.

Because she could still sing well, this writer arranged a recording session for her at Savoy Records. Her earlier albums for them were honest examples of her later career, as moving if not as brilliant as her first Decca recordings. But she hadn't recorded in four years and was understandably wary. She had settled on a repertoire made up of songs—"I Looked Down the Line," "Bring Back Those Days," "God Don't Like It," "Rock Me," etc.—she'd recorded on the first Decca sessions. But it wasn't to be. The day of the scheduled session, she suffered a final stroke, stayed in a coma a few hours, and died early the next morning. Louise Tucker and Walter Stewart, a Philadelphia disc jockey and gospel singer, were among the last to see her.

We saw to it that the national press included her obituary; in Europe, she remained a celebrity, and the Paris *Herald Tribune* gave the announcement special prominence. But at home, Rosetta's demise wasn't much noticed. At her funeral, the church was far from packed, though any old local singer's death usually attracts a regiment of mourners. In her later years, Rosetta had switched from the Holiness to the Baptist Church. And so, the symbol of sanctified singing was given a very middle-class, "seditty" Baptist funeral. A floral display fixed to resemble a guitar was the only flamboyant touch. The preacher delivered a modest sermon, as if he barely knew Rosetta's history. One old friend, Roxie Moore, spoke of Rosetta's childhood in the Holiness Church and, reopening the old wound, insisted that she had meant no harm when she joined the big bands. Louise Tucker, friend in death as well as life, supervised the funeral and sat with the family. The Dixie Hummingbirds acted as pallbearers. The singing was mostly subdued, without any of the flash and bounce that made Rosetta famous. Marie Knight sang "Peace in the Valley," and retired to her seat, dabbing her eyes, knowing Rosetta wouldn't sing it again.

There was one memorable moment. Marion Williams sang "Precious Lord," the song Rosetta used to say, "I want sung when I go." As Marion came to the song's climax, "At the river lord I'll stand," she walked a few steps down the aisle, wailing with such directness that grown men began to weep, holler and pass out. One was Walter Stewart who stood up, shivering, calling out, "Yes! Yes! Yes!" He was surely moved by Marion's singing ("I tell you, mother sang upon our bodies," he'd joke later), but he was also letting out the pity and terror of Rosetta's death. "When I saw Rosetta lying in that hospital," he told some saints after the funeral, "rolling about there in her coma, right there in a hospital ward, one of our *greatest* stars, leaving the world like that . . . all I could think of was that old spiritual line . . . 'I want to die *easy* when I die.' God knows Rosetta didn't."

During the past decade, the "progressive" or "contemporary" choir sound grabbed much of the spotlight from the groups and quartets. Choirs were selling records as early as 1947, when J. Earle Hines and the St. Paul Baptist Choir of Los Angeles recorded "God Be With You." But the St. Paul Choir's repertoire was traditional, and their harmony, typically four part. The proper precursors of the choir era were two East Coast preachers, Reverend Charles Watkins and Professor Charles Taylor. In the mid-fifties, their recordings replete with Afro-Cuban instrumentation and ballad melodies, and their stylized vocal habits (Watkins croons while Taylor hollers, but neither sounds like a typical gospel shouter) set them apart, and even provoked some negative criticism. More commercially successful in accommodating pop mannerisms were Robert Anderson, Sister Wynona Carr, Marie Knight and Sam Cooke; the last three eventually switched fields.

In the late fifties, a six-man group, the Gospel Clefs of Newark became, together with the Staple Singers, gospel's novelty sensation. While the Staples warbled a special blend of male quartet and southern blues, the Clefs, under the direction of Leon Lumkins, demanded attention with their peculiar falsetto harmonies, chord progressions (some rivals dubbed them "Chinese gospel singers") and ballad tunes (their biggest hit, "Open Our Eyes," was revived in 1974 by Earth, Wind and Fire). Lumkins' concepts helped inaugurate gospel's third generation. Obviously inspired by the best of the past—he had originally conceived the group as male Ward Singers—he also incorporated sounds less commonly exploited in gospel: rock and roll, soul jazz, and "semiclassical" anthems. In 1959, in a dazzling transmutation, he turned the staid Anglican anthem "His Yoke Is Easy" into a gospel shout (his group syncopating, "Yes his burden's light, my God's burden is light"); two years later, another group was gospelizing the Hallelujah Chorus.

The new breed of gospel people understood the old songs and testimonies, but they naturally desired a more contemporary gospel that would reflect their experiences and musical tastes. A middle-class gospel audience made for a more self-conscious music. In the sixties, Clinton Utterbach, a conservatory graduate, formed the Utterbach Concert Ensemble. This rather affected name signaled a new image for gospel choirs. The Utterbachs could rock and wail, but their forte was virtuoso arrangements, involving key changes, tricky rhythms and notes communally held for absurdly long periods. When 4/4 time had been the most comfortable signature for older gospel singers, the post-Utterbach choirs became as adventurous as jazz musicians. The freest of all musical times remained the "non-meter" of the gospel solo. A creative singer like Marion Williams, Dorothy Love Coates or Edna Gallmon Cooke might shift the metrical scheme from bar to bar, as variously as Stravinsky does in *Oedipus Rex*. But the choir sounds were too arranged to allow such individual liberties. The focal interest shifted from the individual to a whole ensemble of musical elements. Minor chords and modal progressions, the twin obsessions of recent rock composers, became *de rigueur* in gospel. Hundreds of choir directors in the East and Midwest were liberated by the influences of Utterbach and James Cleveland. Dorothy Love Coates remembers one director telling her, "Darlin', you all can sit down now. It's a new day and my crew's takin' over."

By the early seventies, the choirs had succeeded in their putsch. For some young fans, the gospel sound had to include minor chords and pop melodies: Leon Lumkins' "Open Our Eyes" was now a conservative selection. But the innovations, while gaining some youthful converts, lost most of gospel's outside following. The world might swipe gospel's most distinctive characteristics, but it didn't bother with the church's embezzlements. Even the Edwin Hawkins Singers with the benefits of 16-track recording and pop production budgets couldn't duplicate the success of "O Happy Day."

Other less-fortunate choirs were equally audacious. With the aplomb of gospel singers used to getting by on mother wit and spirit feel, the choir directors with tiny budgets attempted complex effects in record sessions that seldom lasted three hours. As

Reverend Brewster might have told them, "There are so many ways to make a mistake, it's hard to miss one."

Nevertheless the directors realized their goal: choirs as fervent as a shouting congregation, as tight as a jubilee quartet. They had numerous precedents. In the 1920s, preachers like Reverend Gates duplicated a live ambiance by importing into the studios singers who doubled as worshipers. One of Gates' members became the Georgia Peach. Their "Something About the Lord Mighty Sweet" (1934) with its stylized performance of a Dorsey tune may be the first modern gospel record: the live atmosphere implicitly granted the new form an institutional endorsement: if it sounded like church, it had to be church.

Fifty years later, a church setting continues to ratify the vanguard. Choir directors today have to be scholars and diplomats: they must follow all the musical changes while soothing the egos of people dizzied by their first exposure to stardom. The turnover in choir membership can resemble that in salaried groups; the division between professional and amateur has never been less clear. Thus the best choirs of the 1970s were only as good as their leaders. The choir of Brooklyn's Institutional C.O.G.I.C. was dominated by J.C. and Alfred White, nephews of the pastor, Bishop Carl Williams. J.C. served as director, pianist, composer, and lead; Alfred was the organist. For a while Alfred's wife, Doris, led the shouts, but the choir's star was J.C.'s wife, Gloria, who managed to evoke both Ruth Davis and Jacqui Verdell while providing her own sanctified edge. Gloria, Doris, and other soloists (Carolyn White, Rubesteen McClure, etc.) later traveled as evangelists. While retaining the C.O.G.I.C. spirit, Institutional was "the choir with young ideas." In 1971, a streamlined version known as the J. C. White Singers began recording with Max Roach. J.C. and Gloria now pastor a church in Connecticut; Institutional continues to record.

Although graduates of gospel groups, the Whites had considerably altered their styles. In Chicago, the best leads of Milton Bronson's Thompson Community Singers, and Maceo Woods' Christian Tabernacle Choir were also group veterans. But when you heard Vernon and Loretta Oliver, Doris Sykes, George Jordan, Ann Bowden, or reverends Woods and Bronson, the fifties'

gospel mannerisms were unmistakable, perhaps because they
had all come of musical age then. Meanwhile cross-town Charles
Hayes' Cosmopolitan Church of Prayer featured Diane Williams, a young singer who moved and phrased like a latter-day
Dorothy Love and who now invents couplets as savvy as Dot's:

How you gonna pay your rent; all your money's spent?
Maybe you got a gas bill due; maybe you got a light bill too;
Telephone disconnect; waiting on your next pay check.

Charles Fold, formerly musician for Ernestine Rundless'
Meditation Singers, leads a Cincinnati choir which often accompanies James Cleveland, invariably with material that repeats
familiar messages while allowing them to explore shifts in dynamics, intonation, and breath control; the group's most vivid
lead, Rosetta Davis, sounds like 1985's version of Rosetta
Tharpe and Rosa Shaw, the freest of early sanctified women.
Washington's Myrna Summers with her tight nasal sound is a
rangier Shirley Caesar. Her choral opuses like "Uncloudy Day"
fuse a conservatory-trained compositional sense with a commitment to tradition; she has even recorded an *a cappella* solo. One
of her pianists Jeffrey LaValle has gone from C.O.G.I.C. to
Baptist service, and now arranges for the New Jerusalem Baptist
Choir of Flint, Michigan. Robert Mayes, who once accompanied
Willie Mae Ford Smith and Martha Bass, has shaped Chicago's
Christ Universal Temple Ensemble into a disciplined aggrega-
tion, capable of achieving an intimate, conversational manner
that would be remarkable in any group. A similar figure is Washington's Richard Smallwood, who grew up idolizing Little Lucy
Smith, the Roberta Martin Singers' pianist, and accompanied
them with authority when they reunited at the Smithsonian
Institution. Meanwhile his own Singers perform in a style closer
to the seminal modernists, the Walter Hawkins Singers. Like
jazz's young lions, these choir directors have no intention of
sacrificing roots that still nourish them.

Another way of retreading the old wine press is evident in the
work of former pop stars born again as singing pastors. Little
Richard's role as a gospel preacher seems to oblige him to re-

nounce his flamboyant manner and his sexuality. But when he decides to sing, his tremulous whispers, growls and shrieks still recall Marion Williams, "the lady who gave me my *whoo.*" For years Al Green included gospel songs on his Soul albums; and with a gospel singer's *chutzpah,* he would employ his voices— a limber falsetto, a breathless crooner, a growling preacher—in a three-way encounter, alternately exhilarating and schizoid. In time, his tilts at gospel grew less oblique; he seemed genuinely troubled, working out his psychic deliverance in public. Reverend Green's recent albums have not conveyed a blessed assurance. He treats gospel standards as vehicles for his eccentric musings, but when, as in Alex Bradford's "Too Close to Heaven," a virtually fail-safe song, he begins to achieve a more authentic groove, he lets it dissipate in mid-spirit. Church audiences seem baffled by his attempts to out-sanctify the competition one moment, and distribute roses to his fans the next.

As increasing numbers of pop records assimilated the gospel sound, gospel singers responded by adjusting to the requirements of contemporary music. This has proved a mixed blessing; as one singer put it, "They took our gospel singing and made it gospel *music,* but the music used to come from nobody but us." Light, Myrrh, and pre-eminently Word Records have now committed themselves to "gos-pop," a form of rhythmic gospel accentuated by soul music instrumentation, emphatic drumming and walking bass guitars. In the pop field, the typical mix that reduces a vocalist to one element in a musical ensemble may make some sense. But gospel singers really can sing and rock instrumentation cannot equal, much less enhance, their efforts. The corollary of these procedings is that the singers' individual idioms are becoming homogenized; soul cliches like "Put your hands together" and "You all" preclude gospel spontaneity (one self-conscious gos-pop song announces "It's Jesus, Y'All"!). Even the most special stylist can get lost in the jungle of horns, strings and electric machines. That it's affected and uninspired, that the orgasmic cadenzas of the electric guitarist are as vulgar in their way as Liberace's arpeggios, is so much quibbling.

The money today is with rock music and, after the success of "O Happy Day," the dream of most gospel singers is to ride the pop charts.

Paradoxically, the greatest recent gospel seller on the pop charts was Aretha Franklin's return album. She recorded in Los Angeles at James Cleveland's church, accompanied by his choir, performing to an audience that included Gertrude and Clara Ward. And while gospel singers were scampering to record "message" pop tunes, she chose almost her entire repertoire from fifties' gospel. Aretha back in the church was the dream of many fans. The excellent production by Jerry Wexler allowed her much latitude to move at her own pace through standards like Clara Ward's "How I Got Over," Inez Andrews' "Mary Don't You Weep" and a gang of hymns including her earliest gospel hit, "Never Grow Old." Though a gospel lover could note that all the songs had been sung a good deal better by other singers, he'd have to add that most of these singers were now trying to sing semipop songs not nearly as well as Lady Soul can. In an album highlight, "Precious Memories," Aretha moaned, ad libbed and hollered in a manner that nicely conjoined the styles of Mahalia and Clara. There were no epiphanies for the gospel lover—Aretha's 1956 record of "Never Grow Old" remains her best gospel performance—but gospel was not traduced. Its best styles and eras were acknowledged; any novice buying the record would hear honest gospel interpreted by its most successful expatriate. Though Aretha did perform "Precious Lord," sung to the melody of "You've Got a Friend," a Marvin Gaye tune for the hipsters and "You'll Never Walk Alone" for the squares, the album as a whole confirmed her love for the real stuff. In the summer of 1974, she returned to Cleveland's church and led the congregation in Clara Ward's old shout standby, "Let Us All Go Back to the Old Landmark."

Recently some gospel artists have invaded the r. and b. charts, much as Rosetta Tharpe and the Blind Boys did twenty-five years ago. In 1973, after years of trying, Ira

Tucker and the Dixie Hummingbirds made it with "Loves
Me Like a Rock." Hardly a conventional gospel tune, the
song was composed by Paul Simon who once again turned
to the Swan Silvertones' recording "Mary Don't You
Weep" for inspiration. Where he'd earlier utilized a Claude
Jeter ad lib to title "Bridge Over Troubled Waters," now he
used the quartet's chord progressions. On a 1973 album,
Simon employed both the Hummingbirds and Jeter as vocal accompanists. No musical fireworks resulted, but Simon succeeded in advancing the recognition for these
veteran gospel artists; he has recently toured with the excellent young Jessy Dixon Singers. The Birds backed Simon on "Loves Me Like a Rock"; after his single sold a
million copies, they followed up with their own. While
Simon seemed to satirize the confidence that carries his
persona from mother's knees to White House, Tucker's
preacher roars were without irony: "My mama loved me!"
was his message. As a result of "Rock," the Birds have
appeared at a string of coffee houses and record industry
showcases, reliving the Café Society Downtown days with
their promise . . . and ultimate frustration.

Another quartet, the Mighty Clouds of Joy, has gone
even further in their reach for pop prominence. The
Clouds, for fifteen years, have been the most r. and b.-
influenced gospel group. They were the first to carry an
instrumental rhythm section and electric amplification.
Gifted with rousing, athletic singers (their bass doubles as
falsetto), the Clouds made vocal noise of acid-rock dimen-
sions while their lead singer, Joe Ligon, punched a lyric
across with the unsubtle directness of a James Brown. For
most of their career, the group has relied on a set routine
with predictable emotional and rhythmic climaxes culminating in a group shout that resembled the actions of male
Ward Singers. The routines thrilled audiences for years but
of late, the group seemed discouraged. In 1974, producer
Dave Crawford plotted a new musical direction. In their
album, "Time," he gave them a pop production, vastly

superior to the typical gos-pop session, with horns and strings directed at discotheque habituees rather than members of the pastor's Aid Society. The lyrics were nebulously spiritual ("It's So Hard to Be Soft in a Stone World"); the Clouds weren't completely ready to join the Staple Singers on the other side. And the vocal talent was still apparent. The Clouds blended quite as well as the O'Jays or Harold Melvin and the Blue Notes. An auspicious debut in rhythm and blues. But Ligon, particularly, felt out of place in this musical setting. Subsequent Clouds albums include at least one typical shout, the most heartfelt being Ligon's tribute to June Cheeks. While quartets have it worse than ever, careers were recently inaugurated by the Gospel Keynotes with their choir harmonies, frenetic routines and hard country lead Willie Neal Johnson, and by Willie Banks and the Messengers, who project a cooler and more old-timey sound, Banks having sung with the great 1940s quartet, the Flying Clouds.

To commit yourself to soul singing, "spirit feel," perforce limits your professionalism. The peaks achieved tower over other forms of popular music, but inconsistency and mediocrity are more often the rule. Or as one record executive commented, explaining the uneven performance of an artist, "I know that's not professional. But he ain't professional, he's a gospel singer." Sometimes one laughs when a sophisticated performer like Bessie Griffin prays "Help me Lord, I don't know nothing about the world" but she means it. Gospel mirrors show business, but is more properly related to folklore. This explains why the best gospel is also the one closest to the roots of hymns, moans, hollers and shouts. The more worldly stuff demands a discipline, not to mention musical training, antithetical to gospel's nature. It's a wonder to pop performers that gospel singers record so quickly: an average album is recorded in two three-hour sessions. But any more effort will waste energy and attenuate spirit. Recording gospel singers while they're "ready" is not just the quickest but the best way. Forcing them to wait while "laid-back" "head-session" mu-

sicians try to come up with an arrangement simply won't
do.

As if to confirm all this, the biggest recent gospel hit on
the r. and b. charts, Inez Andrews' "Lord Don't Move
the Mountain," did have moderate rock instrumentation,
but the message and song couldn't be more traditional. Inez
Andrews, former lead singer of the Caravans, is an old
gospel warrior, and " 'Mountain' has been with me for
years. I never even bothered to record it. I'd just sing it
when I needed to." She was born poor in Birmingham,
raised with Dorothy Love and Alex Bradford, ("Dot's
mother, Lil McGriff, was a mother to us all"), married
and divorced while still in her teens. She used to support
her children with domestic work: "I'd make eighteen dollars a week. I thought I was saving something. Then I'd
spend seven for baby-sitting and two on the bus." On weekends, she'd sing with local choirs and as occasional under-
study for Dorothy Love with the Original Gospel Harmonettes.

James Cleveland caught her with the Harmonettes and
recruited her in 1956 for the Caravans. The group has
included many great talents (see the chapter on Shirley
Caesar), but Inez became their greatest record seller. Her
first number with them was "Soldiers in the Army," a
Cleveland composition. Its bluesy verses fit Inez' mood and
allowed her to exhibit her mammoth range: a demure contralto bottom, a middle that when clear exhibits mezzo-
soprano coloration but usually stays hoarse and funky . . .
and a thrilling top that defies the hoarseness below and
zooms above the staff. (At the end of "Mary Don't You
Weep," she hollers "Mary," then adds, "I believe I'll call
her a bit louder," and does so. She then appears to scold
the people, "You don't believe me but I think I can call her
a bit louder" and keeps her word. Finally she observes,
"Aw, God's been good to me. I believe I can call her a bit
louder" and tweaks at the air as if plucking a note for
dogs' ears, then ambles offstage, having given up all she in-

tends to.) As remarkable as the range was her affinity for
sorrow songs; for a young woman, she was notably stern
and melancholy. Descending to her knees while the other
Caravans chanted "We've got to hold up the blood-stained
banner," she'd list the obstacles to holding on, "Whah,
mother's gone, whah, father's gone, whah, sister's gone,
whah, brother's gone, whah, I'm outdoors, whah, can't find
a friend." Each "whah" was a shrieking glissando, the
notes smearing across her history. Not pretty sounds but
they comprehended the cry of the motherless child, abandoned wife, betrayed friend.

Inez had then passed from thin to skinny and during a
seven-day stint at the Apollo Theatre, all that catharsis
drained her. "They made me glad twice . . . glad to come
and glad to leave. . . . I know I sang hard. Sam Cooke
did a program with us in Los Angeles and screamed so
much to keep up, he got sick. He said, 'Girl . . . you the
only singer ever put me to bed!' " So to spell herself, after
her performance, she'd return to her seat before the other
Caravans. While Albertina would rock soulfully, her eyes
shut in meditation, and spunky little Dorothy Norwood
would grin out at the people, Inez would recline, legs outstretched and crossed, resting her head on her right hand.
The audience might be screaming, but she made it plain
that enough was enough.

In the early sixties, she left the Caravans and formed
her own group, the Andrewettes. It was an artistic advance but financially, a rear-guard action. One of her singers, Josephine Howard (whose vocal range, bluesy spirit
and hard-luck testimony approximated Inez') once said
"Inez and me liked sausages. We were so poor we'd have
to split halves; she'd like hers boiled. I'd take mine fried."
In the late sixties, she resumed solo work. Her career was
moderately successful, and with four children, a third husband and a new home, she had few complaints. In 1972,
she recorded the moan that had sustained her in the early
days.

Lord don't move the mountain
Give me strength to climb
Lord don't move my stumbling block
Lead me all around.

and found herself on top of the mountain. The single hit
the r. and b. charts for three months, but will last the nine
lives of a gospel standard. It has established Inez as a major
gospel soloist and upped her concert fees. Since then, she
has recorded an obligatory pop song "Looking Back" but
coming in her mid-forties, success won't change her style
or commitment to Lil McGriff's gospel.

In 1979, Inez' old colleague James Cleveland recorded
his biggest hit in years, "I Don't Feel Noways Tired," in
melody and message, "Mountain" 's mirror image. It is as if
Andrews and Cleveland, both Depression children, intuited
the proper theme for the bitter years ahead of us. In 1929,
Blind Willie Johnson's down home moans outsold Bessie
Smith's blues. Almost sixty years later, blacks in a financially depressed period are again turning to the old gospel
messages. The rock instrumentation is almost beside the
point.

The gospel scene has changed greatly since the golden
age of the fifties. The highway, once crowded with great
singers, now affords a living for very few groups: Shirley
Caesar, the Consolers, and a few quartets. Most of the
other great singers either travel seldom (Dorothy Love Coates,
Claude Jeter), perform in the college circuit (Marion Williams)
or Europe (Bessie Griffin), are semiretired (R. H. Harris, Willie
Mae Ford Smith) or priced out of the reach of most congregations (James Cleveland). In many towns, gospel radio programs, once a daily staple, have been exiled to Sundays or the
early morning hours. During a financially depressed time,
the need for gospel messages may increase exponentially, but poor
families can no longer buy the $8.95 albums or $9.00 concert
tickets.

Yet the gospel sound withstood other bad periods. It will

survive, not because the world copies it, but because it exemplifies so profoundly a set of attitudes that has sustained generations of poor blacks. This eclectic, sophisticated extension of spirituals and Dr. Watts hymns retains the strong, cohesive bonds that characterize any body of folklore. Gospel with its freedom of style and gesture allows its singers to show and tell who they are. When Willie Mae Ford Smith says, "I've always sung with my body," she acknowledges one great fact. Gospel allows one to be both *free* and *dignified*. The sanctified mothers who strut and shout in the spirit are also models of social decorum. I said in the introduction that gospel alone among folkloric forms—or, for that matter, most forms of high art—allows women to be peerless artists, not by denying the facts of their womanhood, but rather by declaring and exploiting them. The gospel singer can be sensual and erotic, can testify out of experiences that only a poor black woman would undergo, yet need not make herself ridiculous or pathetic. Similarly, the quartet singer who sweats and works like James Brown retains his dignity because his choice of vocation bespeaks a sense of pride and history.

This sense of vocation displays itself variously. Mahalia Jackson would scold audiences, "You children shouting all right, but you know you don't mean it. Be not deceived, God is not mocked." Shirley Caesar likes to upset folk by calling for the hands of the saved: The room is an ocean of waving arms. Then she asks, "If Jesus came right now, which one of you would be ready to go?" and nary a hand is raised. Essie Moss, the sanctified wife of Bill Moss, leaps on stage spirit filled. "Oh, bless your hearts, beloveds. So glad to be with the saints. You know I ain't like other singers. You can call me up in the hotel at three o'clock in the morning. The rest of them might be carrying on, but me and mine will either be sleeping or calling on Jesus, hallelujah." Here, three of the most flamboyant, corybantic gospel women, women often criticized for violent physical behavior, are announcing they know what they're about. "We ain't crazy, God's spirit is never *un-*

seemly" and only in the spirit are they free to be themselves.

To the gospel lover, rock and soul are for the children. Gospel, like blues and jazz, is the music of grown-ups. If one objects that most of the gospel pioneers started young, the easy reply is that they also grew up early, most of them quitting school and working while in their early teens. They had early the kind of rough experiences that inspire testimonies. It will take the new breed a lot more time to come up with substitutes. But, one says with no optimism, the bad times will come in new ways. One young singer, in her early thirties, has sung for years with style and power, but her manner has also been derivative and shallow. Recently she was afflicted with a serious illness and forced to sing in a wheel chair. It's an awful way of learning to sing "How I Got Over," but gospel singers take tragedy for granted.

Because gospel both utilizes and comprises a body of folklore, it will persist as long as folk remain to live it. Gospel began in the churches of southern states. And, paradoxically, in recent years, regionalism has again become an element in the gospel world. Perhaps because so many great singers are now staying home, cultivating their own gardens by singing in local churches. Or perhaps because the nature of gospel radio programming and concert booking now prevents the fifties' proliferation of talent and songs.

The styles of certain states are well defined. Since southern blacks tend to migrate in predictable fashion, even when they move, they can hear good facsimilies of their native song styles. Many South Carolina and Florida blacks settle in New York and Philadelphia; as do Mississippians in Chicago and Texans in Los Angeles. Certain song styles are universal; no matter what state, the African Methodist Episcopal and Baptist hymnals contain the hymns of those eighteenth-century scribes, Isaac Watts, Charles Wesley, William Cowper, Lowell Mason, John Newton, which are generically known and sung as Dr. Watts'. But certain

distinctions are accepted. Virginia, for example, is celebrated for vivid, melodic jubilee singing (the Silver Leafs
in the twenties, Norfolk Jubilees in the thirties, Golden
Gates in the forties, Harmonizing Four in the fifties),
while South Carolina, Florida and Alabama enjoy a
rougher, more frenetic approach, the growling preacher
styles of men like Silas Steele and Ira Tucker, women like
Dorothy Love and Marion Williams.

At one time, most sanctified churches contained a disciple of Arizona Dranes or Ernestine Washington with
those ladies' nasal twang; while sanctified preachers often
affected a pretentious, somewhat vaudevillian *recitatif,*
first captured in the twenties' recordings of Reverend
F. W. McGee. Today the sanctified choirs sing the compositions of Andraé Crouch and Edwin Hawkins. Commercialized they may be, but both men were raised in
church. One can even argue that the distinctive California
gospel sound of Crouch, Hawkins and the recent Cleveland reflects the folklore of that state. As one journalist
noted, "In a state where everything is turned inside out,
the same mess is bound to go down with black people too."

The great gospel capitals have their own sounds. Detroit seems the most homogenized and, no pun intended,
mechanical: the relations to Motown and Aretha Franklin
are clear. Rosetta Tharpe once said, "St. Louis singers,
they all sing the blues"; though the choirs coexist, St. Louis'
best singers like Willie Mae Ford Smith and Cleophus Robinson tend to confirm her theory. The two greatest gospel
cities are Chicago and Philadelphia. Between them, they've
produced the majority of important soloists, groups and
quartets. Chicago can probably count a greater number but
less variety. Most of its best groups can be seen as offshoots
of the Roberta Martin Singers, while the great Philly
groups—the Ward Singers, Stars of Faith, Davis Sisters,
Imperial Gospel Singers, Angelic Gospel Singers—are more
individually distinctive.

Yet with its modified traditional approach, Chicago maintains
its position as the gospel Mecca. Its latest star is Reverend Clay

Evans, the sixty-year-old pastor of Fellowship Baptist Church. Thirty years ago, Evans was a member of a local group, the Lux Singers, which also included James Cleveland and Imogene Green, but since he had grown up in Tennessee, his style was more rural than either of those Chicago natives. Today his husky, nasal twang makes him the most authentically bluesy male singer on any *Billboard* chart. When satisfied, either by a well-turned phrase or by a lyrical "foretaste of glory divine," his reflex is to "mmm" to himself: within a few measures of any Clay Evans solo, moans and slurs insinuate themselves. Evans' sister, Loudella Reed, is Fellowship's minister of music. After the young peoples' choirs have sung the newer stuff, her pleasure is to set the church afire with hymns: "We call Loudella 'The Gospel Referee'," says Stanley Davis, a Chicago musician. "She can take a moan and change the atmosphere in a second."

Fellowship's most famous member, Reverend Jesse Jackson, has often saluted the Chicago pioneers. The organizational base of his 1984 Presidential campaign was the gospel church: In a form of ecumenism, he united Baptists and Methodists, Pentecostals and Spiritualists, by stressing their universal plight. A typical Jackson rally began with obligatory selections by the local choirs. After they had sung and shouted, he would speak or, rather, preach: His cadences were unmistakably churchy, and his most common phrases came from songs every gospel lover knows, e.g., "Movin' On Up" and "Weeping May Endure for a Night," two phrases most notably—and politically—employed years earlier by Reverend Brewster. Nobody seeing a Jackson rally could doubt that the members of the congregation were enacting revival mannerisms in a political context. They seemed to have agreed beforehand that the old forms would be retained —out of loyalty, gratitude, and sheer expressive convenience— to assert something new and secular.

In those rare moments when the saints of both races worship together, they share in a ubiquitous ecstacy—"It runs from heart to heart"—that constitutes a true democracy of the spirit. Yet, as the 1984 election demonstrated, the political agendas of black and white evangelists are very different. White Pentecostals were trained to quicken at the very mention of Reagan's name while blacks saw him as the focus of social evil in their world—some preachers added "Reaganomics" to all the customary woes afflicting the devout.

Thus it was a major irony that so many gospel singers desired to appear on television programs—"The PTL Club," "The 700 Club," etc.—hosted by white evangelists who would probably consider Reverend Brewster's social gospel a Communist plot. Between Jesse Jackson and Jimmy Swaggart, both populists, both fundamentalists, there was a gap that seemed insurmountable. Likewise, although some black evangelists endorsed the Moral Majority's social agenda, the gospel church gave no signs of abandoning its traditional spirit of acceptance, its adherence to the credo, "Whosoever Will Let Him Come."

At the same time that Jesse Jackson galvanized the black community with his mixture of conservative theology and radical politics, something similar was taking place on the gospel record charts. By far the biggest hit of the 1980s was "(I'm Coming Up) The Rough Side of the Mountain," a duet by F. C. Barnes and Janice Brown, the pastors of Red Budd Holy Church in Rocky Mount, North Carolina. This was traditional gospel with a vengeance, "without form or fashion"—basic rhythm tracks, simple tune, sturdy vocals. "Rough Side" was as much a product of the Reagan Administration as Jackson's campaign; its message confirmed by the latest unemployment figures. In many ghetto shops, it outsold Michael Jackson's *Thriller*.

This astonished pundits who had previously declared contemporary gospel the victor over its traditional antecedents. But older singers were not surprised. "When times get hard," said one, "the people always go back to the Old Landmark." After almost sixty years, gospel music was still performing its social function, conveying good news in bad times. It seemed the news hadn't changed much and neither had the times.

POSTSCRIPT II (1997)

Some years ago, James Cleveland and the Southern California Community Choir were invited to a music festival. This should have been an important gig, a chance to impress big-time agents and promoters. But when it was time for their scheduled appearance, the singers were nowhere to be found. The festival director was livid, and placed a call to Cleveland's producer, Fred Mendelsohn. "This is the most unprofessional thing I've ever seen." But Mendelsohn was blasé. "You don't understand. James is not a professional, he's a gospel singer."

No matter the stylistic developments, the impromptu ad lib quality known as "spirit feel" remains gospel's defining element. The more ambitious choir directors may toy with jazz and classical melodies, or conceive arrangements that resemble symphonic suites in their multiplicity of themes, keys, and mood changes. Yet the urge to break out and shout is barely repressed. The compact between the gospel vanguard and its public remains the same: "We're gonna have a good time." But while the ritual dynamics have scarcely changed, other criteria, political and social, have complicated the current state of gospel to a most vexing degree.

The triumph of Contemporary Gospel is complete and indisputable. Where once the genre could be personified by a soloist or quartet, gospel now means choir. Whether it's Olanda Draper's Memphis chorale backing up Billy Joel at

the Grammy Awards (though Draper, with the most riveting
backstep since Michael Jackson's moonwalk, is a far more
commanding performer) or the Georgia Mass Choir crooning behind Whitney Houston in *The Preacher's Wife*, the
world assumes that if you want Church, you need a choir.

This means that the new star is less often the choir's soloist than its director. Dorothy Love Coates bemoans the su-
perannuated state of her contemporaries: "Nowadays you've
got the audience on the stage. They act like they don't need
us anymore." An even older and more demoralized Claude
Jeter adds, "Some of these folks ain't never double-parked
outside a singer's door." It's true that some of the greatest
singers got their start in a choir. Chicago's First Church of
Deliverance is generally considered the first ensemble of any
kind to broadcast gospel on the radio. But the choir's directors, Ralph Goodpasteur and Julia Mae Kennedy, made sure
that their soloists were tip-top: the debonair crooner, R. L.
Knowles, gospel's first matinée idol and perhaps its first
jazz-imbued stylist (he had migrated from Kansas City), and
Irma Gwynn, who had the vocal quality of Marian Anderson
and Mahalia Jackson's soul. Likewise the St. Paul Baptist
Church Choir of Los Angeles, the first postwar gospel stars,
sang simple quartet harmonies but featured stellar leads like
J. Earle Hines or the indefatigable Sallie Martin.

But where gospel's glory used to be the great variety of its
singers, who had more individual talent than those in any
form of popular music, the singers today are virtually fun-
gible. (Dorothy Morrison, lead on Edwin Hawkins' "O Happy
Day" was quickly forgotten, while the Hawkins family and
their sound dominated gospel for years.) Gospel singers still
exhibit awesome power and range but their common denomi-
nator is the overly busy, annoyingly mannered style I call
the "gospel-gargle" or "Detroit disease" (most of its authors,
like Rance Allen or the Clark Sisters call the Motor City
home). The excessive virtuosity defeats its own purposes,
whether of expressing spirit or asserting self. One Philadelphia old-timer observes "I've never seen a whole generation
sound alike."

Yet new stars appear all the time. John P. Kee, a lead singer, choir director, and composer, grew up in North Carolina, "the 15th of 16 children." He spent some years in New York, working as a backup vocalist for the likes of James Taylor, and claims to have been a drug addict before he got saved. Since James Cleveland's death, Kee has become the Crown Prince of Gospel. His voice is a husky growl like Cleveland's, though better supported and with a sporadic trek into the soprano range. Kee's main contributions are the wedding of quartet and choir (more down-homey than most choirs, slicker and more harmonically open than any quartet) and a form of sacred choreography. His ensembles, which usually include several small children, execute little steps, a cross between the old church-rock and the Bump, the movements so synchronized that they're clearly predetermined. Kee's vision extends from quartet to Detroit gospel; he has produced record sessions for Vanessa Bell Armstrong, some of them featuring gospel rappers.

Though Kee is the most southern of the new stars, his penchant for the dance is shared by New York's Hezekiah Walker, Philadelphia's Walter Stewart, and Chicago's Ricky Dillard. Dillard was featured in Steve Martin's impious *Leap of Faith* (a film so jaundiced about Pentecostal skulduggery that some pastors decreed a boycott). But Dillard must be seen live. A half-shout step will turn into a broad jump; he will rear back 75 degrees, then leap from the soprano section to the second tenor. What makes him so riveting is the investment of aerobic energy with spirit feel. It's as if the Alvin Ailey company had gone free-form, modern dance gone sanctified. Thanks to men like Dillard, the choreographical impulse is now a signature device, a post-modern version of the ring shout.

A genuinely impressive voice belongs to Daryl Coley, a tenor, who ascribes his pop orientation to studio work accompanying Nancy Wilson, though his recordings with the Wilmington-Chester (Pennsylvania) Choir, sound more impassioned. Kirk Franklin, a 24-year-old Texan, who claims Elton John as an inspiration, is the 90's superstar. A short man with an unexceptional voice, he leads a disciplined neo-Hawkins chorale, The Family. Their recording "Why We Sing" (with a lyrical allusion to "His Eye is on the Sparrow") has become the biggest hit since "O Happy Day." It topped the charts in both R. and B. and Contemporary Christian (the trade name for white gospel) and has sold well over a million copies, making it one of those unpredictable cross-overs that fuel the fantasies of gospel entrepreneurs, and tend to occur every 20 years. An older singer advised the money men, "Stop looking to the charts and start looking to the hills."

Franklin notwithstanding, the most successful cross-over act is Take Six. Its members began performing as students at a Seventh-Day Adventist college (signifying their distance from the Baptist or C.O.G.I.C. traditions). While their *a cappella* can summon up memories of Claude Jeter's Swan Silvertones ("Mary Don't You Weep") or Kylo Turner's Pilgrim Travelers ("Something Within"), the Take Six style is equally indebted to the Four Freshmen or Hi-Los. Since gospel soul is only a strand in their collage, quartet lovers are bemused by Take Six's good fortune. It certainly doesn't bode well for any of the traditional groups with their 1 / 4 / 5 chords. The only traditional quartet to break through lately, the Canton Spirituals, was led by a father and son until the old man died. Their style, once *a cappella*, is a groove-heavy version of their fellow Mississippians, the Jackson Southernaires and the Williams Brothers. In between the rock-and-roll, they tell familiar stories of country churches and loving parents.

Another paradoxical combination is the Mississippi Mass Choir, a typical large ensemble, distinguished by the Jackson Southernaires' rhythm section. Their most prominent soloist, Frank Williams, was also the Southernaires' lead, and Malaco Records' a. & r. man. Williams, a rococo lead with a strong tenor, was featured on the choir's biggest hits, "Near the Cross" (yes, the old hymn) and his own composition, "Goodness and Mercy" (one of those plaintive testimonies that sweep the country every decade). The success of Williams' vision proved that choir and quartet crowds were not permanently estranged. Likewise recent hits by Dorothy Norwood ("Victory is Mine"), Dottie Peoples ("On-Time

God") or Shirley Caesar ("Hold My Mule"), in which an old man, who has been testifying about his family's survival, asks a friend to hold his mule while he shouts for joy, could have been recorded in the 1950's, though the background would have been a group or quartet, and the harmonies nowhere as pretentious.

Evidence of the seamless transition between generations is vouchsafed by the Winans clan. Thanks to their children's fame, Mom and Pop Winans now record in a neo-50's style: sanctified mama, quartet dad. The Winans continue to sound like the Temptations, and record for Quincy Jones, their albums polished to an icy sheen. Vicki Winans, the wife of the brothers' main lead Marvin, has pursued her own career, and hosts a syndicated TV show. She is a robust, pretty woman with a sound between Anita Baker and Detroit choir, i.e. some vocal color and a lot of bravura belting. But the Winans of the hour are the brother and sister duo BeBe and CeCe. They began as teen-age vocalists on the ill-fated *PTL Club* where CeCe and Tammy Faye Bakker used to sing and schmooze together. CeCe has grown into a gospel glamour girl, deploying a Broadway Soul approach (she admits that hard gospel is beyond her strength), not unlike that of Whitney Houston, with whom she is frequently teamed. The Winans siblings are not to everyone's taste. "My idea of hell," said one middle-aged fan, "is listening to BeBe and CeCe sing *Heaven*." But it is kind of fun to see Ms. Winans move from the sanctified church into high fashion, thereby living out her old boss Tammy Faye's dream.

Far more exciting is a Georgia country girl, who has recorded under the names Shun Pace Rhodes, La Shun Pace Rhodes, and Shun Pace. A very large woman with an ingratiating smile (Mahalia Jackson on a friendly day), she has the humor and audacity of a jazz stylist. In the midst of "He Keeps Doing Great Things for Me" (a Las Vegasy ballad, in the first place), she asks the church, "Can I do a little jazz?" and proceeds to scat in faux child's voice. She beseeches the crowd to vocalize behind her: "Hold the note, and if you lose a breath, grab one from somebody else." She also likes to draw on folkloric traditions. *A cappella*, she growls her way through "I Know I've Been Changed." Perhaps she owes more to Aretha or Vanessa Bell Armstrong, than to Ruth Davis or Marion Williams, but it remains an astonishing period gesture for the 90's. She testifies about her humble origins with graphic details, e. g., the men in her family were gangsters and drug-dealers till they got saved and became preachers. She praises God for a home with indoor plumbing. (Nowadays gospel singers exult in "telling their business." Jennifer Holiday testifies that Satan ruined her marriage and made her suicidal.) Singlehandedly, Shun Pace reflects the Winans' affinities, as hip as the children, as rooted as the parents.

Both CeCe Winans and Shun Pace appear frequently on Dr. Bobby Jones' television program. Jones, a St. Louis native, with a doctorate in education, has lived for years in Nashville, where his group, New Life, resembles a modern version of the Caravans, whose founder, Albertina Walker, is his inspiration. A dapper fellow, with the unctuous manner of a grade-school principal, Jones relies on strong-voiced young women from the C.O.G.I.C. and Apostolic church, fervent evangelists who gospel-gargle as predictably as everyone else, but who also shout, lay hands on the sick, and speak in tongues. One of them, Beverly Crawford, combines Vanessa Bell Armstrong's technique with Shirley Caesar's stamina. These women offer a startling contrast to their low-keyed, avuncular employer.

Jones' program is easily the finest presentation of gospel in television history. Not so much for the music, which is no better than the time, clearly a silver or bronze, rather than a golden age for gospel. But the interaction of artist and public has never been so well documented, nor has the variety in performing style and physical gesture. Here the genius of the modern choir director becomes manifest. Not merely do the large ensembles execute breathtaking key and metrical changes, they do so while demonstrating a patented choreography, as custom-made as their harmonies. Every choir strives to "get the house," and the inevitable arm-waving and noisy praise that concludes each selection serves as a release mechanism, their spiritual reward for completing their job, their souls intact. Jones also likes to present testifying saints, delirious with joy in the Lord, or at least, with the chance to show out, as well as such vanguard acts as a mime dance group (in white-face, gesticulating to pre-recorded tracks) and instrumental soloists. If that weren't enough, even his commercials are of cultural interest, promoting various black-owned enterprises (usually selling beauty products) with a kind of evangelical fervor that assimilates worship to commerce. (Max Weber would be amazed.)

Contemporary singers have clearly come to terms with the world, bending its musical, physical, rhetorical and mercantile devices to their imperious wills. How has the world responded? While the gospel sound has long ceased being a novelty in pop, it remains a lodestar for certain singers. Rap, a largely West-Indian music, eschews sung vocals, and thus obviates the North American gospel singer. 1970's soul music tends to survive mainly through gospel; although Johnnie Taylor recently scored a surprise comeback on the blues charts (the gospel/blues barrier having also crumbled in reaction to rap). Thanks no doubt to Aretha Franklin's example, a few singers periodically return to gospel, as if fence-straddling were no longer *verboten*. Of course, since Contemporary is so blatantly derived from pop, the embrace of former outcasts is a tacit admission that the two genres complement each other. Singers who insist on their roots include the 50-ish Patti La Belle and the 30-ish Whitney Houston. LaBelle's approach may seem hyperbolic in a rock context but it is the *lingua franca* of Contemporary Gospel. Houston might not be the gospel singer her mother Cissy has been, but she appears more engaged fronting a choir than pledging her love (and she does that best *a cappella* gospel style). Al Green continues to flit between church and boudoir. Mavis Staples has recorded a solo album, accompanied by the organist Lucky Peterson, saluting Mahalia Jackson. In the liner notes she writes that the moment she spelled an ailing Jackson at a Harlem concert, completing "Precious Lord" for the queen, was the high point of her career.

The standard-bearer of pop-gospel remains Aretha Franklin. "Amazing Grace," in which she was accompanied by James Cleveland and the Southern California Community Choir, became her best-selling Atlantic album. For her new label, Arista, she recorded another gospel album, "One Lord, One Faith, One Baptism," this time in her father's church, accompanied on keyboard by the late Thomas Whitfield (formerly the musician-arranger for her most gifted disciple, Vanessa Bell Armstrong) with guest vocals by Mavis Staples and Joe Ligon, lead singer of the Mighty Clouds of Joy, who still sounded uncannily like C. L. Franklin. Despite the presence of Whitfield, not to mention the Contemporary community identified with Detroit, Franklin adhered to the old Ward Singers formula, as she recreated Marion Williams' biggest hits "Surely God is Able" and "Packin' Up." The church has clearly forgiven Aretha. She appears frequently at funeral services singing the Baptist hymns identified with Clara Ward, as if she were the surviving link to the golden age that spawned her.

In 1993, when Marion Williams received the Kennedy Center Honors, Aretha performed in a tribute to the Ward Singers' greatest lead. Once again she sang "Surely God is Able," a reminder of the amazing passage both women had undergone since the 1950s. A few months later she sang at a private concert for President Clinton in the White House. Clinton sat a few yards away from her friend, Reverend Jesse Jackson, the two men as drawn together by one singer as they had been at odds over another, Sister Souljah. Her selections ranged from the hoary ("Drink to Me Only with Thine Eyes") to the maudlin ("Old Man River"). Yet she performed the first ballad with the embellishments of Clara Ward singing "I Heard the Voice of Jesus," which happens to share its melody, and turned the Jerome Kern composition into an evocation of her shouting Baptist grandmother. As a finale, she brought on a choir (what else?) to help her do Marion Williams' "I Was Born to Sing the Gospel," concluding with a swiveling cascade of bent notes that would have impressed Mahalia or Clara. Aretha Franklin was born to sing a lot more than gospel, but at the summit of her career, it remained her aesthetic salvation.

*   *   *

There have never been so many outlets for gospel. Most soul food restaurants offer a Sunday gospel brunch, where the style tends to be resolutely traditional, perhaps because white, or middle-aged black audiences prefer that sound. Traditional groups and even large choirs continue to tour Europe, a trek pioneered by choirs like the First Church of Deliverance under Ralph Goodpasteur, and by groups like the Golden Gate Jubilee Quartet, who have lived in Paris since the 1950's. Particularly successful abroad are the Barrett Sisters, Angelic Gospel Singers, Sensational Nightingales, Bill Moss and the Celestials, Jessy Dixon, and the Johnnie Thompson Singers.

Meanwhile European tourists in New York have made a habit of attending gospel churches in Harlem, seeking an excitement that is bound to seem ersatz or deracinated in Amsterdam and Zurich. The result has been culture shock for both sides. The Europeans like the spirited chorales, but not the lengthy preaching and attention to church business. The congregations like the tourists' love offerings and mere presence—the Europeans frequently outnumber the church flock—but feel patronized and regarded as exotic specimens.

White gospel offers another venue, particularly for singer-composers like Jessy Dixon, Babbie Mason, and Danniebelle Hall, all following in the steps of Andraé Crouch. The gospel sound is so ubiquitous that some white Pentecostal choirs have attempted to duplicate it, among them Nashville's Christ Church. As a rule, Contemporary Christians tend to sound like pop wannabes; and so there are a few Michael Bolton and Mariah Carey sound-a-likes, who attempt soul gospel. The more authentic forms of white gospel, represented by, say, Vestal Goodman, have suffered the same generational rejection as traditional black gospel. Truly fervent white gospel was recorded in the 1950's by Brother Claude Ely, a Pentecostal evangelist from Pucket's Creek,

Virginia. His recordings are filled with ecstatic shrieks and the heavy footfalls of dancing saints. It is most instructive to hear Ely sing a largely black repertory, e.g., "Farther On Up the Road," a Brewster composition recorded only months after the Ward Singers had introduced it. There's plenty of vitality but no improvisation; lots of heart but no soul.

Gospel is increasingly considered a bedrock of African-American culture. Even Louis Farrakhan's Million Man March ended with an overweight tenor belting Andraé Crouch's "To God Be the Glory," while the Muslim shed the happy tears of a Baptist. Academics have recognized the music's significance. Michael W. Harris, an historian at Northwestern University, has written *The Rise of Gospel Blues: The Music of Thomas Andrew Dorsey in the Urban Church*, which focuses on the late 20's and early 30's, when Dorsey kept switching fields. Harris depicts Dorsey as a wily entrepreneur from the start: instructing Theodore Frye, his first vocalist, to employ vaudevillian devices, like strutting up the aisles. The composer of "Precious Lord" seems to have grasped more at Adam Smith's invisible hand than at any let down from heaven. At the Smithsonian Institution, the singer-scholar Bernice Johnson Reagon has directed seminars on the pioneer composers, which have been anthologized in the text, *We'll Understand It Better By and By* (1993); she has also been the narrator of a radio series, *Wade in the Water*, that surveyed the genre's development from lining-out hymns to Contemporary Choir.

Horace Boyer is the only scholar who has been a professional gospel singer. Along with his sibling James, he was a child prodigy. The Boyer Brothers were such big stars in the mid-50's that Alex Bradford sat in on their sessions. Natives of Winter Park, Florida, Horace and James reportedly were the first C.O.G.I.C. children to receive Ph.D.s. Horace teaches at the Amherst branch of the University of Michigan, demonstrating vocally and on piano how gospel used to be. His recent book *How Sweet the Sound* (1995) pays special attention to the music's sanctified origins. Stanley Davis, a Baltimore native, seventeen years Boyer's junior, demonstrates vocal, piano, and choral techniques at Chicago's DePaul and Northwestern universities. Though sympathetic to his generation's sound, Davis has fought hard for Chicago's *grandes dames* like Inez Andrews, Vernon Oliver Price, and Irma Gwynn. He has accompanied the Barrett Sisters, and has a vocal range to rival theirs: on clear days, he can sing an octave over soprano high C. Johnny Lloyd, a Head Start teacher in Philadelphia, is the current head of the Dorsey convention's Soloists Bureau, having been trained by its founder Willie Mae Ford Smith. His idol was the minimally recorded but hugely influential Mary Johnson Davis. He produces annual concerts memorializing her work, and featuring old warriors like Frances Steadman and Charles Banks.*

*   *   *

The mightiest singers continue to fall. Of the eighteen individuals profiled in this book's 1971 edition, twelve have since died. Some enjoyed a biblical span. Thomas A. Dorsey died at 93 (his last years, alas, spent in a coma that was periodically broken by his awakening to croon in falsetto voice the melody of "Precious Lord") and Reverend Brewster at 89 (to the last committed to the civil rights struggle. Toward the end he spoke to the great Memphis singer J. Robert Bradley: "'Well, Mr. Bradley,'—that's how he talks when he wants to sound dignified—'I'm on my back now, floating, watching the stars. But next time you hear from me, I'll be flaunting my way to heaven'").

The gospel mothers enjoyed similar longevity, Willie Mae Ford Smith dying at 89, Sallie Martin at 92. Both were featured in the documentary *Say Amen Somebody* (1982). It was too late to help their careers (the Barrett Sisters benefitted the most from the exposure). But thanks to the film, Mother Smith became at last a celebrity both in St. Louis and around the world. With her huge smile and Ethel

---

*One of the best pieces of gospel journalism was Susan Orlean's 1995 *New Yorker* profile of the Jackson Southernaires. Accompanying the quartet on a tour of southern hamlets, she revealed that the Gospel Highway remains a shabby, pot-holed affair.

Waters-like maternal piety, she became the embodiment of the gospel vocation, a role once held by her disciple Mahalia Jackson. As late as 1988, nearing 84, she could still belt out a song with a teen-ager's volume. Sometimes in her last years she'd hum a Dr. Watts hymn or sing a mid-tempo verse of "My Wild Irish Rose," with more than a hint of vaudevillian brio—returning, as it were, to her primeval roots. (Her brother Prince Ford had danced in Paris with St. Louis' own Josephine Baker.) The bad news is that no records exist of Mother Smith in her prime; the good news is that she died as big a star as if such records existed. Sallie Martin remained crotchety and fidgety to the end. Her ninetieth birthday was celebrated on the *Today* show, and by a convention of white gospel singers, many of whom had purchased Martin and Morris songbooks during the 1940s. In the last weeks of her life, Gregory Cooper, the handsome young man who had served as her accompanist, flack, and companion, was hauled into court, accused of neglecting the old woman. In the midst of the trial, she entered a hospital, and died shortly after. It was a sad departure for a woman whose imperial dignity had previously held firm. (Cooper died a few years later of AIDS.)

In 1989 Bessie Griffin died of breast cancer. During her last years, except for an occasional European tour, her engagements were limited to free-will offerings, where the great contralto was lucky to earn fifty dollars. She felt that the Los Angeles gospel community had abandoned her, and, indeed, few singers visited her during her last months in the hospital. Though when Inez Andrews or Marion Williams called long-distance, her spirit lifted. ("Marion called and prayed for me, and we both got happy. We just had ourselves a crying good time.") It was a typical but final irony that her last album was released two weeks after her death.

Then came a torrent of gospel deaths. Quartet singers: the Fairfield Four's Sam McCrary; the Soul Stirrers' Paul Foster, J. J. Farley, and Roy Crain (leaving "Pop" Harris as the sole survivor); the Dixie Hummingbirds' James Walker (now replaced by a still youthful-sounding Paul Owens, whom he had originally replaced when Owens joined the Swan Silvertones);

the latter group's Louis Johnson; and the Swanee Quintet's Reuben Willingham. Most curious was the death of Wilbur "Little Ax" Broadnax, the short, big-hipped tenor whose relentless drive had powered the Spirit of Memphis, Fairfield Four, Blind Boys, and Golden Echoes. Upon Little Ax's death the name's accuracy became startlingly clear (there had been a brother, Wilmer a.k.a. "Big Ax"), when an autopsy revealed that this hard-singing quartet man was a woman.

Between 1994 and 1996 alone, Willie Mae Ford Smith was joined in death by the gospel singers Iola Pugh of the Consolers, Jeanette Harris of the Golden Harps, Mattie Moss Clark, Cassietta George, Gloria Griffin*, and Jessie Mae Renfro. Robert Anderson's death in 1995 left only Eugene Smith and J. Robert Bradley to represent the tradition of male soloists they had helped inaugurate during the late 30's.

Marion Williams died in 1994. Her career had gone its erratic way for years, with her tearing up a church or jazz festival one month, and going jobless the next. In 1983 diabetic complications resulted in the amputation of a toe; in 1988 she began dialysis treatments three times a week. She continued to record and perform. Two weeks after undergoing her first dialysis treatment, she began a week's tour on a Jazz Boat-Ride, where, according to *The New Yorker's* Whitney Balliett, she outshone everyone from Dizzy Gillespie to Joe Williams, this after having nearly died. In the years between 1982 and 1993, her brilliant soprano voice weak-

---

*Gloria Griffin (1931-95) was one of the last group leads. Born in Mississippi, raised in St. Louis, she joined the Ward Singers as a teen-ager, and later sang with the Caravans. In 1957, she joined the Roberta Martin Singers, and became their star with a series of soulful ballads: "God Specializes," "God is Still on the Throne," and her own composition, "I'm So Grateful." Her alto voice was not large, and, a bit like Dorothy Love Coates, she tended to sing out of her range. But she phrased with such exquisite precision that she resembled a nightclub *diseuse*. Audiences were enthralled by her line-readings; tall, slim, homely and graceful, she was the gospel tragedienne. In her last years, she suffered the usual gospel calamities: no work, car accidents, ill health. But she hadn't lost her power. In 1992 at the Smithsonian Institution, she told the audience, "The doctors said I could never sing another gospel song. But, you know, *Gooooood*, He specializes," then ran up the august aisles and left the audience berserk.

ened (though high C was available, almost to the end.) But her singing evoked a profound sense of time drawing to a close, both her own and the various traditions that she, more than any other singer, had mastered. Often now she sang *a cappella*; her performances of "Death in the Morning" or "Trouble So Hard" sounded like the Platonic ideal of a field recording. One of her last, "My Soul Looks Back," was filled with ancient devices of moaning and verbal interjection combined in a way far more daring than anything one could hear on Bobby Jones. When the recording was played at her funeral, the entire church began rocking and foot-patting, completing the circuit from heart to heart.

The underside of such a huge talent was a penchant for overkill (the gospel singer's universal weakness) and frivolous material. Thus it was a pleasant surprise that when she finally entered the public ken on the soundtrack of the 1991 film *Fried Green Tomatoes*, she did so with "A Charge to Keep I Have" and "Cool Down Yonder," the first a Dr. Watts hymn performed *a cappella*, the second a jubilee quartet song from the 1920s. The world had accepted her at her most authentic. With a revived sense of urgency, she sang the majestic blues of her late years:

> *I surprised myself with the strength God gave me,*
> *Back against the wall, something within me raised me.*
> *Everytime I stumble, I begin to climb,*
> *Enemies tried to grab me but I broke loose every time,*
> *I've come so far, I believe I can run on some more.*

Now the critical plaudits came flooding in. A *New York Times* critic called her "the equal of any blues singer alive"; Whitney Balliett said she was among the greatest jazz singers; a *Rolling Stone* writer described her simply as "the greatest singer ever." In 1993 she became the first singer to win a MacArthur "genius" Award, with a five-year grant of $374,000—an astounding sum for a woman whose existence had been plagued for years by financial insecurity. Other singers took notice: a Brooklyn evangelist commented "I guess this is what we mean by 'after awhile' and 'by and by.'" As

Marion said, her change had come.

In December 1993 she became the first gospel singer to receive the Kennedy Center Honors. She was seated in a box with the Clintons, her fellow honorees (she was the only woman) and her pastor, Mother Irene Oakley. As mentioned earlier, she was saluted by Aretha Franklin and Little Richard, who rushed on stage, "Honey, *you* made me a star because you gave me my high note." Such acknowledgment gladdened all the pioneers long denied their propers. Marion's series of late triumphs seemed to vindicate their patience and endurance.

But this happy development proved a false ending. Marion's feisty spirit had fooled many people, including her doctor. In February 1994 she underwent a quadruple bypass (perhaps not the wisest medical decision for a diabetic whose veins wouldn't heal). She rallied enough to attend her induction into the Philadelphia Walk of Fame, where her name could be found near Clara Ward's. In retrospect this was the one honor she had to witness, the coda to a youth when Clara had nearly "burned me out," or could have, if she hadn't been a genius. She lingered three months, by which time both her legs had been amputated. The MacArthur grant ended with her death; she had enjoyed it for less than a year, and nothing was left for her grand-children. The bluesiest of gospel singers had lived and died a gospel blues. A deceptive reprieve, then a miserable death. Good news and bad times.

*   *   *

Nothing vital stays the same. That traditional gospel would die out, along with its exponents, was to be expected. There do remain a few great soloists (Gladys Beamon Gregory, Irma Gwynn, Inez Andrews, Albertina Walker, Rosie Wallace, Vernon Oliver Price, Emily Bram, and the still soaring Delois Barrett Campbell) and quartets (Ira Tucker's Dixie Hummingbirds, Clarence Fountain's Blind Boys, JoJo Wallace's Nightingales, and a revamped Fairfield Four, still featuring the reverberating bass of Dickie Freeman). To hear him tell it, Reverend Cleophus Robinson is the last master of the gospel blues, "singing as never before," still hoping for stardom: "A man's got to dream, isn't that so?"

Actually the bluesy aspect of gospel has largely disappeared, and the wonderful nineteenth-century hymns survive in garishly updated versions, while most of the contemporary religious ballads—by both black and white composers—are embarrassingly banal, lyrically maladroit, and theologically suspect. But business picks up when the beat starts, whether it is laid down by a quartet's rhythm section or a choir's synthesizer. Gospel still swings the most, still offers—if not the old-time catharsis—the quickest musical route to transcendence.

And that old-time catharsis may be due a revival, as, following the so-called welfare reforms, old-time conditions recur, this time with fewer protections. In 1938, Rosetta Tharpe rejoiced that "He said go down to the welfare, I've got plenty there to spare." But that was then.

The most troubling issue confronting gospel lovers is not aesthetic but political, and is inextricably connected with the AIDS epidemic. The politics of fundamentalists have always been contradictory, the songs and sermons inculcating either passivity or a cloaked form of resistance, the drive for racial tolerance coinciding with absolute intolerance for the unsaved. Dr. King was despised by many preachers, e.g., Reverend J. H. Jackson, former president of the National Baptist Convention, who changed his church's address so it wouldn't read Dr. Martin Luther King Drive. Jackson was a member of the John Birch Society; in 1973, a Yale graduate student in theology, who had been raised in St. Louis, quipped that were the Birchers not so racist, 95% of the Dorsey convention would sign up.

In 1988 the first notable to endorse Pat Robertson's presidential campaign was John Patterson, presiding bishop of the Church of God in Christ, and son-in-law of Bishop C. H. Mason, the denomination's founder. Indeed, for some black fundamentalists, Robertson was the second choice after Jesse Jackson, religious television being (not incidentally) along with soap operas, extremely popular in black homes. Similarly Clarence Thomas became a hero to some church folk who identified with his rhetoric of victimization, and his fundamentalist principles. (Even his white wife was Pentecostal.) In lieu of conservative messages, some ministers now preach a Prosperity Gospel that induces a retreat from politics of any kind. Why go to the trouble of organizing when "whatever the Lord has in store for you is yours," anyway. "Just name it and claim it," provided you tithe: "to get more, you need to give more."

However, by 1996, the Religious Right had scared off many churchgoers, who might otherwise countenance its restrictive morality. Harvey Gantt discerned in the army of believers who supported his rival, Senator Jesse Helms, the same Baptist bigots who had opposed integration. The connection between the Religious Right and the militias (whose congressional advocate, Helen Chenoweth, is a Pentecostal) was another ominous sign. And yet, to be fair, an infusion of politics with religious fervor had defined the civil rights movement, long before zealots started attacking abortion clinics or searching the sky for helicopters.

The church's response to AIDS manifested a similar contradiction between principles and self-interest. The gospel church has long been a refuge for gays and lesbians, some of whom grew up to be among the greatest singers and musicians. Quartets have long muttered homophobic comments about their robed competition, and it is a standard joke that "a choir can't sing without some punk [gay man] on the organ," cueing the mood, inviting the spirit. Everybody knew this but in 1971, merely intimating a gay presence in the church drew opprobrium on this author. Not, however, from James Baldwin. He had observed a nascent gay sensibility in his novel of the sanctified church, "Go Tell It on the Mountain," and throughout his life he remained torn between the richness of the gospel community and the poverty of its unforgiving spirit, the cry of the saints and their soul-crushing commandments. (It's an old criticism. Michael Harris quotes

Daniel Payne, a 19th-century Methodist: "a strong religious feeling coupled with a narrow range of knowledge, often makes one a bigot.")

Deception has always been a religious standby; for some outsiders (like those who used to watch Jimmy Swaggart or Jim Bakker), it's even part of the fun, a homespun magic. For years quartet singers have wailed about their dead mothers while the woman still lived. But the duplicity surrounding AIDS has been of a whole new order, and has claimed far too many victims, who have rightly seen themselves as abandoned. In 1991, James Cleveland, for three decades the King of gospel, and certainly its most innovative figure, died of AIDS, aged 60. He was the most famous of a legion: choir directors and musicians from coast to coast. Under such circumstances it was bitter to hear his Chicago buddies like Reverend Milton Brunson preach that AIDS was God's means of punishing homosexuals (many of whom had sung with Brunson's choir, the Thompson Community Singers). Or to learn that Cleveland's teen-age colleague in the old Lux Singers, Reverend Clay Evans (Jesse Jackson's pastor) had released a vanity album decrying *Homosexuality in the Church.*

All over America, the church turned on the men who, along with the mothers and sisters, had given gospel its special flavor. Nobody was above reproach. Cleveland, like any of the other stricken celebrities, might have educated his huge following but he didn't. Some gay singers preached that the only solution was to give up homosexuality, not that this expeditious counsel helped save *their* lives.* Cleveland's funeral was preached by Reverend E. V. Hill, one of the token black leaders of the militantly homophobic Promise Keepers. (Some recent attempts to draw black men into the church have taken the forms of a muscular, "masculinist" Christianity; a typical appeal being "my Jesus didn't have any sissies or punks around him.") The hypocrisy ran down like drops of blood.

It's possible that the younger gospel singers may not be as

---

*A rare exception is the San Francisco pastor, Yvette Flunder, whose City of Refuge Community Church operates an AIDS clinic, and a shelter for battered women.

gay as their mentors. Leonard Lopate wittily observes that sexual demographics changed when gospel men stopped singing like women, and began mimicking Stevie Wonder. The huge prominence of the Church of God in Christ and other Pentecostal denominations— although they are famously the gayest churches—has fostered a renewed attack on gays. Mattie Moss Clark was the first rebuker; her sanctified disciples have followed suit, joined by younger male singers, some of whom may be figuratively killing their elders, asserting their style and sexuality against the James Clevelands and Alex Bradfords who preceded them. (A similar reaction occurred in the first stages of Castro's Cuba, and Taliban Afghanistan.)

Meanwhile in Los Angeles, Carl Bean, an ex-Bradford Singer, has founded Unity Fellowship, the first black, openly gay church, complete with a large program devoted to AIDS education. Gallows humorists surmised that Cleveland and Bradford would keep feuding in the after-life.

Inez Andrews tells a no-doubt apocryphal tale about a Chicago revival, during which a famous woman evangelist made an altar call. "I'm looking for all the sissies and bull daggers in this building to come up and be saved." "You going?" one fellow asked another. "No, child," was the reply, followed by an echo of "Give Me That Old Time Religion". "If it was good enough for mother, it's good enough for me." With its allusiveness and earthy humor, its nose-thumbing at enemies, its wink at friends—this too is the gospel spirit.

Acknowledgments

During the forty years I've been a gospel lover, many singers have aided me in my research. Besides those already discussed, I've received generous assistance from James Anderson, Robert Anderson, Inez Andrews, Charlie Barnwell, Alberta Carter Bradford, Charles Campbell, Howard Carroll, Carl Coates, Edna Gallmon Cooke, James Davis, Jesse Farley, Mildred Gay, Cassietta George, the Georgia Peach, Louis Gibson, Clay Graham, Gloria Griffin, Gladys Beamon Gregory, Irma Gwynn, Mattie Harper, James Herndon, Josephine Howard, Mildred Miller Howard, Jonathan Jackson, Louis Johnson, Marie Knight, Joe Ligon, Lillian McGriff, Norsalus McKissick, John Myles, Dorothy Norwood, Paul Owens, Kitty Parham, Vernon Oliver Price, Iola Pugh, Sullivan Pugh, Willie Rogers, Myrtle Scott, Eugene Smith, Little Lucy Smith, Lois Snead, Mavis Staples, Roebuck Staples, Frances Steadman, Herman Stevens, Princess Stewart, Johnny Thompson, Jackie Verdell, Henrietta Waddy, James Walker, Joseph Wallace, Rosie Wallace, Delores Washington, Ernestine B. Washington, Kenneth Washington, Robert Washington. Among those involved in gospel production and recording, Robert Banks, Fred Barr, Joe Bostic, John Bowden, Ozzie Cadena, John Hammond, Herman Lubinsky, Fred Mendelsohn, Tillie

Peterson, and Mancel Warwick have been most cooperative. Buddy Franklin, whose knowledge of gospel was immense, was particularly helpful.

Susan Fox prodded, criticized, and encouraged the writing of this book. Her affectionate assistance helped get the work done.

Thank you all.

DISCOGRAPHY

I have restricted this discography to albums currently in print. Thanks to a spate of reissues, many of them import albums, we now have a fairly adequate representation of some classic artists. Not all; there are scandalous gaps.

No matter what genre, there are conspicuous absences. Female groups no longer available include the Imperial Gospel Singers, a Philadelphia group in the Davis Sisters tradition, powered by the piano and vocal drive of the greatly esteemed Rosie Wallace; the Daniels Singers, New York's answer to the Roberta Martin Singers, with East Coast (therefore bluesier) arrangements and a strong lead, Becky Moss; and the Argo Singers, a driving Chicago group over whom the sweet-voiced Lorenza Brown Porter soared with style.

Duos include Brother and Sister Quince, the National Gospel Twins; and the Gay Sisters (Mildred and Evelyn), one-time darlings of the Church of God in Christ, whose repertory included intense Baptist hymns and sanctified shouts, right out of the 1920s. The male gospel group is a late but significant phenomenon. Missing are the Gospel Clefs who, under Leon Lumpkins' tutelage, carried the Reverend Brewster-Clara Ward approach to composition and arrangement one step further; and the Rasberry Singers, also out of the Clara Ward-Marion Williams approach to gospel singing (Raymond Rasberry had accompanied both women). The

Rasberrys were notable for the lead vocals of Carl Hall, the most remarkable male soprano on records (and no slouch when it comes to growl/squalling), and for a relentless drive; they are the most forceful male group, quartet or gospel, I've seen.

Quartet albums were once easy to find, but the discontinuation of labels like Peacock, VeeJay, and Starday-King has led to the disappearance of classic recordings by the Swan Silvertones and Harmonizing Four (once the oldest group on the road, they sang together for over fifty years, featuring, almost to the end, tenor and lead Tommy "Goat" Johnson, baritone Lonnie Smith, father of the jazz organist, and the soulful "Gospel Joe" Williams; their most famous member, Jimmy Jones, was generally regarded as the most powerful quartet basso: while not the vivacious jubilee singers of their first Decca records, they remained the most relaxed of all traveling acts: "the ever-loving Harmonizing Four"), Gospelaires of Dayton, Ohio (who carried the June Cheeks/ Nightingales combination of relentlessly aggressive leads and neo-jubilee backgrounds to the next ecstatic round. Robert Washington could shift from stop to over-drive in seconds), and the Highway QCs (the quartet that produced three Soul Stirrers leads—Sam Cooke, Johnnie Taylor and Willie Rogers—though their long-time lead and manager Spencer Taylor was responsible for their most famous arrangements, somewhere between the Swan Silvertones and the Soul Stirrers). Quartet lovers can point to other acts deserving a reissue.

Choir fans will lament the absence of work by Detroit's Voices of Tabernacle or Southwest Michigan Choir; Los Angeles's Voices of Victory (directed by the influential Thurston Frazier), among others. To these ears, the best choir of all was the St. Paul Church Choir of Los Angeles—one of the first to record modern gospel, and perhaps the first postwar gospel act to be recorded live—which featured leads like Sallie Martin, Cora Martin, Erie Gladney, and the mighty Professor J. Earle Hines, as well as quartet harmonies. They were great stars in the 1940s, but Capitol Records keeps them out of print.

Even the most famous artists aren't fully represented since Savoy and Nashboro deleted albums by their top acts. In redoing this discography, I missed particularly the classic records of the Roberta Martin Singers, the Davis Sisters, and, most of all, the Ward Singers. In retrospect, one recognizes Clara Ward's advance over all preceding religious groups. Not merely are her arrangements still astonishingly fresh and inventive, but her homage to the tradition of Baptist moans, even as her star lead, Marion Williams, supplied the sanctified and quartet elements, makes her group's recorded *oeuvre* incomparably capacious and encyclopedic; *all* of gospel's best qualities can be found in those old Ward Singers records.

This is obviously not a complete discography. Instead, I have listed what I consider the best records available. Listings of artists not previously discussed include a brief analysis.

ROOTS

Arizona Dranes 1926-1928. Herwin 210.

These recordings indicate that something very close to modern gospel was flourishing in the Church of God in Christ seventy years ago. A blind Texan, Arizona Juanita Dranes was associated with the early C.O.G.I.C. luminary Bishop Samuel Crouch (an ancestor of Andraé's). Her gritty, high-pitched twang would be echoed by later C.O.G.I.C. soloists like Ernestine B. Washington, Emily Bram, and Mattie Wigley. Perhaps as notable as her clipped phrasing—bite, bite, bite, with no let-up—is her musicianship. Her kind of barrelhouse piano was already a C.O.G.I.C. standby (T-Bone Walker once said that the first time he heard boogie-woogie piano was in a Texas sanctified church). In addition, Dranes' performances are conceived as arrangements: the interplay of lead voice with background is not haphazard; the piano interludes are exactly placed, and the fervent growls of her back-up group express a conscious, "house-wrecking" temperament. Dranes clearly knew how to build her fire until a Holy Ghost conflagration occurred.

Bessie Johnson 1928-1929. Herwin 202.
One of the early sanctified singers, Bessie Johnson had a rich, commanding contralto. Her preacher growls, like those of other twenties' singers, Sallie Sanders and Reverend Mary Nelson, resemble those of latter-day shouters Ruth Davis and Marion Williams, and suggest how long sanctified women have been employing the originally male characteristics of "hard singing and preaching." In the 1930s, Memphis Minnie, masquerading as "Gospel Minnie," included a growling sermonette in her one religious recording, but even earlier Bessie Smith's "Moan You Moaners" sounded like a more guileful version of Bessie Johnson.

Dr. C. J. Johnson—The Old Time Song Service. Savoy MG 14173.
Dr. Johnson sang the old *a cappella* congregational style. Here his thunderous baritone is recorded in Atlanta, but the results were the same in Brooklyn or Los Angeles: congregations pitched in spontaneously as if nothing had intervened since this style dominated black churches.

How Can I Keep From Singing. Volumes I and II. Yazoo 2020, 2021.
An anthology of white and black religious music from the twenties and thirties. While there is some convergence of repertory (and of the lined-out hymn style) and a universal fervor, the distinctive traits of African-American gospel appear in bold relief: a much vaster range of emotion, vocal color, and rhythmic energy. Some particular classics are Bessie Johnson's finest performance, "Better Things for You," and "Come Let Us Eat Together," a sermon by Reverend E. D. Campbell, whose piercing tenor predicts Archie Brownlee's impassioned shrieks. David Miller, a laconic white troubador ("Lonesome Valley") is another stand-out.

The Document Series

The aim of Document Records, an Austrian label, is to reissue every pre-war race recording, blues and gospel. The sound is barely acceptable and the liner notes invariably uninformed, but there are many treasures here. Gospel fans will particularly enjoy the following anthologies.

Memphis Gospel. Document 5072. (Featuring Bessie Johnson and Mary Nelson).

Gospel Classics (1927-1931). Document 5190.
This album contains the complete recorded *oeuvre* of some pioneer shouters. Jessie May Hill was perhaps the earliest sanctified woman on records: her spectacular "Crucifixion of Christ" set a standard for hard singing echoed twenty-five years later by another C.O.G.I.C. star, Goldia Haynes, who performed the number in Hill style. Laura Henton had a smoother voice, resembling a young Mahalia Jackson, and she sings Lucie Campbell's "Heavenly Sunshine," one of the first gospel songs.

Elder Curry and Elder Beck 1930-1939. Document BDCD-6035.
Elder Charles Beck is a seminal figure in gospel history. During the 1920s, he may have been the best sanctified pianist; his playing was more legato and improvisatory than the herky-jerky ragtime of Arizona Dranes. During the 1930s, he switched to trumpet; the jazz critic Marshall Stearns later compared him to Louis Armstrong. Beck was a relaxed, laid-back vocalist, who may have been the first singer to record modern gospel. He was recording Dorsey tunes and sanctified standards in 1937, a year before Rosetta Tharpe. By 1939 he was singing more Dorsey, accompanied by a small group of women, whose disciplined harmonies anticipated the gospel groups of the mid-40's.

Country Gospel (1946-1953). Document 5221. (Featuring the Two Gospel Keys and Sister O. M. Terrell).
Postwar recordings. Terrell was a local Rosetta Tharpe, too

wild-voiced to reach stardom but great fun. The Two Keys (Emma Daniels and Mother Sally Jones) of Augusta, Georgia (not Atlanta) were among postwar gospel's first stars, best remembered for their hit, "Can't No Grave Hold My Body Down." Their simple guitar and tambourine-whacking remind some critics of white Holiness music. But no white singer of that day sang as freely. The subtle variations throughout their work bespeak "spirit-feel", the raucous, not unfunny moans convey a hint of vaudeville. As late as 1949 the Keys' uncompromising form of street-singing could tear up big city arenas.

Negro Religious Field Records (1934-42). Document 5312.
Wonderful recordings from the Library of Congress. In 1934 Austin Coleman is the fiercest lead singer imaginable: his ecstatic syncopations make later quartet men like Cheeks and Tucker sound timid. Critics detect Cajun and African (natch) influences, and find Coleman archaic. In fact, go into a storefront Fire Baptized church, and you'll find his heirs, admittedly spelling each other: simply listening to him wears one out. In 1942 Bozie Sturdevant is a modern quartet lead, employing all the liberties sanctioned by R. H. Harris. He phrases like Harris on three gospel blues ("Ain't No Grave Can Hold My Body Down" is the most famous), has a tenor quality and vibrato like Harris', a falsetto squeak like Claude Jeter's, and a growling preacher bottom.

Singing The Gospel (1933-36). Document 5326.
Early gospel cuts documenting the gospel revolution wrought by Thomas A. Dorsey and members of the sanctified church. Elder Lightfoot Solomon Michaux (brother of the famous film director Oscar Micheaux) had a large following in Washington D. C., and his "Happy Am I," with its primitive form of choral syncopation, was a surprise cross-over hit during the Depression. Gospel historians will be most challenged by Elder Oscar Sanders and his congregation. They perform two Dorsey songs, "I Claim Jesus First of All," and "Singing in My Soul," in sanctified style: the first recorded evidence that

the union worked. They sound less frantic than Bessie Johnson's ensemble, more geared to new standards of professionalism.

Female Solo Personalities

Gospel Warriors. Spirit Feel 1003.
A series of classic gospel vocalists. Sister Rosetta Tharpe, accompanied only by her guitar, is at her youthful, unadorned best (introducing the first recorded version of "Just a Closer Walk with Thee"). The Georgia Peach (from her first session in 1930 and last one in 1960); Mary Johnson Davis (while shockingly under-recorded, this bluesy soprano was very influential, and found her echoes in Mahalia Jackson's florid curlicues, Clara Ward's intense hymnody, and Marion Williams' startling dynamics); Clara Ward (sequenced so that the Davis influence becomes clear, performing a masterful "Precious Lord" that would later inspire Aretha Franklin's first hit); Marion Williams (roaring like a Baptist deacon in "It's Getting Late in the Evening," discovering the inherent melancholy in "The Storm is Passing Over"); Bessie Griffin (in the best voice of her late years, wailing two of her quartet hits, "I Want to Rest" and the *a cappella* "Well, Well, Well"); Jessie Mae Renfro (who had the twang of her sister C.O.G.I.C. soloists, Ernestine B. Washington and Emily Bram, and a time sense freer than theirs; her huge lyrical voice, hitting immense blue notes without fuss or bother, is most impressive on "I'll Be Satisfied Then" and "I've Had My Chance"); and Frances Steadman (a stylistically absorbing singer with a uniquely deep alto).

The Great Gospel Women. Volumes I and II. Shanachie 6004 and 6017.
On a similar order as *Gospel Warriors*, though with many more vocalists (16 and 17, respectively) and selections (31 and 33). The very greatest are represented by some of their best work: Mahalia Jackson ("These are They," "Pilgrim of Sorrow," "Just Over the Hill," "What Could I Do," and a late church performance, previously unissued, that shows the

queen at her most rambunctious); Marion Williams (the near-reggae "Come Out the Corner," "Nobody Knows Nobody Cares," "There's A Man Going Around," "Pure Gold," and the bluesiest version extant of " Go Down Moses"); Rosetta Tharpe ("I Looked Down the Line," "Nobody's Fault But Mine," and "Peace in the Valley"); Clara Ward ("Just One Moment"); Bessie Griffin ("Since I Met Jesus"); and Edna Gallmon Cooke ("Build Me a Cabin"). But there are also recordings of the C.O.G.I.C. divas, Ernestine B. Washington, Jessie Mae Renfro, Goldia Haynes, and Marie Knight, and some of the major group leads, Roberta Martin (her most famous performance, "What a Friend We Have in Jesus"), Imogene Green (her masterpiece, "Every Now and Then"), Ruth Davis, Dorothy Love Coates, Bessie Folk, and Delois Barrett Campbell. Particular rarities are home recordings of Mary Johnson Davis (her signature "Come Ye Disconsolate") and Myrtle Scott (by legend, Chicago's most soulful singer, who made only two professional recordings).

Inez Andrews

Lord Lift Us Up. Savoy SL 14731.
The Two Sides of Inez Andrews. Shanachie 6019.

Martha Bass

Mother Smith and Her Children. Spirit Feel 6010.

Evangelist Shirley Caesar

Go. Myrrh MSF 6665.
Jesus, I Love Calling Your Name. Myrrh MSB 6721.
I'll Go. Hob 266.
Stranger on the Road. Hob 2144.

Sister Wynona Carr

A Cleveland Baptist with the melismatic aplomb of Rosetta Tharpe and the ready-for-pop contralto of Marie Knight. For some years she was C. L. Franklin's choir director, and helped expose the young Aretha to the wonders of note-bending and moaning. Her performance with the New Bethel Church

Choir of "Our Father" is a revelation, far stronger than any of her studio recordings. She may have sounded too secular for her time, scoring more as a composer ("Lord Jesus," "What Do You Know About Jesus") than as a soloist in those house-wrecking days. Her last gospel record, *The Ball Game*, was her biggest hit, a witty sermon in song. She then entered the pop field, enjoyed a modest success, contracted tuberculosis, retired, and died, aged 50.

Dragnet for Jesus. Specialty SPCD 7016-2.

Dorothy Love Coates

The Best of Dorothy Love-Coates and the Gospel Harmonettes. Nashboro 4508-2.

Edna Gallmon Cooke

Mother Smith and Her Children. Spirit Feel 6010.
The Best of Madame Edna Gallmon Cooke. Nashboro 4008-2.

Aretha Franklin

Amazing Grace. Atlantic SD 2-906.

Cassietta George

A native of Memphis, greatly influenced by Clara Ward, she sang with a female quartet before joining the Caravans. A gifted stylist with a clear small voice, particularly adept at ad-libbed interjections, she was a dynamo in church. Memphis quartet and Chicago gospel trained her to think on her feet.

I Want to See Jesus. Savoy. 14765.

Bessie Griffin

Even Me. Spirit Feel 1009.

Mahalia Jackson

The Apollo Sessions 1946-1951. Volume I. Pair PCD 2-1332.
—*Volume II.* Pair PDK 2 - 1346.
Bless This House. Columbia CL 899.
Live at Newport 1958. Columbia Legacy CK 53629.

Gospels, Spirituals, and Hymns. Columbia Legacy C2T 47083.
—*Volume II.*

Shun Pace Rhodes

He Lives. Savoy SCD 14807.
Shekinah Glory. Savoy SCD 14814.

Willie Mae Ford Smith

Mother Smith and Her Children. Spirit Feel 1010.
I Am Bound for Canaan Land. Savoy SL 14739.

Sister Rosetta Tharpe

Rosetta Tharpe was at her best when left alone, relying solely on her own guitar accompaniment. To these ears the accompaniment of Sammy Price's boogie-woogie trio rendered her brittle and frenetic. Fortunately the Document reissues (as well as those in the *Great Gospel Women)* capture her early glory. A happy surprise is her late work, again unencumbered, before European audiences. Her repertory had scarcely changed in twenty years, and she wails with considerable directness, frequently ad libbing the lyrics as she goes along: on "Jesus Met the Woman at the Well," by continually delaying the resolution, perhaps because she can't remember it, she comes up with something like a 64-bar blues.
Sister Rosetta Tharpe, Volume I (1938-1941). Document 5334.
—*Volume II (1942-44).* Document 5335.
Live in 1960. Southland SCD 1007.
Live at the Hot Club de France. Milan 73138.

Clara Ward

Clara Ward Memorial Album. Savoy MG 14308.
When the Gates Swing Open. Hob HBD 3507.
Receive Me Lord. Nashboro 7124.

Marion Williams

This Too Shall Pass. Nashboro 4515-2.
Born to Sing the Gospel. Shanachie 6009.
Surely God is Able. Spirit Feel 1011.

Can't Keep It to Myself. Shanachie 6007.
My Soul Looks Back 1962-92 (25 selections). Shanachie 6011.
Through Many Dangers 1966-1993 (30 selections). Shanachie 6021.

MALE SOLO PERSONALITIES

The Great Gospel Men. Shanachie 6004.
Female soloists and male quartets are widely known. But the great male soloists remain unsung heroes. They combined the women's passion with the authority customarily invested by black Baptists in male figures. Because several of them were gay, there was an added tension (predictable when men sing in a style generally associated with women) which made their work all the more provocative. This collection includes R. L. Knowles, who, as lead singer of the First Church of Deliverance, is widely credited with introducing the ad lib style in the 1930s; Brother Joe May (the "Thunderbolt of the Middle West" blasting "Move On Up a Little Higher" in a Tennessee church); Professor Alex Bradford (his first recording with the Willie Webb Singers followed by a track where he reaches soprano E above high C; his favorite performance, "Near the Cross," and the briskly contentious "What Folks Say About Me"); James Cleveland, and his colleagues, the great male leads of the Roberta Martin group, Norsalus McKissick (a potential Nat "King" Cole or Billy Eckstine, the one man Mahalia felt could surpass her in a black church) and Eugene Smith. Of particular note are Robert Anderson (roaring in old age through his composition "Prayer Changes Things," wailing in youth, "If Jesus Had to Pray," a gospel masterpiece) and the extraordinary J. Robert Bradley (whose classical training has not interfered with his impeccable singing of hymns and spirituals; nobody can out-moan him).

Dr. Morgan Babb

Like other former quartet men—R. H. Harris, Claude Jeter—Babb performs now as a soloist. His work is solemn, low-keyed, although when appearing with his brothers in the Radio Four, he was an unusually sprightly and melodic lead singer.

Keep Faith. Nashboro 4006-2.

Professor Alex Bradford

Rainbow in the Sky. Specialty SPCD 7015-2.
Too Close. Specialty SPCD 7042-2.

James Cleveland

James Cleveland and the Angelic Choir, Volume III. Savoy
   MG 14076.
James Cleveland and the Angelic Gospel Choir. Savoy RI
   5000.
James Cleveland Sings Solos. Savoy MG 14125.
*James Cleveland Sings with the World's Greatest Gospel
   Choirs.* Savoy SGL 7059.
Hallelujah 'Tis Done (with Cassietta George). Savoy
   SL-14697.

Andraé Crouch

The Best of Andraé. Light LS 5678.

Brother Joe May

Mother Smith and Her Children. Spirit Feel 6010.
The Thunderbolt of the Middle West. Specialty SPCD 7033-2.

Reverend Cleophus Robinson

A native of Mississippi, this St. Louis minister did his best
work with his sister, Josephine James; these records have a
haunting, down-home quality absent in his more commercial work. He remains an exceptional moaner, one of the last
exponents of the gospel blues. His longtime accompanist, the
late Napoleon Brown, a native of Memphis, was a magnificent blues stylist.

Wrapped Up, Tied Up, Tangled Up. Nashboro 4009-2.

Reverend Richard "Mr. Clean" White

A former gang leader turned sanctified preacher, he is an
innovative composer with a voice almost as huge as Brother
Joe May's.

Pray for Me. Savoy SL 14705.

GOSPEL GROUPS

Stars of the Gospel Highway. Spirit Feel 1008.

The artists damaged most by the Contemporary juggernaut were the gospel groups, the small ensembles of four or five singers, invariably accompanied by piano and organ. Here are three of the best: the Roberta Martin Singers (models of understated eloquence with five peerless soloists); the Original Gospel Harmonettes (with Dot Love in fighting form, ad-libbing new verses to her big hits "These are They" and "He's Right on Time"); and the Davis Sisters (at their hard-singing peak with Thelma Davis' "Jesus," Ruth Davis' "Too Close to Heaven," and Imogene Green's "Stand By Me," exhibiting a feral passion as new to gospel as their jazz-imbued harmonies).

The Angelic Gospel Singers

For close to fifty years, the simple approach of the Angelics, divided between old-time Baptist hymn singing and urban blues, has satisfied the South. The founder and surviving member is Margaret Allison, who sings lead and plays a down-home piano. Long-time colleagues were her sister, Josephine MacDowell, who sang a plaintive tenor, and Bernice Cole, a driving alto trained by the Norfolk Jubilees' Norman "Crip" Harris.

The Best of The Angelic Gospel Singers. Nashboro 4509-2.

Reverend F.C. Barnes and Reverend Janice Brown

When It Rains It Pours. AIR/CSR 10041.
The Rough Side of the Mountain. AIR /CSR 10059.

Delois Barrett Campbell and The Barrett Sisters

The Best of Delois Barrett Campbell and the Barrett Sisters. Nashboro 4517-2.

The Caravans

The Best of The Caravans. Savoy SGL 7012.

The Clark Sisters

Gospel. Savoy SL 14753.

The Consolers

The Best of the Consolers. Nashboro 4502-2.

The Davis Sisters

The Best of The Famous Davis Sisters. Savoy SGL 7017.

The Original Gospel Harmonettes

The Best of Dorothy Love Coates and the Original Gospel Harmonettes, Volume I. Specialty SPS 2134.
—*Volume II.* Specialty SPS 2141.
Get on Board. Specialty SPCD 7017-2.

The Roberta Martin Singers

The Best of The Roberta Martin Singers. Savoy SGL 7018.

The Sallie Martin Singers/Cora Martin.

Throw Out the Lifeline (including six solos by Cora Martin, who resembles both Dinah Washington and Sarah Vaughan). Specialty SPCD 7043-2.

The Meditation Singers

Good News. Specialty SPCD-7032-2.

The Stars of Faith

In the Spirit. Nashboro 4519-2.

The Ward Singers

The Best of The Ward Singers of Philadelphia, Pa. Savoy SGL 7015.

QUARTETS

Father and Sons. Spirit Feel 1001.
R. H. Harris' Soul Stirrers were the progenitors of gospel quartet. This album contains eight of their early classics, in-

cluding their first recording and Harris' masterpiece, "Walk Around." The Five Blind Boys of Mississippi made their recording debut with note-for-note copies of the Stirrers' hits. Their lead, Archie Brownlee, combined Harris' phrasing with a hair-raising shriek, while, in calmer moments, he anticipated rhythm-and-blues balladeers of the mid-1950s. The Sensational Nightingales added an East Coast finish to the Texas sound. Their greatest lead, Julius Cheeks briefly toured with the Stirrers; his Nightingales hit, "Somewhere to Lay My Head," remains a rocking wonder.

The Chosen Gospel Singers

The Lifeboat is Coming. Specialty SPCD 7014-2.

The Mighty, Mighty Clouds of Joy

Family Circle. MCA 28008.
The Mighty Clouds Live at the Music Hall. MCA 28017.

The Dixie Hummingbirds

The Best of The Dixie Hummingbirds. MCA 28021.

The Fairfield Four

This quartet recorded for the Library of Congress in 1942, and achieved considerable postwar recognition through a widely syndicated radio broadcast. Originally steeped in the big-voiced jubilee harmonic tradition, they later incorporated gospel mannerisms while retaining their powerhouse sound. The most famous lead was Reverend Sam McCrary, a bluesy Caruso; others included the shouter Edward "Preacher" Thomas and the crooner Willie Love.
Standing on the Rock. Nashboro 4003.

The Five Blind Boys of Alabama

Also known as the Happyland Singers, they have always been a good, harmonically precise quartet. Their lead singer for almost fifty years has been the vocally astonishing Clarence Fountain. Considering their experience as mother lovers— their first record "I Can See Everybody's Mother, I Can't See

Mine" was followed by "When Mother's Gone," "Goodbye Mother," "Mother's on the Train," etc.— it was appropriate that they should appear as a group of Oedipuses in the musical, *Gospel at Colonus.*

The Sermon. Specialty SPCD 7041-2.

The Five Blind Boys of Mississippi

The Best of the Five Blind Boys. MCA 28022.

The Golden Gate Quartet

Ever since the Silver Leafs in the 1920s (whose lead's tremulous head tones were long echoed by Tommy Johnson of the Richmond Harmonizing Four; and whose 1928 arrangement of "Our Father" is imitated here by the Golden Gates), Virginia quartets have featured a loping swing and a concern with vocal coloration that make theirs the quartet tradition closest to jazz. In the 1930s, both the Norfolk Jubilee, a.k.a. Jazz Quartet, and the Golden Gates recorded pop and spirituals with equal aplomb. Although you must turn to *All of My Appointed Time* (see below) to hear the Gates in a deeper, more soul-stirring groove, this album includes thirty-six selections, many of them classics. It would be hard to find more exhilarating teamwork. In their "Golden Gate Gospel Train," they mimic train sounds, then segue into the kind of nonverbal vocalese introduced by the Mills Brothers. The difference is that their mock-saxophones aren't simply playing jazz, they're also moaning; the momentum bespeaks "spirit-feel" more than technique. In "I Looked Down the Road," as many as three vocal situations obtain: a duo by the tenors Henry Owens and William Landford, a baritone part by Bill Johnson, and Orlandus Wilson's basso "boom-boom-boom"s: enough counterpoint to impress any modern choir fan.

The Golden Gate Quartet. RCA CL 42111 (import).
Gospel Train. JSP 602.

The Heavenly Gospel Singers

During the 1930s, the South Carolina quartet style was more

rock-bottomed than the Virginian, more fluid than the Alabaman. The Heavenlys, like most pre-R. H. Harris quartets, did not feature notable leads, although both the growling bass, "Gospel Jimmy" Bryant and his successor, the less frenetic, more legato William Bobo were memorable part-singers. On numbers like their classic "Heavenly Gospel Train," the quartet favored hypnotic vamps which, by intensifying the background parts, hastened the arrival of truly hard leads like Ira Tucker. Their rhythms could be dazzling; whether in their early period ("The Beautiful City") where they took long pauses between beats, or their late, when Bobo would sing double-time against the background's more leisurely tempo. Their repertory included newer tunes, and they stand on the verge of gospel quartet while still featuring the sustained notes and blocked chords that characterize earlier groups— in a word, harmony over expression.

Heavenly Gospel Singers, Volumes I through IV. Document
   5452, 5453, 5454, 5455.

The Jackson Southernaires

Older siblings of the Williams Brothers, they emphasize an understated pulsation and sentimental sermonettes. Willie Banks, lead on their first hit "Too Late," later recorded with his own quartet, the Messengers.

Too Late. MCA 28056.
Greatest Hits. Malaco 4402.

The Sensational Nightingales

The Best of The Sensational Nightingales. MCA 28020.
Greatest Hits. Malaco 4414.

The Pilgrim Jubilees

Fine Mississippi quartet singing led by the two Graham brothers, Clay and Cleve. The Jubes' work is subtly propulsive, they have the most intriguing time sense of any current quartet. Excellent guitar.

Homecoming. Nashboro 4510-2.

The Pilgrim Travelers

Walking Rhythm. Specialty SPCD 7041-2.
Better Than That. Specialty SPCD 7053-2.
The Best of the Pilgrim Travelers. Specialty SPCD 7204-2.

The Soul Stirrers

Shine on Me. Featuring R. H. Harris. Specialty SPCD 7013-2.
*Jesus Gave Me Water. Featuring Sam Cooke, Paul Foster,
    and Julius Cheeks.* Specialty SPCD 7031-2.
*Heaven is My Home. Featuring Paul Foster and Johnnie
    Taylor.* Specialty SPCD 7040-2.
The Gospel Soul of Sam Cooke with The Soul Stirrers.
    Specialty SPS 2116.

The Spartanburg Famous Four

*The Spartanburg Famous Four, Shelby Gospel Four, Gospel
    Light Jubilee Singers, 1938-39.* Document 5445.
Three 1930s Carolina quartets that exhibit the traits of the
Heavenly Gospel Singers. The Spartanburgs' lead, Bus Porter, liked to interpolate falsetto doodles, part-scat, part-moan,
into his spirited solos. He stands out with the Golden Gates'
Owens and Landford as the most distinctive quartet lead of
the pre-gospel era.

The Swan Silvertones

Love Lifted Me. Specialty SPS 2122.
My Rock. Specialty SPS 2148.
Heavenly Light. Specialty SPCD 7044-2.
Reverend Claude Jeter: Yesterday and Today. Shanachie
6010.

The Swanee Quintet

The funkiest, countriest quartet. As a church once rocked to
guitarist William "Pee Wee" Crawford's vamps, the late
Reuben Willingham quipped, "This may not be a Fish Fry,
but it sure got soul." The Augusta-based Swanees maintained
the same background—Charlie Barnwell, Rufus Washington

and the good-humored falsetto James "Big Red" Anderson —for over thirty years. Some of James Brown's grooves were first set down by his friends, the Swanees. Veteran leads included Willingham, Johnny Jones (the finest singer in the post Sam Cooke tradition, with a range from baritone to high falsetto, and a more vivid, sanctified persona than his idol Cooke) and Percy Griffin.

The Best of the Swanee Quintet. Nashboro 4503-2.

The Fabulous Violinaires of Detroit

Very hip quartet (an early member was Wilson Pickett), using adventurous harmonies (they may have been the first to feature screaming falsettos) and intense leads in the Julius Cheeks tradition by Robert Blair.

Today is the Day. Malaco 4399.

The Sensational Williams Brothers

Hand in Hand. Malaco 4409.

The Wright Brothers

Mitchell's Christian Singers, Volume IV (1940) The Wright Brothers Gospel Singers (1940-c. 1948). Document DOCD - 5496.

This is a major re-issue. It is charming to hear Mitchell's Christian Singers, the most artless and homespun quartet, attempt the switched-on bravura of the Golden Gates or Heavenlys, including some sanctified syncopation in "Kneel Down and Pray." But The Wright Brothers (see page 44) steal the show. They offer perhaps the first *gospel* quartet recordings. Not only the repertory they choose but the fervor of each member, particularly the falsetto and bass, anticipate post-war groups like the Pilgrim Travelers and Swan Silvertones. "Wake Me, Shake Me," with its tenors yodelling in the background, predicts the post-war falsetto harmonies of the Violinaires, Nightingales, Clouds of Joy, and Gospel Keynotes (the last two, Texas groups). With a background vamp and a heartfelt lead, "After Awhile" is as intense as anything the Pilgrim Travelers would record six years later.

Not surprisingly, the Travelers' leads, Barber and Turner, grew up in Cleveland, Texas, the Wrights' homebase. "Walk Around," the Wrights' arrangement of R. H. Harris' masterpiece, contains some precocious ad-libbing. With the Wrights, the gospel sound had arrived.

CHOIRS

The Charles Fold Singers

This Too Will Pass. Savoy SGL 7072.

The Banks Brothers and The Greater Harvest Baptist Choir

The Banks Brothers are a Baptist duo trained by Mary Johnson Davis; Charles Banks sings a tasteful lead reminiscent of Robert Anderson. The choir makes up in spirit for technical lackings.
It Took A Miracle. Savoy MG 14102.

Donald Vails and The Choraleers

Since moving from Atlanta to Detroit, Vails has become that city's pre-eminent choral director. His sound juxtaposes florid leads with decorous backgrounds.
Sinner Man. Savoy SG 70191.

The Florida Mass Choir

The Florida Mass Choir. Savoy SGL 14770.

The Georgia Mass Choir

Under the direction of James Bignon and Milt Biggham, this choir stays true to its southern roots with songs and leads reminiscent of 1950s gospel and occasional dips into folkloric, *a cappella* material.
Hold On Help is On the Way. Savoy SGL 7098.

The Edwin Hawkins Singers

The Best of The Edwin Hawkins Singers. Savoy SG 7077.

The Walter Hawkins Singers

Love Alive. Light LS 5686.

The Institutional Church Choir of Brooklyn

This Is The Answer. Savoy MG 7008.

The Mississippi Mass Choir

Live in Jackson, Mississippi. Malaco 6003.

The New Jerusalem Baptist Church Choir

I Can't Feel at Home. Savoy SGL 7050.

The O'Neal Twins and The Interfaith Choir of St. Louis

Their unusual vocal sound is based on the blend between brother Edward's raucous and brother Edgar's cooler version of the same voice. The Interfaith Choir always includes a few of the city's gifted soloists.
Jesus Dropped the Charges. Savoy SGL 7065.

Dorothy Norwood and The Atlanta Combined Choirs

This big hit is yet another gospel record about thankless children and put-upon mothers. Norwood is noted for her stories ("Johnny and Jesus," "The Old Lady's House," etc.) She has a harsh, gravelly voice that, to everyone's amazement, has actually improved with the years: "Some days now, I almost call myself singing."
The Denied Mother. Savoy MG 14140.

The Thompson Community Singers

It's Gonna Rain, with Jessy Dixon. Myrrh MSB 6966.

ANTHOLOGIES

The Gospel Sound. Columbia Legacy C2K 57160.
A companion to this book, originally issued in 1972, this anthology includes recordings from the twenties to the sixties. Among the highlights are some of the best performances of Blind Willie Johnson ("Motherless Children," "If I Had My

Way"), Reverend J. M. Gates ("Down Here Lord Waiting on You"), Arizona Dranes ("Witness") and from the Columbia-era, Bill Landford-less Golden Gates ("Anyhow" and the exhilarating albeit misogynistic "Jezebel": "nine days she lay in Jerusalem streets, her flesh was too filthy for the dogs to eat"). The modern performers include Mahalia Jackson, Marion Williams, Dorothy Love Coates (her composition, "The Strange Man," offers a kind of feminist alternative to "Jezebel"), the Dixie Hummingbirds, and the Staple Singers.

The Gospel Sound of Spirit Feel. Spirit Feel 1012.
Another companion to this book, featuring the greatest soloists (Jackson, Williams, Tharpe, Ward, Renfro, Ernestine Washington), quartets (Hummingbirds, Soul Stirrers, Nightingales, and—shockingly—the only Spirit of Memphis track currently available, "I'll Tell It," Silas Steele's last recording), and male soloists like Anderson, McKissick, and Charles Taylor.

Precious Lord: The Beloved Gospel Songs of Thomas A. Dorsey. Columbia Legacy CK 57164.
Marion Williams, Alex Bradford, R. H. Harris, the Dixie Hummingbirds, and Bessie Griffin perform Dorsey classics. On two selections, Dorsey is reunited with Sallie Martin, whom he accompanies on piano in a style straight out of 1920s vaudeville.

The Great 1955 Shrine Concert. Specialty SPCD 7045-2.
This spectacular album documents a typical concert of gospel's golden era. Some of the greatest talents are here, filled with youthful energy and the blood lust of contenders fighting for a crown. The Pilgrim Travelers sound a bit tired but Sam Cooke has seldom sung harder than on "Nearer to Thee," while his co-lead, Paul Foster, is most soulful on "Be With Me Jesus." Dorothy Love wails, preaches, chants, and swings in a style that hasn't changed in forty years. Brother Joe May is slinkily seductive on "It's a Long, Long Way." But

the standouts may be the Caravans, appearing shortly after James Cleveland joined the group. Cassietta George, Johneron Davis, and Louise McDowell are seraphic tribunes behind his rollicking "What Kind of Man is This" (the arrangement that inspired Ray Charles' "This Little Gal of Mine"), while the group founder, Albertina Walker, has seldom sounded as commanding as she does on "Since I Met Jesus," perhaps her most thrilling performance on record.

The Soul of Chicago. Shanachie 6008.
Chicago, gospel's Mecca and Vatican, remains the one city where traditional singers comprise a community, and retain a small but steady audience. The artists included, all in their 60s or 70s, could still summon an old-time power in 1992. Among them, Jeanette Harris and the Golden Harps (featuring Harris and Cheryl, her daughter by R. H. Harris); the Gay Sisters; Robert Anderson; Delois Barrett Campbell; Reverend Samuel Patterson (a sanctified guitarist whose voice sounds eerily like B. B. King's), and four unheralded soloists: Vernon Oliver Price, the last of the great sanctified women in the Ernestine Washington-Goldia Haynes tradition (she is also Jeanette Harris' sister-in-law, and the mother of Louis Price, former lead singer of the Temptations), who has supported herself for years as an unofficial school guidance counselor, and—living the life she sings about—running a prison ministry; Irma Gwynn, the last surviving member of Clarence Cobbs' ensemble of virtuosic soloists (she has a majestic contralto, à la Marian Anderson, true gospel soul, and a distinctive sense of time); Lucy Smith Collier, best known as Chicago's premier organist and longtime musician for her stepmother Roberta Martin (now hobbled by a stroke, she remains a great singer, a wildly acrobatic melismatist with a voice like the young Dinah Washington); and Gladys Beamon Gregory (a gorgeous voice, undamaged by the years, perhaps because she spent them working as an office manager, rather than exhausting herself on the gospel highway), who may be the last of the classic soloists.

Gospel at Newport. Vanguard 77014-2.
Between 1959 and 1966, the Newport Folk Festival frequently presented gospel groups. While the acts usually had to generate their own energy, working against the folkies' off-time clapping, "spirit-feel" proved sufficient. The Dixie Hummingbirds' "Christian's Automobile" may be the best example of Ira Tucker's pyrotechnics. Other highlights: the Swan Silvertones' harmonic precision; a youthful Alex Bradford belting a Dorsey standard with a Philadelphia choir; Dorothy Love Coates in a rather dour, school-marmish mode; and Mavis Staples singing her favorite hard gospel song, "Pray On My Child."

All of My Appointed Time: Forty Years of a cappela *Gospel.*
     Jass J-CD-640.
This anthology, compiled by the author, opens with two uncharacteristically churchy recordings by the Golden Gates ("Standing By the Bedside," "Listen to the Lambs"). The Kings of Harmony are still regarded as peerless housewreckers. The recordings here, "Precious Lord" (led by Walter Latimore) and "God Shall Wipe All Tears Away" (led by Carey "Squeaky" Bradley), may be the first instances of hard gospel quartet on record. Another Alabama quartet, the Blue Jays began singing in the pre-gospel era. They are represented by their best gospel work, "Canaan" and "Standing on the Highway" with leads by the monolithic Silas Steele. The Soul Stirrers, whose loose time and switch-lead tactics influenced the Blue Jays, perform "Well Well Well," an unusually sober and folkloric recording, for once evocative of an older quartet tradition, and "I'm Gonna Tell God," which features compelling work by Leroy Taylor. Side Two salutes women artists. The Georgia Peach, perhaps the first woman to record the newer gospel repertory, frequently performed with male quartets; here she sings the 1930s quartet standard "Here Am I Send Me." Jeanette Harris and the Golden Harps were considered the champion female quartet. Harris's raspy vocals and showmanship contrast with Ann Grant's more stately and resonant second-lead. *A cappella*

solos have long held a place in the church and are currently being recorded about as often as unaccompanied group vocals (which means, for both, hardly at all). Bessie Griffin, formerly of New Orleans' Southern Harps, recreates her biggest quartet hit, "The Lord Will Make a Way." As a girl in Miami, Marion Williams idolized the Kings of Harmony. Her two solos here, "They Led My Lord Away" and the album's title selection, combine the melancholy lyricism of R. H. Harris with Silas Steele's Burning Bush authority.

VIDEOS

The Old Time Camp Meeting Songs. Rev. Timothy Flemming and the congregation of Mt. Carmel Baptist Church. GSR 011. (2740 Greenbriar Pkwy, Suite 253. Atlanta Georgia 30331) Though Mount Carmel, with thousands of members, is one of Atlanta's super-churches, its pastor was raised in the country and is a master of the older forms of congregational singing. For this video, he requested that his members wear the overalls, gingham dresses, and bonnets of their ancestors. Under his guidance, the music produced is indistinguishable from that of C. J. Johnson (whose widow, Elizabeth, joins Flemming on several selections). He growls and moans with great force, a cross between Blind Willie Johnson and C. L. Franklin: among others, the lining-out hymn "Lord I Come to Thee," "Jesus is Keeping Me Alive," and "Be Still, God will Fight Your Battles"(aggressively sung despite its quietist message) have a classic sound. But what makes the video priceless is the sight of people weeping, exulting, shouting, and falling out: the gap between past and present is erased. The video ends with Deacon Willie Gilmer, whose reminiscences should intrigue any cultural historian ("Our parents used to whip us, *not* rape us"; nowadays men are thrown out of church for attacking boys, women for training their daughters for the streets.)The way he worries a word ("early, *early*") or prolongs a note demonstrates the route taken by early jazz.

ADDENDA

Sister Ernestine Washington 1943-1948. Document DOCD 5462.
Spectacular performance by the grand dame of the Church of God in Christ. Her singular achievement was to wed sanctified bravura to the legato soul of her Baptist inspiration, Roberta Martin.

Selah Jubilee Singers Volume II 1941-1944. Document DOCD 5500.
Like Madame Washington, the Selahs were stationed in Brooklyn, N.Y. Always a precision group, their musicianship increased exponentially in 1944 when Norman "Crip" Harris joined them. On selections like "Cool Down Yonder" or "When Was Jesus Born," he anticipates the virtuosic lead of his disciple Ira Tucker, while his intricate background arrangements will startle modern choir directors. The Selahs don't offer soul—they call themselves "spirit-killers"—but instead a technical polish and folksy vaudeville that may be truer to the quartet's original vision. Spirit-feel they leave to the competition.

INDEX OF NAMES

(Page numbers in italic type denote a major treatment.)

INDEX OF NAMES II

INDEX OF SONG TITLES

About the Author

Anthony Heilbut received his Ph.D. in English from Harvard and has taught at New York University and Hunter College. He is also the author of *Exiled in Paradise: German Refugee Artists and Intellectuals in America from the 1930s to the Present* (1983; 1997); and *Thomas Mann: Eros and Literature* (1996); and of numerous articles on literary and social issues for *The New Yorker, The New York Times Book Review, The Nation, The Village Voice,* and *Humanities*. Mr. Heilbut has produced or compiled forty albums, among them winners of the Grammy Award and the Grand Prix du Disque. He is the founder of Spirit Feel Records, a small label distributed by Shanachie, nine of whose albums have received "Five Stars" from *Rolling Stone. Pulse* called the latest release, Marion Williams' *Through Many Dangers,* "a touchstone of American music, and perhaps the greatest gospel album ever produced."